SCHOOL OF
ORIENTAL AND AFRICAN STUDIES
UNIVERSITY OF LONDON

London Oriental Series
Volume 31

LONDON ORIENTAL SERIES · VOLUME 31

QURANIC STUDIES

SOURCES AND METHODS OF SCRIPTURAL INTERPRETATION

BY

JOHN WANSBROUGH

Reader in Arabic
School of Oriental and African Studies
University of London

OXFORD UNIVERSITY PRESS

1977

Oxford University Press, Walton Street, Oxford OX2 6DP

OXFORD LONDON GLASGOW NEW YORK
TORONTO MELBOURNE WELLINGTON CAPE TOWN
IBADAN NAIROBI DAR ES SALAAM LUSAKA ADDIS ABABA
KUALA LUMPUR SINGAPORE JAKARTA HONG KONG TOKYO
DELHI BOMBAY CALCUTTA MADRAS KARACHI

ISBN 0 19 713588 9

Printed in Great Britain
at the University Press, Oxford
by Vivian Ridler
Printer to the University

London Oriental Series

No. 1 PHONETICS IN ANCIENT INDIA
W. SIDNEY ALLEN

No. 2 THE DIACRITICAL POINT AND THE ACCENTS IN SYRIAC
J. B. SEGAL

†No. 3 THE MANICHAEAN HYMN CYCLES IN PARTHIAN
MARY BOYCE

†No. 4 THE BACKGROUND OF THE REBELLION OF AN LU-SHAN
EDWIN G. PULLEYBLANK

*No. 5 SOCIAL POLICY AND SOCIAL CHANGE IN WESTERN INDIA 1817–1830
KENNETH BALLHATCHET

No. 6 THE HEVAJRA TANTRA
D. L. SNELLGROVE. Two volumes

No. 7 THE GĀNDHĀRĪ DHARMAPADA
Edited with an Introduction and Commentary by JOHN BROUGH

*No. 8 THE HISTORY OF THE CAUCASIAN ALBANIANS BY MOVSĒS DASXURANÇI
Translated by C. J. F. DOWSETT

†No. 9 KURDISH DIALECT STUDIES, Vol. I
D. N. MACKENZIE

†No. 10 KURDISH DIALECT STUDIES, Vol. II
D. N. MACKENZIE

No. 11 NINETEENTH-CENTURY MALAYA
The Origins of British Political Control
C. D. COWAN

No. 12 THE HEBREW PASSOVER FROM THE EARLIEST TIMES TO A.D. 70
J. B. SEGAL

†No. 13 THE MORPHOLOGY OF THE TIGRE NOUN
F. R. PALMER

*No. 14 JAINA YOGA
A Survey of the Mediaeval Śrāvakācāras
R. WILLIAMS

†No. 15 TIDDIM CHIN
A Descriptive Analysis of Two Texts
EUGÉNIE J. A. HENDERSON

* These volumes are out of print.

† These volumes obtainable only from the School of Oriental and African Studies.

*No. 16 NESHRĪ'S HISTORY OF THE OTTOMANS
The Sources and Development of the Text
V. L. MÉNAGE

No. 17 EASTERN ARABIAN DIALECT STUDIES
T. M. JOHNSTONE

No. 18 THE NINE WAYS OF BON
Excerpts from gZi-brjid
Edited and translated by DAVID L. SNELGROVE

†No. 19 TIBETAN TEXTS CONCERNING KHOTAN
R. E. EMMERICK

†No. 20 SAKA GRAMMATICAL STUDIES
R. E. EMMERICK

†No. 21 THE BOOK OF ZAMBASTA
A Khotanese Poem on Buddhism
Edited and translated by R. E. EMMERICK

†No. 22 THE 'SŪTRA OF THE CAUSES AND EFFECTS OF ACTIONS' IN SOGDIAN
Edited by D. N. MACKENZIE

†No. 23 THE KHOTANESE ŚŪRANGAMASAMĀDHISŪTRA
R. E. EMMERICK

No. 24 A DICTIONARY OF THE MON INSCRIPTIONS FROM THE SIXTH TO THE SIXTEENTH CENTURIES
Incorporating materials collected by the late C. O. Blagden
H. L. SHORTO

No. 25 THE FINANCIAL SYSTEM OF EGYPT A.H. 564–741/A.D. 1169–1341
HASSANEIN M. RABIE

†No. 26 THE TREASURY OF GOOD SAYINGS: A TIBETAN HISTORY OF BON
SAMTEN G. KARMAY

No. 27 POPULATION PRESSURE IN RURAL ANATOLIA 1450–1600
M. A. COOK

No. 28 THE MODAL SYSTEM OF ARAB AND PERSIAN MUSIC A.D. 1250–1300
O. WRIGHT

No. 29 THE *SHEN TZU* FRAGMENTS
P. M. THOMPSON

No. 30 JOGJAKARTA UNDER SULTAN MANGKUBUMI 1749–1792
A History of the Division of Java
M. C. RICKLEFS

* This volume is out of print.

† These volumes obtainable only from the School of Oriental and African Studies.

CONTENTS

FOR MY WIFE

PREFACE

DESPITE long reflection, many false starts, and unceasing efforts at clearer formulation, these studies remain essays. Time and industry, together with the mechanism of cross-reference, have served perhaps to make of them one essay, but not to eliminate the basic etymological sense of that term. This estimate, intended neither to disarm nor to discourage, is the consequence as much of an experimental method as of an inordinate quantity of literary material to be examined. To argue a case for the Qur'ān as scripture may seem gratuitous. As the record of Muslim revelation the book requires no introduction. As a document susceptible of analysis by the instruments and techniques of Biblical criticism it is virtually unknown. The doctrinal obstacles that have traditionally impeded such investigation are, on the other hand, very well known. Not merely dogmas such as those defining scripture as the uncreated Word of God and acknowledging its formal and substantive inimitability, but also the entire corpus of Islamic historiography, by providing a more or less coherent and plausible report of the circumstances of the Quranic revelation, have discouraged examination of the document as representative of a traditional literary type. But historiography, like other kinds of literature, derives an important share of its momentum from the rhetorical devices upon which it depends for expression, that is, upon techniques designed, developed, or borrowed to enhance and to interpret its communication. Historical reports of the Quranic revelation are no exception, and it seemed to me that a structural analysis, not only of the text of scripture but also of the other evidence associated with its genesis and with its interpretation, might produce some useful comparisons with the traditional historiography.

I have thus proposed for the study of Islamic monotheism a threefold division into its principal components: scriptural canon, prophetology, and sacred language. Examination of these, in the first three chapters of this book, will, I hope, provide an adequate introduction to my main concern, which is the development of scriptural exegesis. There the treatment is typological, though I have sought to elicit an at least provisional chronology. Provisional too are my views on the elaboration of the canon, on its precise relation to the much larger corpus of prophetical literature, and on the environment which produced the final forms of both. Such problems as attend a typological description of the traditional components of salvation history of the decisive factors in community formation, the boundaries between orthodoxy and heterodoxy resulting from formulation of a fixed identity and elaboration of a historical image, and the articulation of a dogmatic theology as final stage and permanent emblem of the religious establishment, await clarification and eventual (tentative) solutions. These may be found, I suspect, in the Islamic literature of polemic, both sectarian and interconfessional, and it is my intention to devote a second volume to analysis of that literature. The interesting hypotheses of such scholars as Schoeps and Rabin, following upon the theories of Harnack and Schlatter, with regard to the sectarian catenations from which Islam in the end emerged, or constituted the final expression, deserve notice. There the essential difficulty lies in identifying the several shared theologoumena as products of historical diffusion rather than of polygenesis. All such efforts at historical reconstruction (*wie es eigentlich gewesen*) tend to be reductive, and here one senses the spectre of that (possibly very real) dichotomy in early Christian history: Jerusalem *Urgemeinde* opposed to Hellenistic *kerygma* (Bultmann). The basic problems associated with that opposition, whether social or doctrinal, seem in retrospect to reflect disputes about eschatology, much as the development of Rabbinic Judaism has been defined as reaction to or residue from extreme expressions of eschatological belief/activity. Now, in the formation of the Muslim community an eschatological factor is hardly perceptible, though much has been made of the presence in Muslim scripture of eschatological formulae (Casanova and Andrae). In my view it is unlikely to have been an eschatological community which served either as model or as point of departure for Islam, but rather one of or a combination of others of the traditional types, e.g. ritualist, scripturalist, primitivist.

That argument does not, however, find a place in these essays. My aim here is a systematic study of the formal properties of scriptural authority, as merely one (though possibly the major one) factor contributing to the emergence of an independent and self-conscious religious community. The literary uses, and hence communal functions, of scripture might be (roughly) isolated as four: polemic, liturgical, didactic, and juridical, in descending order of importance and (approximate) chronological order of appearance. I believe that this set of priorities can be demonstrated from the Muslim exegetical literature, examination of which constitutes half the bulk of my book. The material adduced is intended to represent a cross-section of Quranic commentary prior to the monumental work of Ṭabarī (d. 923). Save for a kind of philosophical exegesis belonging to a later period, the typology set out here includes the principal lines of inquiry applied to the text of Muslim scripture: haggadic, halakhic, masoretic, rhetorical, and allegorical. The manner in which the concept of authority was progressively articulated by means of these exegetical types is the formative principle and the purpose of my exposition, though it is of course possible to interpret the evidence differently. It is, on the other hand, quite impossible to mistake the chronology of the sources or to ignore the presence of *Nachdichtung* in traditionist literary forms. Tradition implies, and actively involves, historicization, and the growth of a polemical motif into a historical fact is a process hardly requiring demonstration, e.g. the patriarchal narratives of the Old Testament. History, like poetry, is mimetic and produces as many necessary truths as it contains fortuitous facts (Lessing).

Pressed into the service of salvation history these two categories tend to coalesce: everything becomes relevant, the most insignificant scraps of information fall into place as components of the grand design. And it is that design which scriptural exegesis is intended to illustrate, by recourse to a range of standard hermeneutical techniques, all of ancient lineage and indisputable merit. Islamic adaptation of these was a fairly uncomplicated process of direct appropriation, and thus its analysis contains no surprises. It can, on the other hand, be argued that the data of the theodicy (as set out in Chapter I) limited from the outset its historical development: the expression of communal purpose and authority could hardly have been different from what it became (Weber). Sectarian forms of Islam reflect an equally predictable pattern of divergence from what became the normative (Sunnī) expression. Again, the problem of diffusion and polygenesis. Some aid towards a solution may be sought in the lexicon of exegesis, where terminological calques could, and probably do, indicate a community of scholarship. I have examined these, but am unable to identify one single path of diffusion. The marginalia of Judaeo-Christian history, what might be called 'the sectarian milieu', await systematic exposition. That the wait promises to be a long one is most persuasively illustrated in the quite extraordinary literature generated by discovery of the Dead Sea Scrolls. Comforted by speculative scholarship of such quality and quantity, I feel no special compulsion to apologize for the conjectural nature of my own efforts to depict the origins of Islam.

The final draft of this work was completed in July 1972, and I have thus not taken account of studies published since that date (and quite possibly of several published before that date). The sources employed in Chapter IV are in part still in manuscript, and I am pleased to acknowledge the helpfulness of the staffs of the several libraries in Istanbul listed in the Bibliography and of the British Museum. I should also like to express here my gratitude to Simon Hopkins, who read and commented upon the final version of these studies, having been for many years as my student exposed to the cruder formulations of my earliest thoughts on the subject. I think he is not satisfied with the result, but then, neither am I. Finally, I wish to thank the School of Oriental and African Studies for granting me leave to work in Istanbul, for including this book in the London Oriental Series, and for meeting the expense of publication.

J. W.

July 1975

ABBREVIATIONS

AJSLL	*American Journal of Semitic Languages and Literatures*
AO	*Acta Orientalia*
BO	*Bibliotheca Orientalis*
BSOAS	*Bulletin of the School of Oriental and African Studies*
BSS	T. Nöldeke, *Beiträge zur Semitischen Sprachwissenschaft*
CHB	*Cambridge History of the Bible*
EI	*Encyclopaedia of Islam*, second edition, Leiden 1960–
GAL	C. Brockelmann, *Geschichte der Arabischen Literatur*
GAS	F. Sezgin, *Geschichte des Arabischen Schrifttums*
GdQ	T. Nöldeke and F. Schwally, *Geschichte des Qorans* i–ii, G. Bergsträsser and O. Pretzl, *Geschichte des Qorans* iii
GVG	C. Brockelmann, *Grundriss der Vergleichenden Grammatik der Semitischen Sprachen*
HUCA	*Hebrew Union College Annual*
IC	*Islamic Culture*
IQ	*Islamic Quarterly*
JA	*Journal Asiatique*
JAOS	*Journal of the American Oriental Society*
JNES	*Journal of Near Eastern Studies*
JQR	*Jewish Quarterly Review*
JRAS	*Journal of the Royal Asiatic Society*
JSS	*Journal of Semitic Studies*
MSOS	*Mitteilungen des Seminars für Orientalische Sprachen*
MW	*Muslim World*
NBSS	T. Nöldeke, *Neue Beiträge zur Semitischen Sprachwissenschaft*
OLZ	*Orientalistische Literaturzeitung*
PAAJR	*Proceedings of the American Academy for Jewish Research*
REI	*Revue des Études Islamiques*
REJ	*Revue des Études Juives*
RO	*Rocznik Orientalistyczny*
SALP	N. Abbott, *Studies in Arabic Literary Papyri*
SI	*Studia Islamica*
VT	*Vetus Testamentum*
WI	*Die Welt des Islams*
WZKM	*Wiener Zeitschrift für die Kunde des Morgenlandes*
ZA	*Zeitschrift für Assyriologie*
ZDMG	*Zeitschrift der Deutschen Morgenländischen Gesellschaft*
ZS	*Zeitschrift für Semitistik*

BIBLIOGRAPHY

Abbott, N. *SALP* I: *Historical Texts*, Oriental Institute Publications lxxv, University of Chicago, 1957

—— *SALP* II: *Qur'ānic Commentary and Tradition*, Oriental Institute Publications lxxvi, University of Chicago, 1967. See Wansbrough, *BSOAS* xxxi (1968) 613–16

ʿAbd al-Bāqī, M. *Muʿjam gharīb al-Qur'ān*, Cairo, 1950

ʿAbd al-Jabbār. *Tanzīh al-Qur'ān*, Beirut, n.d.

—— *Tathbīt dalā'il al-nubuwwa*, MS. Shehid Ali Pasha 1575

Abū ʿUbayd. *Kitāb al-nāsikh wal-mansūkh*, MS. Ahmet III, 143

—— See A. Spitaler, 'Ein Kapitel aus den Faḍā'il al-Qur'ān von Abū ʿUbaid al-Qāsim ibn Sallām', in *Documenta Islamica Inedita*, Berlin, 1952, 1–24

Abū ʿUbayda. *Majāz al-Qur'ān*, Cairo, 1954–62

Ahrens, K. 'Christliches im Qoran', *ZDMG* lxxxiv (1930) 15–68, 148–90

Allard, M. 'Une Méthode nouvelle pour l'étude du Coran, *SI* xvi (1961) 5–21

—— *Analyse conceptuelle du Coran sur cartes perforées*, Paris, 1963

Altmann, A. 'Saadya's theory of revelation: its origin and background', in *Saadya Studies*, Manchester, 1943, 4–25

Andrae, T. *Die person Muhammeds in lehre und glauben seiner gemeinde*, Stockholm, 1918

Ashʿarī. *Kitāb maqālāt al-islāmiyyīn*, Bibliotheca Islamica I, Wiesbaden, 1963

Asín Palacios, M. *La Escatologia Musulmana en la Divina Comedia*, Madrid, 1961.

Auerbach, E. *Mimesis*, Bern, 1967

Augapfel, J. 'Das *Kitāb* im Qur'ān', *WZKM* xxix (1915) 384–93

Bacher, W. 'Die Anfänge der hebräischen Grammatik', *ZDMG* xlix (1895) 1–62, 335–92

—— *Die exegetische Terminologie der jüdischen Traditionsliteratur* i–ii, Leipzig, 1899–1905

Baghdādī, ʿAbd al-Qāhir. *Kitāb al-nāsikh wal-mansūkh*, MS. Beyazit Umumi 445

Baljon, J. 'The "Amr of God" in the Qur'ān', *AO* xxiii (1958) 7–18

Bāqillānī. *Iʿjāz al-Qur'ān*, Cairo, 1963

Barr, J. *The Semantics of Biblical Language*, Oxford, 1961

—— *Comparative Philology and the Text of the Old Testament*, Oxford, 1968

Barth, J. 'Studien zur Kritik und Exegese des Qorans', *Der Islam* vi (1915–16) 113–48

Bayḍāwī. *Anwār al-tanzīl*, Bulaq, 1330

Beck, E. 'Die Kodizesvarianten der Amṣār', *Orientalia* xvi (1947) 353–76

—— 'Die Gestalt des Abraham am Wendepunkt der Entwicklung Muhammeds', *Le Muséon* lxv (1952) 73–94

Becker, C. H. 'Der Islam als Problem', *Der Islam* i (1910) 1–21 (*Islamstudien* I, Leipzig, 1924, 1–23)
—— 'Christliche Polemik und Islamische Dogmenbildung', *ZA* xxvi (1911) 175–95 (*Islamstudien* I, 432–49)
—— 'Ubi sunt qui ante nos in mundo fuere', in *Festschrift E. Kuhn*, Breslau, 1916 87–105 (*Islamstudien* I, 501–19)
—— 'Prinzipielles zu Lammens Sīrastudien', *Der Islam* iv (1913) 263–9 (*Islamstudien* I, 520–7: 'Grundsätzliches zur Leben-Muhammed-Forschung')
—— *Beiträge zur Geschichte Ägyptens unter dem Islam* i–ii, Strassburg, 1902–3
Bell, R. *Bell's Introduction to the Qur'ān*, ed. W. M. Watt, Edinburgh, 1970
Ben-Zvi, I. 'Les Origines de l'établissement des tribus d'Israël en Arabie', *Le Muséon* lxxiv (1961) 143–90
Bergsträsser, G. *Einführung in die semitischen Sprachen*, München, 1928
—— *Hebräische Grammatik* i, Leipzig, 1918
—— 'Die Koranlesung des Ḥasan von Baṣra', *Islamica* ii (1926) 11–57
—— 'Anfänge und Charakter des juristischen Denkens im Islam', *Der Islam* xiv (1925) 76–81
—— and Pretzl, O. *Geschichte des Qorans* III: Die Geschichte des Korantexts, Leipzig, 1938
Bevan, A. 'Mohammed's Ascension', in *Studien zur Semitischen Philologie und Religionsgeschichte Julius Wellhausen . . . gewidmet*, Giessen, 1914, 49–61
Birkeland, H. *Altarabische Pausalformen*, Oslo, 1940
—— *The Legend of the Opening of Muhammed's Breast*, Oslo, 1955
—— *Old Muslim Opposition against Interpretation of the Koran*, Oslo, 1955
—— *The Lord Guideth: Studies on Primitive Islam*, Oslo, 1956
—— 'The interpretation of Sūrah 107', *SI* ix (1958) 13–29
Björkman, W. *Beiträge zur Geschichte der Staatskanzlei im islamischen Ägypten*, Hamburg, 1928
Blachère, R. *Introduction au Coran*, Paris, 1959
—— *Histoire de la littérature arabe* i–iii, Paris, 1952–66
Black, M. *An Aramaic approach to the Gospels and Acts*, Oxford, 1967
Blanc, H. *Communal Dialects in Baghdad*, Cambridge, Mass., 1964
Blau, J. *A Grammar of Christian Arabic, based mainly on South Palestinian Texts from the first Millennium*, CSCO Subsidia 27–9, Louvain, 1966–7. *See* Wansbrough, *BSOAS* xxxi (1968) 610–13
—— *On Pseudo-corrections in some Semitic Languages*, Jerusalem, 1970
—— *The Emergence and Linguistic Background of Judaeo-Arabic*, Oxford, 1965
—— 'The role of the bedouins as arbiters in linguistic questions and the Mas'ala Az-Zunbūriyya', *JSS* viii (1963) 42–51
—— 'Some problems of the formation of the old Semitic languages in the light of Arabic dialects', in *Proceedings of the International Conference on Semitic Studies*, Jerusalem, 1965
—— 'L'Apparition du type linguistique néo-arabe', *REI* xxxvi (1969) 191–201
—— 'Judaeo-Arabic in its linguistic setting', *PAAJR* xxxvi (1968) 1–12
—— 'On the problem of the synthetic character of Classical Arabic as against Judaeo-Arabic (Middle Arabic)', *JQR* lxiii (1972) 29–38

Bloch, A. *Vers und Sprache im Altarabischen*, Acta Tropica Supplementum 5, Basel, 1946

Bonebakker, S. *Some Early Definitions of the Tawriya and Ṣafadī's 'Faḍḍ al-Xitām 'an at-tawriya wa'l-istixdām'*, The Hague–Paris, 1966

Bouman, J. *Le Conflit autour du Coran et la solution d'al-Bāqillānī*, Amsterdam, 1959

—— 'The Doctrine of 'Abd al-Djabbār on the Qur'ān as the created word of Allāh', in *Verbum: Essays . . . Dedicated to Dr. H. W. Obbink*, Utrecht, 1964, 67–86

Bräunlich, E. 'Versuch einer literargeschichtlichen Betrachtungsweise altarabischer Poesien', *Der Islam* xxiv (1937) 201–69

—— 'Zur Frage der Echtheit der altarabischen Poesie', *OLZ* (1926) 825–33

Bravmann, M. 'On the spiritual background of early Islam and the history of its principal concepts', *Le Muséon* lxiv (1951) 317–56

Brockelmann, C. *Geschichte der arabischen Literatur*, Leiden, 1937–49

—— *Grundriss der vergleichenden Grammatik der Semitischen Sprachen* I–II, Berlin, 1908–13

Buhl, F. 'Über Vergleichungen und Gleichnisse im Qur'ān', *AO* ii (1924) 1–11

—— 'Zur Kuranexegese', *AO* iii (1925) 97–108

—— 'Ein paar Beiträge zur Kritik der Geschichte Muhammed's', in *Orientalische Studien Theodor Nöldeke . . . gewidmet*, Giessen, 1906, i, 7–22

Bukhārī. *Ṣaḥīḥ* iii, Leiden, 1868

Burton, J. 'Those are the high-flying cranes', *JSS* xv (1970) 246–65

—— 'The collection of the Qur'ān', *Glasgow University Oriental Society, Transactions* xxiii, 1969–70 (1972) 42–60

Caetani, L. *Annali dell'Islam* I, Milan, 1905

Caskel, W. 'Aijām al-'Arab: Studien zur altarabischen Epik', *Islamica* iii Suppl. (1931) 1–99

—— 'Zur Beduinisierung Arabiens', *ZDMG* ciii (1953) *28–36*

Cerulli, E. *Il 'Libro della Scala' e la questione delle fonti arabo-spagnole della Divina Commedia*, Studi e Testi 150, Città del Vaticano, 1949

Chapira, B. 'Légendes bibliques attribuées a Ka'b el-Aḥbār', *REJ* lxix (1919) 86–107, lxx (1920) 37–43

Cohen, A. 'Arabisms in Rabbinic literature', *JQR* iii (1912–13) 221–33

Cohen, D. 'Koinè, langues communes et dialectes arabes', *Arabica* ix (1962) 119–44

Corré, A. 'Phonemic problems in the Masora', in *Essays Presented to Chief Rabbi Israel Brodie*, London, 1968, 59–66

Corriente, F. 'On the functional yield of some synthetic devices in Arabic and Semitic morphology', *JQR* lxii (1971) 20–50

Culley, R. *Oral Formulaic Language in the Biblical Psalms*, Toronto, 1967

Curtius, E. *Europäische Literatur und Lateinisches Mittelalter*, Bern, 1948

Dānī. *Kitāb al-taysīr fī 'l-qirā'āt al-sab'*, Istanbul, 1930

Daube, D. 'Rabbinic methods of interpretation and Hellenistic rhetoric', *HUCA* xxii (1949) 239–64

DeGoeje, M. 'Die Berufung Mohammed's', in *Orientalische Studien Theodor Nöldeke . . . gewidmet*, Giessen, 1906, i, 1–5

Derenbourg, J. 'Quelques remarques sur la declinaison arabe', *JA* iv (1844) 209–20

Derrett, J. *Law in the New Testament*, London, 1970

Dīnawarī. *Tafsīr al-wāḍiḥ*, MS. Ayasofya 221–2

Dozy, R. *Supplément aux Dictionnaires Arabes*, Leiden, 1967

Eissfeldt, O. *Einleitung in das Alte Testament*, Tübingen, 1956

Elbogen, I. *Der jüdische Gottesdienst in seiner geschichtlichen Entwicklung*, Frankfurt, 1931

Farrā'. *Ma'ānī 'l-Qur'ān*, Cairo, 1955–, and MS. Nurosmaniye 459

Ferguson, C. 'The Arabic Koine', *Language* xxxv (1959) 616–30

Fischer, A. 'Arab. aysh', *ZDMG* lix (1905) 807–18

—— 'Usaiịid, usw.', *ZDMG* lvi (1902) 581

—— 'Eine Qorān-Interpolation', in *Orientalische Studien Theodor Nöldeke . . . gewidmet*, 1906, i, 33–55

—— 'Die Mas'ala Zunbūrīja', in *A Volume of Oriental Studies Presented to E. G. Browne*, Cambridge, 1922, 150–6

Fischer, W. 'Ein Stück vorklassischer, arabischer Kunstprosa in der Umm Ma'bad-Legende', in *Festschrift W. Eilers*, Wiesbaden, 1967, 318–24

—— 'Silbenstruktur und Vokalismus im Arabischen', *ZDMG* cxvii (1967) 30–77

Frye, N. *Anatomy of Criticism*, Princeton, 1957

Fück, J. *'Arabīya; recherches sur l'histoire de la langue et du style arabe*, tr. C. Denizeau, Paris, 1955

Galliner, S. *Saadia Al-fajjūmī's arabische Psalmenübersetzung und Commentar* (*Psalm 73–89*), Berlin, 1903

Garbell, I. 'Remarks on the historical phonology of an East Mediterranean Arabic dialect', *Word* xiv (1958) 303–37

Geiger, A. *Was hat Mohammed aus dem Judenthume aufgenommen?*, Leipzig, 1902

Gerhardsson, B. *Memory and Manuscript: Oral Tradition and Written Transmission in Rabbinic Judaism and Early Christianity*, Copenhagen, 1964

Gertner, M. 'The Masorah and the Levites: an essay in the history of a concept', *VT* x (1960) 241–72

—— 'Terms of scriptural interpretation: a study in Hebrew semantics', *BSOAS* (1962) 1–27

—— 'The terms pharisaioi, gazarenoi, hupokritai: their semantic complexity and conceptual correlation', *BSOAS* xxvi (1963) 245–58

—— 'On translating medieval Hebrew writing', *JRAS* (1963) 163–93

Goitein, S. 'Ramadan, the Muslim month of fasting', in *Studies in Islamic History and Institutions*, Leiden, 1966, 90–110

—— 'A turning-point in the history of the Muslim state', *IC* xxiii (1949) 120–35 (*Studies* 149–67)

—— 'The Birth-hour of Muslim law', *MW* I (1960) 23–9 (*Studies* 126–34)

Goldziher, I. *Abhandlungen zur Arabischen Philologie* i–ii, Leiden, 1896–99

—— *Die Richtungen der islamischen Koranauslegung*, Leiden, 1920

—— *Muhammedanische Studien* i–ii, Halle, 1889–90

—— *Die Ẓāhiriten*, Leipzig, 1884

—— *Vorlesungen über den Islam*, Heidelberg, 1910

—— *Gesammelte Schriften* i–v, ed. J. Desomogyi, Hildesheim, 1967–70 (*GS*)

— 'Beiträge zur Geschichte der Sprachgelehrsamkeit bei den Arabern I–III', *SKAW* lxvii (1871) 207–51, lxxii (1872) 587–631, lxxiii (1873) 511–52 (*GS* i, 7–51, 91–135, 187–228)

—— 'Linguistisches aus der Literatur der muhammedanischen Mystik', *ZDMG* xxvi (1872) 764–85 (*GS* i, 165–86)

—— 'Über muhammedanische Polemik gegen Ahl al-kitāb', *ZDMG* xxxii (1878) 341–87 (*GS* ii, 1–47)

—— 'Das Princip des Istiṣḥāb in der muhammedanischen Gesetzwissenschaft', *WZKM* i (1887) 228–36 (*GS* ii, 182–90)

— 'Die Ginnen der Dichter', *ZDMG* xlv (1891) 685–90 (*GS* ii, 400–5)

— 'Der Chaṭīb bei den alten Arabern', *WZKM* vi (1892) 97–102 (*GS* iii, 27–32)

—— 'Usages juifs d'après la littérature religieuse des Musulmans', *REJ* xxviii (1894) 75–94 (*GS* iii, 322–41)

—— 'Neue Materialien zur Litteratur des Überlieferungswesens bei den Muhammedanern', *ZDMG* l (1896) 465–506 (*GS* iv, 69–110)

—— 'Mélanges judéo-arabes', *REJ* xliii (1901) 1–14 (*GS* iv, 263–76)

—— 'Neutestamentliche Elemente in der Traditionslitteratur des Islam', *Oriens Christianus* (1902) 390–7 (*GS* iv, 315–22)

—— 'Die Bedeutung der Nachmittagszeit im Islam', *Archiv für Religionswissenschaft* ix (1906) 294–302 (*GS* v, 23–31)

—— 'Aus der Theologie des Fachr al-dīn al-Rāzī', *Der Islam* iii (1912) 213–47 (*GS* v, 237–71)

—— 'Bemerkungen zur neuhebräischen Poesie', *JQR* xiv (1902) 719–36

—— 'Kämpfe um die Stellung des Ḥadīt im Islam', *ZDMG* lxi (1907) 860–72 (*GS* v, 86–98)

Götz, M. 'Māturīdī und sein Kitāb Ta'wīlāt al-Qur'ān', *Der Islam* xli (1965) 27–70

Grohmann, A. *Einführung und Chrestomathie zur arabischen Papyruskunde*, Prague, 1955

Grunebaum, G. von. *A Tenth-century Document of Arabic Literary Theory and Criticism*, Chicago, 1950

—— *Kritik und Dichtkunst: Studien zur arabischen Literaturgeschichte*, Wiesbaden, 1955

Grünbaum, M. *Neue Beiträge zur semitischen Sagenkunde*, Leipzig, 1893

Guidi, M. *La lotta tra l'Islam e il Manicheismo*, Rome, 1927

Hasan, A. 'The theory of naskh', *Islamic Studies* iv (1965) 181–200

Heinrichs, W. *Arabische Dichtung und Griechische Poetik*, Beirut, 1969. See Wansbrough, *BSOAS* xxxiii (1970) 615–17

Heller, B. 'Récits et personnages bibliques dans la légende mahométane', *REJ* lxxxv (1928) 113–36

—— 'La Légende biblique dans l'Islam', *REJ* xcviii (1934) 1–18

Hibatallāh. *Kitāb al-nāsikh wal-mansūkh*, Cairo, 1960

Hirschberg, J. *Jüdische und christliche Lehren im vor- und frühislamischen Arabien*, Cracow, 1939
Hirschfeld, H. 'Historical and legendary controversies between Mohammed and the Rabbis', *JQR* x (1897–8) 100–16
—— 'Mohammedan criticism of the Bible', *JQR* xiii (1900–1) 222–40
—— *New Researches into the Composition and Exegesis of the Qoran*, London, 1902
Horovitz, J. *Koranische Untersuchungen*, Berlin–Leipzig, 1926
—— 'Zur Muhammadlegende', *Der Islam* v (1915) 41–53
—— 'Muhammeds Himmelfahrt', *Der Islam* ix (1919) 159–83
—— 'Biblische Nachwirkungen in der Sīra', *Der Islam* xii (1922) 184–9
Horst, H. 'Zur Überlieferung im Korankommentar aṭ-Ṭabarīs', *ZDMG* ciii (1953) 290–307
Ḥusayn, Ṭāhā. 'La Rhétorique arabe de Djaḥiz à ʿAbd al-Ḳāhir', in Ḳudama b. Djaʿfar: *Naḳd an-nathr*, Cairo, 1933, 3–24
Hyman, A. 'Maimonides' "Thirteen Principles"', *Jewish Medieval and Renaissance Studies*, Cambridge, Mass., 1967, 119–44
Ibn ʿAbbās. *Kitāb bayān lughāt al-Qur'ān*, MS. Esad Efendi 91
—— *Kitāb gharīb al-Qur'ān*, MS. Atif Efendi 2815
—— *'Masā'il Nāfiʿ b. Azraq'*: see ʿAbd al-Bāqī, *Muʿjam gharīb al-Qur'ān*, 234–92
Ibn ʿAbd Rabbih. *Al-ʿIqd al-farīd*, Bulaq, 1293
Ibn Abī 'l-Iṣbaʿ. *Badīʿ al-Qur'ān*, Cairo, 1957
Ibn Anbārī. *Al-Inṣāf fī masā'il al-khilāf*, Cairo, 1961
Ibn ʿArabī. *Aḥkām al-Qur'ān*, Cairo, 1331
—— *Sharḥ* to Tirmidhī, *Ṣaḥīḥ*, Cairo, 1934
Ibn Athīr. *Kitāb al-kāmil*, Leiden, 1851–76
Ibn Ḥazm. *Kitāb al-fiṣal wal-milal*, Cairo, 1321
Ibn Hishām. See Ibn Isḥāq
Ibn Hishām al-Anṣārī. *Mughnī 'l-labīb*, Cairo, 1969
Ibn Isḥāq. *Al-Sīra al-nabawiyya* (Ibn Hishām), Cairo, 1955
Ibn Kalbī, Hishām. *Kitāb al-Aṣnām*, Cairo, 1924
Ibn Kammūna (Saʿd b. Manṣūr). *Tanqīḥ al-abḥāth lil-milal al-thalāth*, Berkeley–Los Angeles, 1967
Ibn Kathīr. *Tafsīr*, Beirut, 1966
Ibn Munayyir. 'Al-Intiṣāf': *sharḥ* to Zamakhsharī, *Al-Kashshāf*, Beirut, 1967
Ibn Muʿtazz. *Kitāb al-Badīʿ*, London, 1935
Ibn Muqaffaʿ. 'Risālat fil-Ṣaḥāba', in M. Kurd ʿAlī, *Rasā'il al-bulaghā'*, Cairo, 1946, 117–34
Ibn Qutayba. *Ta'wīl Mushkil al-Qur'ān*, Cairo, 1954
Ibn Saʿd. *Ṭabaqāt*, Cairo, 1939
Ibn Wahb. *Al-Burhān fī wujūh al-bayān*, Baghdad, 1967
Ibn Abī Dāwūd. See Jeffery, *Materials*
Iṣfahānī, Rāghib. *Ḥall mutashābihāt al-Qur'ān*, MS. Ragip Pasha 180
Izutsu, T. *Ethico-religious concepts in the Qur'ān*, Montreal, 1966
Jāḥiẓ. 'Kitāb ḥujaj al-nubuwwa', in *Rasā'il*, Cairo, 1933, 117–54

—— *Al-Bayān wal-tabyīn* i–iii, Cairo, 1947

—— 'Kitāb al-tarbīʿ wal-tadwīr', in *Tria Opuscula*, Leiden, 1903, 86–107

Jaʿfar al-Ṣādiq. *Tafsīr*, MS. Nafiz Pasha 65

Jaṣṣāṣ. *Aḥkām al-Qurʾān*, Istanbul, 1335–8

Jastrow, M. *A Dictionary of the Targumim*, New York, 1950

Jeffery, A. *Materials for the history of the text of the Qurʾān* (inc. Ibn Abī Dāwūd, *Kitāb al-maṣāḥif*), Leiden, 1937

—— 'The Qur'ān as scripture', *MW* xl (1950) 41–55, 106–34, 185–206, 257–75

Jensen, P. 'Das Leben Muhammeds und die David-Sage', *Der Islam* xii (1922) 84–97

Johnson, A. 'Mashal', in *Wisdom in Israel and in the ancient Near East*, Suppl. *VT* iii (1960) 162–9

Jones, J. 'The chronology of the *maghāzī*—a textual survey', *BSOAS* xix (1957) 245–80

Jullandri, R. 'Qur'ānic exegesis and classical tafsīr', *IQ* xii (1968) 71–119

Jurjānī. *Asrār al-balāgha*, Istanbul, 1954

—— *Dalāʾil iʿjāz al-Qurʾān*, Cairo, 1372

Kahle, P. 'The Arabic readers of the Koran', *JNES* viii (1949) 65–71

Kalbī, Muḥammad. *Tafsīr*, MS. Ayasofya 118, Hamidiye 40

Katsch, A. *Judaism in Islam*, New York, 1954

Khoury, A. *Les Théologiens byzantins et l'Islam*, Louvain–Paris, 1969. See Wansbrough, *BSOAS* xxxiii (1970) 391–3

Khurasānī, ʿAṭā' (Pseudo). *Tafsīr (ikhtilāf)*, MS. Ahmet III, 310

Kisā'ī. *Kitāb Mushtabihāt al-Qurʾān*, MS. Beyazit Umumi 436

Kister, M. 'You shall only set out for three mosques': a study of an early tradition', *Le Muséon* lxxxii (1969) 173–96

—— 'A bag of meat: a study of an early *ḥadīth*', *BSOAS* xxxiii (1970) 267–75

—— 'Al-taḥannuth: an inquiry into the meaning of a term', *BSOAS* xxxi (1968) 223–36

—— '*Al-ḥīra*: some notes on its relations with Arabia', *Arabica* xv (1968) 143–69

Koch, K. *The Growth of the Biblical Tradition*, London, 1969

Kofler, H. 'Reste altarabischer Dialekte', *WZKM* xlvii (1940) 61–130, 233–62, xlviii (1941) 52–88, 247–74, xlix (1942) 15–30, 234–56

Kluge, F. and Götze, A. *Etymologisches Wörterbuch der deutschen Sprache*, Berlin 1953

Kopf, L. 'Religious influences on medieval Arabic philology', *SI* v (1956) 33–59

—— 'The treatment of foreign words in medieval Arabic lexicology', *Scripta Hierosolymitana* ix (1961) 191–205

Krauss, S. 'Talmudische Nachrichten über Arabien', *ZDMG* lxx (1916) 321–53, lxxi (1917) 268–9

Künstlinger, D. ' "Kitāb" und "ahlu l-kitābi" im Ḳurān', *RO* iv (1926) 238–47

—— ' "Islām", "Muslim", "Aslama" im Ḳurān'. *RO* xi (1935) 128–37

—— 'Die Namen der Gottes-Schriften im Qurān', *RO* xiii (1937) 72–84

—— ' 'Uzair ist der Sohn Allāh's', *OLZ* (1932) 381–3

—— 'Sabʿan min al-mathānī', *OLZ* (1937) 596–8

Lammens, H. *L'Arabie occidentale avant l'hégire*, Beirut, 1928

Lauterbach, J. *Saadja Al-fajjūmī's arabische Psalmenübersetzung und Commentar (Psalm 107–24)*, Berlin, 1903

Lausberg, H. *Handbuch der literarischen Rhetorik*, München, 1960

Lehmann, E., and Pedersen, J. 'Der Beweis für die Auferstehung im Koran, *Der Islam* v (1914) 54–61

Lidzbarski, M. 'Salām und Islām', *ZS* i (1922) 85–96

Lindblom, J. 'Wisdom in the Old Testament prophets', in *Wisdom in Israel and in the ancient Near East*, Suppl. *VT* iii (1960) 192–204

Loewe, R. 'The "Plain" meaning of scripture in early Jewish exegesis', in *Papers of the Institute of Jewish Studies*, Jerusalem, 1965, 140–85

—— 'The medieval history of the Latin Vulgate', *CHB* ii, Cambridge, 1969, 102–54

Maʿarrī. *Risālat al-ghufrān*, Cairo, 1950

Anon. *Kitāb al-Mabānī*, Cairo, 1954 (Jeffery, *Two Muqaddimas*)

Malaṭī. *Kitāb al-tanbīh wal-radd ʿalā ahl al-ahwāʾ wal-bidaʿ*, Bibliotheca Islamica IX, Istanbul, 1936

Maimonides. *Dalālat al-ḥāʾirīn* i–iii, Paris, 1856–66 (S. Munk)

—— *Iggeret Teman*, New York, 1952 (A. Halkin)

Mālik b. Anas. *Al-Muwaṭṭaʾ*, Cairo, 1951

Margoliouth, D. 'Omar's instructions to the kadi', *JRAS* (1910) 307–26

—— 'The origins of Arabic poetry', *JRAS* (1925) 417–49

Massignon, L. *Recueil de textes inédits concernant l'histoire de la mystique en pays d'Islam* i, Paris, 1929

Masson, D. *Le Coran et la révélation judéo-chrétienne: études comparées*, Paris, 1958

Mann, J. *The Jews in Egypt and in Palestine under the Fatimids* i–ii, Oxford, 1920–2

Māturīdī. *Kitāb Taʾwīlāt al-Qurʾān*, MS. Medine 179, 180

Mehren, A. von. *Die Rhetorik der Araber*, Kopenhagen–Wien, 1853

Metzger, B. *The Text of the New Testament*, Oxford, 1968

Mirsky, A. 'Biblical variants in medieval Hebrew poetry', *Textus* iii (1963) 159–62

Mittwoch, E. 'Die Berliner arabische Handschrift Ahlwardt No. 683', in *A Volume of Oriental Studies Presented to E. G. Browne*, Cambridge, 1922, 339–44

Monroe, J. 'Oral composition in Pre-Islamic poetry', *Journal of Arabic Literature* iii (1972) 1–53

Moubarac, Y. *Abraham dans le Coran*, Paris, 1958

Moscati, S. (ed.). *An Introduction to the Comparative Grammar of the Semitic Languages*, Wiesbaden, 1964

—— (ed.). *Linguistica Semitica; presente e futuro*, Studi Semitici 4, Rome, 1961

Mowinckel, S. 'Psalm criticism between 1900 and 1935', *VT* v (1955) 13–33

Muilenburg, J. 'A study in Hebrew rhetoric: repetition and style', Suppl. *VT* i (1953) 97–111

Müller, F. *Untersuchungen zur Reimprosa im Koran*, Bonn, 1969. See Wansbrough, *BSOAS* xxxiii (1970) 389–91

Murtaḍā, Sharīf. *Amālī*, Cairo, 1954
Muqātil b. Sulaymān. *Tafsīr*, MS. Hasan Hüsnü 17
—— *Kitāb tafsīr al-khamsmi'at āya min al-Qur'ān*, MS. British Museum Or. 6333
—— *Kitāb al-Ashbāh wal-naẓīr fī tafsīr al-Qur'ān*, MS. Beyazit Umumi 561
Muslim. *Ṣaḥīḥ* viii, Cairo, 1332
Naḥḥās. *Kitāb al-nāsikh wal-mansūkh*, Cairo, 1938
Nöldeke, T. *Beiträge zur Kenntnis der Poesie der alten Araber*, Hannover, 1864
—— *Delectus Veterum Carminum Arabicorum*, Berlin 1890
—— *Zur Grammatik des classischen Arabisch* (ed. Spitaler), Darmstadt, 1963
—— *Beiträge zur semitischen Sprachwissenschaft*, Strassburg, 1904
—— *Neue Beiträge zur semitischen Sprachwissenschaft*, Strassburg, 1910
—— and Schwally, F. *Geschichte des Qorans* i–ii, Leipzig, 1909–19. See Bergsträsser-Pretzl
Norden, E. *Die Antike Kunstprosa*, Stuttgart, 1958
Norris, H. 'New evidence on the life of ʿAbdullāh B. Yāsīn and the origins of the the Almoravid movement', *Journal of African History* xii (1971) 255–68
Nyberg, H. 'Zum Kampf zwischen Islam und Manichäismus', *OLZ* xxxii (1929) 425–41
Obermann, J. 'Political theology in early Islam: Ḥasan al-Baṣrī's treatise on qadar', *JAOS* lv (1935) 138–62
—— 'Koran and Agada: the events at Mount Sinai', *AJSLL* lvii (1941) 23–48
—— 'Islamic origins: a study in background and foundation', in *The Arab Heritage*, Princeton, 1944, 58–120
Ory, S. 'Un Nouveau Type de muṣḥaf: Inventaire des Corans en rouleaux de provenance damascaine, conservés à Istanbul', *REI* xxxiii (1965) 87–149
O'Shaughnessy, T. *The Koranic Concept of the Word of God*, Rome, 1948
—— 'The seven names for Hell in the Qur'ān', *BSOAS* xxiv (1961) 444–69
—— *Muhammad's Thoughts on Death: a Thematic Study of the Qur'anic Data*, Leiden, 1969. See Wansbrough, *BSOAS* xxxiii (1970) 613–15
Paret, R. 'Der Koran als Geschichtsquelle', *Der Islam* xxxvii (1961) 26–42
—— *Der Koran: Kommentar und Konkordanz*, Stuttgart, 1971
Pedersen, J. *Israel* i–iv, London–Copenhagen, 1926–40
—— 'The Islamic preacher: wāʿiẓ, mudhakkir, qāṣṣ', in *Goldziher Memoria Volume* i, Budapest, 1948, 226–51
—— 'The criticism of the Islamic preacher', *WI* ii (1953) 215–31
—— See Lehmann, E.
Perlmann, M. 'Another Kaʿb al-Aḥbār story', *JQR* xlv (1954) 48–58
Qarṭājannī. See Heinrichs, W., *Arabische Dichtung*
Qalqashandī. *Ṣubḥ al-aʿshā*, Cairo, 1914–20
Qāsim b. Ibrāhīm. *Kitāb al-radd ʿalā 'l-zindīq* (see Guidi, M.)
Qazwīnī. *Shurūḥ al-talkhīṣ* i–iv, Cairo, 1937
Qummī. *Tafsīr*, Najaf, 1386
Qurṭubī. *Al-Jāmi ʿli-aḥkām al-Qur'ān*, Cairo, 1967

Rabin, C. *Ancient West-Arabian*, London, 1951
—— 'The beginnings of Classical Arabic', *SI* iv (1955) 19–37
—— *Qumran Studies*, Oxford, 1957
—— 'The historical background of Qumran Hebrew', *Scripta Hierosolymitana* iv (1958/1965) 144–61
Rad, G. von. *Old Testament Theology* i–ii, Edinburgh, 1962–5
Reckendorf, H. *Die Syntaktischen Verhältnisse des Arabischen* i–ii, Leiden, 1895–8
—— *Arabische Syntax*, Heidelberg, 1921
Reuschel, W. 'Wa-kāna llāhu ʿalīman raḥīman', in *Studia Orientalia in Memoriam Caroli Brockelmann*, Halle, 1968, 147–53
Richter, W. *Exegese als Literaturwissenschaft*, Göttingen, 1971
Ritter, H. 'Studien zur Geschichte der islamischen Frömmigkeit I. Ḥasan al-Baṣrī, *Der Islam* xxi (1933) 1–83
Rosenthal, F. 'The influence of the Biblical tradition on Muslim historiography', in *Historians of the Middle East*, London, 1962, 35–45
Saadya. *Kitāb al-Amānāt wal-iʿtiqādāt*, Leiden, 1880
—— See Galliner, S., and Lauterbach, J.
Sabbagh, T. *La Métaphore dans le Coran*, Paris, 1943
Schacht, J. *The Origins of Muhammadan Jurisprudence*, Oxford, 1953
—— *An Introduction to Islamic Law*, Oxford, 1964
Schapiro, I. *Die haggadischen Elemente im erzählenden Teil des Korans* i, Leipzig, 1907
Schoeps, H. *Theologie und Geschichte des Judenchristentums*, Tübingen, 1949
Schreiner, M. 'Zur Geschichte der Polemik zwischen Juden und Muhammedanern', *ZDMG* xlii (1888) 591–675
Schrieke, B. 'Die Himmelsreise Muhammeds', *Der Islam* vi (1915–16) 1–30
Schwarz, M. 'The Letter of al-Ḥasan al-Baṣrī', *Oriens* xx (1967/9) 15–30
Schwarzbaum, H. 'The Jewish and Moslem versions of some theodicy legends', *Fabula* iii (1959–60) 119–69
Seeligmann, I. 'Voraussetzungen der Midraschexegese', Suppl. *VT* i (1953) 150–81
Segal, M. *A Grammar of Mishnaic Hebrew*, Oxford, 1927
Sellheim, R. 'Prophet, Caliph und Geschichte: Die Muhammad-Biographie des Ibn Isḥāq', *Oriens* xviii–xix (1965–6/67) 33–91
Semaan, K. 'Al-Nāsikh wal-mansūkh', *IQ* vi (1961) 11–29
Serjeant, R. 'The "Constitution of Medina" ', *IQ* viii (1964) 3–16
Sezgin, F. *Geschichte des Arabischen Schrifttums* i, Leiden, 1967
Shāfiʿī. *Al-Risāla*, Cairo, 1940
—— *Aḥkām al-Qurʾān* (Bayhaqī), Cairo, 1951–2
Shahid, I. 'A contribution to Koranic exegesis', in *Arabic and Islamic Studies in Honor of Hamilton A. R. Gibb*, Leiden, 1965, 563–80
Shahrastānī. *Kitāb al-Milal wal-niḥal*, Cairo, 1321
Sidersky, D. *Les Origines des légendes musulmanes dans le Coran*, Paris, 1933
Sister, M. 'Metaphern und Vergleiche im Koran' *MSOS* xxxiv (1931) 104–54

Speyer, H. *Die Biblischen Erzählungen im Qoran*, Hildesheim, 1961
Spitaler, A. Review of Fück, *'Arabīya*, in *BO* x (1953) 144–50
—— Review of Bloch, *Vers und Sprache*, in *Oriens* ii (1949) 317–22
—— 'Arabisch', in *Linguistica Semitica*, 115–38 (see Moscati, S.)
—— See Nöldeke, *Zur Grammatik*
Steinschneider, M. *Polemische und apologetische Literatur in arabischer Sprache*, Leipzig, 1877
Stetter, E. *Topoi und Schemata im ḥadīṯ*, Tübingen, 1965
Stieglecker, H. *Die Glaubenslehren des Islam* i–iv, Paderborn, 1959–62
Strack, H. *Introduction to the Talmud and Midrash*, Philadelphia, 1945
Subkī. *Shurūḥ al-talkhīṣ* i–iv (see Qazwīnī)
Sufyān Thawrī. *Tafsīr al-Qur'ān al-karīm*, Rampur, 1965
Suhaylī. *Al-Rawḍ al-unuf*, Cairo, 1332
Suyūṭī. *Al-Itqān fī 'ulūm al-Qur'ān*, Cairo, 1967
—— *Al-Muzhir fī 'ulūm al-lugha*, Cairo, 1958
—— and Maḥallī. *Tafsīr al-Jalālayn*, Damascus, 1385
Ṭabarī. *Annales*, Leiden, 1879–1901
—— *Tafsīr*, Cairo, 1321–8
—— *Kitāb Ikhtilāf al-fuqahā'* (J. Schacht), Leiden, 1933
Tahānawī. *Kitāb Kashshāf iṣṭilāḥāt al-funūn*, Calcutta, 1862
Tirmidhī. *Ṣaḥīḥ* xi–xii, Cairo, 1934
Torrey, C. *The Jewish Foundation of Islam*, New York, 1967
Tustarī. *Tafsīr al-Qur'ān al-'aẓīm*, Cairo, 1329
Tyan, E. 'Méthodologie et sources du droit en Islam', *SI* x (1959) 79–109
Ullendorff, E. 'Is Biblical Hebrew a language?', *BSOAS* xxxiv (1971) 241–55
Ullmann, M. *Untersuchungen zur Rağazpoesie*, Wiesbaden, 1966
Vajda, G. 'Juifs et Musulmans selon le ḥadīṯ', *JA* ccxxix (1937) 57–127
Vermes, G. *Scripture and Tradition in Judaism*, Leiden, 1961
—— 'The use of bar nash/bar nashā in Jewish Aramaic', in Black, *An Aramaic Approach*, 310–28
—— 'Bible and Midrash: early Old Testament exegesis', *CHB* i, Cambridge, 1970, 199–231
Vollers, K. 'Arabisch und Semitisch: Gedanken über eine Revision der semitischen Lautgesetze', *ZA* ix (1894) 165–217
—— Review of Nöldeke, *Zur Grammatik*, in *ZA* xii (1897) 125–39
—— *Volkssprache und Schriftsprache im alten Arabien*, Strassburg, 1906
Vossler, K. *Einführung ins Vulgärlatein* (H. Schmeck), München, 1954
Wāḥidī. *Kitāb Asbāb al-nuzūl*, Cairo, 1315
Wansbrough, J. 'A Note on Arabic rhetoric', in *Lebende Antike: Symposion für Rudolf Sühnel*, Berlin, 1967, 55–63
—— 'Arabic rhetoric and Qur'anic exegesis', *BSOAS* xxxi (1968) 469–85
—— 'Majāz al-qur'ān: periphrastic exegesis', *BSOAS* xxxiii (1970) 247–66
Wāqidī. *Kitāb al-Maghāzī* (M. Jones), London, 1966. See Wansbrough, *BSOAS* xxxi (1968) 148–9

Watt, W. 'Early discussions about the Qur'ān', *MW* xl (1950) 27–40, 96–105
—— 'The dating of the Qur'ān: a review of Richard Bell's theories', *JRAS* (1957) 46–56
—— 'The Materials used by Ibn Isḥāq', in *Historians of the Middle East*, London, 1962, 23–34
Wehr, H. Review of Fück, *'Arabīya*, in *ZDMG* cii (1952) 179–86
Weil, G. *Die grammatischen Schulen von Kufa und Basra*, Leiden, 1913
—— *Grundriss und System der altarabischen Metren*, Wiesbaden, 1958
Weinreich, U. *Languages in contact*, The Hague–Paris, 1968
Weisgerber, L. *Deutsch als Volksname*, Stuttgart, 1953
Weisweiler, M. "Abdalqāhir al-Curcānī's Werk über die Unnachahmlichkeit des Korans und seine syntaktisch-stilistischen Lehren, *Oriens* xi (1958) 77–121
Wellhausen, J. *Reste arabischen Heidentums*, Berlin, 1927
—— *Prolegomena zur ältesten Geschichte des Islams*, Skizzen und Vorarbeiten VI, Berlin, 1899
—— *Das arabische Reich und sein Sturz*, Berlin, 1902
Wensinck, A. 'Muhammed und die Propheten', *AO* ii (1924) 168–98
—— *A Handbook of Early Muhammadan Tradition*, Leiden, 1927
—— *The Muslim Creed*, Cambridge, 1932
Westermann, C. *Grundformen prophetischer Rede*, München, 1968
Wetzstein, I. 'Sprachliches aus den Zeltlagern der syrischen Wüste', *ZDMG* xxii 1868) 69–194
Widengren, G. *Muhammad, the Apostle of God, and his Ascension*, Uppsala–Wiesbaden, 1955
—— 'Oral tradition and written literature among the Hebrews in the light of Arabic evidence, with special regard to prose narratives', *AO* xxiii (1959) 201–62
Wieder, N. *The Judean Scrolls and Karaism*, London, 1962
Wild, S. *Das Kitāb al-'Ain und die arabische Lexikographie*, Wiesbaden, 1965
Würthwein, E. *The Text of the Old Testament*, Oxford, 1957
Zabīdī. *Tāj al-'Arūs*, Cairo, 1306–7
Zajjāj. *Kitāb I'rāb al-Qur'ān wa-ma'ānīhi*, MS. Ahmet III, 122–3, Nurosmaniye 115
Zamakhsharī. *Al-Kashshāf 'an ḥaqā'iq al-tanzīl* i–iv, Beirut, 1967
—— *Al-Mufaṣṣal*, Christiana, 1879
Zuhrī. *Kitāb Tanzīl al-Qur'ān*, Beirut, 1963
Zunz, L. *Die Gottesdienstlichen Vorträge der Juden*, Frankfurt, 1892

I

REVELATION AND CANON

1. THE DOCUMENT

ONCE separated from an extensive corpus of prophetical *logia*, the Islamic revelation became scripture and in time, starting from the fact itself of literary stabilization, was seen to contain a logical structure of its own. By the very achievement of canonicity the document of revelation was assured a kind of independence, both of historical traditions commonly adduced to explain its existence and of external criteria recruited to facilitate its understanding. But the elaborate and imposing edifice of classical Quranic scholarship is hardly monolithic, and discernible lines of cleavage correspond to the number of options left open to the most fundamental lines of inquiry. Both formally and conceptually, Muslim scripture drew upon a traditional stock of monotheistic imagery, which may be described as schemata of revelation. Analysis of the Quranic application of these shows that they have been adapted to the essentially paraenetic character of that document, and that, for example, originally narrative material was reduced almost invariably to a series of discrete and parabolic utterances. An illustration is *Sūrat Yūsuf*, often cited as a single instance of complete and sustained narrative in the Qur'ān. In fact, without benefit of exegesis the Quranic story of Joseph is anything but clear, a consequence in part of its elliptical presentation and in part of occasional allusion to extra-Biblical tradition, e.g. verses 24, 67, 77.[1] It may, indeed, be supposed that the public for whom Muslim scripture was intended could be expected to supply the missing detail. A distinctly referential, as contrasted with expository, style characterizes Quranic treatment of most of what I have alluded to as schemata of revelation, exhibited there as components of earlier established literary types. The technique by which a theme is repeatedly signalled but seldom developed may be observed from an examination in their Quranic form of those themes traditionally associated with literature of prophetical expression. Not merely the principal themes, but also the rhetorical conventions by which they are linked and in which they are clothed, the variant traditions in which they have been preserved, as well as the incidence of exegetical gloss and linguistic assimilation, comprise the areas of investigation undertaken in the first part of these studies.

[1] See below, IV pp. 136–7.

Four characteristic examples are found in the imagery appropriate to the theodicy: retribution, sign, exile, and covenant. These themes, which constitute by far the major part of the Quranic message, depend upon a limited lexical range with correspondingly high ratios of frequency and distribution. The result is not unexpected: a very repetitive style which could indicate either a long period of oral transmission or an original series of unco-ordinated pericopes, or both.[1] The imagery associated with divine retribution turns principally upon four substantives: *umma* (nation), *awwalūn* (predecessors), *qarn* (generation), and *qarya* (abode), accompanied by such finite verbs as *khalā*, *maḍā*, and *halaka* (signifying decease). Of the many contexts containing these locutions those which are not anonymous were analysed by Horovitz, described as *Straflegenden*, and ingeniously related to the seven *mathānī* (Q. 15: 87, possibly 39: 23).[2] Emphasis upon the dramatis personae of those *Straflegenden*, which I should prefer to call retribution pericopes, led Horovitz to postulate a number of Biblical calques, in turn adduced as evidence of the Arabian prophet's increasing knowledge of Hebrew scripture. This kind of argument was a corollary of that scholar's acceptance of the Nöldeke–Schwally chronology of revelation, a feasible but hardly the only method of interpreting the Quranic data.[3] The phrases تلك أمة قد خلت (Q. 2: 134, 141), لكل أمة أجل (Q. 7: 34, 10: 49), لكل أمة رسول (Q. 10: 47, cf. 16: 36, with *shahīd* 16: 89, with *nadhīr* 35: 24), لقد أرسلنا الى أمم من قبلك (Q. 16: 63, cf. 29: 18, 41: 25), etc., are to be understood as hortatory or admonishing, and of eschatological rather than historical significance. Of similar application is imagery developed round the concept *awwalūn*, as بل قالوا مثل ما قال الأولون (Q. 23: 81), إنْ هذا الا أساطير الأولين (Q. 8: 38, cf. 3: 136), فقد مضت سنة الأولين (Q. 6: 25), ولقد أرسلنا من قبلك فى شيع الأولين (Q. 15: 10, cf. 54: 51), ومضى مثل الأولين Q. 43: 8, cf. 13: 6), in which the implicit reference to history is attenuated by the eschatological framework. The locution كم أهلكنا من قبلهم من قرن (Q. 6: 6, 19: 74, 98, etc.) is always anonymous, as are almost all constructions based on the plural *qurūn* (e.g. Q. 10: 13, 32: 26. 36: 31, etc.). Similarly وما أهلكنا من قرية (Q. 7: 4), وكم من قرية أهلكناها (Q. 15: 4), and with the plural مهلك القرى (Q. 6: 131, 28: 59).

It may seem useful to distinguish between these general thematic formulations and those narrative conventions employed to introduce or to conclude actual accounts of divine retribution found in the Qur'ān, such as كذلك نقصّ عليك من أنباء ما قد سبق (Q. 20: 99, cf. 7: 101, 11: 100, etc.),

[1] See below, pp. 20, 46–52.

[2] *Untersuchungen*, 10–32.

[3] See below, pp. 38–43.

or لقد كان فى قصصهم عبرة (Q. 12: 111). The phrase فانظروا كيف كان عاقبة الذين من قبل is either of anonymous application (Q. 30: 42) or specific (e.g. Moses, in Q. 40: 21), like several of the narrative formulae.[1] Closely related to the imagery of retribution and containing an allusion to what might be regarded as its *Sitz im Leben* is Q. 27: 34 قالت ان الملوك اذا دخلوا قرية أفسدوها وجعلوا أعزة أهلها أذلة وكذلك يفعلون. In the context of Solomon's letter to the queen of Sabā' a threat of destruction is seen to be of secular origin, but employing the 'abode' (*qarya*) image, the one of most frequent occurrence among the Quranic formulae for divine retribution. It is, on the other hand, hardly likely, in view of the *basmala*, that we are here offered even the reminiscence of an authentic document, and the expression 'when they enter a village they destroy it' is probably to be interpreted as *Nachdichtung* derived from precisely that formula.[2] It would anyway appear that the conventional designation of this theme adopted by exegetes was *umam khāliya* (the nations which have perished), e.g. by Muqātil b. Sulaymān ad Q. 18: 9 and 55 to gloss *āyātinā* (our signs) and *sunnat al-awwalīn* (the way of the predecessors), respectively.[3] *Umam khāliya* may be thought to exhibit the motif: *Ubi sunt qui ante nos in mundo fuere* characteristic of Wisdom literature, despite absence in the Quranic text of an exact equivalent to *Ubi sunt*.[4] Identification and historicity of the *umam khāliya* were problems posed and solved in the literature of haggadic exegesis.[5] In Muslim scripture itself they represent merely perpetuation of a literary type.

The nations perished in many ways, each an expression of divine vengeance. Here the Quranic vocabulary draws amply upon the lexicon of literary Arabic. Based upon only a few finite verbs, of which the most common are *ja'ala*, *akhadha*, *arsala*, and *waqa'a* (all containing the connotation: to set in motion), the primary concepts *'āqiba* (destiny) and *'adhāb* (retribution) are realized as a series of variations upon the theme of natural disaster: e.g. *rajfa* (Q. 7: 78), *ṭūfān* (29: 14), *rijz* (2: 59), *maṭar* (26: 173), *ḥāṣib* (17: 68), *rīḥ 'aqīm* (51: 41), *qāṣif min al-rīḥ* (17: 69), *ḥijāra min sijjīl* (11: 82), *ḥijāra min ṭīn* (51: 33), *sayl al-'arim* (34: 16), *rīḥ ṣarṣar* (41: 16), *fāra 'l-tannūr* (11: 40), *mā' munhamir* (54: 11), *jarād wa-qummal wa-ḍafādi' wa-dam* (7: 133), *sinīn wa-naqṣ min al-thamarāt* (7: 130), *ṣā'iqa* (2: 55); but occasionally also as more direct intervention: e.g. *la'na* (28: 42), *ṣayḥa* (11: 67), *zajra* (37: 19), *ṣākhkha* (80: 33), used to convey the notion of curse, as

1 See below, pp. 18–20.
2 *Pace* Horovitz, op. cit. 35.
3 *Tafsīr*, MS H. Hüsnü 17, 167v, 170v; see also the references in Goldziher, *Abhandungen* II, xvi–xviii: *qubūriyyāt*.
4 Becker, 'Ubi sunt', esp. 509; cf. Horovitz, op. cit. 16, 21, 29; and for poetic treatment, Hirschberg, *Lehren*, 53–7.
5 See below, IV pp. 135–6.

well as generic terms like *ṭā'if* (68: 19), *ṭāghiya* (69: 5), *baṭsha* (44: 16), or *karb* (37: 115). The significance of this imagery is typological and the punishments exemplary, of the kind referred to in Q. 13. 6 وقد خلت من قبلهم المثلات and 34: 19 وجعلناهم أحاديث. Both frequency and distribution of the selected lexica suggest originally distinct pericopes.

To be contrasted with the *exempla* afforded by the *umam khāliya* are the concepts of trial and ordeal exhibited in the verbs *balā* and *fatana* with God as subject, e.g. وفى ذلكم بلاء من ربّكم (Q. 2: 49), فأما الانسان اذا ما ابتلاه ربّه (Q. 89: 15), ولقد فتنّا الذين من قبلهم (Q. 29: 3), and especially كل نفس ذائقة الموت ونبلوكم بالشر والخير فتنة والينا ترجعون (Q. 21: 35). Similar constructions with *aḍalla* (cause to err) may also be adduced, e.g. كذلك يضلّ الله من يشاء (Q. 74: 31). Divine justice is here mitigated by what seems clearly to be a reflex of the Biblical election tradition, evident in passages where Abraham (Q. 2: 124) or David (38: 24) or Solomon (38: 34) is object of the trial. Not unexpected is the occasional allusion in these contexts to its corollary, the remnant tradition (*baqīya*, *bāqiya*, *bāqiyūn*): general in Q. 11: 116 القرون من قبلكم اولوا بقية and specific in 26: 120 and 37: 77 (Noah), 43: 28 (Abraham), 2: 248 (Moses and Aaron), 69: 8 (ʿĀd), and 53: 51 (Thamūd), the two last negatively expressed and thus belonging to the *umam khāliya*. The appearance in Muslim scripture of these two Biblical motifs may, in my opinion, be interpreted as *Bildungserlebnis* imperfectly assimilated.

Of quite different character is treatment of the retribution theme reflected in the locution *ayyām allāh* (days/battles of God). In Quranic usage *yawm* may be merely chronological and quantitative, as in Q. 2: 196, 41: 9–10, etc., but the context is more often eschatological, e.g. من قبل ان يأتى يوم لا مردّ له من الله (Q. 30: 43, cf. 14: 44) and in phrases like نسيتم لقاء يومكم (Q. 32: 14) and لكم ميعاد يوم (34: 30). Its typical function as complement to *umma* is evident in الأيام الخالية (Q. 69: 24) and مثل أيام الذين خلوا من قبلهم (10: 102). In Q. 45: 14 الذين لا يرجون أيام الله the plural *ayyām* is the equivalent of the eschatological singular in the examples above and of the Biblical יום יהוה. With one exception (Job 24: 1) Biblical usage favours the singular, which may of course refer to a historical event, e.g. Isaiah 9: 3 יום מדין, a synonym of מלחמה (Judges 8: 13). But the days/battles of Israel are also those of God (Numbers 21: 14 מלחמת יהוה) a concept very likely the source of *ayyām* not only in Q. 45: 14 (above), but also in 3: 140 وتلك الأيام نداولها بين الناس and 14: 5 اخرج قومك من الظلمات الى النور وذكّرهم بأيام الله, the latter addressed to Moses. Now, the existence in Arabic of a profane tradition (*ayyām al-ʿarab*) might be thought to provide an alternative source for the Quranic locution, much as it appears to have been the source of 'epic' motifs in classical Islamic historiography.[1] The possibility of contamination may not be excluded, and conceptual transfer within the Arabic lexicon from secular to divine (battle) is scarcely difficult. Against the non-occurrence of *malḥama* in Muslim scripture may be set its primary use (in the plural: *malāḥim*) as designation of apocalyptica,[2] as well as the semantic equivalence of the cognate roots felt by Saadya in his translation of Psalm 109: 3 and of Exodus 15: 3.[3] Like the remnant imagery contained in *baqīya:yeter/she'ar*, the equivalence *ayyām:milḥamot* exhibits theological elaboration of a Wisdom motif (*Ubi sunt*), of which a search for the origins might seem superfluous. In prophetical language, as opposed to that of apocalyptic, the imagery of retribution belongs to the oracular judgement (e.g. *massa* in Isaiah and the later prophets), and it is that literary type which is perpetuated in the Qur'ān.

For expression of the 'sign' as manifestation of the deity and as credential of the prophet, the lexical range is somewhat wider than for the theme of retribution. One may distinguish between Quranic terms for sign and descriptions of them. The latter fall into four groups, of which the most frequent is imagery drawn from the phenomena of divine creation, exhibiting variations upon the motif of Q. 3: 190 انّ فى خلق السموات والأرض واختلاف آلّيل والنهار لآيات لأولى الألباب. In addition to the blessings and disasters of nature events of an unusual character (*khāriq lil-ʿāda*) are introduced, e.g. splitting of the moon (Q. 54: 1, cf. 55: 37, 84: 1) and crumbling of mountains (Q. 77: 10, cf. 59: 21, 7: 143). Different from but related to those are instances of more personal intervention in the laws of nature by its creator, e.g. nourishment (Q. 7: 32, cf. 2: 257), clothing (7: 26), treasure (11: 12, cf. 9: 34, 43: 33–5), hosts (36: 28, 48: 4, cf. 3: 12, 5: 52), sanctuaries (2: 158), but also the *exempla* of salvation history: Noah and his people (25: 37), Joseph and his brothers (12: 7), Jesus and his mother (23: 50), the men of the Cave (18: 9).

Rather more important to the elaboration of dogma are two other categories of sign, which may be designated respectively guidance and scripture. To the former belong *rūḥ*, *amr*, *kalima/kalimāt*, *ḥukm/ḥikma*, *shirʿa*, *minhāj*, *miṣbāḥ/nūr*, *mawʿiẓa*, *waʿd/waʿīd*, *barāʾa*, *adhān*, but also *rasūl/risāla*, *bashīr*, *nadhīr*, *nabī/nubuwwa*, and *malak/malāʾika*. To the latter may be reckoned *kitāb/kutub*, *qur'ān*, *injīl*, *tawrāt*, *furqān*, *zabūr/*

[1] See Caskel, 'Aijām al-ʿArab', 1–99; and below, IV pp. 125, 140.

[2] Cf. Dozy, *Supplément* ii, 522, and *kutub malḥama* with *sefer milḥamot*, Numbers 21: 14; and Goldziher, *Richtungen*, 57, but also 66 n. 5, where, however, I should equate *malāḥim* with the Quranic *ayyām allāh*, not merely with 'Nachrichten apokalyptischer Art'.

[3] Lauterbach, *Saadja*, vi, 25 n. 3; Rabin, *Qumran*, 118–19.

zubur, *ṣuḥuf*, *sūra/suwar*. It would be misleading to propose a rigorously schematic distinction between the two sets of lexica, in which semantic boundaries tend to be blurred by contextual similarity. References in scripture to scripture pose a particular kind of problem, related to the role of proof-texts in Islamic prophetology.[1] Collocation of sign as guidance and sign as scripture is of comparatively high frequency in the Qur'ān, e.g. *kalimāt* with *kitāb* (Q. 18: 27), *ḥikma* with *kitāb*, *tawrāt*, and *injīl* (3: 48, 5: 110, etc.), *ḥukm* with *kitāb* and *nubuwwa* (3: 79, 6: 89, etc.). *Rūḥ* and *amr*, though not formally linked with 'scriptural' signs, appear in contexts determined by finite verbs signifying revelation, e.g. *awḥā* (Q. 42: 52) and *anzala* (65: 5), as do general terms for 'guidance' like *rushd*, *hudā*, *bayān/tibyān*, and even *raḥma* (mercy). *Rasūl* (messenger) is of course found in combination with nearly all the words of both categories. From collocations of this kind one might infer that the Quranic concept of theophany is basically scriptural, an argument commonly referred to a tradition of rhetorical accomplishment among speakers of Arabic.[2]

'Sign' is generally conveyed in Muslim scripture by *āya*, which in Q. 38: 29 may be understood to signify 'verse of the revealed book' كتاب أنزلناه اليك مبارك ليدبّروا آياته. Elsewhere, however, *āya* is merely '*exemplum*' and from analogous contexts attracts a number of synonyms, e.g. *'alāmāt* (Q. 16: 6, curiously only once, though this is the most common equivalent in exegetical literature), *'ibra* (12: 111), *uswa* (60: 4), *ḥadīth* (45: 6), *mathal* (43: 57), *tadhkira* (20: 3), *dhikr* (3: 58), *dhikrā* (50: 37), *bayyina* (20: 133), *burhān* (4: 174), *sulṭān* (30: 35), *nabā'* (38: 67), *sha'ā'ir* (22: 36), *ashrāṭ* (47: 18), *āthār* (30: 50). In Q. 48: 29 *sīmā* and *athar* are not synonyms of *āya*, but signify rather 'imprint'.[3] Save for *Sūrat Raḥmān* (verse 13 and *passim*: فبأى الآء ربّكما تكذّبان) it is *āya/āyāt* which bears the burden of a Quranic refrain: ان فى ذلك لآية (sing. Q. 2: 248, *sūras* 16 and 26 *passim*; plural 10: 67, *sūra* 30 *passim*; six occurrences with *'ibra*, e.g. 3: 13). The locution belongs to the imagery of prophetical expression, e.g. Isaiah 37: 30 וזה לך האות, and may announce a miracle: e.g. Isaiah 7: 14 לכן יתן אדני הוא לכם אות and Q. 18: 9 أم حسبت ان أصحاب الكهف والرقيم كانوا من آياتنا عجباً.[4]

It is precisely in contexts characterized by the equivalence sign: miracle, demanded as credential of the prophet, that the lexical range is widest. Introduced by such conjunctive particles as *lawlā*, *lawmā*, *law anna*, *ḥattā*,

[1] See below, II pp. 63–5.

[2] See below, II pp. 79–81.

[3] *Pace* Hirschfeld, *Researches*, 96–7 n. 75 where read *sīmā* or *āya*, but see also 45–6, 60–1; cf. *'unwān al-sujūd* in Nöldeke, *Delectus*, 77, line 14.

[4] Cf. Westermann, *Grundformen*, 113–4; Quranic usage, it may be observed, partakes of both *Heilsankündigung* and *Gerichtsankündigung*.

matā, or by a simple imperative, the demands include gardens, springs, fire, victory, angels, messengers, and (!) scripture (*kitāb*, *ṣuḥuf*, *sūra*, *qur'ān*). The formulae range from a modest reproach, e.g. لولا أنزل عليه آية من ربه (Q. 10: 20, 13: 7, etc., cf. 20: 33) to the elaborate inventory of Q. 17: 90–3:

We will not believe you until you cause a spring to erupt from the earth, or till you have a garden with palms and grapes in which you can make rivers flow, or till you cause heaven to collapse, as you claim, or bring us face to face with God and the angels, or till you own a house of gold, or ascend into heaven, nor will we believe your ascension until you send down to us a book that we can read.

The scripture:miracle imagery is of course that underlying the *taḥaddī* (challenge) verses.[1] Relation to the Quranic version of the *Ubi sunt* motif was achieved by allusion to earlier scriptural (!) revelations, e.g. Q. 21: 5 بل قالوا أضغاث أحلام بل افتراه بل هو شاعر فليأتنا بآية كما أرسل الأولون and 37: 168 لو انّ عندنا ذكرا من الأولين. In this context the not quite unexpected disclaimer of miracles and refusal 'to grant a sign' (cf. John 6: 28–32, Matthew 16: 1–4, Luke 11: 29–32), e.g. Q. 7: 203 واذا لم تأتهم بآية قالوا لولا اجتبيتها and 40: 78 وما كان لرسول ان يأتى بآية الا بإذن الله is further evidence of conformity to scriptural archetype.

A third theme contributory to the Quranic theodicy is that of exile. A primary source for the imagery is a description of Abraham's withdrawal in search of God from the environment familiar to him قال أراغب انت عن الهتى يا ابراهيم لئن لم تنته لارجمنك واهجرنى مليا . . . . واعتزلكم وما تدعون من دون الله (Q. 19: 46, 48). Use of *i'tazala* (withdrew) may be compared with Q. 18: 16, where the flight of the men of the Cave from persecution is so named. But it is the verb *hajara*, imperative here (leave me!), which exemplifies the Quranic concept of displacement, whether for the sake of worship, of redemption, or of bearing witness (martyrdom). Employment of the imperative for that classical instance of exile (cf. Genesis 12: 1 *lekh lekha*) becomes in Q. 73: 10 an expression of general paraenesis واصبر على ما يقولون واهجرهم هجرا جميلا (cf. *lekh/halokh*, Isaiah 6: 9, Jeremiah 2: 1, Ezekiel 3: 4, Amos 7: 17, etc.). The active participle of the first form appears in Q. 59: 9, but of most frequent occurrence are the perfect, imperfect, and active participle of the verb's third derived form, e.g. Q. 2: 218 انّ الذين آمنوا والذين هاجروا وجاهدوا فى سبيل الله and 4: 100 ومن يهاجر فى سبيل الله يجد فى الأرض مراغما كثيرا

[1] See below, II pp. 78–9.

وسعة ومن يخرج من بيته مهاجرا الى الله ورسوله. The parallelism of *yuhājir* and *yakhruj* exhibited in Q. 4: 100 is attested elsewhere, e.g. 2: 74, 60: 1, and in 4: 66 with the imperative *ukhrujū*. A fourth derived form with God as subject appears in Q. 8: 5 كما أخرجك ربّك من بيتك بالحق. The latter construction, accompanied by the participle *muhājir*, is especially conspicuous in a context containing the only Quranic instance of *jalā'* as exile ولولا ان كتب الله عليهم الجلاء لعذبهم فى الدنيا (Q. 59: 3, cf. verses 2, 8, 9, 11). There, the notion of exile, though an act of God, is not an imperative addressed to a prophet, but belongs instead to the vocabulary of prophetical threats (cf. *golah*, Nahum v: 10, Amos 1: 15, etc.). *Sūrat Barā'a* contains a number of parallel constructions with *kharaja* and *nafara* signifying movement towards, or at the behest of, God, e.g. the imperative in Q. 9: 38 اذا قيل لكم انفروا فى سبيل الله (cf. verses 39, 41–2, 46–7, 81, 122). The imperative of *farra* in Q. 51: 50 ففرّوا الى الله is isolated. Of Moses and Lot the verb *asrā* is used, often glossed 'in the night', e.g. Q. 44: 23 فأسر بعبادى ليلا (cf. 20: 77, 26: 52, and *lekh lekha* in Exodus 3: 10, 16, 4: 12, etc.), and 11: 81 فأسر بأهلك بقطع من الليل (cf. 15: 65). It is that locution which was employed for the *isrā'* verse (Q 17: 1), a Mosaic reference appropriated in exegetical literature to the biography of the Arabian prophet.[1] The divine imperative may also express the notion of movement combined with the imagery of retribution, as in Q. 3: 137 فسيروا فى الأرض فانظروا كيف كان عاقبة المكذبين (cf. 6: 11, 16: 36, etc., and in the imperfect: 12: 109, 30: 9, and *passim*), and especially 34: 18, following upon the devastation wrought by the deluge (verse 16: *sayl al-'arim*). The verb *sāra* occurs once (Q. 28: 29 Moses) in the perfect, and to indicate movement at the command of God, a notion symbolized in exegetical literature by the non-Quranic substantive *hijra*.[2]

The unilateral character of the imperative is reflected in the fourth theme here proposed to illustrate the Quranic theodicy: the covenant. The *locus classicus* is Q. 3: 81 واذ أخذ الله ميثاق النبيين amplified in 33: 7 by reference to Noah, Abraham, Moses, and Jesus, and employed in the exegetical tradition to depict the origins of prophecy in Arabia.[3] The finite verb form *akhadha* (took), with God as agent or one of His retributive 'signs' as source of action (e.g. Q. 11: 102, 22: 48, and 11: 57, 2: 55, respectively), invariably expresses unilateral imposition, and is thus used in the two passages cited above, as well as in most other locutions based on *mīthāq*, when the latter refers to a covenant between God and man

[1] See below, II pp. 67–8.
[2] Cf. Wensinck, 'Propheten', 189–90.
[3] Ibn Hishām, *Sīra* i, 233–4.

(Q. 2: 63, 83, 84, 93, 3: 187, 4: 154, 5: 12, 14, 70, 7: 169, 57: 8). The divine covenant is also called *ʿahd*, for which the perfect of the verb *ʿahida*, with God as agent, expresses a unilateral function, e.g. Q. 2: 125, 3: 183, etc. (36: 60 has *lam* with the jussive). A complementary and bilateral concept of *ʿahd* is exhibited in the use of third form perfect *ʿāhada*, with God as object, e.g. Q. 9: 75 ومنهم من عاهد الله. While the substantive *ʿahd* seldom occurs with the finite verb *ʿahida* (but cf. Q. 2: 124–5), there is a single instance of *mīthāq* governed by an otherwise unattested *wāthaqa*, with God as agent (Q. 5: 7). As designations of the divine covenant *ʿahd* and *mīthāq* can be synonymous, e.g. in Q. 2: 27 الذين ينقضون عهد الله من بعد ميثاقه (cf. 13: 20, 25), though it is not impossible that here *mīthāq* refers to (written?) corroboration of a covenant already articulated, an interpretation supported to some extent by Q. 7: 169 ألم يؤخذ عليهم ميثاق الكتاب, as well as by derivatives like *wathāq* (47: 4, 89: 26) and (*ʿurwa*) *wuthqā* (2: 256, 31: 22). In his translation of the Psalter, Saadya rendered 111: 5 יזכר לעולם בריתו in Arabic as ידכרך בה אלי אלאבד עהדה.[1] Like Biblical *berit*, both *ʿahd* and *mīthāq* may designate a covenantal relation between men, as in Q. 8: 56 الذين عاهدت منهم ثم ينقضون عهدهم فى كل مرة وهم لا يتقون and 8: 72 وان استنصروكم فى الدين فعليكم النصر الا على قوم بينكم وبينهم ميثاق, respectively. In the former passage use of the third derived form (*ʿāhadta*) is characteristic of the secular application of *ʿahd* (e.g. Q. 2: 100, 177, 9: 1, 4, 7), as it is also of the bilateral covenant (cf. Q. 9: 75 above, and 16: 91, 33: 15, 23, 48: 10) between God and man. For the latter an eighth derived form of *akhadha* is also attested, e.g. Q. 19: 78 أطلع الغيب ام اتخذ عند الرحمن عهدا (cf. 19: 87, 2: 80).

The Quranic covenant imagery may reflect development from profane legal terminology by the introduction of divine sanction, though it is of interest to note that in the 'Umma document(s)' preserved in the *Sīra* of Ibn Hishām neither *ʿahd* nor *mīthāq* occurs: the finite verb *ʿāhada* (!) appears once and the document itself is called *ṣaḥīfa*, a neutral term.[2] On the other hand, conceptual transfer from profane to divine imagery, and vice versa, may be inferred from modification of a formula such as إنّ العهد كان مسؤلا (Q. 17: 34) to وكان عهد الله مسؤلا (33: 15), or from the interpolation *min allāh* after each of the only three instances of *mawthiq* (Q. 12: 66, 80), the last of which, significantly, is object of the verb *akhadha* with Jacob as agent. The observation of Horovitz on a distinction between

[1] Lauterbach, *Saadja*, x, 34 n. 4.

[2] See Serjeant, 'Constitution', 3–16; it may well be that the Quranic plural *ṣuḥuf* is a reference not merely to 'scripture' but to covenant, cf. esp. Q. 87: 18–19, i.e. 'the first *ṣuḥuf*, those of Abraham and Moses'.

mīthāq as calque of *berit* and/or *diatheke* and *mīthāq* as 'Terminus der arabischen Rechtssprache' is superfluous: *berit* readily provides a *Vorlage* for either usage, and *loci probantes* for secular treaty relations will not be older than the Qur'ān document.[1] Similarly Jeffery, in a rather impressionistic treatment of some of the covenant verses, asserted that *mīthāq* and *'ahd* were also employed outside scripture (but when?). The description there of accompanying finite verb-forms is inadequately differentiated, and to adduce Q. 6: 89 (3: 81 would have been more appropriate!) as belonging to the covenant imagery must mean that 'covenant' included the gifts of scripture and prophecy, and will thus have been relevant only to Jews and Christians, not to all of the *umam khāliya*.[2] Elsewhere the author's search for parallels to/sources for the Muslim concept of scripture took him far beyond the Judaeo-Christian tradition.[3] Such investigation may be of considerable value for studies in comparative religion,[4] but of rather less for the literary analysis of scripture, especially in the light of the very explicit Quranic data. The source of the covenant imagery was clearly Biblical, and predominantly Pentateuchal. That the Mosaic covenant reflected in Muslim scripture should exhibit haggadic accretion and even conceptual deformation is hardly surprising, but worthy of remark: neither the Deuteronomic nor the Rabbinic interpretation of covenant was restricted to the express content of the Decalogue.[5]

Some evidence for determination of a *Sitz im Leben* may, however, be available for other Quranic terms appropriate to the covenant relationship. As against two instances, both secular, of *dhimma* (Q. 9: 8, 10), the Umma document contains وانّ ذمة الله واحدة: and the locution *ḥabl allāh* (Q. 3: 103) is paralleled in 3: 112 by *ḥabl min allāh* and *ḥabl min al-nās*, with which may be compared *ḥibāl* in the account of 'Aqaba.[6] Moreover, *amāna*, used of the covenant between God and man in Q. 23: 8 and 70: 32 والذين هم لأماناتهم وعهدهم راعون (cf. 2: 283 and 4: 58, where it is exclusively secular; but also Nehemiah 10: 1, in which the purpose of אמנה was adherence to God's law), is widely attested in later chancery usage.[7] Other essentially neutral terms, like *bāya'a* (acknowledge authority) and *aymān* (oaths), may in Quranic usage be lent divine sanction by occurring in context with *'ahd* and its derivatives, e.g. Q. 48: 10 إنّ الذين يبايعونك انما يبايعون الله . . . ومن أوفى بما عاهد عليه الله and 16: 91 واوفوا بعهد الله اذا عاهدتم ولا تنقضوا الأيمان بعد توكيدها, respectively.

1 *Untersuchungen*, 51.
2 'Scripture', 119–21, 127–9.
3 Jeffery, op. cit., 41–55, but cf. also 202 n. 40.
4 See below, II p. 61.
5 Cf. Obermann, 'Agada', esp. 29–47.
6 Ibn Hishām, *Sīra* I, 502, 442, respectively.
7 Qalqashandī, *Ṣubḥ* XIII, 321–51.

Covenant is related in the Quranic theodicy to the *exempla* of salvation history, to those representatives of the *umam khāliya* from which a remnant survived. Reference is general in Q. 33: 15 ولقد كانوا عاهدوا الله من قبل لا يولّون الأدبار وكان عهد الله مسؤلا (cf. 2: 286, in which covenant is depicted as 'burden'/'yoke': *iṣr*), and specific in 33: 7 واذ أخذنا من النبيين ميثاقهم ومنك ومن نوح وابراهيم وموسى وعيسى ابن مريم وأخذنا منهم ميثاقا غليظا. The context is didactic rather than historical, and the concept limited to the Patriarchal and Sinai traditions. Allusion to Adam's negligence ولقد عهدنا الى آدم من قبل فنسى ولم نجد له عزما (Q. 20: 115) reflects an admonition attested elsewhere in prophetical literature, e.g. Jeremiah 22: 9 and Hosea 6: 7.[1] Exhortation to observe and to keep the covenant (*rāʿā/awfā*) is frequent, but it is the Patriarchal and Mosaic covenants which were to be observed. A single reference to a Christian covenant (Q. 5: 14) like inclusion of Jesus in Q. 33: 7 (above), represents chronological extension, not historical development. The complementary concepts of fulfilment and renewal characteristic of the writing prophets (Jeremiah 31: 31 ברית חדשה) and of the evangelists (Luke 22: 20 καινὴ διαθήκη) are not stressed in the covenantal imagery of the Qur'ān.[2] Unlike the conceptual distinction recognized in Old Testament theology between the Deuteronomic and Priestly notions of covenant,[3] the difference of semantic functions between Quranic *akhadha* and *ʿahida*, on the one hand, and *ʿāhada* on the other, is almost purely formal. Possibly separate traditions of bilateral and unilateral covenants coalesce in the Quranic imagery to produce the concept of submission explicit in the term *islām*. The covenant terminology might appear, moreover, to support the derivation of *aslama* from *salām* proposed by Lidzbarski, namely, 'to enter into a state of peace', or perhaps 'of salvation', exhibiting the equivalence *berit: shalom*.[4] Reflex of *berit* is exhibited in two occurrences of the cognate *barā'a*: Q. 9: 1 براءة من الله ورسوله الى الذين عاهدتم من المشركين and 54: 43 أكفاركم خير من اولئكم ام لكم براءة فى الزبر, the former in a context (Q. 9: 1–10) which provided the *locus probans* for juridical theory on the scope of secular treaty relations. The clearly formulaic expression of the entire passage might, indeed, be thought to provide some evidence of a *Sitz im Leben* for the covenant as set out in Muslim scripture, similar

[1] See Speyer, *Erzählungen*, 66–7.

[2] Cf. von Rad, *Theology* ii, 212–17, 247, 268–72, but also i, 306–18.

[3] Von Rad, op. cit. i, 129–35.

[4] 'Salām', 85–90; Pedersen, *Israel* i–ii, 263–335; and Künstlinger, 'Islām', 128–37, esp. 133–4; rejected by Horovitz, *Untersuchungen*, 54–5, and Katsch, *Judaism*, 104–5, as well as by Bravmann, who detected a reflex of Arabian conduct in warfare, 'Background', 324–43.

to the role of legalistic and cultic elements in the formulation of the Hebrew covenant tradition.[1]

. . . . .

The presence in the Qur'ān of literary convention was recognized by exponents of what I have described as rhetorical exegesis.[2] The schemata of revelation include a number of conventions typically employed to introduce the major themes of the Quranic theodicy. Exhibiting a comparatively limited lexical range, those formulae serve to confirm the impression of a composition made up of originally unrelated pericopes. From the very high ratios of frequency and distribution e.g. for *qul* and *ayyuhā*, one must expect a degree of contextual overlapping. From a formal point of view, however, the conventions can be identified as apodictic, supplicatory, and narrative. As such they may be regarded as symbolic of the basic, often minimal, units of expression in prophetical literature. Seldom reducible, they frequently mirror a pre-literary form, and occasionally a discernible function in language other than scripture. For example, the covenant with Adam (Q. 20: 115) referred to above was described by Zamakhsharī as reflex of a royal messenger formula يقال فى أوامر الملوك ووصاياهم: تقدم الملك الى فلان وأوعز اليه وعزم عليه وعهد اليه.[3] Similarly, Q. 27: 34 depicting the arrival of Solomon's letter in Sabā' might be thought to contain incipient elements of the Quranic retribution imagery. The problem here, and in general, is the difficulty in dating *loci probantes* from profane Arabic literature. In its earliest stages that literature is essentially exegetical, even when not avowedly concerned to elucidate scripture, and genuinely independent witness to the *usus loquendi* is indeed rare.

Easily the most expressive example of the Quranic messenger formula is Q. 19: 17–21, in which Mary is informed by the Spirit of God (traditionally understood to be the angel Gabriel) that she is to bear a son. The passage may be analysed as follows:[4]

v. 17 Commission (*Beauftragung*)

فأرسلنا اليها روحنا فتمثل لها بشرا سويا

v. 19 Delivery (*Überbringung*)

قال انما أنا رسول ربّك لاهب لك غلاما زكيا

v. 21 Message (*Ausrichtung*)

قال كذلك قال ربّك هو علىّ هيّن ولنجعله آية للناس ورحمة منا وكان أمرا مقضيا.

The utterance of the messenger (*Botenspruch*) is contained in verses 19

[1] Cf. Buhl, 'Kuranexegese', 97–106; and Koch, *Growth*, 21–2, 29–33.

[2] See below, IV pp. 227–39.

[3] *Kashshāf* iii, 90–1 ad loc.

[4] Cf. Westermann, *Grundformen*, 72–3.

and 21 (verses 18 and 20 report Mary's reaction to the incident), and the messenger formula proper (*Botenformel*) may be isolated as كذلك قال ربّك, i.e. כה אמר יהוה.[1] The locution *kadhālika qāla rabbuki(ka)* is employed also in Q. 19: 9 for a similar message delivered to Zechariah, and in 51: 30 to Abraham, suggesting thus a stereotype for identical situations. Of related application is كذلك حقت كلمت الله in Q. 10: 33 and 40: 6. In what may be the same function *kadhālika* appears in a pausal context (followed by *wa-qad*) in Q. 18: 91, and as *corroboratio* in the queen of Sabā''s observation on the conduct of kings: 27: 34 وكذلك يفعلون.[2] The demonstrative *kadhālika*, often synonymous with *kamā* in reference to an earlier, analogous event, may occur with finite verbs and God as agent, e.g. Q. 11: 102 وكذلك أخذ ربّك اذا أخذ القرى and 18: 19 وكذلك بعثناهم, with which may be compared 2: 286 كما حملته على الذين من قبلنا and 4: 47 كما لعنّا أصحاب السبت. More often, however, the function of *kadhālika* is that of presentative, employed to introduce utterances both exemplary and general, e.g. كذلك يبيّن الله آياته (Q. 2: 187, 3: 103, etc.), وكذلك نفصّل الآيات (6: 55, 7: 32, etc., and with *nuṣarrif* 7: 58), or the refrain إنّا كذلك نجزى المحسنين (37: 80, 105, 110, 121, 131).[3] As in the prophetical literature of the Old Testament the messenger formula, also designated formula of legitimation (*corroboratio*), may be merely understood, and constructions including only the term of commission, e.g. *laqad ataynā*, *laqad arsalnā* (Q. 2: 87, 27: 15, 31: 12, and 30: 47, 40: 23, 29: 14, respectively), are common in Muslim scripture.

The most frequent by far of Quranic apodictic formulae is *qul* (say, speak!), a locution which dispenses altogether with the messenger formula as set out above. The observation of Horovitz that all of the Qur'ān must be regarded as the utterance of God is doctrinally sound but for a form-critical approach very frustrating.[4] Since, however, it has never been possible to insist that production of the Quranic revelation was analogous to that of the Hebrew prophetical literature, problems pertaining to the development of literary forms are difficult to define, let alone solve. Westermann's chronological formulation 'prophetisches Wort *als* Botenwort' presupposes just such a discernible development, attested by the various forms in which the word of God was uttered, from the Pentateuch

[1] Westermann, op. cit. 107 ff.

[2] According to Ibn Qutayba, *wa-kadhālika* in Q. 27: 34 was preceded by a pause and introduced a fresh proposition, uttered by God, *Ta'wīl* 226–7. Similarly, a pause after *kadhālika* in the *Botenformel*, e.g. Q. 19: 9, was the subject of exegetical dispute, see below, IV pp. 224–5.

[3] Cf. Koch, *Growth*, 212: *lakhen*; *kadhālika* so employed was usually interpreted *hākadhā*, see below, IV pp. 129–30.

[4] *Untersuchungen*, 5.

through the prophetical books to Chronicles.[1] By contrast, the Qur'ān exhibits a variety of recognizable literary forms in no recognizable order. Less dogmatic than Horovitz, Suyūṭī adduced five passages in Muslim scripture whose attribution to God was at least disputed: Q. 6: 104, 114 were the words of the Arabian prophet; 19: 64 (but, curiously, not 19: 9, 21 and 51: 30) were the words of Gabriel; 37: 164–66 were ascribed to the angels; finally, verse 4 of the *Fātiḥa* may have been uttered by the faithful (*'ibād*) or could, by insertion (*taqdīr*) of the imperative *qūlū*, be attributed to God, a process applicable also to the two passages ascribed to the prophet.[2] The mechanism of insertion, developed by the masoretes,[3] must surely account for some at least of the 350-odd occurrences of an imperative form of *qāla* (speak).[4]

Its functions are several, but it would be an exaggeration to describe its over-all effect as successful replacement of typically prophetical expressions by the direct speech of God. The theological implications of the inverse development in Hebrew scripture could provoke an impression that Muslim scripture represented a conscious return to the unmediated theophany of the Hexateuch.[5] That would, I think, be misleading, even were the mechanism of divine imperatives consistently applied, which clearly it was not. The role of the prophet in Islam is too central to allow of such an interpretation, however much the Muslim doctrine of scripture as the word of God might appear to lend it support.[6] What might be construed as a logical contradiction between the two views is reflected in the functions of *qul*. It is, for example, employed to introduce mention of God in the third person, as in Q. 2: 120, 140, 7: 28–9, 13: 36, 27: 93, etc., though such passages are far fewer in number than those without an introductory *qul*, perhaps best exemplified in utterances of the type: *wa*(*kāna*) *allāh 'alīm*/*raḥīm*/*ḥakīm*, etc. *Qul* may preface an apodosis after statements beginning *yas'alūnaka* (they ask you), often of halakhic content, as in the series Q. 2: 218–22, or 4: 176 and 5: 4, but also in matters eschatological (7: 187) and anecdotal (18: 83).[7] *Qul* commonly serves to indicate liturgical instructions, frequently prayer e.g. Q. 3: 26, 10: 104, 13: 16, and especially *sūra*s 112, 113, and 114.[8] Finally, but most significantly, *qul* may introduce statements not predicable of the deity and usually containing finite verb-forms like 'I fear' (Q. 6: 15), 'I have been ordered' (13: 36), 'If I err' (34: 50), but also descriptions of the type 'I am only a warner' (38: 65, etc.), as

[1] *Grundformen*, 70–1 (italics mine).
[2] *Itqān, naw'* 10: I, 99–101.
[3] See below, IV pp. 219–24.
[4] Cf. Nöldeke, 'Zur Sprache des Korans', *NBSS*, 8; *GdQ* ii, 36, 42.
[5] See Koch, *Growth*, 216 ff; von Rad, *Theology* ii, 33–49.
[6] See below, p. 38, and II, pp. 55–6, 77–8.
[7] For the manner in which *yas'alūnaka* may generate an aetiological legend, see Horovitz, *Untersuchungen*, 6, and below, IV pp. 122–6.
[8] *Pace* Nöldeke, *NBSS*, 8.

well as stereotype formulae like 'God suffices as witness between us' (29: 52). It is for these last categories that the possibility of interpolation suggests itself, but to insist upon such in a text characterized by the absence of logical structure, as contrasted with stylistic homogeneity, would be superfluous.[1]

A somewhat less common apodictic formula is the vocative *yā ayyuhā*. Though from the observations so far made this locution could be seen to require a preceding *qul*, it is in fact so provided only six times, four of which contain declarations in the first person that could not be ascribed to God (Q. 7: 158, 10: 104, 22: 49, 109: 1–2). It would thus not be impossible to see in that phrase the primary form of prophetical announcement in Muslim scripture. Most often the formula introduces an imperative (e.g. Q. 35: 3) or a prohibitive (24: 27), but also a conditional construction (8: 29), and occasionally a nominal (33: 50) or interrogative sentence (61: 10). The addressees may be either 'you people' without qualification (*al-nās*, cf. also *al-mala'*, *al-insān*), or 'you believers/disbelievers/Jews/scriptuaries' (*alladhīna āmanū/kafarū/hādū/ūtū 'l-kitāb*), or finally, one of several epithets referring to God's messengers, e.g. *rasūl*, *rusul*, *mursalūn*, *nabī*, *muzammil*, *muddaththir*, etc. Utterances addressed to members of the latter group might of course be interpreted as containing implicitly the divine imperative, and hence equivalent to expressions prefaced by *qul*. Though it is possible to argue that use of the vocative dispenses with a specific phrase of legitimation (*corroboratio*), such as the messenger formula, the two elements are by no means mutually exclusive.[2] Some vocative constructions appear invariably in contexts containing also the imperative *qul*, e.g. four of the five occurrences of *yā banī ādam* (Q. 7: 26, 27, 31, 35; the fifth is 36: 60). Despite the plural and the assertion of Nöldeke–Schwally to the contrary, I am inclined to relate this locution to the vocative *ben adam* characteristic of Ezekiel (2: 1 and *passim*, cf. also Daniel 8: 17), where modification of the messenger formula is not infrequent, e.g. 3: 11 ודברת אליהם ואמרת אליהם כה אמר אדני יהוה and 11: 5 ויאמר אלי אמר כה אמר יהוה.[3]

A third vocative found in the Qur'ān is the Wisdom formula *yā bunayya* (Q. 11: 42, 12: 5, 31: 13, 16, 17, 37: 102), attested also in the plural *yā baniyya* (Q. 12: 67, 87 where Jacob addresses his sons; 2: 132 where Isaac and Jacob are addressed by Abraham). Unlike the corresponding Hebrew locutions (Proverbs *passim*: שמע בני/שמעו בנים/ועתה בנים) the Quranic ones

[1] See below, pp. 46–7.

[2] Cf. Koch, *Growth*, 210–11.

[3] *GdQ* i, 242 n. 1: their proposed alternative appears only twice in the vocative, Q. 82: 6, 84: 6 *yā insān*, and can hardly be said to represent a functional counterpart of the common address in Ezekiel; nor, it may be added, was *ben adam* in Ezekiel rendered in the Targum by *bar nashā/bar nash* (i.e. *insān*), but by *bar adam*: see Vermes, 'Jewish Aramaic', 328.

are only formally linked to Wisdom: in Q. 31: 12–13 ولقد آتينا لقمن الحكمة واذ قال لقمن لابنه وهو يعظه يا بنىّ لا تشرك بالله . . . ., and introduce exhortations and admonitions of a distinctly monotheistic flavour.[1] Similarly related to Wisdom literature is the formula: *am ḥasiba/ḥasibta/ḥasibtum an* (e.g. Q. 29: 4, 45: 21, 47: 29, 18: 9, 2: 214, 3: 142, 9: 16, and the variations in 23: 115, 29: 2 'did you suppose that', etc.), in consequence of which the prophetical announcement becomes a rhetorical question.[2] This attenuated form of imperative is also encountered in the later prophets, e.g. Ezekiel 8: 6 בן־אדם הראה אתה and 8: 17 הראית בן־אדם, where apodictic formulae are often of a character almost conversational. To relate the juxtaposition in the Qur'ān of such a variety of forms to a history of the prophetical office would be a hazardous, if not quite futile, undertaking. The conceptual and formal transfer of terminology, very likely in both directions, between the roles of envoy as royal agent and as divine mediator had been effected in Semitic literature long before the composition of Muslim scripture.[3] It is to that tradition, rather than to one fabricated from the data of Arabic literature, that a literary history of the Qur'ān must inevitably lead.

Analysis of the Quranic formulae of supplication reveals a similar set of problems. Evidence of such pre-Islamic liturgical practices as might be presumed to offer a recognizable source for the Quranic references is encased in a pseudo-historical projection of Islamic scriptural exegesis. Its classical formulation is found in the *Kitāb al-Aṣnām* of Hishām b. al-Kalbī (d. 204/819).[4] There Arabian litholatry is described as the consequence of strife among the descendants of Ishmael in Mecca, their dispersion from that sanctuary with relics of the Ka'ba in their possession, and continued observance of the traditional cultic procedures at these several monuments 'in memory of and abiding affection for Mecca'.[5] It is, then, not surprising to find that such ritual phenomena as honouring the sanctuary (*ta'ẓīm al-bayt*) by circumambulation (*ṭawāf, dawār*), station (*wuqūf*), sacrifice (*ihdā' al-budn*), and pilgrimage (*ḥajj, 'umra*) were in fact derived from the covenant (*'ahd*) imposed by God upon Abraham and Ishmael at the Ka'ba. Some admixture of alien and distorted observance (مع إدخالهم فيه ما ليس منه) was inevitable, though such appears to have consisted largely in neglect of the originally symbolic function of the bits of masonry detached by departing factions from the sanctuary at Mecca. Originally unitarian formulae of supplication, like the *tasmiya* and *talbiya*, were thus preserved,

[1] Cf. Lindblom, 'Wisdom', 192–204 for the link between Wisdom and monotheism; Goldziher, 'Polemik', 354–5; Horovitz, *Untersuchungen*, 132–6; cf. also Nöldeke, *Delectus*, 1 line 8.

[2] Cf. Proverbs 20: 9; and von Rad, *Theology* ii, 68 on Job 4: 17.

[3] See Westermann, *Grundformen*, 82.

[4] *GAS* i, 268–71.

[5] *Kitāb al-Aṣnām*, 6.

but at the cost of adulteration by polytheistic foci.[1] The strongly exegetical character of Hishām's description of pagan practices is clear from his account of the introduction of such by ʿAmr b. Rabīʿa/ʿAmr b. Luhayy, where the classification of sacrificial animals reflects the allusions of Q. 5: 153 (*baḥīra, sā'iba, waṣīla, ḥāmī*).[2]

The use of this and related material by Wellhausen and Lammens resulted in a portrait of the Jāhiliyya that, in accordance with the best principles of Biblical literary (documentary) criticism by which the earliest ascertainable form of report becomes synonymous with event, made the transition from pagan to Islamic worship a logical and almost predictable process.[3] The antonomastic development which produced Allāh as the Islamic name for God was seen to provide reasonable support for the social evolution inferred from the exegetical literature.[4] The Quranic forms of address employed for supplication admit of the same interpretation, and it is thus not difficult to postulate as *Sitz im Leben* for the expressions *yā rabbanā* (address) and *yā ʿibādī* (response) the *usus loquendi* of the Arabian *kāhin*.[5] Indeed, the most frequent supplicatory formula in the Qur'ān is *rabbī/rabbanā*, without the vocative particle but often made asseverative by a prefixed *qul* (Q. 13: 30) or *qul inna* (34: 39). Both *rabbī* and *rabbanā* may introduce a petition formulated as imperative, e.g. Q. 3: 194, 7: 126, 14: 41, 19: 6, 10. The response, introduced by *yā ʿibādī*, may also include an imperative, e.g. Q. 29: 56, 39: 10, 53, 43: 68. One is, moreover, not surprised to find the locution *allāhumma*, an alleged vocative form of *allāh* and attested in the Qur'ān (3: 26, 5: 114, 8: 32, 10: 10, 39: 46), contained in the polytheistic *talbiya* of Nizār.[6] For the Muslim *talbiya*, which is non-Quranic, a secular origin is plausible: لبّيك is, however, functionally comparable to Biblical אשריך (Deuteronomy 33: 29, etc.).[7]

In Quranic usage both *rabb* and *allāh* (or a pronominal substitute) in combination with the verbal nouns *ḥamd* or *subḥān* (denoting gratitude or praise) generate a number of exclamatory constructions, e.g. *al-ḥamdu lillāh, lahu 'l-ḥamd, bi-ḥamdi rabbika, bi-ḥamdika*, etc., or *subḥāna 'llāh, subḥāna 'lladhī, subḥāna rabbika, subḥānaka*, etc. All of these reflect an obviously liturgical origin, though hardly attested in Hishām's description of Arabian paganism, save in the antithesis *kufrānika:subḥānika* and the parallelism *tasbīḥ:tahlīl*, both in verse.[8] With the exception of Q. 3: 188 (and possibly 61: 6) finite verb forms of the root *ḥ-m-d* do not occur in the Qur'ān, though of the root *s-b-ḥ* finite forms are common. An interesting

[1] *Kitāb al-Aṣnām*, 7.
[2] *Kitāb al-Aṣnām*, 8, 58.
[3] *Reste*, esp. 10–64; *Arabie*, esp. 101–79; see below, IV pp. 138–40.
[4] Wellhausen, *Reste*, 218; see below, III pp. 93–9, IV pp. 122–7.
[5] Lammens, *Arabie*, 152; Wellhausen, *Reste*, 145.
[6] *Kitāb al-Aṣnām*, 7.
[7] Wellhausen, *Reste*, 111.
[8] *Kitāb al-Aṣnām*, 26, 39, respectively.

feature of scriptural syntax is the predominantly liturgical use of the emphatic particle *iyyā*, with pronominal suffix designating the object of worship, fear, service, etc., before the verbs: *ʿabada* (Q. 1: 5, 34: 40, 10: 28, 28: 63, 2: 172, 16: 114, 41: 37, 29: 56), *daʿā* (6: 41), *rahiba* (2: 40, 16: 51), *ittaqā* (2: 41), and *istaʿāna* (1: 5).[1]

The primary function of Quranic supplicatory formulae is the *invocatio*, expressed in the *tahlīl* لا اله الا الله (Q. 37: 35 and variations *passim*), in the *tasmiya* ذكر اسم الله (e.g. 5: 4), in the *takbīr* ولذكر الله أكبر (e.g. 29: 45), or in the introductory imperative to *Sūrat Ikhlāṣ* قل هو الله أحد. As song of praise (hymn) the *invocatio* seems likely to belong to a cultic tradition, related to sanctuary and public worship.[2] Some support for that conjecture might be found in the relation of the *tahlīl* to sacrificial prescription, i.e. *uhilla* in Q. 2: 173, 5: 3, 6: 145, 16: 115, and glossed in 6: 121 مما لم يذكر اسم الله عليه. The alternative is to postulate an origin in private devotion. While evidence for a cultic background is more abundant, it has been transmitted in a manner so overlaid with retroflective exegesis (*Nachdichtung*) as to be nearly unintelligible. Solution to this kind of problem is often frustrated by the impossibility of isolating a satisfactory prehistory for what in the exegetical tradition have become highly charged technical terms. A perfect illustration is provided in Kister's study of *taḥannuth*, in which the author argues persuasively in favour of the equivalence *taḥannuth*:*taʿabbud*, accepting the latter as designation of cultic practices connected with the pre-Islamic sanctuary at Mecca.[3] On the other hand, the notion of informal, private devotion contained in the Hebrew cognate (?) *teḥinnah* is rather older than Kister, following Goitein, appears to accept, though that in itself does not of course justify identification of the two terms.[4] It is merely that references adduced to support the equivalence *taḥannuth*:*taʿabbud*/*tabarrur* are drawn from a literary tradition which stresses the exclusively Arabian sources of Islam.[5]

The fragmentary character of Muslim scripture can nowhere be more clearly observed than in those passages traditionally described as narrative. These consist in fact not so much of narrative as of *exempla*, of the sort alluded to in the Qur'ān itself as 'signs' (*āyāt*), and hardly qualify even for the epithet 'legend'.[6] Exhibiting a limited number of themes, the *exempla* achieve a kind of stylistic uniformity by resort to a scarcely varied stock of rhetorical convention. An instance is the serial employment of the presentative *wa-idh* (cf. Hebrew ועתה) in *Sūrat Baqara*, e.g. verses 30, 34,

[1] Cf. Fischer, 'Zunburīja', 153–5.
[2] See Koch, *Growth*, 161–6: *tehillah*.
[3] 'Taḥannuth', 223–36.
[4] Kister, op. cit. 231 n. 51; see Elbogen, *Gottesdienst*, 73–81, and 265: *taḥanun*.
[5] See below, IV pp. 122–7.
[6] Cf. Horovitz, *Untersuchungen*, 7 ff.

49–51, 53–5, 58, 60–1, 63, 67, 72, 83–4, 93, 124–7, relieved by *idh* alone in 131 and 133, and not noticeably different from constructions with *wa-idhā* in the same contexts, e.g. 76, 91, 117.[1] While the effect is tedious in the extreme, by means of this deictic formula, of far higher frequency than any other, a number of disparate topics, abruptly introduced and as abruptly dismissed, is mechanically linked. Dismissal is commonly effected by the locution ان ّ فى ذلك لآية (e.g. Q. 2: 248), with minor variations, e.g. *ʿibra* (3: 13), *tadhkira* (69: 12).[2]

These basic 'narrative' conventions are supplemented by others, which may be distinguished as interrogative, imperative, and simple declarative, exhibiting thus the grammatical types already encountered for apodictic and supplicatory formulae. Since, indeed, the so-called narrative sections of the Qur'ān are of essentially symbolic character adduced to illustrate the eschatological value of the theodicy, it is not surprising to find such remarkable conformity. Formally interrogative locutions function almost exclusively as rhetorical questions, e.g. هل أتاك حديث/نباء preceding mention of Abraham, Moses, Pharaoh, Thamūd, and other representatives of the *umam khāliya* (Q. 20: 9, 51: 24, 79: 15, 85: 17, 38: 21, and the variation ألم يأتك نباء 9: 70, 14: 29). A parallel concluding formula may be seen in فبأى حديث بعده يؤمنون (Q. 7: 185, 77: 50), where *ḥadīth* must, as elsewhere, be understood not as *historia* but as *exemplum*, as in 34: 19 وجعلناهم أحاديث. Similarly, *nabā'* and *qiṣṣa* in phrases of formulaic character signify *exempla*, e.g. Q. 18: 13 نحن نقصّ عليك نباءهم and 12: 3 نحن نقصّ عليك أحسن القصص. A finite verb of the second derived form *nabba'a*, imperative in Q. 15: 49, 51 and imperfect in 5: 105, 6: 60, 108, etc., supports that interpretation, as does the concluding formula تلك/ذلك من أنباء (e.g. Q. 11: 49, 12: 102), where *anbā'* may be seen as equivalent to *āyāt* (signs). The rhetorical question is also posed in the locutions ألم تر الى/ان (e.g. Q. 4: 44, 40: 69, 14: 19, 22: 18), أولم يروا الى/ان (e.g. 13: 41, 34: 9), and أولم يسيروا فى الأرض (e.g. 30: 9, 35: 44). Imperative formations with the verbs *dhakara* and *dhakkara* (recall, remind) serve also to introduce *exempla*, as in the series واذكر فى الكتاب (Q. 19: 16, 41, 51, 54, 56) and واذكر عبدنا (Q. 38: 17, 41, 45, cf. verse 48), but especially 14: 5 وذكرهم بأيام الله. Similarly, the imperative construction *fanẓur kayf* (see how, consider what) with *ʿāqiba* (destiny, Q. 7: 103), with *āyāt* (signs, 6: 46), or with *amthāl* (similes/parables, 17: 48), may introducc or conclude mention of the *exempla* which characterize this very allusive version of

[1] See Nöldeke, *Zur Grammatik*, 108–9; Reckendorf, *Verhältnisse*, 475–80.
[2] Horovitz, op. cit. 6, 13–4.

Heilsgeschichte. Their paideutic function is explicit in such formulae as واضرب لهم مثلا (strike for them a parable, Q. 18: 32, 45, 36: 13), واتل عليهم نباء (recite to them the example, 5: 27, 10: 71, 26: 69), and تلك آيات الله نتلوها (these are the signs of God which we recite, 2: 252, 3: 108, 45: 6). Functionally related to the imperative constructions is the use in *Sūrat Ṣāffāt* of the phrase *salām ʿalā* (*benedictio*) to introduce the figures of Noah, Abraham, Moses, Aaron, etc. (Q. 37: 79, 109, 120, 130).

Despite the uniformity of introductory and concluding formulae, it is hardly possible to regard these as fixing the limits of recognizable narrative units.[1] It is even more difficult to reconstruct from the elliptically drawn *exempla* themselves a form which might plausibly represent an earlier stage of transmission. Quranic allusion presupposes familiarity with the narrative material of Judaeo-Christian scripture, which was not so much reformulated as merely referred to. Narrative structure on the other hand, absent in the text of scripture, emerged in the literature of haggadic exegesis, in which the many lacunae were more or less satisfactorily filled.[2] Determination of a likely *Sitz im Leben* for the Quranic forms turns, then, upon the possibility of regarding the *exempla* as originally distinct pericopes of essentially homiletic purpose. There are, of course, several situations at least in which such pericopes might or could have originated. But taken together, the quantity of reference, the mechanically repetitious employment of rhetorical convention, and the stridently polemical style, all suggest a strongly sectarian atmosphere, in which a corpus of familiar scripture was being pressed into the service of as yet unfamiliar doctrine. The implications of that hypothesis for a textual history of Muslim scripture remain to be examined.

. . . . .

The Quranic masorah is traditionally restricted to a series of more or less standard deviations from the canonical text.[3] Such material as was alleged by some to have a claim to canonical status, but which in the event was not included in the definitive text, tended to be relegated to discussion of specifically halakhic questions or to argument arising out of sectarian interests.[4] The problem of 'variants' can be usefully approached by distinguishing between variant readings, the proper concern of the masoretes, and variant traditions. In the Muslim exegetical literature the latter were explained, or evaded, by reference to the chronology of revelation, by means of which unmistakable repetition in the Quranic text

[1] Cf. Koch, *Growth*, 115–18; Torrey's sociological observations are of little value for a literary analysis, *Foundation*, 105–16.

[2] See below, IV pp. 127–9.

[3] See Jeffery, *Materials*; and *GdQ* iii.

[4] *GdQ* i, 234–61, ii, 33–8, 81–112.

could be justified. Versions of the chronology, together with traditions relating to the modes of revelation, have been considered adequate criteria for describing the collection and preservation of that text by the Muslim community.[1] But variant traditions are present in such quantity as to deserve some attention in a description of the process by which revelation became canon. Unlike the minutiae to be gained from *variae lectiones*,[2] analysis of variant traditions will not support the theory of an *Urtext* nor even that of a composite edition produced by deliberations in committee, both of which may, not surprisingly, be traced to Rabbinic *Vorlagen*.[3] Such analysis indicates, rather, the existence of independent, possibly regional, traditions incorporated more or less intact into the canonical compilation, itself the product of expansion and strife within the Muslim community. Now, that kind of variant is found for most of the *exempla* adduced to illustrate the *umam khāliya* theme, of which those relating to the mission of the prophet Shuʿayb offer a typical instance. It may be conceded that the kind of analysis undertaken will in no small measure determine the results. For the Quranic material pertaining to Abraham, the studies of Beck and Moubarac were developed from a wholly arbitrary adherence to the traditional chronology of revelation and ended in a 'historical' survey of the prophet's 'changing attitude towards the patriarchs'.[4] Demonstration of the 'historical development of Abraham in the Qur'ān', for Moubarac the evolution of a composite figure out of an originally dual image, required not only a verifiable chronology of revelation but also the structural unity of the canon. Both were asserted; neither was proved.[5]

A literary analysis, as contrasted with a historical or theological one, may properly disregard such criteria. For Shuʿayb the scriptural account exists in three complete versions: Q. 7: 85–93, 11: 84–95, and 26: 176–90; and in abridged form (introductory and concluding formulae only) in 29: 36–7. Between the three versions an internal relationship may be set out as follows.

A

I And to Midian their brother Shuʿayb. (7: 85)

II (He said) if some of you believe in that with which I have been sent, and others of you do not, then have patience until God judges between us, for He is the best of judges. (7:87)

[1] See below, pp. 33–46. [2] See below, IV pp. 203–8.

[3] Cf. Eissfeldt, *Einleitung*, 695–707; and see below, pp. 45–52.

[4] Beck, 'Abraham', 73–94; Moubarac, *Abraham*, esp. 31–50, 91–5, 163–75.

[5] Moubarac, *Abraham*, 139, admitted the difficulty of eliciting from the document of revelation a 'theology of history' as contrasted with 'reports of a historical nature': 'Ou encore, il y a dans le Coran une histoire de la religion plutôt qu'une religion de l'histoire'.

III My people, worship God, for you have no other than Him. And a sign has come to you from your Lord. Give full measure and weight, and do not cheat your fellows of their property, nor work evil in the land, now that matters have been put right. There will be benefit to you if you have faith. So occupy not any path, seeking to make it devious, and threatening and barring from the way of God him who believes. (7: 85–6)

IV But remember that you were few and He increased you, and consider the destiny of those who work evil. (7: 86)

V And the assembly of those of his people who regarded themselves as authorities said: We will expel you from our midst, Shuʿayb, and those who believe with you, unless you return to our law. (7: 88)

VI He replied: And if we do not wish to? We should be guilty of denying God were we to return to your law after He delivered us. It is not for us to return unless our Lord God wishes it. His wisdom comprehends all things, upon God do we rely. Lord, judge in truth between our people and ourselves, for You are the best of judges. (7: 88–9)

VII And the assembly of those of his people who did not accept said: If you follow Shuʿayb then you are lost. (7: 90)

VIII So disaster overtook them and they were left prostrate in their place. Those who rejected Shuʿayb were as though they had not been, those who rejected Shuʿayb were indeed lost. (7: 91–2)

IX And he turned away from them saying: My people, I brought you messages from my Lord and advised you, so how shall I have pity on a people who does not accept? (7: 93)

B

I And to Midian their brother Shuʿayb. (11: 84)

II (He said) My people, do you not see that I bear a sign from my Lord, Who has provided well for me. I do not wish to oppose you in that which I forbid, but only to put things right so far as I can. And my success lies with God upon Whom I rely and towards Whom I turn. (11: 88)

III My people, worship God, for you have no other than Him. Give not short measure and weight, for I see you in wealth and fear for you the punishment of the last day. My people, give full measure and weight in equity, and do not cheat your fellows of their property, nor work evil in the land. That which abides with God will be a benefit to you, if you have faith. For I cannot preserve you. (11:84–6)

IV My people, let not rejection of me make you guilty, lest that afflict you which afflicted the people of Noah or of Hūd or of Ṣāliḥ, nor are the people of Lot irrelevant. (11: 89)

V They replied: Shuʿayb, does your prayer command that we abandon that which our fathers worshipped or that we (do not) conduct our affairs as we wish? But are you not clement and righteous? (11: 87)

VI (He said) Ask forgiveness of your Lord and turn towards Him. My Lord is merciful (and) loving. He said: My people, is my family dearer to you than God, for you have cast Him behind you. My Lord understands that which you do. (11: 90, 92)

VII They replied: Shuʿayb, we do not understand much of what you say and regard you as without support. Were it not for your family, we would stone you, for you have no power over us. (11: 91)

VIII And when Our decree was uttered We delivered Shuʿayb and those who had faith with him, as a mercy from Us. And disaster overtook those who had done wrong and they were left prostrate in their place. As though they had not been, Midian perished as Thamūd had perished. (11: 94–5)

IX (He said) My people, do in your position (as) I do. You will know him to whom a grievous punishment comes, and who it is who lies. And watch, for I watch with you. (11: 93)

C

I . . .

II (Shuʿayb said) I am a messenger entrusted to you. (26: 178)

III Thus said Shuʿayb to them: Will you not fear? Fear God and obey (me). For that I ask of you no reward. I have no reward but with the Lord of the universe. Give full measure, and be not of those who cause loss. Weigh in straightforward equity. And do not cheat your fellows of their property, nor work evil in the land. (26: 177, 179–83)

IV And fear Him Who created you and those who went before. (26: 184)

V They replied: You are one of the possessed. And are only a mortal like ourselves, and we think you a liar. But if you speak the truth, then let some part of heaven fall upon us. (26: 185–7)

VI . . .

VII . . .

VIII The men of the copse rejected the messengers. Thus they rejected him, and the punishment of the last day, a momentous day, overtook them. In that there is a sign, but most of them have no faith. (26:176, 189–80).

IX He said: My Lord knows best what you have done. (26: 188)

The isolation and order of components proposed here, though not always coincident with verse juncture and sequence, correspond to a scheme widely attested in the literature of prophetical expression.[1] From the analysis version A emerges as the most coherent and version C the

[1] See Westermann, *Grundformen*, 79–82; Koch, *Growth*, 190–4.

least. Absence in the latter of element I, the formula of commission (*Beauftragung*), and the presence there of the simple presentative *idh qāla* (thus he said: at the beginning of element III) suggest a primitive and probably earlier formulation. The commission itself, which appears not only in versions A and B, but also in the summary account at Q. 29: 36–7, is a stereotype phrase employed exclusively for the non-Biblical 'prophets': والى . . . . . أخاهم . . . . قال يا قوم اعبدوا الله (Q. 7: 65, 11: 50—Hūd to 'Ād; 7: 73, 11: 61—Ṣāliḥ to Thamūd; 7: 85, 11: 84, 29: 36—Shu'ayb to Midian), and might well be thought an editorial interpolation designed precisely to introduce reports of prophetical missions, themselves cast in informal dialogue.

Element II, the *corroboratio* (*Botenformel*), is not necessarily out of place in the canonical sequence of A and B, but is probably nearer its original position in C, where it introduces the substance of the message, which is element III: the diatribe or accusation (*Scheltwort/Anklage*).[1] Only in version B is the diatribe not immediately followed by element IV: the threat or prediction of disaster (*Drohwort/Unheilsankündigung*).[2] Also in version B that prediction is specified as the destiny of those who rejected the warnings of Noah and Lot, and of the Arabian prophets Hūd and Ṣāliḥ, while in versions A and C allusion to the fate of the *umam khāliya* is general. Thus version B, rather than A, might represent the final shape of the tradition, a possibility strengthened by the form if not the position of element II: in C merely *rasūl amīn*, in A *billadhī ursiltu bihi*, and in B *bayyina min rabbī* (which however occurs, slightly varied, in element III of version A: *bayyina min rabbikum*).

In elements V, VI, and VII, which constitute the altercation, dialogue is prominent. Version C contains only element V, the contestation (*Bestreitung*), elaborated in A and B to include a counter-argument or justification (*Begründung*), and a third component (element VII) which might be described as the resignation and which concludes the dispute. Here, however, version A exhibits a context more even and consistent than B, as well as a more sophisticated argument. Element VIII signals reversion from dialogue to narrative, in order to describe rejection of God's message and fulfilment of the threat (element IV), the dominant motif of the Quranic *exempla*. The position of element IX, the epilogue or final assessment, is logical only in version A. From the canonical verse sequence of versions B and C, and from its absence in Q. 29: 36–7, one might conclude that it was a late and optional embellishment.

As set out in the diatribe (element III), the primary transgressions of Shu'ayb's people were three: failure to observe fair practice in what appear to be basic mercantile transactions اوفوا الكيل والميزان (cf. especially Q. 83:

[1] Westermann, *Grundformen*, 46–9.

[2] Westermann, loc. cit.

2–3, but also 6: 152, 17: 35, and 12: 59, 88; and *passim* in the negotiations between Joseph and his brothers); lack of equity in questions of property ولا تبخسوا الناس أشياءهم (cf. Q. 2: 282, 11: 15); and apparently a general inclination to damage and injury لا تفسدوا فى الأرض or لا تعثوا فى الأرض مفسدين (the latter, attested otherwise only at Q. 2: 60, evidently restricted to the Shuʿayb traditions). From indications such as these it is of course quite impossible to identify either the people or the prophet.[1] Other allusions are similarly unhelpful, e.g. the concept of 'reform' (*iṣlāḥ*) in Q. 7: 85 and 11: 88, but not in version C, or inclusion of the men of the copse among the *aḥzāb* in Q. 38: 13 (cf. also 15: 78) or with others of the *umam khāliya* in 50: 14 (cf. also the Midianites in 9: 70). But Quranic references to Midian belong as often to the Mosaic traditions, and the story of Shuʿayb must be regarded as a parable, its exemplary function of greater moment than its improbable historicity. Admonitions on equity in the matter of weights and measures represent a Pentateuchal motif, developed in the prophetical literature (Leviticus 19: 35–6, Deuteronomy 25: 13–16, and cf. Amos 8: 5, Micah 6: 11). The Shuʿayb traditions exhibit little by way of historical development but ample evidence of literary elaboration, drawn from recognizable and well-established types of prophetical report. Such elaboration is characteristic of Muslim scripture, in which a comparatively small number of themes is preserved in varying stages of literary achievement.

The effect of variant traditions may be differently illustrated, and assessed. Majority opinion in the exegetical literature accepts that the passage Q. 55: 46–77 describes four gardens, whose identification as stages of celestial reward for the faithful became a significant exercise in eschatological writing. Early on, but with little effect upon the verses as source of doctrinal and allegorical speculation, a dissenting view was recorded, namely, that the dual form *jannatāni* in Q. 55: 46 was demanded by the scheme obtaining there for verse juncture, but in fact represented the singular *janna*, as in Q. 79: 41 ولمن خاف مقام ربّه جنتان: قال الفراء أراد جنة كقوله فإن الجنة هى المأوى فثنى لاجل الفاصلة.[2] Applied also and for the same reason to Q. 55: 62 that stricture would halve the total number of gardens, a result confirmed by examination of the parallel descriptions of the two pairs. Each contains sixteen verses (i.e. Q. 55: 46–61 and 62–77), half of which consist of the recurring phrase فبأى الآء ربّكما تكذّبان, employed thirty-one times in the entire *sūra* but nowhere else in the text

[1] Cf. Geiger, *Was hat Mohammed*, 170–7; *GdQ* i, 151 n. 9; Horovitz, *Untersuchungen*, 93–4, 119–20, 138; Torrey, *Foundation*, 71; Speyer, *Erzählungen*, 251–4.

[2] Farrā', *apud* Suyūṭī, *Itqān* iii, 299; employing the same criteria but ignoring the masoretic tradition, Müller, *Reimprosa*, 132–3, reached a similar conclusion; cf. *BSOAS* xxxiii (1970) 389–91.

of scripture (cf. the related locutions in Q. 7: 69, 74, 53: 55). Formally, its function is to stress the dual inflexion characteristic of this passage. Structurally, it produces the effect of a litany, and its similarity to כי לעולם חסדו which performs the same function in Psalm 136 has been noted.[1] I should like here to insist upon the term litany rather than refrain. The role of the latter in the Qur'ān and elsewhere, is that of concluding formula, which does not adequately describe employment of the device in this passage.[2] There the construction is based upon eight uniformly short verses, which are those of the second description (Q. 55: 62–77), expanded formally and conceptually in the somewhat less uniform verses of the first description (Q. 55: 46–61), the whole enveloped and punctuated by the element: Then which of your Lord's bounties do you deny? In the order of the canon the two sets of eight verses are as follows.

A

46. And to him who fears the presence of his Lord, two gardens.
48. Of many varieties/colours.
50. With two springs flowing.
52. Of every fruit two kinds.
54. Reclining on beds with linings of brocade, the fruit of the two gardens near by.
56. With chaste maidens, untouched before by men or jinn.
58. As though of ruby and pearl.
60. Can the reward for goodness be other than goodness?

B

62. And besides them, two gardens.
64. Of deep green.
66. With two springs bubbling.
68. With fruit and palms and pomegranates.
70. With pure (and) beautiful ones.
72. Pure white, reserved in chambers.
74. Untouched before by men or jinn.
76. Reclining on green cushions and fine carpets.

The contrapuntal scheme is not perfectly executed, but sufficiently so to have prompted Zamakhsharī to qualify the descriptive components of version B as just inferior to those of version A.[3] That implied of course

[1] Hirschfeld, *Researches*, 73 n. 20, though of the calque I am less certain than the author; cf. also Speyer, *Erzählungen*, 29.

[2] Ibn Qutayba described the formula as a marker (*fāṣila*) between each pair of divine favours, *Ta'wīl*, 181; cf. *GdQ* i, 42; Koch, *Growth*, 96; Eissfeldt, *Einleitung*, 71–3: *Strophenbau*.

[3] *Kashshāf* iv, 454: *ad min dūni himā* in verse 62.

acceptance of the canonical order of the two descriptions, but from the same evidence it could be argued that version A represents an elaboration of version B, both by rhetorical device and exegetical gloss. Whether the embellishment is to be understood as purely literary or as a reflex of what may have been the liturgical function of these verses, is difficult to determine. If a cultic context can be envisaged, it would seem that the descriptions of paradise were recited in inverse order to the canon. More likely, however, is juxtaposition in the canon of two closely related variant traditions, contaminated by recitation in identical contexts, or produced from a single tradition by oral transmission. Imagery based on a pair of gardens appears elsewhere, e.g. Q. 34: 15–16 and 18: 32–3, though in the latter instance the parable is weakened by defective syntactical distribution.[1] In neither passage did the imagery provoke eschatological speculation, whereas Quranic garden imagery based upon the singular *janna* (e.g. *aṣḥāb al-janna* Q. 2: 82 and *passim*; and the parables 2: 265–6, 68: 17–33)[2] or the plural *jannāt* (e.g. the formula جنات تجرى من تحتها الأنهار Q. 2: 25 and *passim*; *jannāt ʿadn* 9: 72 and *passim*; *jannāt al-naʿīm* 10: 9, and *jannāt wa-ʿuyūn* 51: 15), did provide the traditional points of departure for such. It may well be that the dual *jannatāni* of Q. 55: 46 and 62 was, implicitly, never understood as anything but singular.

. . . . .

From Zamakhsharī's pun on *min dūni himā* (Q. 55: 62) it is legitimate to infer a consciously formulated correspondence between the descriptions in verses 46–60 and 62–76. Whether that correspondence is exclusively rhetorical, or rhetorical and exegetical, will depend upon the more general problem of recognizing in the canonical text such phenomena as paraphrase, gloss, and interpolation. That problem was adumbrated by Fischer in his analysis of Q. 101: 8–11, where the exegetical function of the locution *mā adrāka mā* (how do you know what . . . is?) is convincingly demonstrated.[3] Reverberation of the exegetical equivalence *hāwiya*: abyss/hellfire found expression elsewhere, e.g. in an elegy ascribed to Waraqa b. Nawfal من الناس جبارا الى النار هاويا;[4] and an ironic utterance attributed to ʿAbīd b. Abraṣ, describing his narrow escape from eternal damnation أخبرك انّى دخلت الهاوية,[5] both emphasizing, incidentally, the triptosy of its scriptural

[1] Cf. Speyer, *Erzählungen*, 433–4; and below, IV p. 128.

[2] Horovitz, *Untersuchungen*, 11.

[3] 'Eine Qoran-Interpolation', 33–55; though it is easier to identify than to date interpolations, the objections to Fischer's proposal articulated by Barth and Torrey are, in my opinion, unacceptable: references in Paret, *Der Koran*, 518–19; and O'Shaughnessy, 'Seven Names', 449–51.

[4] Ibn Hishām, *Sīra* i, 232 line 5.

[5] Maʿarrī, *Risālat al-Ghufrān*, 178 top.

occurrence.[1] That the phrase *mā adrāka mā* is of hermeneutical, not merely lexical, moment is evident from its thirteen occurrences in the Qur'ān where, in addition to such *hapax legomena* as *hāwiya* (Q. 101: 10), *saqar* (74: 27), *ʿilliyūn* (83: 19), etc., expressions like *yawm al-dīn* (82: 17–18), *yawm al-faṣl* (77: 14), and *ʿaqaba* (90: 12) are glossed. But traditional accommodation of the phrase was designed to expel doubts about just whose utterance it represented: God's, prophet's, or commentator's. Rāghib Iṣfahānī declared, for example, that whenever God preceded mention of any topic with *mā adrāka mā*, He explained it, but that when He employed the expression *mā yudrīka*, the matter was left unexplained.[2] The fact that the two formulae are anyway not functionally comparable is less relevant than the manner in which *mā adrāka mā* was there unequivocally assumed to be the word of God. The *mā yudrīka* construction, always completed by *laʿalla* (how do you know whether?), is predicative rather than explicative (Q. 33: 63, 42: 17, 80: 3), as Iṣfahānī inadvertently observed.

Some instances of apostrophe might be thought to signal commentary to the text of revelation, e.g. in Q. 16: 51 وقال الله لا تتخذوا الاهين اثنين/انما هو الاه واحد/فاياى فارهبون where the middle term in the third person contrasts with the imperative construction as a whole: 'God said: do not take unto yourselves two gods/for He is only one god/so have fear of Me (alone)'. Such, in my opinion, is not to be confused with a passage like Q. 25: 45–56, in which mention of God alternates between first and third person, exhibiting the abrupt transition characteristic of so much of Quranic style, and indicating not juxtaposition of text and commentary but rather, of fragments from independent traditions. That the apostrophic *qul* must in those contexts impossibly predicable of God be an interpolation has been proposed; similarly the locution *min allāh* after *mawthiq* in Q. 12: 66, 80, by means of which that otherwise unattested designation of covenant could be unambiguously related to *mīthāq*.

In the examples of variant traditions adduced above, those describing the mission of Shuʿayb might be held to contain traces of exegetical activity. Element I (formula of commission) appears in versions A and B only, and may represent a gloss of the introductory *idh qāla* of version C. Element IV (threat/prediction of disaster), in A and C a general reference to the *umam khāliya*, becomes in B specific enumeration of the fates of those who rejected Noah, Hūd, Ṣāliḥ, and Lot. On the other hand, elaboration of element V in version C to the series V–VII (altercation) in versions A and B is more likely to be evidence of independent origins. Now, in the passage containing parallel descriptions of the two gardens, the precise relationship between corresponding elements is rather more problematic, since, as I have intimated, the possibility of proliferation from a single

[1] Fischer, 'Eine Qoran-Interpolation', 43–4.

[2] *Apud* Suyūṭī, *Itqān* ii, 139.

tradition cannot be ruled out.[1] However, a tendency towards clarification as well as conceptual enhancement is discernible in a comparison of verse 64 (*mudhāmmatāni*) with verse 48 (*dhawātā afnānin*: interpreting *afnān* as *alwān*),[2] of verse 66 (*naḍḍākhatāni*) with verse 50 (*tajriyāni*), or of verse 68 (*fākihatun wa-nakhlun wa-rummānun*) with verse 52 (*min kulli fākihatin zawjāni*). Thus set out the evidence would appear to support the hypothesis of an earlier composition for version B, though the remaining parts of the two descriptions suggest other possibilities. For example, subsumption in verse 56 of all the elements of verses 70, 72, 74 might indicate originally distinct traditions, as could the presence in version A of verses 58 and 60, both without obvious counterparts in version B. But I am inclined to see in verse 58 (*al-yāqūt wal-marjān*) an elaboration of *ḥūr* in verse 72, and to interpret verse 54 as a conscious reformulation of the clumsier imagery of verse 76. A paraphrase of version B in version A might none the less be of liturgical, rather than exclusively exegetical origin. The rhetorical question of verse 60 exhibits a common Quranic device, already noticed, and serves to stress the eschatological content of the entire passage. As such it would belong to the exegetical tradition, the concern of which it was to underline the relation of this particular instance of double garden imagery with the concept of celestial reward elsewhere illustrated by the forms *janna* and *jannāt*.

. . . . .

I have drawn attention to the allusive treatment in the Qur'ān of the schemata of revelation. The style is best observed in the so-called 'narrative' passages, of which the Shuʿayb traditions offer typical illustration. Indeed, each of the themes representative of the Quranic theodicy exhibits a recognizable literary type in a state of suspended development. A degree of uniformity was achieved by recourse to a limited number of rhetorical conventions. Specifically stylistic problems provoke other more general ones relating to assimilation and the mimetic process. For example, traces in the retribution imagery of election and remnant traditions associated with the salvation history of Israel distinguish the role of that nation in the theodicy from those of the *umam khāliya*, themselves elected but vanished without survivors. A consequence of that distinction is the purely exemplary function of parables containing the accounts of non-Biblical prophets, and a concomitant failure to assimilate Arabian elements to the Judaeo-Christian legacy. An example of partial assimilation may be seen in the imagery developed round the concept 'days/battles of God'. Not unexpectedly, the injunction *wa-dhakkirhum bi-ayyām allāh* in Q. 14: 5 is addressed to Moses. But elsewhere the terms *ayyām* and *ayyām allāh* are of general application, and the possibility of contamination by the

[1] Cf. Koch, *Growth*, 90–1.

[2] Zamakhsharī, *Kashshāf* iv, 452 ad loc.

autochthonic *ayyām al-ʿarab* has been noted. Other instances of more and less successful assimilation to the native linguistic tradition are provided by the Quranic imagery relating to angelology and resurrection.

Anonymous and collective reference in Muslim scripture to angels (*malak/malāʾika*) is abundant, relieved very rarely by specific designation, e.g. Q. 2: 98, 102.[1] In the exegetical literature the vague and general became explicit and specific (*taʿyīn*), and a series of dogmas elaborated with reference to the role and rank of angels in the hierarchy of creation.[2] The function of angels as mediators between God and men, and by extension emissaries and agents of revelation, is a significant component of Islamic prophetology (cf. e.g. Q. 17: 95, 22: 75, 35: 1, 41: 14).[3] Terms other than *malak* were in the exegetical tradition subsumed under this rubric, as for example, *zabāniyya* in Q. 96: 18, interpreted by Zamakhsharī as 'angels of retribution' (*malāʾikat al-ʿadhāb*).[4] Rather less arbitrary was application of that procedure to the epithet *muqarrabūn*. In four passages (Q. 56: 11, 88, 83: 21, 28), the notion of propinquity to God as reward for piety is clearly conveyed, expressed in 56: 7–11 as a tripartite distribution of benefit, of which *muqarrabūn* represent the highest order. Twice (Q. 7: 114, 26: 42) the same image is employed in a secular setting, promise of reward being the utterance of Pharaoh. Thus the transfer of function achieved by derivatives of the root *q-r-b* attested in prophetical and Rabbinic literature is reflected in Quranic usage, though I should be reluctant to interpret the courtly environment of Q. 7: 114 and 26: 42 as exhibiting a genuine *Sitz im Leben* for the Arabic metaphor.[5] As in the imagery associated with the messenger as both royal and divine agent, that relating to admission into the royal and into the divine presence may be thought a calque of the semantic evolution already complete in Biblical Hebrew, e.g. Esther 1: 14 as contrasted with Jeremiah 30: 21.

In two further Quranic passages (3: 45 and 4: 172), both traditional sources of Muslim Christology, the content of *muqarrabūn* is extended to include not only an élite among the saved, but also Jesus and certain of the angels. Express reference in Q. 4: 172 to *malāʾika muqarrabūn* became in the exegetical tradition the occasion of another and different link with Biblical imagery. Zamakhsharī identified these 'angels drawn near' with the cherubim round the throne of God 'like Gabriel, Michael, Isrāfīl, and others of their rank' وهم الملائكة الكروبيون الذين حول العرش كجبريل وميكائيل واسرافيل ومن فى طبقتهم.[6] In Arabic lexicography approximation

[1] See Wensinck, *Creed*, 198–202 and references; also Vajda, *EI*, s.v. Hārūt wa-Mārūt.

[2] Wensinck, loc. cit.; Geiger, *Was hat Mohammed*, 80–2; for *taʿyīn*, see below, IV pp. 135–6.

[3] See below, II pp. 55, 61–3.

[4] *Kashshāf* iv, 779 ad loc.

[5] Speyer, *Erzählungen*, 266, 299–300; von Rad, *Theology* ii, 218–9.

[6] *Kashshāf* i, 596 ad loc.; cf. Speyer, op. cit., 26–7 for Rabbinic parallels; and Goldziher, 'Polemik', 371, for *karūbiyyūn* and Isrāfīl in Arabic versions of Genesis 3: 24.

of the roots *q-r-b* and *k-r-b* was seen to conform to a series of semantic conclusions drawn from the behaviour of morphemes of intensity (*mubālagha*), by which *karūbiyyūn* must represent those of the *muqarrabūn* 'nearest the throne of God' and, hence, the principal of the angels, among whom were Gabriel, Michael, and Isrāfīl.[1] The linguistic laws by which that accommodation of a non-linguistic calque was justified are only partially attested: the measure *fa'ūl* and the affix *-iyy* may be so interpreted, but not the relation *k/q*.[2] Juxtaposition of three originally unrelated elements: the pious, the archangels, and the cherubim, is of course logically unsatisfactory, but for the assimilation of Biblical exegesis to the Arabic linguistic tradition, an instructive example indeed.

The lexical range of Quranic resurrection imagery is rather wider. The primary concept is that of resurrection as a second creation, derived from the vocabulary appropriate to the acts of God in nature.[3] Typical formulations are لقد جئتمونا كما خلقناكم أول مرة (Q. 18: 48), منها خلقناكم وفيها نعيدكم ومنها نخرجكم تارة أخرى (20: 55), قل يحييها الذى أنشاها أول مرة (36: 79), and قل الله يبدؤ الخلق ثم يعيده (10: 34 and *passim*). Express reference to *khalq jadīd* (fresh creation) occurs consistently in a context of altercation about the promised resurrection, e.g. Q. 13: 5, 17: 49, 98, 32: 10, 34: 7 (variation *khalq ākhar* in 23: 14), and in 50: 15 paired with *khalq awwal* (first creation). With derivatives of such verbs as *ansha'a* (in Q. 36: 79, above), *anshara*, and *akhraja* (signifying erect, elicit, evoke), imagery designed to convey production of life out of death is varied and extended: *nash'a ūlā* (56: 62), *nash'a ukhrā* (53: 47), *nash'a ākhira* (29: 20), *inshā'* (56: 35), *nushūr* (25: 3, 35: 9), *khurūj* (50: 11, 42), etc. Of highest frequency, however, are constructions based on the antithesis *ḥayy*:*mayyit*, occurring with *akhraja* in Q. 6: 95 and 10: 31, but mostly with finite verb-forms of the same roots, e.g. Q. 2: 259, 22: 6, 30: 50, and explicitly linked with *khalq* in 2: 164 and 46: 33.[4] The categorical statement in the song of Moses אני אמית ואחיה (Deuteronomy 32: 39) appears verbatim in Q. 2: 259 أنا أحيى وأميت.[5] The hymnic context of the Biblical passages, reflected in the liturgical application of תחית המתים, may be seen also in Quranic usage, where the epithet 'bringer of life and death/death and life' is often introduced by the *invocatio*, e.g. *allāh*, *huwa*, *wa-huwa 'lladhī*, etc. (Q. 30: 40, 10: 56, 23: 80).[6] Related to that particular image is the concept, but

[1] Zabīdī, *Tāj al-'Arūs* i, 454 s.v. *karūbiyyūn*.
[2] Cf. Vollers, *Volkssprache*, 11; *GVG* i, 121–2.
[3] Cf. Lehmann–Pedersen, 'Auferstehung', 54–61; Wensinck, 'Propheten', 182–4.
[4] See the passages adduced in Müller, *Reimprosa*, 128–9; O'Shaughnessy, *Death*, 32, 45–6, 50; cf. *BSOAS* xxxiii (1970) 613–5.
[5] Cf. also the third person construction in Q. 53: 44 with the song of Hannah, 1 Samuel 2: 6, adduced Speyer, *Erzählungen*, 445.
[6] Cf. Elbogen, *Gottesdienst*, 29, 32, 44; Geiger, *Was hat Mohammed*, 70, 76–8, 202.

not the cognate, of 'dry bones' reclothed with flesh at the command of God עצמות יבשות (Ezekiel 37: 1–14), e.g. Q. 23: 14 فخلقنا المضغة عظاما فكسونا العظام لحما and 36: 78 من يحيى العظام وهى رميم. Rhetorical emphasis upon the corporeal aspect of resurrection is exhibited also in the collocation 'dust and bones' (*turāb wa-ʿiẓām*, e.g. Q. 23: 82), an expression of incredulity rather than a divine reminder of mortality.[1] Quranic expression of the latter is contained in Q. 22: 5 فانا خلقناكم من تراب. In Muslim scripture the fact of resurrection is presupposed: it is the point of departure for polemic rather than the result of thematic development, and formulations of doubt are stereotype.

Of somewhat different character are four other terms appropriate to the Quranic resurrection imagery: *baʿth*, *ḥashr*, *rajʿ*, and *qiyāma*. The basic notion of dispatch common to the first three of these is exhibited in scriptural usage, but is in each case dominated by association with the symbolism of the day of judgement. Such is achieved by juxtaposition of finite forms with the substantive *yawm* (day), e.g. يوم يبعثهم الله (Q. 56: 6, 18), الى يوم يُبعثون (7: 14, 15: 36, etc.). يوم نحشر المتقين (19: 85), ويوم نحشرهم جميعا (10: 28, etc.), ويوم يُرجعون اليه (24: 64, cf. 2: 281). The day is occasionally specified as *yawm al-qiyāma*, as in Q. 23: 16, 17: 97, but the ambiguity inherent in *baʿatha* (as a synonym of *arsala*: send) may have effected what appears to be a gloss (*ḥayyan*: alive) in Q. 19: 15 and 33 ويوم يبعث/أبعث حيّا. Similarly Q. 22: 7 وان الله يبعث من فى القبور where the locution 'those in their graves' restricts the semantic range of *yabʿath* (sends, hence resurrects) in a manner appropriate to the exegetical gloss. The metaphorical value of the image is thus diminished, or eliminated, as in Zamakhsharī's interpretation of the isolated instance of *yawm al-khurūj* (Q. 50: 42: day of emergence) as 'they emerge from their graves', which, though rendering *yawm al-khurūj* unequivocally as 'day of resurrection', destroys the more sophisticated metaphorical function of *akhraja* and its derivatives.[2] The same ambiguity in *ḥashara* (gather) and *rajaʿa* (return) is reduced by employment of parallel constructions with *ilayhi* (to Him), e.g. *ilayhi tuḥsharūn* (Q. 5: 96, 58: 9, etc.) and *ilayhi turjaʿūn* (2: 28, 10: 56, etc.). *Status constuctus* with *yawm* and the verbal noun is explicit only for *baʿth* فهذا يوم البعث (Q. 30: 56), but the contexts of Q. 50: 44 يوم تشقق الأرض عنهم سراعا ذلك حشر علينا يسير and 86: 8–9 إنّه على رجعه لقادر يوم تبلى السرائر perform a similar service for *ḥashr* and *rajʿ*, respectively.

Of the four terms *qiyāma* is unique, and for two reasons: the verbal noun itself occurs only in *status constructus* with *yawm*, and, with two

[1] O'Shaughnessy, *Death*, 46–9; cf. Speyer, op. cit. 72–3 ad Genesis 3: 19.

[2] *Kashshāf* iv, 393 ad loc.

exceptions, finite forms of the root *q-w-m* do not explicitly describe the fact of resurrection. The locution *yawm taqūm al-sāʿa* (Q. 30: 12, 14, 55, 40: 46, 45: 27) reflects *al-sāʿa qāʾima* of 18: 36 and 41: 50, in which the agent is the (final) Hour. Similarly, combinations of the imperfect with *ḥisāb* (reckoning) in Q. 14: 41, *ashhād* (witnesses) in 40: 51, *rūḥ* (spirit) and *malāʾika* (angels) in 73: 38. Only in Q. 39: 68 فإذا هم قيام ينظرون and 83: 6 يوم يقوم الناس لربّ العالمين is the act of rising/standing predicated of men. On the other hand, ratios of frequency and distribution for *yawm al-qiyāma* are high (seventy times in *sūra*s ranging from the second to the seventy-fifth), and corresponding collocation with derivatives of *baʿth* and *ḥashr* has been noted. Against the possibility of generation from the finite constructions *yawma yaqūmu/taqūmu* may be set the likelihood of *yawm al-qiyāma* as an incompletely assimilated borrowing. A calque of Syriac *qeyamta*, indicating presumably a loan-translation of Greek *anastasis*, would produce a significant polarity within the Quranic resurrection imagery.[1] The major implication need not, however, be a dual source for the theological concept, namely תחית המתים and ἀνάστασις,[2] but rather, or also, further evidence of the polemical environment in which the scripture of Islam came into being.

2. ITS COMPOSITION

Procedures of transmission and preservation demand that the word of God conform to recognizable patterns of human utterance. From the foregoing analysis of rhetorical schemata and of variant tradition, exegetical gloss, and conceptual assimilation, it may be supposed that the Quranic revelation is no exception to the general rule. But the mimetic process is a complex one. Isolation of such monotheist imagery as is characteristic of themes like divine retribution and sign, covenant and exile, indicates the perpetuation in Muslim scripture of established literary types. And yet, the merely allusive style of that document would appear to preclude positing the relationship of figural interpretation (typology) admitted to exist between the Old and New Testaments. The pattern of fulfilment (*figuram implere*) cannot, or at least hardly, be elicited from a comparison of Muslim with Hebrew scripture. That this is not merely a negative inference from the absence of an explicit connection of the sort established between the Christian and Hebrew scriptures ought to be clear from examination of the Quranic forms themselves, which reflect, but do not develop, most of the themes traditionally associated with literature of prophetical expression. If the claim to place the Qurʾān within that clearly defined literary tradition is conceded, it would none the less be inaccurate to describe that document as exhibiting essentially a calque of earlier fixed forms. The relationship

[1] Ahrens, 'Christliches im Qoran', 32.

[2] Cf. Black, *Aramaic Approach*, 281.

is rather more complicated, due at least in part to the origins of Muslim scripture in polemic. Illustration of that is provided by analysis of the confused and conflicting theories about the manner of its composition.

Muslim views on the mechanics of revelation consist for the most part of exegetical speculation on the content of Q. 42: 51. That verse may be set out as follows.

It is not granted to any man	وما كان لبشر
that God address him except:	أن يكلمه الله الا
(A) directly	(A) وحيا
(B) or from behind a screen	(B) أو من وراء حجاب
(C) or by sending a messenger	(C) أو يرسل رسولا
who utters with His permission	فيوحى بإذنه
that which He wishes	ما يشاء
He is indeed exalted and wise.	إنّه علىّ حكيم

A primary difficulty in this passage is its implication for a fundamental dilemma of Islamic theology: revelation as the unmediated speech of God, or revelation as the prophetical (angelic) report of God's speech. My translation of element (A) diverges from the *consensus doctorum* of Muslim tradition, according to which *waḥy* is synonymous with *ilhām* (inspiration), the verbal noun of Quranic *alhama* (91: 8, a *hapax legomenon*).[1] It seems clear, however, from element (C), in which the pronominal components of *fa-yūḥiya* and *bi-idhnihi* can hardly share a single referent, that the use here of *awḥā* is 'to reveal/present oneself' and, in conjunction with *kallama*, 'to utter directly (without mediation)'. That interpretation has the additional advantage of offering the required degree of contrast between the three (!) alternative kinds of theophany. Zamakhsharī, drawing upon the imagery of delegated authority (*wakīl*, *rasūl*), permitted element (C) to be so interpreted, but alluded in the same passage to what had become a traditional link between elements (A) and (C), namely, that the concept *waḥy* presupposed dispatch (*irsāl*) of a messenger.[2] Now, that Quranic *awḥā* may in some contexts be a synonym of *arsala* is clear from the very next verse (Q. 42: 52) كذلك أوحينا اليك روحا من أمرنا (cf. 17: 86, 41: 12). Application of the equivalence to elements (A) and (C) of Q. 42: 51, producing ultimately an interpretation of nearly the same currency as *waḥy*: *ilhām*, may, I suspect, be traced to the elliptical style of earlier exegetes. Muḥammad Kalbī, for example, glossed 'We reveal to you' with 'We send Gabriel to you with it' in the sense of 'to inform you of it'.[3] Muqātil b. Sulaymān improved upon

[1] e.g. Zamakhsharī, *Kashshāf* iv, 233 ad loc. Ibn Qutayba, on the other hand, was doubtful, *Ta'wīl*, 78, 83. See below, II pp. 58–9.

[2] *Kashshāf*, loc. cit.; the equation *waḥy*: *irsāl* may be compared with Zamakhsharī's observations on the messenger formula as derived from royal protocol, see above, p. 12.

[3] *Tafsir*, MS Ayasofya 118, 135ʳ *ad* Q. 12: 102.

that method by adding to his own gloss 'God revealed to him' the phrase 'Gabriel came to him and informed him of it'.[1] But that *waḥy* may signify communication, without recourse to an emissary, is confirmed not only by Q. 42: 51 but also by the use of *awḥā* in 6: 19, 112, 12: 3, 18: 27, etc.[2]

The significance of the tripartite description of the word of God in Q. 42: 51 lies in its allusion to the uniqueness of the Mosaic revelation, explicitly adduced three times by Zamakhsharī in his commentary to this verse. According to that exposition divine communication to all prophets other than Moses was conveyed by an emissary (mode C); Moses and the angels alone was/are addressed by God, but indirectly (mode B); the Jewish claim that Moses had been directly and personally spoken to by God (mode A) was denied. This report, adduced without authentication, is found also in Muqātil, and is symptomatic of the polemical atmosphere in which Muslim views were formulated.[3]

The exact nature of that polemic emerges from examination of the imagery employed for mode (B). Quranic *ḥijāb* (screen) may be of literal application (Q. 33: 53) or metaphorical (19: 17, 38: 32, 83: 15); its function in 7:46 is eschatological, and in 17: 45 and 41:5 it is a reflex of Biblical *masveh/kalymma*.[4] In Q. 42: 51, however, the symbolism is Rabbinic, being the locution מאחורי הוילון descriptive of the distinction between Israelite and foreign prophets in their reception of the word of God.[5] And within the circle of Hebrew prophets the Biblical distinction accorded Moses (Exodus 33: 11, Numbers 12: 8, Deuteronomy 34: 10) and elaborated in the Rabbinic tradition,[6] is also and not unexpectedly found in Muslim exegesis, e.g. *ad* Q. 2: 253, 4: 164 (وكلّم الله موسى تكليما), 7:143–4, 28: 30, where it reflects a transition from mode (B) to mode (A).[7] Biblical attestation of the unique relationship between God and Moses found a second expression in the criterion of angelic mediator, essential to all but the Mosaic revelation and, as mode (C) of Q. 42: 51, of considerable significance in the development of Muslim prophetology.[8] The unmediated theophany of the Pentateuch and earlier prophets was recast in prophetical literature proper, to which the Qur'ān may be reckoned, by recourse to the messenger formulae and the divine imperative.[9] Quranic *waḥy* in its final form was an inclusive concept, expanded by Suyūṭī to cover not only the express utterance of

[1] *Tafsīr*, MS. H. Hüsnü 17, 172v *ad* Q. 18: 86.

[2] For *waḥy* in the profane tradition, cf. Goldziher, *Studien* ii, 7 n. 1.

[3] *Kashshāf* iv, 233–4; *Tafsīr*, MS H. Hüsnü 17, 277v ad loc; cf. Geiger, *Was hat Mohammed*, 78–80, and Speyer, *Erzählungen*, 299–301.

[4] See below, II pp. 72–3.

[5] Speyer, op. cit. 420; Horovitz, *Untersuchungen*, 52–3; Jeffery, 'Scripture', 200 n. 34.

[6] Cf. Saadya, *Kitāb al-Amānāt*, 118–25, 132–5; Maimonides, *Dalālat* ii, chs. 33–4; Altmann, 'Theory', 19–21; Speyer, op. cit. 419.

[7] Zamakhsharī, *Kashshāf* i, 297 *ad* Q. 2: 253; Bāqillānī, *I'jāz*, 15; Suyūṭī, *Itqān* i, 129; Sharīf Murtaḍā, *Āmālī* ii, 312 *ad* Q. 4: 164; *GdQ* i, 23.

[8] See below, II pp. 58–61.

[9] Cf. Koch, *Growth*, 187; and above, pp. 12–15.

God but also that which men among themselves perceived to be His intention (i.e. inspiration).[1] As set out in Q. 42: 51, and shorn of profane and rhetorical amplification, the notion drew almost certainly upon Rabbinic formulations of the Mosaic tradition, even to the extent of adopting in modified form arguments designed originally to demonstrate the pre-creation of the Torah.[2]

Muslim discussion of the mode of Quranic revelation is characterized by a predominant concern to distinguish it from the manner in which the Torah was revealed. Expressed in the polarity *jumla* (integral): *munajjam* (serial), the distinction derived moment from a widely accepted interpretation of Q. 25: 32 وقال الذين كفروا لولا نزل عليه القرآن جملة واحدة كذلك لنثبت به فؤادك ورتّلناه ترتيلا. The necessary link between the locution *jumlatan wāḥidatan* (all of one piece) and the Mosaic revelation was provided by interpreting *alladhīna kafarū* (those who reject/disbelieve) as reference to the Jews. In a prophetical *ḥadīth* traced to ʿAbdallāh b. ʿAbbās such was the primary interpretation, *mushrikūn* (polytheists) being adduced as an alternative. For Zamakhsharī the roles were reversed. The spokesmen are Quraysh or, it is said (*wa-qīla*), the Jews. The contrast may be understood as polemical rather than historical, and exhibits a major theme of Muslim exegetical literature.[3] Priority of the Jews over Quraysh in that particular context was early attested, e.g. in Kalbī's gloss to Q. 17: 2 وآتينا موسى الكتاب/أعطينا موسى التوراة جملة واحدة. Quranic proof-texts for this interpretation, containing reference to the Mosaic tablets (*alwāḥ*, e.g. Q. 7: 144–5, 150, 154, 171), were easily found and frequently adduced, as in Suyūṭī.[4] Preoccupation with the precise difference between the two revelations generated a number of near-synonyms for the adverbial *munajjaman* (also *nujūman*): in the second half of Q. 25: 32 the term *tartīlan*, properly an elocutionary designation (*taflīj al-asnān*) was often interpreted as a reference to serial revelation; from Q. 17: 106 وقرآنا فرّقناه لتقرأه على الناس على مكث ونزّلناه تنزيلا the expressions *mufarraqan* (separately) and *tanzīlan* (by descent) could be seen to embody the same concept.[5] Similarly, *nujūman*, somewhat arbitrarily related to Quranic بمواقع النجوم (56: 75), became the point of departure for speculation on the likely extent/capacity of an in-

[1] *Itqān* i, 128, on the doubtful authority of Zuhrī.

[2] See Ibn Wahb, *Burhān*, 139–41; *GdQ* i, 21 n. 2, 46; Horovitz, op. cit. 67–8; and below, II pp. 83–4.

[3] Suyūṭī, *Itqān* i, 122; Zamakhsharī, *Kashshāf* iii, 278 ad loc; and see below, IV pp. 122–6.

[4] Kalbī, *Tafsir*, MS Hamidiye 40, 174v; *Itqān* i, 122–3; cf. Geiger, *Was hat Mohammed*, 151.

[5] Zamakhsharī, *Kashshāf* iii, 278–9 *ad* Q. 25: 32; cf. ibid iv, 637 for *tartīlan* in Q. 73: 4; Suyūṭī, *Itqān* i, 117–18.

stalment (*najm*), generally agreed to contain about five verses. The notion of a time-lag may also be elicited from Q. 20: 114 ولا تعجل بالقرآن من قبل أن يقضى اليك وحيه in which the terms *qur'ān* (publication) and *waḥy* (communication) are balanced by implicit reference to a period required for hearing, understanding, and learning the content of each revelation.[1]

The antithesis *jumla*:*munajjam* was further differentiated. Lest the concept of piecemeal revelation be seen to thrown doubt upon the origins of Muslim scripture, two verses شهر رمضان الذى أنزل فيه القرآن (Q. 2: 185) and إنّا أنزلناه فى ليلة القدر (97: 1) were adduced and interpreted to demonstrate that the Quranic revelation had consisted of two separate processes: transfer in its entirety to the nearest heaven and thence serially to the prophet during a period of approximately twenty years انه نزل الى السماء الدنيا ليلة القدر جملة واحدة ثم نزل بعد ذلك منجما فى عشرين سنة.[2] The chronological expressions in the two verses, Ramaḍān and Laylat al-qadr, did not remain exclusive to the Muslim revelation: the scriptures of Abraham, of Moses, of David, and of Jesus had also been revealed at ascertainable dates in Ramaḍān.[3] But it is the Mosaic revelation which furnished almost alone a *point d'appui* in the polemical discourse, exhibiting the Rabbinic (and Patristic) view of the origins of the Pentateuch.[4] On the other hand, references to Christian scripture in the Qur'ān provoked inevitably a similar description, as in Suyūṭī, where the interpretation of Q. 3: 3 stressed that both Torah and Gospel (*injīl*) had been revealed all of a piece, or in the observation of Ibn Isḥāq on the material contained in the revelation to Jesus وقد كان فيما بلغنى عما كان وضع عيسى ابن مريم فيما جاءه من الله فى الانجيل لأهل الانجيل.[5] Despite polemical reiteration some confusion persisted, ultimately to be clarified or evaded by resort to rationalizing argument drawn from outside scripture. The *munajjam* concept was after all not exclusively Quranic: in his commentary to the Psalter Saadya explained repetition as the consequence of separate occasions of revelation to David, much as could be found in the Torah, itself a product of serial revelation תורה מגלה נתנה.[6]

The dual character of the Quranic revelation was seen to be an honour

[1] Suyūṭī, *Itqān* i, 124–5; Zamakhsharī, *Kashshāf* iii, 90 *ad* Q. 20: 114.

[2] Suyūṭī, *Itqān* i, 116; cf. *GdQ* i, 80; the accusative pronoun in Q. 97: 1 is in Suyūṭī's discussion understood to refer to the Qur'ān, though Gabriel was occasionally made the referent, see below, II pp. 61–2.

[3] Suyūṭī, *Itqān* i, 120; a variant tradition in the anonymous *Kitāb al-Mabānī*, 235.

[4] Cf. Eissfeldt, *Einleitung*, 695–8, citing *inter alia* Talm. Babl. Baba Batra 14b; and see Goitein, 'Ramadan', 90–110.

[5] *Itqān* iii, 343; apud Ibn Hishām, *Sīra* i, 232.

[6] Lauterbach, *Saadja*, 23 n. 9; Speyer, *Erzählungen*, 423 n. 2, citing Talm. Babl. Giṭṭim 60a.

(*tashrīf*) bestowed by God upon its recipient: by virtue of the integral transfer of the word to the nearest heaven, Muhammad was made the equal (*taswiya*) of Moses, above whom he was subsequently elevated (*tafḍīl*) as a result of the serial transfer وفيه ايضا التسوية بين نبينا وبين موسى فى إنزاله كتابه جملة والتفضيل لمحمد فى إنزاله عليه منجما ليحفظه. Precise reasons for the second process were of three kinds: (a) Muhammad, being illiterate, required time to learn; (b) the Qur'ān, containing abrogating and abrogated parts, revised formulations, and direct answers to specific questions, must of necessity have been serially revealed; (c) conversion of the Arabian heathen had perforce to proceed by gentle and humane stages.[1] The extent to which those views reflect doctrinal disputes of a most significant kind for the historical image of the Muslim community will be made clear in the following chapters.

. . . .

From the axiomatic position achieved by the principle of serial revelation it followed that that process should be described: temporally and spatially fixed. The demand was met, indeed exceeded, by a supply of data formulated to provide a meticulous chronology of the Quranic revelation. Technically designated *akhbār/asbāb al-nuzūl* (reports about/causes of revelation), this material found its most succinct expression in halakhic exegesis, bearing eloquent witness to the many, often contradictory, uses to which a single instance of revelation might be put.[2] The arbitrary character of these data is best observed in the pseudo-historical literature which accompanied, possibly preceded, the efforts of the halakhists to distribute meaningfully the Quranic revelation over a period of twenty/twenty-five years following the call of the Arabian prophet. The traditional principle informing that literature, namely, that a chronology of revelation is possible, has to my knowledge never been questioned.[3]

A typical illustration is found in the accounts of an interview of Ja'far b. Abī Ṭālib with a/the ruler of Ethiopia (*najāshī*). The episode is one in a narrative series treating of the Muslim emigration/exile to that country (*al-hijra al-ūlā*) and of the dispatch by Quraysh of a mission to secure return of the emigrants to Mecca. In the presence of those envoys Ja'far was summoned to explain the circumstances of himself and his companions. His response may be set out as follows.

1. We were a people, a folk in ignorance.
2. Worshipping idols.
3. And eating carrion.
4. Frequenting prostitutes.

[1] Suyūṭī, *Itqān* i, 82, 119, 121, 124.
[2] See below, IV pp. 177–8.
[3] *GdQ* i, 58–65; cf. below, IV pp. 126–7.

5. And severing ties of kinship.
6. Violating the rules of security.
7. The powerful among us oppressing the weak.

Thus we were until:

1. God sent to us a messenger chosen from our midst, whose background, honesty, faithfulness, and continence we knew.
2. Who called us to God, to associate no one with Him, to worship Him, to rid ourselves of the stones and images which we and our fathers had been worshipping. He commanded us to worship God alone and to associate nothing with Him.
3. (And he commanded us) to abstain from that which is forbidden and from blood.
4. And he forbade us prostitutes.
5. (And he commanded us) to observe the ties of kinship.
6. And to abide by the rules of security.
7. (And he forbade us) to devour the property of orphans.
8. And he commanded us to speak honestly and to act in good faith; and (to abstain from) false speech and the slander of honourable women.
9. And he commanded us to fulfil the duties of prayer, almsgiving, and fasting.

Recounted on the authority of an eye-witness (*scil.* Umm Salama) to the event, this version was adduced in the earliest biography of the Arabian prophet.[1]

The substance of Jaʿfar's recital, designated by the tradent 'the principles of Islam' (*umūr al-islām*), is not unlike prescriptions of essentials for the new faith published from time to time by the Christian apostles (e.g. Acts 15: 20, 28–9). Formally, a degree of dramatic tension is achieved by the syntactical balance developed round the phrase 'Thus we were until'. The counterpoint consists almost entirely of locutions attested at least once, in some cases frequently, in the canonical text of the Quranic revelation:

1. كنّا قوما أهل جاهلية may be thought to reflect أراكم قوما تجهلون (Q. 11: 29, 46: 23, cf. 7: 138, 27: 55), or even one of the four occurrences of *jāhiliyya* (interpreted as a collective: Q. 3: 154, 5: 50, 33: 33, 48: 26). حتى بعث الله الينا رسولا منّا is of common occurrence, e.g. هو الذى بعث فى الأمّيّين رسولا منهم (Q. 62: 2, cf. 3: 164, 9: 128). Of the four qualities attributed to the prophet: *nasab*, *ṣidq*, *amāna*, and *ʿafāf*, only the last is not attested in scripture, though the remaining three nowhere appear as a collective designation of prophetical credentials (cf. 4: 58).

2. نعبد الأصنام is found in Q. 14: 35 and 26: 71, invariably related to the

[1] Ibn Hishām, *Sīra* i, 336; to underline the contrapuntal style of the oration I have rearranged just slightly the components of the second series, which includes two items not listed in the first. Variant and parallel traditions are found elsewhere, see Caetani, *Annali* i, 266–7.

story of Abraham (cf. 6: 74 and the imagery of 19: 42–9). The somewhat awkward statement فدعانا الى الله لنوحّده ونعبده ونخلع ما كنّا نعبد نحن وأباؤنا من دونه من الحجارة والأوثان is such that it could provoke a reply like Q. 11: 62, but neither *khalaʿa* (rid) nor *ḥijāra* (stones) is so used in the Qur'ān. *Awthān* (images, idols) is attested (Q. 29: 17, 25), but not a finite form of *waḥḥada*. More easily placed is the paraphrase وأمرنا ان نعبد الله وحده لا نشرك به شيئا, reflecting Q. 7: 70 and 3: 64.

3. The phrase ونأكل الميتة belongs to the series of prohibitions articulated in Q. 2: 173, 5: 3, 6: 145, 16: 115, but for the complement in the contrapuntal scheme neither *kaff* (abstention) nor *maḥārim* (prohibitions) is Quranic, and the plural *dimā'* is not used of sacrificial blood.

4. ونأتي الفواحش is frequently attested in the singular (e.g. Q. 4: 15, 19, 25) and the prohibition occurs (with *ḥarrama*) in the plural in Q. 7: 33.

5. ونقطع الأرحام appears as an admonition in Q. 47: 22, but the locution صلة الرحم is not scriptural (cf. however Q. 4: 1).

6. The term جوار is itself not found in scripture, but the exhortation here reflects the contents of Q. 4: 36, and finite forms of the verb are employed metaphorically (!) in 23: 88.

7. ويأكل القوى منّا الضعيف is not scriptural, but its complement أكل مال اليتيم appears verbatim (plural) in Q. 4: 10, and varied slightly in 6: 152 and 17: 34.

8. This and the following injunctions are not adduced in Jaʿfar's description of the Meccans prior to the appearance of the prophet, and thus intrude upon the contrapuntal scheme of items (1) to (7). Their phraseology is, however, Quranic: صدق الحديث may be related to لسان صدق Q. 19: 50; قول الزور occurs in 22: 30 (with *awthān*, cf. 58: 2); قذف المحصنات reflects الذين يرمون لمحصنات in 24: 4, 23 (with *ramā*; *qadhafa* is not so used in scripture).

9. الصلاة والزكاة appear almost invariably together (e.g. Q. 2: 43, 19: 31, 55), and صيام separately (e.g. 2: 183) or with related injunctions (e.g. 2: 196 with *ḥajj*, *ṣadaqa*, and *nusuk*), but the combination of fasting with prayer and almsgiving is not attested in scripture.

Now, the exact relationship between this very concise catechism and the canonical text of the Quranic revelation is not immediately clear. Acceptance of the historicity of Jaʿfar's interview with the Najāshī must lead one to suppose either that the injunctions here expressed had been the subject of revelations before the emigration to Ethiopia, or that they represent prophetical *logia* later confirmed by or incorporated into the text of scripture. On the other hand, the structure of the report suggests a careful rhetorical formulation of Quranic material generally supposed to have been revealed after the date of that event. Three further points in the interview deserve notice.[1] Asked by the ruler to recite something from the revelation sent to their prophet, Ja'far produced the beginning of *Sūrat Maryam* (صدرا من كهيعص), at which the Najāshī, greatly moved, declared: This is, indeed, from the same source as that which Jesus uttered (ليخرج من مشكاة واحدة). Interrogated next day on his attitude towards Jesus, Ja'far replied: He is the servant of God, His messenger, and His spirit, His word which He bestowed upon the unblemished virgin Mary (هو عبد الله ورسوله وروحه و كلمته ألقاها الى مريم العذراء البتول). Explicit mention of the nineteenth *sūra*, possible allusion to the imagery of Q. 24: 35, and almost certain reference to 4: 171–2 (but cf. also 19: 17, 30) might be thought to strengthen the inference that the author of this report was familiar with a fairly extensive range of Quranic diction. The positivist Caetani, failing to recognize the literary form and reacting to what he regarded as anachronism, dismissed the account in the *Sīra* in favour of the terse version in Ṭabarī of the arrival of a delegation from Quraysh, in which appears no reference to a conversation between Ja'far and the Najāshī.[2] Caetani's rejection reflects his approval of a chronology of revelation in which *Sūrat Maryam*, or at least its beginning, was Meccan, but in which much of the content of Ja'far's confession of faith included material agreed to have been revealed in Medina. The quite arbitrary character of that chronology is clear from even a cursory examination of Muslim scholarship. In his commentary to the *Sīra*, Suhaylī regarded the account of Ja'far and the Najāshī as unexceptionable.[3] Qummī stated explicitly *Sūrat Maryam*, not merely its beginning, and adduced the Muslim catechism in a form almost identical to that of an Apostolic promulgation.[4] Ibn al-Athīr included an account varying only slightly from that of the *Sīra*.[5] And Suyūṭī cited the episode approvingly.[6] It can, of course, be argued that reports (*akhbār*) about and occasions/causes (*asbāb*) of revelation are not quite the same thing, and thus, that halakhic exegesis may disregard as fictive, or at least irrelevant, the data found in haggadic literature of the kind exhibited in the *Sīra*. But in practice such was seldom the case, and the foregoing analysis may be thought to have suggested the interdependence of source materials traditionally adduced as evidence of independent corroboration.

[1] *Sīra* i, 336–7.

[2] *Annali* i, 277–8, mentioning only Q. 4: 171–2; Ṭabarī, *Annales* I/1189; similarly *GdQ* i, 130; cf. Buhl, 'Beiträge', 13–22.

[3] *Al-Rawḍ al-unuf* i, 213.

[4] *Tafsīr* i, 176–9 *ad* Q. 5: 82.

[5] *Al-Kāmil* ii, 60–3.

[6] *Itqān* i, 50.

I have proposed that one might interpret Jaʿfar's recital as a report of prophetical *logia* exhibiting a stage of transmission prior to their incorporation into the Quranic canon. An essential feature of that report, and one characteristic of the *Sīra* as a type of exegetical literature, is the *narratio*. This device, common in Biblical literature, provides a context of historical circumstance or, at least, vaguely historical allusion, into which or by means of which reports of a prophet's deeds (מעשים) or words (דברים) may be introduced. For Hebrew scripture the priority in time of such reports over the actual reproduction in literary form of prophetical utterances has been established.[1] To postulate a similar, if not identical, process for Muslim scripture seems to me not unjustified, though in this particular instance complicated by the redaction history of the *Sīra* itself.[2] The fairly consistent application of a contrapuntal scheme in Jaʿfar's confession reveals, indeed, a preoccupation with rhetorical niceties, but certainly does not preclude the possibility of oral transmission or delivery. Use of counterpoint might even be interpreted as a mnemonic device calculated to assist such. As set out in this episode the promulgation of basic Muslim doctrine has the inestimable advantage of clarity and cohesion over its disjointed and dispersed occurrence in the canonical text of scripture. That difference may, at least superficially, indicate a composition posterior to the several revelations contained there. From the same and similar evidence, however, a rather more complex relationship between the canonical traditions is discernible. In the narrative structure of the latter, revelations of exclusively regulative content are presented in a manner which conforms to that characteristic of the Quranic theodicy as a whole, of which the retribution pericopes (e.g. Shuʿayb) are examples.

In the story of Jaʿfar and the Najāshī three distinct but related themes may be seen: exile from the homeland, enumeration of the basic ingredients of monotheism, and external recognition of the prophet's credentials. In that way three purely literary functions—typological, exegetical, and aetiological—combine to produce a narrative history. The same process can be observed in treatment of passages whose content is not regulative but paraenetic: for example, in the relation of *Sūra* 105 to the Affair of the Elephant.[3] Whatever the sense, or variant readings, generated by the phrase *aṣḥāb al-fīl*, the literary tradition represents the elaboration of three themes: holy war (Abraha's campaign), the inviolate sanctuary and its protectors (Mecca and Quraysh), and the action of God in history (birds as bearers of plague). By means of these, the elliptical Quranic passage was incorporated into salvation history as an episode both lively and easily understood. Here too, as in the story of Jaʿfar, relationship to the canon is not merely causal, and an attempt to adduce it as illustrative of the

[1] See von Rad, *Theology* ii, 34–9.
[2] See below, IV pp. 127, 140–3.
[3] Ibn Hishām, *Sīra* i, 43–61.

chronology of revelation was rejected by Suyūṭī.[1] Both episodes are characterized by action which is symbolic and which takes precedence over the direct speech of the corresponding canonical passages. The contrast between parallel formulations, canonical and non-canonical, may be likened to that which obtains between the narrative framework (*Fremdbericht*) and the dialogue (*Ich-Bericht*) observed in the retribution pericopes.

In all of this material, whether or not ultimately incorporated into the canon, the organizing principle was the same: movement in history as an act of God. From the foregoing analyses it may be agreed that the patterns upon which description of that movement drew were ancient and well established. Their literary formulation might seem to make superfluous the question of historicity. And it is not merely the chronology of revelation, as a recognized component of the Quranic masorah, which is problematic. Traditional discussions of the modes of revelation would appear to have derived considerable impetus from polemic about the precise distinction between the Muslim and Hebrew scriptures. Indeed, the history of the canon itself provokes the question at least of methodological, if not substantial, assimilation of earlier descriptive techniques. Assimilation of the sort encountered here need not, of course, be defined in terms of a rigorous distinction between *Urerlebnis* and *Bildungserlebnis*. A literary analysis can, after all, only reveal what seems to be the essential role of historiography, namely, the unceasing reinterpretation of tradition. It need hardly be added that both method and material are almost infinitely transferable.

. . . .

In the exegetical literature formation of the Quranic canon is ascribed to one of two processes: either official recognition of a corpus left intact by the Arabian prophet (*Urtext*), or imposition of a uniform recension produced by an officially constituted body with concomitant suppression of earlier and variant versions ('Uthmanic codex). The two processes may appear as separate, if not quite mutually exclusive, traditions, or together as two stages in a single tradition, the consequence of more or less successful harmonization. Critical analysis of the tradition(s) is set out in the second part of the fundamental work of Nöldeke–Schwally, in which may be read the authors' concluding judgement on the diametrical opposition between formation of the Quranic canon and that of the Jewish and Christian scriptures: 'Die Entstehung des muhammedanischen Kanons ist völlig abweichend, man könnte sagen entgegengesetzt verlaufen. Er ist nicht das Werk mehrerer Schriftsteller, sondern eines einzigen Mannes und deshalb in der kurzen Spanne eines Menschenalters zustande gekommen'.[2] Now,

[1] *Itqān* i, 90; cf. Horovitz, *Untersuchungen*, 10–11, 96–8; Blachère, *Histoire* iii, 788 n. 3.

[2] *GdQ* ii, 120.

it seems to me at least arguable that the evidence of the Qur'ān itself, quite apart from that of the exegetical tradition, lends little support to that assertion. It may, indeed, appear from my description of that document that the Muslim scripture is not only composite, but also, and such can be inferred from a typological analysis of Quranic exegesis, that the period required for its achievement was rather more than a single generation.[1]

Traditional material relating to the canon must be assessed not merely in respect of its intrinsic merit, but equally by reference to a series of data extrinsic to the process itself of canonization but relevant none the less to canonicity. It would seem not unreasonable to assume that the latter presupposed acceptance by the Muslim community of the Quranic revelation as normative for its religious life. And yet, Schacht's studies of the early development of legal doctrine within the community demonstrate that, with very few exceptions, Muslim jurisprudence was not derived from the contents of the Qur'ān.[2] It may be added that those few exceptions are themselves hardly evidence for existence of the canon, and further observed that even where doctrine was alleged to draw upon scripture, such is not necessarily proof of the earlier existence of the scriptural source.[3] Derivation of law from scripture (halakhic exegesis) was a phenomenon of the third/ninth century, and while the obvious inference is admittedly an *argumentum e silentio*, the chronology of the source material demands that it be mentioned. A similar kind of negative evidence is absence of any reference to the Qur'ān in the *Fiqh Akbar I*, dated by Wensinck to about the middle of the second/eighth century.[4] Moreover, stabilization of the text of scripture (masoretic exegesis) was an activity whose literary expression is also not attested before the third/ninth century, and the appearance of the classical *maṣāḥif* literature (*variae lectiones*) was even later.[5] It is of course neither possible, nor necessary, to maintain that the material of the canon did not, in some form, exist prior to that period of intensive literary activity, but establishment of a standard text such as is implied by the 'Uthmanic recension traditions can hardly have been earlier.

One has further to consider the actual significance of the textual variants exhibited in these traditions. From the material assembled by Bergsträsser and Pretzl, and in more detail by Jeffery, it could well be asked to what extent any of the variants, or variant codices (?), may be said to represent traditions genuinely independent of the 'Uthmanic recension.[6] The infinitesimal differences are not such as would seem to have necessitated suppression of the non-'Uthmanic versions, the more so since a minimal standard deviation from the canon was accommodated by the several inter-

[1] See below, IV pp. 145–8.
[2] *Origins*, *passim* but esp. 224–7.
[3] Cf. Strack, *Introduction*, 10.
[4] *Creed*, 102–24.
[5] See Jeffery, *Materials*, 1–16.
[6] *GdQ* iii, 57–115; *Materials*, 19–355.

pretations of the *aḥruf* doctrine.[1] The choice between interpreting those codices as conscious (i.e. exegetical) variations upon the ʿUthmanic recension, or as having in common with that recension an earlier *Vorlage*, is not an easy one. What might be considered a special category of variant codex, the 'metropolitan codices' (*maṣāḥif al-amṣār*), do not display the differences either among themselves or from the ʿUthmanic recension which are alleged to have provoked the editorial measures attributed to the third caliph.[2] The tradition itself of separate collections of *amṣār*-variants, far from being attributable to so early an authority as the Damascene *muqriʾ* Ibn ʿĀmir (d. 118/736), appears not to be more ancient than Farrāʾ (d. 207/822) or possibly than his teacher Kisāʾī (d. 189/804). Fixed terminology, like reference to the ʿUthmanic recension as *imām*, or to *muṣḥaf* as codex, in contrast to the plural *maṣāḥif* not as codices but as variants, can also not be dated earlier than the beginning of the third/ninth century.[3] The random predominance of Medinese readings in both Sībawayh and Farrāʾ, where one might have expected reflections of practice in Basra and Kufa, cannot but provoke the impression that concern with the text of scripture did not precede by much the appearance of the masoretic literature as it has in fact been preserved. Failure to situate regionally actual manuscripts of the Qurʾān by collating them with collections of 'metropolitan' variants might be thought to confirm that impression.[4]

Now, confronted by the ʿUthmanic recension traditions one is compelled to assume either that suppression of substantial deviations was so instantly and universally successful that no trace of serious opposition remained, or that the story was a fiction designed to serve another purpose. The first possibility is, however, belied by the chronological sequence of literature on the Qurʾān, of which none may be described as presupposing a standard or *ne varietur* text as early as the middle of the first/seventh century, and further, by absence of explicit reference to a canon in contexts where such ought to appear. The second possibility, on the other hand, gives rise to some interesting but naturally inconclusive speculation on the means to which a newly independent religious community might have recourse in the effort to describe its origins. I have alluded to the likelihood of a Rabbinic model for the account of an authoritative text produced in committee, namely the Jamnia tradition on the canonization of Hebrew scripture.[5] Similarly, the Muslim tradition of an *Urtext*, whether conceived of as independent or as a stage preliminary to ʿUthmān's editorial work, might be thought to reflect Rabbinic views on the Mosaic reception of the Torah. That conjecture derives some support from the relationship

[1] *GdQ* iii, 186–90, 213–28.
[2] Cf. the lists in Ibn Abī Dāwūd, apud Jeffery, *Materials*, 39–49; and *GdQ* iii, 6–19.
[3] *GdQ* iii, 9 n. 4; Jeffery, op. cit. 13; Beck, 'Kodizesvarianten', 353–76.
[4] *GdQ* iii, 270: 'dass fast alle Kodizes einen Mischtext aufweisen'.
[5] See above, p. 21.

between Moses and Muhammad as recipients of the word of God, integral to Muslim discussion of the modes of revelation. The primary source of strength for the *Urtext* tradition may be found in the concept of 'the final review' (العرضة الأخيرة), representing the culmination of a series of encounters between the prophet and the angel Gabriel for periodic organization of the material so far revealed 'in order that abrogated matter might be distinguished from that which remained effective' (التى بيّن فيها ما نسخ وما بقى) or 'abrogated distinguished from its replacement' (ما نسخ وما بدل).[1] The significant element in these descriptions is reference to the doctrine of abrogation (*naskh*) and hence the implications of the *Urtext* theory for halakhic exegesis.[2] Later formulations of that doctrine required that the process of abrogation be incomplete upon the death of the prophet and concomitantly that definitive organization of the text of revelation be postponed until after that date. The ʿUthmanic recension story may be regarded as the means by which that end was attained.[3]

Thus could the two canon traditions be seen as complementary rather than contradictory, though the actual instrument of harmonization was the celebrated codex of Ḥafṣa, which provided a tidy sequence of events covering the period from the death of the prophet to the action of the caliph ʿUthmān.[4] It is, however, not absolutely necessary to select only one of two interpretations: the ʿUthmanic recension story as a reflex of the Rabbinic academy at Jamnia, or as a logical construction of the halakhists. The technical term employed to describe ʿUthmān's editorial work, *scil. jamʿ*, was used with a semantic latitude capable of accommodating a number of related but quite distinct actions. Suyūṭī's synthesis includes all of them: in *nawʿ* 18 he assumed throughout the equivalence *jamʿ* : *tartīb* (arrangement), but distinguished arrangement/collection between two covers (i.e. in codex form), internal arrangement of *sūra*s, and arrangement of/restriction to readings confirmed by the authority of the prophet, and insisted as well upon the difference between order of revelation (*tartīb al-nuzūl*) and order of recitation (*tartīb al-tilāwa*).[5] In *nawʿ* 20, traditions were adduced in which *jamʿ* could be interpreted as preservation/memorization (*ḥifẓ*), as recording by writing (*kitāba*), or as hearing and obeying (*al-samʿ wal-ṭāʿa lahu*).[6] Such a spectrum of meaning, besides reflecting a series of doctrinal positions in that long discussion, attests surely to uncertainty about the process by which revelation became canon.

I have in the preceding pages attempted to show that the structure itself

[1] Suyūṭī, *Itqān* i, 142, and *Kitāb al-Mabānī*, 26, respectively.
[2] See below, IV pp. 192–201.
[3] Cf. Burton, 'Cranes', 246–65, esp. 260; id. 'Collection', 42–60.
[4] *GdQ* ii, 20–3, 91, 114–15.
[5] *Itqān* i, 164–83; cf. also *Kitāb al-Mabānī*, ch. III, 39–77.
[6] *Itqān* i, 199–206.

of Muslim scripture lends little support to the theory of a deliberate edition. Particularly in the *exempla* of salvation history, characterized by variant traditions, but also in passages of exclusively paraenetic or eschatological content, ellipsis and repetition are such as to suggest not the carefully executed project of one or of many men, but rather the product of an organic development from originally independent traditions during a long period of transmission. That such traditions might have been of local/regional character is not impossible, but in view of the inconclusive nature of the so-called 'metropolitan codices' regional distribution of the variant traditions could hardly be justified. An alternative and less refractory hypothesis is one already advanced: juxtaposition of independent pericopes to some extent unified by means of a limited number of rhetorical conventions. Such might be held to account both for the repetitive character of the document and for what is undeniably its stylistic homogeneity, the latter quality in part a consequence of the former.[1] The content of these pericopes may be described as prophetical *logia* whose formulation exhibits a number of recognizable literary types based on what I have designated schemata of revelation. In canonical form these *logia* are expressed, not quite consistently, as the direct utterance of God, but outside the canon take the form of reports about such utterances. An example of the latter was seen in the story of Jaʿfar b. Abī Ṭālib and the Najāshī.

Whether one is justified in equating non-canonical with pre-canonical is a historical problem complicated rather than clarified by the evolution of exegetical literature. Of the earliest form of that literature, described below as narrative/haggadic, we have no specimens which do not exhibit traces of redaction characteristic of the third/ninth century. Thus the forms in which prophetical *logia* were likely to have been transmitted display a version of scripture which is unmistakably canonical. Primacy of the *narratio* is none the less evident, and stylistic as well as explicative elements indicate oral transmission.[2] Again, Jaʿfar's recital is instructive, for there material of an ethical and regulative nature was presented in a form both hortatory and entertaining, but above all, owing to the contrapuntal scheme employed, in a manner both easy to understand and to remember. The use of symmetry as a mnemonic technique in oral transmission is of course widely attested.[3] Repeated application of conventional formulae of introduction and conclusion, refrains, litanies, and the structural balance observable in related pericopes perform an identical service. It might, on the other hand, be more accurate to speak not of oral transmission but of oral delivery. Resort to mnemonic device and symmetrical structure does not preclude the existence of written *Vorlagen*, indeed, in many instances

[1] See below, III pp. 117–18.
[2] See below, IV pp. 129–31, 145–8.
[3] Cf. Gerhardsson, *Memory*, 147, but see the entire section 136–56.

presupposes such. Coexistence of textual transmission and oral tradition may be substantiated not only by the technique of dictation, but also by reference to the exigencies of typically cultic situations (liturgical and didactic), in which the more appropriate oral delivery exhibits a refinement of simple and straightforward recitation from memorized texts. That the many techniques associated with refined and sophisticated oral delivery could ultimately be incorporated into an improved text may be cited as evidence of rhetorical development, but not of change from exclusively oral to exclusively written transmission.[1]

Related to procedures of transmission and delivery are the techniques of oral and written composition. Though from the point of view of historical reconstruction it is unquestionably useful, perhaps imperative, to keep separate the discussion of each, mention at least of the problems relating to composition is not unjustified. Both the very high frequency and the uniform distribution in the Qur'ān of formulae and of 'formulaic systems' could indicate not only a long period of oral transmission but also of oral composition.[2] Analysis of formulaic language in Muslim scripture would include statistics for the thematic permutations which I have described as variant traditions, as well as for the schemata adduced to illustrate the theodicy. Equally important are the rhyme-phrases employed in Quranic periodization, which exhibit, in addition to the stressed syllable of the rhyme itself, fairly uniform length and thus a nearly constant metrical value.[3] Those phrases are most conspicuous in passages of halakhic and narrative content, where they serve as both conjunctive and disjunctive markers.[4] Now, all of that material—theme, schemata, and rhyme-phrase—may be described as components of formulaic systems, but not necessarily as proof of oral composition. The imagery and lexicon of Muslim scripture are almost exclusively archetypal and suggest, if they do not presuppose, some contact with literary precursors. The dichotomy postulated between 'borrowing' and 'traditional language' is possibly misleading and certainly an oversimplification: like most linguistic expression the structure of monotheist revelation contains very little that is not 'traditional language'.[5] For the Quranic revelation ascription to Biblical archetypes has been, perhaps unnecessarily, complicated by the existence of a native Arabic tradition of monotheistic (*ḥanīfī*) poetry.[6] The authenticity of that poetry has been disputed; its importance to the Muslim exegetical tradition cannot be. But the sources of archetypal

[1] Gerhardsson, loc. cit.; cf. Widengren, 'Oral tradition', esp. 201–32.

[2] Cf. Culley, *Formulaic language*, 10–20, 21–7; Muilenburg, 'Hebrew rhetoric', 97–111.

[3] The criteria for detection and assessment of formulaic language were after all derived from oral poetry, see references in Culley, loc. cit.; and Monroe, 'Oral composition', 1–53.

[4] See below, III pp. 112, 115–6.

[5] Cf. Culley, op. cit. 112–19.

[6] See below, III pp. 96–7.

imagery in the Qur'ān are not thereby concealed, nor is the sheer quantity of reference to Patriarchal narrative in any way diminished (Moses: 502 verses in 36 *sūras*, Abraham: 245 verses in 25 *sūras*, Noah: 131 verses in 28 *sūras*).[1] Elaboration of the corpus of prophetical *logia* from which the Quranic canon was eventually separated may have been essentially a product of oral composition. Emergence of the canon itself, however, represented application of considerable literary technique. Not the least of the problems provoked by its final form is the erratic distribution of obviously related pericopes.[2]

Analysis of its parts does not thus necessarily explain existence of the whole. Lack of such over-all logical structure in the Qur'ān as is found in the Jewish and Christian canons, is reflected in traditions which attempt to postulate a correspondence (vaguely defined and somewhat contrived) between parts of the Muslim canon and the earlier scriptures, e.g. قال رسول الله أعطيتُ السبع الطول مكان التوراة والمائين مكان الانجيل والمثانى مكان الزبور وفضّلتُ بالمفصل.[3] The descriptive terms are merely quantitative and the correspondence quite arbitrary, but that it should have been adduced at all is worthy of remark.

The fact of canonicity may be seen as a kind of watershed in the transmission history of the Quranic revelation.[4] Development beyond that point, which I should hesitate to set before the end of the second/eighth century, is to be elicited from a study of exegesis and commentary. Description of the course of events up to that date is, I have more than once suggested, frustrated by the form in which pertinent witness has been preserved. Any attempt at reconstruction is thus hazardous, being limited to tenuous conclusions from literary analogies. If the pericope hypothesis is acknowledged to make some sense of the Quranic data themselves, it requires none the less to be supplemented by a notion of the environment in which prophetical *logia* might have been preserved and transmitted. Now, what could be seen as obviously analogous circumstances, namely those obtaining for preservation and transmission of both Rabbinic and Apostolic formulations of the word of God, presuppose for both an authoritative centre of such activity, which was Jerusalem.[5] Despite implicit emphasis upon the role of Medina in the 'Uthmanic recension traditions, evidence for a single centre of activity is not easily found in the pre-canonical transmission history of the

[1] Moubarac, *Abraham*, 27–9.

[2] Cf. *GdQ* ii, 63–8: with regard to 64 n. 1 it may be observed that Geiger's proposal that the Mishnah tractates were arranged in descending order of their length was ultimately rejected by Strack, who suggested that their sequence corresponded to that of legal problems in the Pentateuch, see *Introduction*, 27–8.

[3] *Kitāb al-Mabānī*, 235; variants and discussion in Suyūṭī, *Itqān* i, 163, 177–81.

[4] Cf. Koch, *Growth*, 106–8; and Vermes, *Scripture*, esp. 127–77.

[5] Cf. Gerhardsson, *Memory*, 214–20.

Qur'ān, nor, for that matter, in the early development of Islamic jurisprudence.[1] If the origins of exegetical literature may in fact be located in Mesopotamia, that is the paradoxical corollary of a social and political development, the literary description of which was designed precisely to demonstrate that the story of Islam was conterminous with the history of the Arabian peninsula, and especially of the Hijaz in the first/seventh century. As such the descriptive material need not be discounted, but can by no means be accepted as constituting disinterested historiography. Thus the fact of the Mesopotamian environment emerges, perhaps not quite accidentally, and must be adduced as criterion for assessing any evidence which purports to describe the circumstances of Islam prior to the third/ninth century.[2]

Enough has been said of the canonization traditions to indicate their contradictory, and probably polemical, character. Proposed as alternative was the concept of an organic development exhibiting gradual juxtaposition of originally separate collections of *logia*. The failure to eliminate repetition in the canon might be attributed to the status which these *logia* had already achieved in the several (!) communities within which they originated and by whose members they were transmitted. Here 'community' need not be understood as a regional specification, though such is not impossible. I should be inclined to postulate the growth of *logia* collections in environments essentially sectarian but within the mainstream of oriental monotheism. Such an environment could be inferred from the evidence of parallels proposed by Rabin between Islamic terminology and that of the Qumran sect.[3] But some of that material reflects polygenesis rather than diffusion through historical contact, e.g. the light imagery and the personification of evil.[4] And resemblance can be deceptive: rather than in the cognate *fassara* I am tempted to see a methodological reflex of Qumranic *pesher* in the Muslim term *ta'wīl*, and thus an 'inverted' semantic relationship between *pesher* and *tafsīr*, similar to that found by Rabin to obtain between Qumranic and Rabbinic terminology.[5] The primary difficulty, however, in this and all such expositions aimed at demonstrating historical diffusion lies in their uncritical assent to the traditional chronology of Islamic origins, resulting inevitably in socio-psychological analyses of data whose literary, rather than historical, character is patent.[6] Some scholars, among them Ben-Zvi and Katsch, have been excessively generous in their assessment of the documentary value of Islamic source materials for the existence and cultural significance (!) of Jewish communities in the Hijaz,

[1] See Schacht, *Origins*, 8, 213.

[2] On geographical factors in the assessment of legal source materials, cf. Schacht, *Origins*, 188–9, 223, 228.

[3] *Qumran*, 112–30.

[4] *Qumran*, 114–15 and 122, resp.

[5] *Qumran*, 96–7, 108–11, 117; cf. below, IV p. 246.

[6] e.g. Rabin, *Qumran*, 120–7; cf. my observations in *BSOAS* xxxiii (1970) 613–14.

about which Jewish sources are themselves silent.[1] References in Rabbinic literature to Arabia are of remarkably little worth for purposes of historical reconstruction, and especially for the Hijaz in the sixth and seventh centuries.[2] The incompatibility of Islamic and Jewish sources was only partially neutralized, but the tyranny of the 'Hijazi origins of Islam' fully demonstrated, by insistence upon a major Jewish immigration into central Arabia.[3] Some of the material assembled by Rabin, such as apocalyptic concepts and embellishments to prophetology, represent of course diffusion through contact, but do not require an exodus from Judaea into the Arabian desert.[4]

Development and perpetuation of a *logia* tradition by the sectarian group/community, wherever it (they) may have been situated, can be ascribed to the exigencies of cult or of instruction, but probably not to the requirements of legislative or judicial authority. The latter must be regarded as the agent itself of canonization and posterior to the liturgical and didactic functions of the tradition. The entire process of canonization will thus be seen as a protracted one of community formation (*Gemeindebildung*).[5] The essentially cultic/didactic role of the *logia* tradition is explicit even in the term *qur'ān* (*lectio*, *legenda*), which may be said to form within the lexicon of the canonization traditions a kind of binary opposition with the term *muṣḥaf* (codex).[6] In that context the reproach levelled at the caliph 'Uthmān is instructive: كان القرآن كتبا فتركتها الا واحدا.[7] The caliph's reply that that the Qur'ān (*sic*) was in fact one and had been sent from One, exhibiting a post-canonical stage of the discussion, cannot delete the impression that *qur'ān* originally designated any one of several *logia* collections. Such is of course confirmed by the *maṣāḥif* literature. Canonicity once achieved, *qur'ān* and *muṣḥaf* became synonymous as designations of revelation. That function had, however, to be shared with a third term: *sunna* (*exemplum*), in which was symbolized the definitive enthronement of revelation as canon for the Islamic community. The act found succinct expression in Suyūṭī, in his observation on a typology of revelation (*kalām allāh*) articulated by Juwaynī: قلتُ القرآن هو القسم الثانى والقسم الأول هو السنة كما ورد ان جبريل كان ينزل بالسنة كما ينزل بالقرآن ومن هنا جاز رواية

[1] Ben Zvi, 'Les Origines', esp. 178–90; Katsch, *Judaism*, xxv.

[2] Cf. Krauss, 'Nachrichten', 321–53; Cohen, 'Arabisms', 221–33; Steinschneider, *Polemische Literatur*, Anhang VII, esp. 244–73; Hirschberg, *Lehren*, 14–26, but see below, III pp. 96–7.

[3] See especially Torrey, *Foundation*, 1–27; but also Obermann, 'Islamic Origins', 58–120.

[4] *Qumran*, 118–21, 128; cf. Wieder, *Scrolls*, 4: on the messianic symbolism of 'wilderness'.

[5] Cf. Koch, *Growth*, 44; Seeligmann, 'Midraschexegese', 150–81.

[6] Horovitz, *Untersuchungen*, 74.

[7] Ṭabarī, *Annales* I/2952; cf. *GdQ* ii, 50, 90.

السنة بالمعنى لان جبريل أداه بالمعنى ولم تجز القراءة بالمعنى لان جبريل أداه باللفظ.[1] The distinction between permitted modes of transmission (*litteratim* and paraphrastic) was merely formal recognition of a principle which remained almost purely theoretical. In practice Sunna, as revelation, was transmitted with infinite care, and was the primary instrument by which the Quranic revelation was linked with the historical figure of an Arabian prophet. Inherent in the reports pertaining to that process are two factors worthy of remark: the immediacy and practicability of *ius consuetudinis* as articulated in the Sunna; and consistent emphasis upon the role of Medina as its source and paradigm.[2]

Formulation of the Sunna as embodiment of prophetical practice/judgement cannot be dated before the beginning of the third/ninth century, and thus may be seen as coincident with recognition of the Qur'ān as the canonical collection of prophetical *logia*. Juxtaposition of the two revelations as equally authoritative need not, in my opinion, be understood to imply that Qur'ān yielded a position already secure to the encroachments of Sunna.[3] It can indeed be argued that the opposite was so: that canonization of the Quranic revelation could only have been effected within the community once its content could be related to that of the *prophetical* Sunna and, perhaps more important, to the historical figure delineated there. Acknowledgement of a prophet as source of regulative prescription for the religious life of the community may be thought to reflect traditional notions of charismatic authority. That such should entail discussion of the emblems, and in particular the credentials, of prophethood cannot be surprising. In Muslim literature a not inconsiderable portion of that discussion was concerned to establish the role of scripture as testimony to prophethood, and it is that function of the Quranic revelation which forms the subject of the following chapter.

[1] *Itqān* i, 128; and Goldziher, 'Kämpfe', 86–98.
[2] Goldziher, *Studien* ii, 11–22.
[3] Pace Goldziher, *Studien* ii, 20; see below, IV pp. 174–5, 176–7.

II

EMBLEMS OF PROPHETHOOD

A MARKED feature of Islamic prophetology is its ethnic orientation, nowhere more clearly expressed than in the Quranic concept of *umam khāliya*.[1] But the scriptural imagery did not quite imply ethnic exclusiveness, and even an apparently unambiguous passage like Q. 14: 4 وما أرسلنا من رسول الا بلسان قومه could be adduced in support either of the ethnocentric nature of the prophet's mission (by stressing the basically Arabic content of revelation) or as divine proof of its universality (by stressing the inclusion of non-Arabic idiom).[2] Commentary on Q. 14: 4 consists largely of speculation about the language(s) of scripture and of God, a topic complicated by controversy over the origins of classical Arabic.[3] Apart from the diametrically opposed possibilities of that particular verse, it may be asserted that Quranic imagery underlining the ethnocentric position of prophets is both uniform and consistent, e.g. ولكل أمة رسول (Q. 10: 47), ولكل قوم هاد (13: 8), وان من أمة الا خلا فيها نذير (35:24), ونزعنا من كل أمة شهيدا (28: 75). These aphoristic formulations, slightly modified, are reflected in the retribution pericopes, especially in the conventions employed to introduce the themes of commission and of rejection. For example, in Q. 16: 113 ولقد جاءهم رسول منهم فكذّبوه (cf. 23: 44, 30: 47, 38: 4, 50: 2, 71: 1) is emphasized the prophet's membership of the community to which he has been sent, as also in the designation *akh* (brother) employed in conjunction with *ahl* (people) and *aṣḥāb* (members/companions) in the commission formulae.[4] Both components, membership and rejection, belong of course to the traditional imagery of prophetical experience, e.g. Deuteronomy 18: 18, Matthew 5: 12, Luke 6: 23. Application of the same or similar descriptions not only to B. Isrā'īl but to the entire range of *umam khāliya* exhibits the attenuated election tradition found in Rabbinic and Christian literature, according to which every nation was recipient of a prophet, e.g. Numbers Rabba 20: כשם שהעמיד מלכים וחכמים ונביאים לישראל כוהעמיד לאומות הע ולם.[5] That *ummot ha-ʿolam*, moreover, is reflected in Quranic *ummiyyūn* (gentiles)

[1] See above, I pp. 2–5.
[2] Cf. Suyūṭī, *Itqān* ii, 106–7.
[3] See below, p. 81, and III pp. 93–106.
[4] See above, I pp. 24–5.
[5] Speyer, *Erzählungen*, 417–18; cf. Andrae, *Person*, 292–3, adducing other parallels; Horovitz, *Untersuchungen*, 46; Wensinck, 'Propheten', 185.

can hardly be doubted, and not only in Q. 3: 30, 75 and 62: 2, but also in 2: 78.[1] Reference to *ummiyyūn* among Jews, as in Q. 2: 78, may of course be a reflex of *ʿam ha-areṣ*, but probably in the sense of exclusion or separation, as in Ezra 10: 11 and sectarian (Pharisaic, Qumranic, Karaite) applications, invariably abusive.[2] Whether, on the other hand, the locution الرسول النبى الأمّىّ (Q. 7: 157–8) belongs properly to this instance of linguistic and conceptual assimilation is a separate problem; its common interpretation suggests a parallel to if not a calque of *ʿam ha-areṣ*.[3]

From the notion of a prophet for every nation the universal character of each prophet's mission may be elicited, as was argued for Q. 14: 4, or by reference to the *epitheta ornantia lil-ʿālamīn* (21: 107, 25: 1) and *ʿalā ʾl-ʿālamīn* (3: 33, 6: 86). An internal relationship governing the dispatch and destiny of all prophets may be seen in the concept *fatra* (Q. 5: 19), understood there to ensure that no nation be without a prophet. A unique instance of transition from ethnocentric to universal mission is explicit in scriptural references to the figure of Abraham, e.g. Q. 3: 67 ما كان ابراهيم يهوديا ولا نصرانيا ولكن كان حنيفا مسلما and 16: 120 ان ابراهيم كان أمة قانتا لله حنيفا. The imagery is traditional, exhibited in the evolution from God-seeker to patriarch to the Pauline concept 'father of all the faithful' (e.g. Romans 4: 9–12).[4] For the epithet *umma* in Q. 16: 120 Zamakhsharī provided the gloss *maʾmūm/imām* (*exemplum*: cf. 2: 124), a conclusion of methodological if not material interest: the obvious *Vorlage* in Genesis 12: 2 ואעשך לגוי גדול was not thereby concealed.[5]

Rigorous and consistent distinction between the designations *nabī* and *rasūl* is not justified by Quranic usage, though something is to be said for linking the term *rasūl* (apostle, messenger) with the concept of mission to a specific nation (*umma*).[6] Like *nadhīr*, *mundhir*, *bashīr*, *mubashshir*, and even *ʿabd*, the denomination *rasūl* is basically functional; the only generic term for prophet is the Hebrew loan *nabī*. But while, or perhaps because, Quranic *nabī* is used only of Biblical figures, the generic employed in exegetical literature was *mursal*, a Quranic term (e.g. Q. 7: 75) understood

[1] *Pace* Horovitz, op. cit. 53.

[2] Cf. Rabin, *Qumran*, 12–18, 61–4; his reference 125 n. 2 to Q. 2: 78 must (?) be to that use of *ʿam ha-areṣ*; see Wieder, *Scrolls*, 153–6, and the references in Paret, *Der Koran*, 21–2 ad loc.; from the context of Q. 2: 78–9 inference of an allusion to sectarian strife within the Jewish community seems justified: for the vituperative epithets in that kind of polemic cf. Wieder, op. cit. 129–60.

[3] See below, p. 63.

[4] Gerhardsson, *Memory*, 287–8; Beck, 'Abraham', 89–94; Moubarac, *Abraham*, 99–118, but also 140–8: stressing, curiously, Abraham's role as recipient of revelation; cf. also Chapira, 'Légendes', 86–107, 37–43.

[5] *Kashshāf* ii, 641–2 ad loc.; cf. Geiger, *Was hat Mohammed*, 26–8, 201; Torrey, *Foundation*, 38; Katsch, *Judaism*, 75–6.

[6] Cf. Wensinck, 'Propheten', 171–5; and the modifications proposed thereto by Horovitz, *Untersuchungen*, 48–9.

to include both *nabī* and *rasūl*, as in Suyūṭī's enumeration of those mentioned in Muslim scripture.[1] Election to prophethood, a divine and unilateral act, is regularly expressed by one of three verbs: *ikhtāra* (Q. 20: 13 Moses), *ijtabā* (6: 87 Ishmael and Hebrew prophets), and *iṣṭafā* (2: 130 Abraham), each employed collectively as well as individually. The generally factitive verb *jaʿala*, with an appropriate objective complement, may perform the same function (e.g. Q. 19: 31, 26: 21), and an isolated instance of *iṣṭanaʿa* (20: 41 Moses) may be so interpreted. That the passive participle *mukhlaṣ* is included in the election imagery, as proposed by Lidzbarski, can be inferred from Q. 19: 51 (Moses), possibly from 12: 24 (Joseph), but not in the sense of prophetical election for the several occurrences of the plural (e.g. 37: 40), in which the image is that of the community of worshippers.[2] The single occurrence of the participle *muṣṭafayn* (Q. 38: 47 plural) is, however, a reference to prophetical election. The very large and merely symbolic numbers related of prophets in the Muslim tradition appear to reflect discussion of the respective merits of angels and prophets, a relationship derived from the semantic proximity of *malak* to *rasūl* (cf. Malachi 3: 1 הנני שלח מלאכי) and crystallized in the messenger formulae.[3] In Q. 40: 78, a passage commonly adduced in argument for an infinite number of divine messengers, the plural *rusul* is employed, and glossed *nabī* in the exegetical tradition.[4]

Of the later doctrinal development which granted the Arabian prophet superiority (*sayyid al-mursalīn*) over God's other emissaries, there is no unequivocal trace in Muslim scripture.[5] Indeed, such statements as Q. 2: 285 لا نفرّق بين احد من رسله (similarly 2: 136, 3: 83) clearly make the opposite point, namely, that among prophets there was no distinction in rank. That view is also emphasized in Q. 41: 43 ما يقال لك الا ما قد قيل للرسل من قبلك and 46: 9 قل ما كنت بدعا من الرسل in both of which the addressee was traditionally seen to be Muhammad. In flat contradiction to such passages is Q. 17: 55 ولقد فضّلنا بعض النبيين على بعض (cf. the imagery in 17: 21) and by implication 4: 125 فاتخذ الله ابراهيم خليلا (identical phraseology differently applied in 17: 73, 25: 28), of which the latter may be compared with אברהם אהבי of Isaiah 41: 8.[6] Moreover, Q. 4: 171–2 and 19: 19 may be thought to accord a special distinction to Jesus, while a number of verses

1 *Itqān* iv, 58–67; cf. Speyer, *Erzählungen*, 416 n. 1.
2 'Salām und Islām', 95–6.
3 See above, I pp. 12–13; cf. Horovitz, op. cit. 46; Wensinck, op. cit. 184, and id. *Creed*, 200–2, 204.
4 e.g. Zamakhsharī, *Kashshāf* iv, 180 ad loc.
5 See Andrae, *Person*, 245–89, esp. 247–50 for Sulamī's systematic elaboration of that argument.
6 Cf. Geiger, *Was hat Mohammed*, 119–20; Speyer, *Erzählungen*, 173.

based on the imagery of Q. 2: 253 (those prophets to whom God spoke) allude to Adam (2: 31, 37), Abraham (2: 124), but especially Moses (4: 164, 7: 143, 26: 10, 27: 8–12, 28: 30–5), reflecting thus the data of the exegetical tradition.[1] Such as it is, the scriptural material may be enlisted to support the particular position of Moses in the prophetical hierarchy, but hardly that of Muhammad. The paradigm was not only Biblical, but Rabbinic.[2]

The certainty that already in the Hexateuch the figure of Moses was the product of literary elaboration is of some relevance to a description of the analogous process for Muhammad.[3] There, however, the literary development is confined to the non-canonical revelation: the prophetical Sunna together with a Muhammadan *evangelium* formulated as a history of the Hijazi Arabs.[4] Like its Mosaic *Vorbild* the portrait of Muhammad emerged gradually and in response to the needs of a religious community.[5] But unlike the Hexateuch, from which could be inferred at least the outlines of a historical portrait of Moses, the role of the Qur'ān in the delineation of an Arabian prophet was peripheral: evidence of a divine communication but not a report of its circumstances. The historical value of Muslim scripture lies, it seems to me, not in its role as source for the biography of Muhammad, but rather as source for the concepts eventually applied to composition of the Muslim theology of prophethood. The latter are both directly accessible in the text of scripture and susceptible of schematic realization, while the very notion of biographical data in the Qur'ān depends upon exegetical principles derived from material external to the canon. The satisfaction with a century of Quranic studies expressed by Paret is thus in my opinion hardly justified.[6] His recognition of the arbitrary value of *variae lectiones* and of the real contrast between orthographic and interpretative variants, as well as of the problems posed by parallel passages, could have provoked some doubt about the reliability of the ʿUthmanic recension traditions, rather than questions about Muhammad's articulation of dogma.[7] Further, his distinction between an 'äusserer Geschichtsablauf' and an 'innere Einstellung', and his admission that only for the latter can the Qur'ān be of some documentary value, is merely a reflex of the now well-established method of psychological description.[8]

That the prophetical Sunna itself contains ample evidence of community practice (*ius consuetudinis*: *sunna muttabaʿa*) as well as practice ascribed

[1] See above, I pp. 35–8; and cf. Torrey, *Foundation*, 75–82 *vs.* Wellhausen.

[2] Cf. Speyer, op. cit. 419–20; Jeffery, 'Scripture', 108–9, 126–7; Katsch, *Judaism*, 172–3.

[3] Von Rad, *Theology* i, 289–96.

[4] See below, pp. 65–73.

[5] Cf. Andrae, *Person*, 186.

[6] 'Der Koran als Geschichtsquelle', 24–42.

[7] Paret, op. cit. 28, 31–2.

[8] Paret, op. cit. 33 ff; see above, I pp. 43–4, 51–2.

specifically to the prophet (*sunnat al-nabī*) is clear from the well-known document conveying the caliph ʿUmar's instructions to the *qāḍī* Abū Mūsa ʾl-Ashʿarī, in some recensions of which *sunna* was transmitted (or glossed) *sunnat al-nabī*.[1] I consider at least questionable Margoliouth's assumption that the two sources of law were (*a*) texts of the Qur'ān, and (*b*) practice.[2] From the document itself it is impossible to insist upon a neat distinction between community and prophetical practice, or between 'texts of the Qur'ān' and what I have in the foregoing pages designated prophetical *logia*. *Qur'ān* was anyway glossed or transmitted in some recensions *kitāb allāh*, which may not have been the same thing.[3] The purpose of the caliph's letter was of course justification of resort to analogy, and the authenticity of the document may well be doubted.[4] The contrast between *sunna* as practice of the community and *sunna* as practice of the prophet, analogous to the Talmudic distinction between *minhag* and *halakhah*,[5] could be and was neutralized by recourse to a simple and transparent expedient: elevation of all statutes, whatever their origin, to the status of revelation vouchsafed to a single identifiable recipient. A Muslim formulation of that dogma reads وقال صلى الله عليه وسلم ألا أنى اوتيتُ القرآن ومثله معه يعنى السنة.[6] Recognition of the (prophetical) Sunna as Mishnah may be regarded as yet another element in what could be described as the 'Mosaic syndrome' of Muslim prophetology. Within the community the didactic principle of *imitatio magistri* (الأصل الاقتداء) was realized as *magister dixit* (cf. הלכה למשה מסיני), in the form of symbolic acts (سنة فعلية: מעשים) and sayings (سنة قولية: דברים).[7]

Co-ordination of the Quranic revelation with that process of *Gemeindebildung* was the achievement of haggadic exegesis, in which the essentially anonymous references of the text of revelation were carefully related to the originally independent figure of the Arabian prophet. The haggadic literary devices were many and varied.[8] The extent to which the haggadists were concerned primarily to elucidate a fixed scriptural text has perhaps been exaggerated.[9] To describe at least part of Ibn Isḥāq's activity, for example, as exegetical (*tafsīr*) is convenient but, if the technical term is construed in its traditional sense (*explication de texte*), possibly misleading.

[1] Margoliouth, 'Omar's instructions', esp. 309–10.

[2] Margoliouth, op. cit. 313.

[3] See below, pp. 74–6.

[4] Cf. the author's appropriate observations, 326; and see below, IV pp. 158–9.

[5] See below, IV pp. 199–200.

[6] Suyūṭī, *Itqān* iv, 174; cf. above, I pp. 51–2; Goldziher, *Studien* ii, 20; Andrae, *Person*, 179–80; Schacht, *Origins*, 149: the tradition was known to Ibn Qutayba but not to Shāfiʿī.

[7] Cf. Strack, *Introduction*, 9, 17; Gerhardsson, *Memory*, 82, 120–1.

[8] See below, IV pp. 122–48.

[9] Cf. Becker, 'Grundsätzliches', 520–7; Watt, 'Materials', 23–34; and my observations in *BSOAS* xxxi (1968) 148–9.

In this context Sellheim's structural analysis of the *Sīra* deserves notice.[1] The author's discernment of a three-tiered composition (pp. 48–9) derives from a separation of three kinds of material: the Hijazi environment (*Grundschicht*: pp. 73–8), prophetical legend (*erste Schicht*: pp. 53–73), and justification of the ʿAbbāsid *dawla* (*zweite Schicht*: pp. 49–53). The taxonomy depends upon material distinctions rather than formal (stylistic) ones, and appears to be at least partly informed by relation to the agreed data of Ibn Isḥāq's own career. As such it is a valuable contribution towards solving the familiar problems about motives and materials in the earliest stages of Islamic historiography.[2] Now, the Muslim concept of *Heilsgeschichte* depended, not unexpectedly, upon the didactic value of *exempla*, and those constitute in turn a major portion of scripture.[3] Whether such reflect Muhammad's idea(s) of history is irrelevant. That they represent the organizing principle of Ibn Isḥāq's composition is relevant: the figure of an Arabian prophet, warts and all, might be thought to provoke the question not so much of historicity as of faithfulness to the traditional (Judaeo-Christian) concept of prophethood. From the point of view of form-criticism Sellheim's *Grundschicht* may be a misnomer, if by 'basic' he would propose a contrast between a nucleus of historical 'truth' and, on the one hand, the embroidery of prophetical legend (*erste Schicht*) and, on the other, the transparent motives of political patronage (*zweite Schicht*). All three of the structural levels exhibit a single impulse, namely, a concern to locate the origins of Islam in the Hijaz. The emergence of an Arabian prophetical tradition, of which the earliest agent appears to have been the *Sīra* of Ibn Isḥāq, may well have contributed to its author's dispute about methodology with Mālik b. Anas and his subsequent departure from Medina. Indeed, an important problem in the analysis of the *Sīra*, and one only alluded to by Sellheim, is Ibn Isḥāq's treatment of material preserved also as the canonical text of revelation.[4]

. . . . .

From the Quranic data themselves emerge several characteristics employed by the exegetes to establish a relation between the utterance of God and its appointed recipient. These concern modes of revelation and came to figure significantly in the literary elaboration of a biography appropriate to the prophet of Islam.[5] As was noted, exegetical discussions of Q. 42: 51 stressed the equivalence *waḥy*:*ilhām*, from which it was inferred that one mode of revelation consisted in divine 'inspiration'. That justification for

1 'Die Muhammad-Biographie', 33–91.

2 Cf. Rosenthal, 'Influence', 35–45.

3 E.g. the employment of *ʿibra* by Ṭabarī, *Annales* I/78, cited by Rosenthal, op. cit. 38–9; cf. Abbott, *SALP* i, 6–9.

4 Sellheim, op. cit. 47, 91; see below, IV pp. 127–9.

5 See above, I pp. 34–8.

this inference had to be based on extra-canonical usage is clear from the single (problematic) occurrence in scripture of *alhama* فألهمها فجورها وتقواها (Q. 91: 8), itself the subject of dispute between two interpretations: informed/communicated by God, or created/implanted in the soul by God. In the lexicon of scriptural exegesis, as contrasted with that of philosophy, it was the former interpretation which prevailed, attested as early as Kalbī, *ad* Q. 12: 15 وأوحينا اليه الى يوسف أرسل اليه جبريل ويقال ألهمه, though only as one alternative to the rendering of *awḥā* as *irsāl* (dispatch).[1] In later usage *ilhām* is unambiguously inspiration, e.g. in Suyūṭī ألهم الله الخلفاء الراشدين ذلك.[2] What appears very likely to have been the source of the semantic juxtaposition of *waḥy* and *ilhām* is reflected in a passage from the seventh/thirteenth-century theologian Ibn Qudāma 'l-Maqdisī ثم يلزمكم ان تقولوا ان الشعر قرآنا (*sic*) لان الله عز وجل ألهم قول الشعر وأقدر عليه كما ألهم جبريل في قولكم.[3] It seems not unreasonable to regard *ilhām* in the sense of inspiration a borrowing from the terminology of (profane) rhetoric and the several attempts (not supported by Zamakhsharī and the Mu'tazila) to preserve a distinction between *ilhām* and *waḥy* (as dispatch) a reaction to the source of that borrowing and ensuing confusion.[4] Other terms appropriate to the modes of revelation may be thought to corroborate this argument.

Even the word *tanzīl*, a scriptural convention for 'revelation' (e.g. Q. 69: 40–3), could be employed to describe poetic inspiration (*scil.* of Ḥassān b. Thābit).[5] Of significance in this respect is collocation of the verb *tanazzala* (descend) with satanic agents (*shayāṭīn*) in Q. 26: 210, 221–2, exhibiting the specifically Quranic imagery in which *shayṭān* was identified as an agent of evil.[6] That this was not always so is clear from the report, adduced by *inter alios* Suyūṭī, according to which delay in revelation to the prophet Muhammad was the result of desertion by his *shayṭān*: اشتقى النبى فلم يقم ليلة او ليلتين فأتته امراة فقالت يا محمد ما أرى شيطانك الا قد تركك.[7] Ṭabarī's reports on the satanic agents operative in the utterances of false prophets reflect of course Islamic doctrine on the modes of revelation.

1 *Tafsīr*, MS Ayasofya 118, 129r; but cf. the same author's interpretation of *awḥā* in Q. 12: 102 as *akhbara*, above, I p. 34.

2 *Itqān* i, 164.

3 Goldziher, *Abhandlungen* i, 6 n. 5; see also Heinrichs, *Arabische Dichtung*, 35–6; cf. *BSOAS* xxxiii (1970) 616.

4 Pace Heinrichs, loc. cit.

5 See Jeffery, 'Scripture', 190; Blachère, *Histoire* ii, 333; Shahid, 'Contribution', 573.

6 Shahid, 'Contribution', 569–72, 577–8.

7 *Itqān* i, 91; Zamakhsharī, *Kashshāf* iv, 765–6 *ad* Q. 93: 3 identifying the woman as Umm Jamīl/Jumayl, wife of Abū Lahab; for the several traditions in Ṭabarī, cf. Birkeland, *The Lord guideth*, 13–8; and Bukhārī: 'Der Schaitan der Propheten ist der Engel Gabriel', cited Wellhausen, *Reste*, 134 n. 2.

The essentially neutral content of *shayṭān* (daemonic as opposed to diabolical) in the passages from Suyūṭī and Bukhārī could be interpreted as evidence of a situation in which prophetic and poetic inspiration were, if not identical, at least closely related.[1] That the tale reported of the poet Umayya b. Abī 'l-Ṣalt, in which his breast was opened and filled (with the gift of inspiration), should figure among the infancy stories of the prophet Muhammad might be thought to have similar significance.[2] Negative statements in scripture traditionally associated with the Arabian prophet, such as Q. 69: 41 وما هو بقول شاعر, 69: 42, ولا بقول كاهن, and 37: 36 أإنا لتاركوا الهتنا لشاعر مجنون, as well as the celebrated attack on the 'poets' (26: 221–7), exhibit exceptive constructions in which the content of the message rather than the source or mode of inspiration is impugned.[3] References to the prophet as visionary (2 Samuel 24: 11), as seer (1 Samuel 9: 9), as mad (Hosea 9: 7), anyway contain such traditional imagery as seriously to diminish the impact of whatever invective they might bear, perfectly expressed in Q. 51: 52 كذلك ما أتى الذين من قبلهم من رسول الا قالوا ساحر أو مجنون. Instructive examples of parallel phraseology for divine and satanic inspiration are generated by Quranic application of the verb *alqā* (literally to cast, but often synonymous with *arsala*, or with *awḥā*, in the sense of dispatch), e.g. Q. 40: 15 يلقى الروح من أمره (cf. 4: 171; and a similar construction with *nafakha* 21: 91), 20: 39 وألقيت عليك محبة منّى and 8: 12 سألقى فى قلوب الذين كفروا الرعب.[4] The imagery was perpetuated in the exegetical tradition, e.g. أو يحفظ فى اللوح المحفوظ فينزل الى الرسول ويلقيه عليه describing the activity of Gabriel.[5] In Q. 22: 52, however, that same activity is attributed to a satanic agent ألقى الشيطان فى امنيته . . . فينسخ الله ما يلقى الشيطان (cf. 22: 53, and 20: 87 with reference to *al-sāmirī*).[6] The centrality of Q. 22: 52 in discussions of the Islamic theory of abrogation has been demonstrated by Burton, and it seems clear that pertinent interpretation of satanic *alqā* required that it be understood as counterpoint to *ansā* (to make forget), e.g. Q. 6: 68, 12: 42, 18: 63, 58: 19.[7] The significance in those discussions of satanic, as opposed to divine, agency consists in the light it throws upon the semantic

[1] Goldziher, *Abhandlungen* i, 107–8; cf. Jeffery, 'Scripture', 191 n. 10.

[2] Goldziher, *Abhandlungen* i, 3, 213; Horovitz, 'Himmelfahrt', 171–3; see below, pp. 66–7.

[3] *Pace* Shahid, 'Contribution', 568–72.

[4] Cf. Goldziher, *Abhandlungen* i, 5, 7 on *nafakha/nafatha*.

[5] Suyūṭī, *Itqān* i, 125.

[6] Cf. Geiger, *Was hat Mohammed*, 163–4; Horovitz, *Untersuchungen*, 114–15; and the literature cited Paret, *Der Koran*, 334–7, esp. Yahuda, 'The Golden Calf and the Sāmirī'.

[7] 'Cranes', 253–4, 265; see below, IV pp. 195–6.

evolution of *shayṭān*: from poetic muse to God's particular adversary, from *shayṭān* as *jinnī* to *shayṭān* as *iblīs*.[1]

The parallel and easily confused sources of prophetical and poetic inspiration noticed here have an approximate Biblical counterpart in conflicting reports on the motive of the Davidic census, related in 2 Samuel 24: 1–9 and 1 Chronicles 21: 1–7 (cf. 1 Samuel 16: 14 on Saul and the two spirits of God). Quranic adaptation of the Judaeo-Christian Satan will not have been a consequence merely of antonomasia, nor yet of an attempt to separate prophet from poet (for both might be divinely inspired), but rather, of a persuasion that all inspiration required an *intermediary*. It may also be observed that Widengren's description of the prophet as recipient of revelation concedes but nominal recognition of this very characteristic element in the Muslim concept of scripture by stressing inordinately his movement towards and confrontation with God.[2] That imagery, too, belongs to the exegetical tradition, but seldom, save in allegorical and sectarian interpretation, impinges upon scholarly understanding of the modes of revelation. Whatever body of prophetical 'wisdom' might from time to time have been regarded as supplementary to the contents of scripture, it was with an organized corpus of recognizable *logia* that the mainstream of Islamic theology was concerned, and not with a source of concealed wisdom for the elect. The appearance, at several levels of popular and sectarian theology, of elements drawn from the inexhaustible pool of Oriental Gnostic concepts is undeniable, but did not much influence the stability of orthodox Muslim doctrine regarding the content and mode of the Quranic revelation.[3]

The agency of mediation is symbolized, somewhat ingenuously, in two scriptural passages: Q. 6: 112 وكذلك جعلنا لكل نبى عدوا شياطين الانس والجن يوحى بعضهم الى. بعض زخرف القول and 72: 27–8 الا من ارتضى من رسول فانه يسلك من بين يديه ومن خلفه رصدا ليعلم ان قد أبلغوا رسالات ربهم While the first postulates for every prophet (*nabī*) a satanic tempter hostile to the divine mission with which he has been entrusted, the second provides for a guardian angel (*raṣad*) to ensure that the mission is fulfilled: رصد حفظة من الملائكة يحفظونه من الشياطين.[4] This anthropomorphic expression of the sources of divine communication found significant elaboration in Muslim views on the part played by the angel Gabriel in the process of revelation. In Juwaynī's typology it is made quite clear that Gabriel was the agent of transmission for both Qur'ān and Sunna, the former literally

[1] Cf. Goldziher, *Abhandlungen* i, 7, 106–17; id. 'Ginnen', 685–90; Geiger, *Was hat Mohammed*, 98–100; Horovitz, *Untersuchungen*, 87, 120–1; Ahrens, 'Christliches im Qoran', 176.

[2] *Apostle of God*, 124–7, 207–8.

[3] Widengren, op. cit. 100 n. 2.

[4] Zamakhsharī, *Kashshāf* iv, 633 *ad* Q. 72: 27–8.

(*bil-lafẓ*) and the latter conceptually (*bil-maʿnā*).[1] While later exegetes appear to have agreed upon the Qur'ān as referent for the accusative pronoun in Q. 97: 1, Barth's proposal that it was Gabriel dispatched by God in Laylat al-qadr is not only likely from the point of view of syntax, but is supported by Kalbī's interpretation of a similar construction in Q. 12: 2 إنا أنزلناه قرآنا عربيا يقول إنا أنزلنا جبريل بالقرآن على محمد على مجرى لغة العربية.[2] Explicit mention of Gabriel in Muslim scripture (Q. 2: 97–8, 66: 4) would seem hardly to bear the burden of exegesis produced to depict his central role in the mechanics of revelation: Zamakhsharī found it worth while to explain that the accusative pronoun in فانه نزّله على قلبك بإذن الله referred to the Qur'ān.[3] But paucity of reference could be and was compensated for by identifying Gabriel with the Spirit, e.g. *rūḥ al-qudus* (Q. 2: 253, 5: 110, 16: 102), *al-rūḥ al-amīn* (26: 193), *rūḥanā* (19: 17), *al-rūḥ* (40: 15 etc.), an equation difficult to reconcile with Q. 17: 85 and the elaborate story of Muhammad, Gabriel, and the rabbis of Yathrib.[4] In the light of both Biblical and Rabbinic allusions to Gabriel, the Muslim allegation that he was regarded by the Jews as an enemy poses something of a problem. Most of the reasons usually adduced to support this contention are set out in Zamakhsharī: (*a*) that Gabriel had revealed to the Jewish prophet (*sic*, cf. Jeremiah 27) God's intention to destroy the Temple through the agency of Nebuchadnezzar; (*b*) that God had commanded Gabriel to establish prophethood among the Jews but he had taken it elsewhere (*scil.* to the Arabs); (*c*) that he had revealed the secrets of the Jews to Muhammad. These details, together with an account of an altercation between ʿUmar and the rabbis of Yathrib about the relative merits of Gabriel and Michael, were tenuously attached to the Quranic phrase (2: 97): Say, who is an enemy of Gabriel? Itself polemical in tone, the phrase might be thought to reflect the several versions of a test of 'true prophethood' imposed by the Jews of Yathrib/Medina upon Muhammad or by Quraysh with their assistance, in each instance thwarted by the intervention of Gabriel on behalf of the Arabian prophet.[5] This interpretation would point to the third of the three reasons for hostility between Gabriel and the Jews, namely, that he had revealed their secrets to Muhammad. The nature of the polemic must, I think, be understood as exclusively Judaeo-Muslim, and the role of Quraysh seen as a literary embellishment designed to show that opposition to Muhammad was (also) Arabian. Gabriel's position in Muslim prophetology is, after all,

[1] Cited above, I pp. 51–2.
[2] See above, I pp. 34–5; Barth, 'Studien', 119; Kalbī, *Tafsīr*, MS Ayasofya 118, 128r.
[3] *Kashshāf* i, 169 *ad* Q. 2: 97.
[4] See below, IV pp. 122–6.
[5] *Kashshāf*, loc. cit.; cf. Suyūṭī, *Itqān* i, 97.

not qualitatively different from that predicated of him in Daniel 8: 15, 9: 21, possibly 10: 9 ff., and in Rabbinic literature.[1]

In Muslim, as in Rabbinic, tradition one of Gabriel's primary functions is that of pedagogue: as he had been guide and mentor to Joseph (Targum Pseudo-Jonathan *ad* Genesis 37: 15; Talmud Babl. Sotah 36b) and to Moses (Exodus Rabba I 67b), so too for Muhammad he performed the rites of initiation into prophethood, instructed him concerning ablutions and the times of prayer, guided him during his ascension to heaven, and arranged for him the content of revelation during meetings in Ramaḍān.[2] For the Arabian prophet that instruction was of particular significance since, according to the traditional interpretation of *ummī* in Q. 7: 157–8 he was illiterate: الذى لا يكتب ولا يقرأ. The manner in which this dogma influenced discussion of the modes of revelation has been noticed.[3] The consequent postulation of an equivalence *ummī*: *'am ha-areṣ* may reflect a misunderstanding of Q. 2: 78.[4] On the other hand, a similar dogmatic impulse in Patristic literature, according to which Jesus and the apostles were described as *anthropoi agrammatoi*, was adduced by Wensinck.[5] The basis in Christian scripture for that view, e.g. John 7: 15, Acts 4: 13, might be thought to exhibit a specifically anti-Rabbinic (Pharisaic) tendency. An analogous orientation in Muslim tradition is illustrated by several elements in the Muhammadan *evangelium*.[6]

. . . . .

The same Quranic passage (7: 157) provided a point of departure for the allegation that the Arabian prophet had been prognosticated in Hebrew and Christian scripture: الرسول النبى الأمّىّ الذى يجدونه مكتوبا عندهم فى التوراة والانجيل. Despite the further charge that sectaries of both religions had falsified and concealed (*taḥrīf*, *kitmān*) those parts of their scripture which predicted the coming of Muhammad, the search for proof-texts (*testimonia*) was notably successful.[7] Since the technique itself had clearly been developed and refined in the crucible of Judaeo-Christian polemic (cf. Luke 24: 27), it is of some interest that its earliest attestation in Muslim literature should be an interpretation of Ahmad/Muhammad as the Paraclete of John 15: 23–16: 1.[8] On the other hand, the classical *loci probantes* from Hebrew scripture were (curiously, in

[1] Cf. Geiger, *Was hat Mohammed*, 12–15, 200; Katsch, *Judaism*, 85–91; Horovitz, *Untersuchungen*, 46, 107; Pedersen, *EI*, s.v. Djabrā'īl.

[2] References in Wensinck, *Handbook*, 59; see above, I p. 37.

[3] See above, I p. 36: *munajjam* opposed to *jumla*.

[4] See above, pp. 53–4; cf. *GdQ* i, 14.

[5] 'Propheten', 191–2.

[6] Cf. Koch, *Growth*, 88; Gerhardsson, *Memory*, 12–3; and see below, pp. 70–1.

[7] See below, IV pp. 189–90.

[8] Ibn Hishām, *Sīra* i, 232–3; cf. *GdQ* i, 9–10 n. 1; and bibliographical references *GAS* i, 289.

the light of Christian figural interpretation of the imagery in Isaiah, Jeremiah, etc.) not the prophetical books, but, rather, passages from the Torah, e.g. Genesis 17: 20, Deuteronomy 18: 15, 33: 2, all objects of later and detailed refutation by Maimonides.[1] But in the later efflorescence of that polemic references to Isaiah especially, but also to the other prophets and of course the Psalter, were abundant.[2] The passages adduced consisted of such as were traditionally recognized (by Jewish and Christian exegetes) to contain obviously messianic symbolism, and their use by Muslim polemicists displays familiarity with both substance and techniques of Biblical exegesis. One example was the attention devoted to numerical value of the letters in the name(s) of the Arabian prophet, AḤMaD (Q. 61: 6) and MuḤaMMaD (3: 144, 33: 40, 47: 2, 48: 29), the results of which calculations were seen to correspond to (numerical) equivalents in selected Biblical phraseology, e.g. Genesis 17: 20. Mention of this device (*ḥisāb al-jummal*) is attested in the earliest Quranic exegesis and related there to Jewish practice (*scil.* נוטריקון and גימטריא).[3]

In Muslim scripture itself both Ahmad (Q. 61: 6 ومبشرا برسول يأتي من بعدي اسمه أحمد) and Muhammad (33: 40 ما كان محمد أبا احد من رجالكم ولكن رسول الله وخاتم النبيين) occur in contexts exhibiting distinctly messianic imagery. The locution 'seal of the prophets', traditionally interpreted as reference to the last link in a chain of prophetical election (آخر الأنبياء), can, if somewhat arbitrarily, be related to occurrence of finite forms of the verb *khatama* in the sense 'to place a seal upon' (Q. 2: 7, 6: 46, 36: 65, 42: 24, 45: 23). As such it was synonymous with Quranic *ṭabaʿa* (e.g. 9: 93), and that equivalence (طابع:خاتم) was incorporated into the exegetical tradition.[4] The eschatological significance of Q. 33: 40 is, however, unmistakable, and the verse might be understood to constitute an exception to the attested principle that a prophet be elected from within his own community: thus, 'Muhammad is not the father of anyone of you, but rather the messenger of God and seal of the prophets'. That Q. 33: 40 contains one of the four occurrences in scripture of the name Muhammad suggests a particular polemic, in which not only the credentials but also the identity of the Arabian prophet was in dispute. The calque proposed by Hirschfeld, חותם (Haggai 2: 23, cf. Jeremiah 22: 24), required that the Arabic cognate be interpreted, indeed, as signet (*ṭabʿ*)

[1] *Iggeret Teman*, 36–7; cf. Steinschneider, *Polemische Literatur*, 326–7.

[2] See Steinschneider, op. cit. 325–9, 389–92, and separate entries nos. 2, 14/66, 105; Goldziher, 'Polemik', 372–9; Schreiner, 'Zur Geschichte', 595, 599–601, 613, 625–8, 642–7.

[3] e.g. Kalbī, *Tafsīr ad* Q. 3: 7, MS Ayasofya 118, 29ʳ; Muqātil, *Tafsir* intro. and *ad* Q. 3: 7, MS H. Hüsnü 17, 2ʳ, 35ᵛ; cf. Bacher, *Terminologie* i, 127, ii, 27–8, respectively.

[4] e.g. Zamakhsharī, *Kashshāf* iii, 544–5 *ad* Q. 33: 40.

indicating divine election.[1] That put forward by Horovitz, σφραγίς (1 Corinthians 9: 2, cf. Romans 4: 11) equated *khātam* with *muṣaddiq* (*corroboratio*), that is, verification of earlier prophets and scriptures, a frequent Quranic usage (e.g. 2:101, 3: 81).[2] The teleological interpretation suggested by Jeffery, τέλος νόμου (Romans 10: 4, cf. Daniel 9: 24) was in harmony with traditional Muslim exegesis, as well as attested in Manichean literature.[3] Only the last proposal would seem to do justice to the eschatological flavour of Q. 33: 40, and of 61: 6 where, incidentally, it is Jesus, not 'he who shall come after me', who is designated *muṣaddiq*.

Both verses contain the kind of material from which the Islamic *Prophetenkultus* was elaborated, and might be thought to refute the view that the latter was diametrically opposed to the Quranic portrait of an Arabian prophet.[4] The inherent weakness of that view is its dependence upon a clear distinction between a later, sectarian (even extremist) development of the concept θεῖος ἄνθρωπος, and an original, factual, and sober account of the pious man summoned by God. So tidy a dichotomy is supported neither by the content of revelation nor the chronology of early Islamic literature. Despite protests of the type 'I am only . . .'/'I am nothing but . . .' (e.g. Q. 7: 188, 18: 110; the type is formulaic, cf. 26: 115 for Noah, and 19: 19 for Gabriel!), the biography of Muhammad formulated in exegetical literature cannot be said either to distort or to contradict scriptural data on the words and deeds of prophets in general. Indeed, from the point of view of a literary analysis, it can be argued that the principal difference between the text of scripture and the Muhammadan *evangelium* lies merely in the canonical status of the former. Thematic and exemplary treatment of prophethood in the Qur'ān was reformulated in the *evangelium* (*sunna/sīra*) as the personal history of Muhammad.[5]

. . . . .

As in the classical literature of Hebrew prophecy, accounts of the prophetical call in Muslim scripture begin abruptly with one or another of the formulae of commission, and dispense with description of whatever preparation may have preceded the call.[6] I should hesitate, however, to concede *e silentio* there was no such preparation for the reception of revelation.[7] For the pre-classical period of Hebrew prophecy evidence of such was occasionally transmitted, e.g. for Samuel (1 Samuel 1: 20–8, 2: 18–21, 3: 1–4), presumably in the original documents underlying the Elijah/Elisha cycles, but especially for Moses (Exodus 1: 8–3: 1 ff.).[8] The infancy

[1] *Researches*, 23; cf. Goldziher, 'Bemerkungen zur neuhebräischen Poesie', 724–6, for the poetic use of *khatam*: *misrah* (Isaiah 9: 6).

[2] *Untersuchungen*, 53–4.

[3] 'Scripture', 266–7.

[4] Andrae, *Person*, 292–3.

[5] See Horovitz, 'Biblische Nachwirkungen', 184–9, on the rather facile equations of Jensen, 'Das Leben Muhammeds', 84–97.

[6] See above, I pp. 12, 23–5.

[7] *Pace* von Rad, *Theology* ii, 50–9.

[8] Cf. Eissfeldt, *Einleitung*, 349–56.

stories of Samuel and Moses have at least two motifs in common: election/dedication at birth, and a mode of life designed to induce responsiveness to the word of God. The importance of the Mosaic *exemplum*, which also dominated Jewish prophetology, in both Muslim scripture and exegesis has been noticed.[1] That the two motifs should figure in the *evangelium infantiae* of the Arabian prophet is not unexpected, though it is of course quite possible that the immediate *Vorbild* was not Moses.[2] It may, on the other hand, also not have been Jesus. The typology of such motifs, as set out by Andrae, may be understood to represent or to be drawn from a pool of narrative ingredients traditionally appropriate to the lives of holy men.[3] The manner in which these could be adapted to a particular ambient emerges from Kister's study of the descriptive terminology employed in accounts of Muhammad's piety prior to his call.[4] Collation of Gospel material with Islamic tradition, as undertaken by Goldziher, is obviously of value but could be misleading.[5] As a distinct literary type the *Evangelion* was not restricted to the Christian canon, but represented the historicization of *logia* traditions found not only in Biblical but also in Rabbinic and Gnostic literature.[6] The Muslim term pertinent to that genre is *mab'ath* (mission), in which historical development is symbolized in the thematic polarity: promise–fulfilment. The ingredients of the Muhammedan *evangelium* vary from one collection to another, but most had achieved literary stabilization by the beginning of the third/ninth century.

Literary transmission did not necessarily entail a fixed order, and fluctuation of three elements in particular has been remarked and analysed, namely, the purification, the beatific vision, and the ascension/nocturnal journey.[7] The Quranic evidence for each of those incidents in the life of Muhammad is tenuous indeed, and such agreement as does exist in exegetical literature on chapter and verse exhibits acceptance of several arbitrary connections between scripture and the prophetical *evangelium*. For example, the ritual opening of the breast, or purification, reflects undoubtedly a formula for the origin of poetic inspiration, and juxtaposition of its Muhammadan version to Q. 94: 1–3 rests upon the semantic equivalence *shaqq baṭn*:*sharḥ ṣadr*. Now, Schrieke has argued persuasively that such and similar rituals are almost invariably preliminary to an ascension (confrontation with deity), indicating thus a syndrome whose internal logic requires no scriptural support.[8] The exegetical (as opposed to historical)

[1] See above, pp. 55–6, and I pp. 35–8; cf. Maimonides, *Dalāla* ii, chs. 32–45, esp. 36.
[2] Ibn Hishām, *Sīra* i, 155–7, 235. [3] *Person*, 28–56. [4] 'Taḥannuth', 223–36.
[5] *Studien* ii, 382–93; id. 'Neutestamentliche Elemente', 390–7.
[6] Cf. Koch, *Growth*, 59–60.
[7] See Bevan, 'Mohammed's ascension', 51–61; Schrieke, 'Himmelsreise Muhammeds', 1–30; Horovitz, 'Muhammeds Himmelfahrt', 159–83.
[8] 'Himmelsreise Muhammeds', 6–9; cf. also Widengren, *Apostle of God*, 80–95, 199–216 on the ascension as a literary *topos*; Birkeland, *The Lord guideth*, 39–55, speaks, however, of the theological distortion of 'an original experience of God in the Prophet's

link between ritual purification and Q. 94: 1–3 ألم نشرح لك صدرك ووضعنا عنك وزرك الذى انقض ظهرك is none the less a legitimate one, and was of particular value in discussions of the dogma relating to prophetical perfection/infallibility (*ʿiṣma*).[1] First articulated in *Fiqh Akbar II* (dated by Wensinck towards the middle of the fourth/tenth century), the dogma exhibits elements of both sectarian emphasis upon the qualities of the imamate and of Rabbinic views on the kings and prophets of Israel.[2] Application to the Quranic text enabled exegetes to identify the 'burden' (*wizr*) of Q. 94: 2 with apparent mention of earlier transgression (*dhanb*) and error (*ḍalāl*) in the life of the Arabian prophet (e.g. Q. 40: 55, 48: 2, 93: 7), necessitating in turn postulation of the earliest possible date in his life for the act of purification. In the *evangelium* itself the dogma found elaboration in the story of the attempt by Quraysh to seduce Muhammad with offers of power and wealth, to which naturally he did not succumb.[3] Similarly, the second element in the syndrome of prophetical initiation, the beatific vision, may exist independent of scriptural support, which, however, could be and often was adduced in discussions not so much of Muhammad's prophetical experience as of whether and when the faithful might be expected to see God.[4] Those verses which were considered relevant to Muhammad's vision, e.g. Q. 53: 11–18, 81: 19–25, 48: 27, were the object of extensive and contradictory exegesis, resolved, save in the *litteratim* theses of the mystics, by resort to compromise in the form of a spiritual vision (رؤية فى القلب cf. ראית הלב).[5] The vision was intimately related to the third element in the syndrome of initiation: the ascension. That ascension (*miʿrāj*) and noctural journey (*isrāʾ*) exhibit fissiparous production from a single tradition seems clear: their not quite consistently separate treatment in exegetical literature betokens a concern for chronological development in the *evangelium*, in which the ascension was combined with the already preposited ritual of purification.[6]

The Quranic verse to which that exegetical tradition was invariably attached is 17: 1 سبحان الذى أسرى بعبده ليلا من المسجد الحرام الى المسجد الأقصا. The anonymity of this reference was conceded only by Bevan.[7]

own life'; id. 'Legend', 6–12, distinguished the *shaqq baṭn* version as an 'investigation' motif, separate from the purification and prior to the vocation.

[1] Cf. Andrae, *Person*, 134–9; Birkeland, 'Legend', 42–7, on the transition *shaqq*: *sharḥ*.

[2] *Creed*, 192: articles 8–9, commentary 217–18.

[3] Ibn Hishām, *Sīra* i, 295–7; cf. Matthew 4: 1–11, etc.; and see below, IV p. 122.

[4] Wensinck, *Creed*, 63–6.

[5] Andrae, *Person*, 68–85; Widengren, 'Oral tradition', 258–60; Goldziher, *Richtungen*, 105–6; a rationalistic interpretation worthy of Nöldeke may be read, appropriately, in DeGoeje, 'Die Berufung Mohammed's', 1–5.

[6] Schrieke, 'Himmelsreise Muhammeds', 14; Horovitz, 'Muhammeds Himmelfahrt', 174–5; Birkeland, 'Legend', 54–60.

[7] 'Mohammed's ascension', 53–4.

The alternative, namely, that *ʿabd* can only be Muhammad, implies submission to an interpretation of all the Quranic data which, in my opinion, has yet to be demonstrated.[1] Far from providing unambiguous witness to the Arabian prophet, this particular scriptural image (أسرى بعبده ليلا) is employed, in but slightly varying forms, only to describe Moses' departure from Egypt (Q. 20: 77, 26: 52, 44: 23; *laylan* may reflect the imagery of Exodus 12: 29–34).[2] Moreover, the introductory formula سبحان الذى is most probably of cultic origin and general application.[3] Without specification of the terminal points in the journey من المسجد الحرام الى المسجد الأقصا, probably a gloss, identification of *ʿabd* with Moses might be thought confirmed by the following verses (17: 2 ff.).[4] On the other hand and without exception, it is with Q. 17: 1 that the *isrāʾ*, and more often than not the *miʿrāj*, are linked in the exegetical tradition. In the light of the clearly Mosaic formulation of Muslim prophetology, that connection can hardly be described as arbitrary or fortuitous, but may reflect as well a mixture of motifs.[5] Sudden transport by the spirit of God from one place to another is a motif not uncommon in the literature of prophetical expression (e.g. Elijah: 1 Kings 18: 12, 2 Kings 2: 11, 16; Ezekiel 2: 12, 8: 3, 11: 1, 43: 5; cf. 2 Corinthians 12: 2–4), and it may be that some such instance of divine intervention lay behind the hymnic imagery of Q. 17: 1.[6]

That transposition of imagery, from what must have been in origin a reference to the Mosaic exodus to an expression of ecstatic movement, can have been effected only by means of the phrase 'from the sacred mosque to the furthest mosque' which, I have noted, may be an exegetical gloss designed to accommodate within the canonical text the ascension episode of the Muhammadan *evangelium*. Allusion in Q. 17: 60 to a vision (وما جعلنا الرؤيا التى أريناك الا فتنة للناس) and in 17: 93 to an ascension (أو ترقى

[1] Cf. *GdQ* i, 134–7, ii, 85–8; Widengren, *Apostle of God*, 96–114; Schrieke, 'Himmelsreise Muhammeds', 13 n. 6; Horovitz, 'Muhammeds Himmelfahrt', 160–1: uncharacteristically ingenuous, and ironic in the light of his further observation on another identification (162), 'Dass auch die europäische Forschung sie bisher ohne Nachprüfung übernommen hat, beweist nur, dass sie sich keineswegs überall von dem Banne der islamischen Tradition befreit hat'.

[2] A related locution is used twice of Lot's departure from Sodom, Q. 11: 81, 15: 65; see above, I p. 8.

[3] See above, I pp. 17–18.

[4] All of Q. 17: 1 was judged an interpolation by *GdQ* i, 136–7, though Weil's proposal of a forgery was rejected, *GdQ* ii, 85–8.

[5] e.g. the pseudepigraphic Assumptio Mosis, cf. Eissfeldt, *Einleitung*, 770–1; Moubarac's linking, *Abraham*, 59–60, of Q. 17: 1 with the Abraham traditions is in my opinion unjustified, though it was of course a Meccan sanctuary tradition which facilitated interpretation of *masjid ḥarām* and *masjid aqṣā* as toponyms, cf. *Abraham*, 53–81. The Biblical Abraham was not merely a seeker of God, but also a founder of sanctuaries, e.g. Genesis 12: 7, 8, 13: 4, 18, 22: 9.

[6] Cf. *GdQ* i, 134 n. 7.

في السماء) are hardly relevant to the content of 17: 1. Both are polemical and the latter hypothetical, as is the ascension imagery in Q. 6: 35 and 15: 14. In the exegetical tradition the sacred mosque was identified as the Kaʿba in Mecca and the furthest mosque simply as Jerusalem.[1] In Jerusalem the Rock (*ṣakhra*) might also be specified, but relation of the ascension as well as the nocturnal journey to Q. 17: 1 would appear to support identification of the furthest mosque with heaven.[2] A corresponding spiritualization of the point of departure (!) for both is discernible in statements ascribed to ʿAbdallāh b. ʿAbbās, according to which it was the spirit (*rūḥ*) of Muhammad which made the journey from a point depicted not specifically as the sacred mosque, but more generally as sacred enclave (*ḥaram*).[3] But a tendency in the opposite direction, namely, to fix the terminal points of the journey at the Kaʿba (Mecca) and at the Aqṣā mosque (Jerusalem) attests to the political significance of Islamic sanctuaries and only incidentally to the exegesis of Q. 17: 1.[4] The link between revelation and the *evangelium* was, however, not neglected. The celebrated tradition prescribing three pilgrimages (لا تشدّ الرحال الا الى ثلاثة مساجد) appears in Muqātil's discussion of Q. 17: 1, together with several stories about the sanctity of Jerusalem, exhibiting conflation of *masjid al-aqṣā* with *ṣakhra bayt al-maqdis*.[5] One is tempted, if not quite constrained, to see in those sanctuary traditions the origin of the *isrā'/miʿrāj* story, imposed upon Q. 17: 1 much in the way *Sūrat al-Fīl* was made the peg for a similar sanctuary tradition concerning Mecca.[6] If, indeed, the exegesis did not in both instances precede the revelation, it would none the less appear to have originated independently of the verses it purported to explain. That same ambivalent relationship between scripture and interpretation holds for much of the content of the Muhammadan *evangelium*.

Attached also to Q. 17: 1 is a characteristic example of prophetical *vaticinatio ex eventu* (*akhbār al-ghayb*): Quraysh, appropriately astonished by Muhammad's report of his nocturnal journey, challenged him to describe a caravan of theirs at that moment returning to Mecca from Syria (*sic*). This the prophet duly met, adding details of its leading camel and predicting its arrival in Mecca next morning.[7] That the source of the

[1] e.g. Zamakhsharī, *Kashshāf* ii, 647 *ad* Q. 17: 1; cf. Horovitz, *Untersuchungen*, 140–1.
[2] See Schrieke, 'Himmelsreise Muhammeds', 13–15; Horovitz, 'Muhammeds Himmelfahrt', 162–9: the Rabbinic/Christian concept of 'celestial Jerusalem'.
[3] Zamakhsharī, loc. cit.; Kalbī, *Tafsīr ad* Q. 17: 1, MS. Ayasofya 118, 156^{r}: possibly to accommodate a report that the prophet had begun the night in the house of Umm Hāni' bint Abī Ṭālib.
[4] See Kister, 'Three mosques', 173–96: the traditions adduce, inconsistently, both the Aqṣā mosque and the Dome of the Rock. Cf. Paret, *Der Koran*, 295–6.
[5] *Tafsīr*, MS H. Hüsnü 17, 157^{v}–8^{r}.
[6] *Pace* Birkeland, *The Lord guideth*, 100–1; see above, I p. 42.
[7] Ibn Hishām, *Sīra* i, 402–3, and most commentaries ad loc., e.g. Zamakhsharī, *Kashshāf* ii, 647; see below, IV pp. 120–1.

anecdote is the *evangelium*, not the document of revelation, is clear from its inclusion in treatises on the proofs of prophethood (*dalā'il al-nubuwwa*).[1] A product of haggadic exegesis, its function was primarily entertainment, but the concluding formula 'and still they did not believe' signals its incorporation into the mass of criteria assembled to distinguish the true from the false prophet, i.e. fulfilment of the prediction (e.g. Deuteronomy 18: 22). The classic reference in scripture for the *vaticinatio* is of course Q. 30: 1–4, the dominant interpretation of which provided not only evidence of genuine prophethood but also comment on the course of Oriental history.[2] The range of *akhbār al-ghayb* includes another kind of utterance, which might be designated figural (typological). An example was the warning given by Muhammad's camel at Ḥudaybiya to halt and negotiate at the perimeter of the Meccan *ḥaram*, interpreted by the prophet as manifestation of the force which had arrested Abraha's elephant.[3] That an animal should have been appointed instrument of God's will (cf. Numbers 22: 22–35) is in this particular context less significant than the fact that Muhammad alone could understand and explain the camel's action to his puzzled companions.

Situations in which the inscrutable wisdom of the prophet was demonstrated are not uncommon. A familiar *mise en scène* is the confrontation between Muhammad and the rabbis, in which the agency of Gabriel was central. In one such episode Muhammad proved himself able, without the aid of Gabriel, to confound the rabbis, namely, in the case of the couple taken in adultery. The story is conventionally formulated in terms of a prophetical test, based on two alternatives: if Muhammad elected to punish the couple by flogging, public humiliation, and banishment (comprehended in the term *tajbiya*) he was clearly a king; if, on the other hand, he sentenced them to death by stoning he must be a prophet. His first step was to engage the Medinese rabbis in dispute, during which he could display his superior knowledge of God's law. In one account it was Muhammad who got the rabbi 'Abdallāh b. Ṣūriyā to admit that the stoning punishment was attested in the Torah; in another it was the Jewish convert to Islam, 'Abdallāh b. Salām, who revealed the treachery of an unnamed rabbi who had, during the dispute with Muhammad, held his hand over the relevant passage in the Mosaic law. Muhammad thus triumphed, and the couple was stoned at the gate of his mosque in Medina.[4] Traditions relating this story to the ertswhile Quranic 'stoning verse' (*āyat al-rajm*) belong to the principal *loci probantes* in discussions of the Islamic doctrine of

[1] e.g. 'Abd al-Jabbār, *Tathbīt dalā'il nubuwwat sayyidinā Muḥammad*, MS Shehid Ali Pasha 1575, 22r.

[2] See below, IV pp. 144–5.

[3] Ibn Hishām, *Sīra* ii, 310; Wāqidī, *Kitāb al-maghāzī*, 587; cf. Vermes, *Scripture*, 135–40.

[4] Ibn Hishām, *Sīra* i, 564–6; cf. Hirschfeld, 'Controversies', 109–16.

abrogation.[1] The *Sitz im Leben* of the story itself, however, is the Muhammadan *evangelium* developed out of Judaeo-Muslim polemic. Elements like the marital status (*iḥṣān*) of the accused couple and the rabbi's concealment (*kitmān*) of the pertinent portion of the Torah with his hand exhibit a secondary stage of accretion, in which doctrinal significance preceded polemical value. The latter is reflected in its anti-Rabbinic flavour, common to a wide range of anecdotes in the *evangelium*, and might be thought to share a symbolic quality with the adulteress pericope in the gospel of John (7: 53–8: 11). The intentions of the two stories are admittedly opposed: the action of Jesus was to supersede the Mosaic law, that of Muhammad to revive it (فأنا أول من أحيا أمر الله وكتابه وعمل به), to rescue it from dereliction at the hands of faithless custodians.[2] None the less, the anti-Pharisaic propaganda of the one is reflected in the anti-Rabbinic propaganda of the other. That John 7: 53–8: 11 was itself drawn, perhaps later than formation of the Christian canon, from a pool of narrative elements traditionally associated with opposition to established authority has been proposed.[3] A theme common to all such material was public demonstration of true prophethood, one which could hardly have real significance outside the Judaic tradition. Halakhic elaboration of the theme stressed two different but related aspects: the source of prophetical authority and the extent of prophetical jurisdiction.[4] In its primitive and unembellished haggadic form, however, the theme is essentially apologetic, and reflects a widespread and popular literary type.

Importance of the Mosaic law is exemplified in yet another component of the Muhammadan *evangelium*: the story of the prophet's abstention from food sacrificed to idols.[5] Kister demonstrated that conflicting versions of the tradition exhibit the entire range of feasible positions with regard to the onset of Muhammad's perfection/infallibility (*ʿiṣma*), and in particular whether it began before or at the moment of his prophetical calling. With the gradual crystallizing of Islamic orthodoxy the quality of *ʿiṣma* was seen to be conterminous with the life of the prophet, conforming thus to other data in the *evangelium*.[6] But the substance of the argument about food was susceptible of halakhic extension, as formulated in the complementary prescriptions of Q. 6: 118 (eat of that over which God's name has been uttered) and 6: 121 (eat not of that over which God's name has not been uttered). The sacrificial ordinances were thus neither dissolved as in the

[1] Cf. references in Wensinck, *Handbook*, 221–2; Goldziher, 'Usages juifs', 79; Hirschfeld, *Researches*, 137; *GdQ* i, 248–52; Schacht, *Origins*, 53 n. 4, 73–4, 191 n. 5.
[2] Ibn Hishām, *Sīra* i, 566.
[3] See Metzger, *New Testament*, 223–4 and references 273; but cf. Derrett, *Law*, 156–88; Torrey, *Foundation*, 149–50.
[4] See below, IV pp. 192–6.
[5] Kister, 'Bag of meat', 267–75.
[6] Cf. above, pp. 65–7; Birkeland, *The Lord Guideth*, 28–32.

Synoptic tradition (Matthew 15: 10–20, Mark 7: 14–23), nor figuratively transposed as in Pauline doctrine (1 Corinthians 8), but rather, epitomized as in the Apostolic promulgations to proselytes (Acts 15: 20, 28–9, 21: 25).[1] In the Muhammadan anecdote not adjustment of but adherence to the Mosaic law was stressed (e.g. Leviticus 17: 7), in particular by the Arabian prophet, whose exemplary figure was being delineated for edification of the community. Now, discussions of their precise relation to the Mosaic law were characteristic of sectarian literature emanating from communities in the Judaeo-Christian environment, and inclusion of this anecdote in the Muhammadan *evangelium* might be thought to reflect a similar concern. Specific mention of idols in connection with dietary laws, e.g. Q. 22: 30 وأحلت لكم الأنعام الا ما يتلى عليكم فاجتنبوا الرجس من الأوثان can of course be, and often was, construed as allusion to the practices of pagan Arabia. But here, as elsewhere in the historicization of prophetical *logia*, even persuasive elements of local colour must be judged against the possibility of assimilation from a literary source.

Like the Muslim canon, the Muhammadan *evangelium* applied directly and graphically figures from Biblical imagery. In the story of the first public recitations from revelation it is told how Quraysh, sceptical and stubborn, taunt Muhammad with their refusal to listen to and understand his proclamations. Thereupon was revealed the verse واذا قرأت القرآن جعلنا بينك وبين الذين لا يؤمنون بالآخرة حجابا مستورا (Q. 17: 45).[2] The setting is contrived and the motivation transparent, but the required exegetical peg was provided: the obdurate audience rendered victim of its own utterance. Veils were placed over their hearts and deafness in their ears, and a screen erected between themselves and the prophet. The Quranic imagery (Q. 17: 45–6, 18: 57, 6: 25, and in the mouths of the scoffers 41: 5) is developed round the motif 'hardening of the heart', condensed in 5: 13 وجعلنا قلوبهم قاسية. In the literature of prophetical expression the classic example is Isaiah 6: 9–10, where, during the commissioning of the prophet, the plight of Israel is so described.[3] The rather ingenuous point of departure for the anecdote in the Muhammadan *evangelium*, namely the assertion by Quraysh that their hearts were veiled and their ears deafened, is contained not only in Q. 41: 5, but also 2: 88 وقالوا قلوبنا غلف. The latter verse, however was traditionally interpreted as reference to the Jews (cf. Leviticus 26: 41 לבבם הערל), the transfer of imagery to Quraysh being a frequently attested

[1] *Pace* Geiger, *Was hat Mohammed*, 197; cf. Katsch, *Judaism*, 121–4; Gerhardsson, *Memory*, 314–18.

[2] Ibn Hishām, *Sīra* i, 314–17.

[3] Cf. von Rad, *Theology* ii, 151–5.

device of the exegetical tradition.[1] The Biblical motif is also Mosaic, e.g. Exodus 4: 21 ואני אחזק את־לבו (referring to Pharaoh), and Pauline exegesis of Exodus 34: 33–5 linked the veil (מסוה) of Moses with the obduracy of Israel (2 Corinthians 3: 12–18 κάλυμμα).[2] The dual function of the veil, symbolic of both the hardened heart and the protected messenger of God, found expression also in Muslim scriptural interpretation. In his commentary to Q. 17: 45 Ṭabarī explained *ḥijāb* as *kinān* (veil, derived from *akinna* in the following verse, cf. Q. 6: 25, 18: 57, 41: 5), or as *sātir* (screen) and glossed the entire locution 'screened from the people, who could thus not see him' (مستورا عن العباد فلا يرونه).[3] This additional interpretative element was elaborated in later exegesis, where the *ḥijāb* was seen as a shield to protect the prophet from attempts on his life.[4] Interpretation of *ḥijāb* as *sātir* (screen) might, conversely, be applied metaphorically, as in Saadya's Arabic rendering of Psalm 88: 15 (תסתיר פניך ממני) as ולא תחגב רחמתך.[5] In Q. 17: 45 the Mosaic *Vorbild* is unmistakable, and the functional equivalence of *ḥijāb*: *masveh* (Exodus 34: 33–5) merely another instance of resort to traditional imagery in the elaboration of Muslim prophetology.

. . . . .

The ambivalent relationship between scriptural data on the qualities of prophethood and the material of the Muhammadan *evangelium* is especially conspicuous in Muslim discussions of prophetical thaumaturgy. The latter consists exclusively of not very convincingly adapted stereotypes of miracles traditionally associated with men of God, and catalogued in the *dalā'il al-nubuwwa* literature.[6] The arbitrary assignment of Quranic chapter and verse to those components of the *evangelium* has been noted. Despite elaboration of a systematic test by means of which the acceptability of a miracle could be determined, the theological relevance of that material remained minimal.[7] Neither eliminated nor replaced, it was instead superseded by refinement of a dogma in which the document of revelation could play a rather more central part, and by which the role of the Arabian prophet could be assessed in terms of historical perspective. Adduced by Jāḥiẓ, that dogma found rudimentary expression in the typology set out by

[1] Cf. Geiger, *Was hat Mohammed*, 12; Goldziher, *Richtungen*, 175–6.
[2] Horovitz, *Untersuchungen*, 30; Gerhardsson, *Memory*, 285–6; Ahrens, 'Christliches im Qoran', 170.
[3] *Tafsīr* xv, 66.
[4] e.g. Ibn Kathīr, *Tafsīr* iv, 314; Suyūṭī, in *Tafsīr al-Jalālayn*, 386, both *ad* Q. 17: 47; the story, without scriptural reference, is retailed in Ibn Hishām, *Sīra* i, 355–6, where the agent of the assassination attempt is identified as the wife of Abū Lahab; cf. the commentaries to Q. 93: 3, and above, p. 59.
[5] Galliner, *Saadja*, xxiv, 8, 47, n. 7.
[6] e.g. Abū Nu'aym and Bayhaqī, cited Andrae, *Person*, 57–91.
[7] Cf. Andrae, *Person*, 101–3, citing Ījī, *Kitāb al-Mawāqif*.

Ibn Qutayba: the miracles (signs) of Moses were characteristic of an age of sorcery (*zaman al-siḥr*), those of Jesus of an age of medicine (*zaman al-ṭibb*), that (*sic*) of Muhammad of an age of eloquence (*zaman al-bayān*).[1] Emphasis upon the single miracle of Muhammad, the book revealed to him by God, might be thought to contradict the data of the Muhammadan *evangelium*, while attesting simultaneously to the general validity of miracles as proof of prophethood. Application of that criterion was consistent, even when tradition provided no explicit record of a miracle, as in the case of Shuʿayb, e.g. Zamakhsharī's unequivocal assertion *ad* Q. 7: 85 with reference to the locution قد جاءتكم بينة من ربّكم.[2] Derivation of the procedure from a Christian *Vorlage* is hardly necessary, despite the nature of the material upon which the Muhammadan *evangelium* drew. The judgement of Horovitz, that the Christian origin of the infancy and other stories was so pronounced as to preclude their employment by the Muslim adversaries of John of Damascus, is somewhat ingenuous. One could as easily argue that the content of the Qur'ān, which consists almost exclusively of elements adapted from the Judaeo-Christian tradition, must have disabled its sectaries in controversy with Jews and Christians.[3] The role of the miracle as prophetical credential was of such currency in the formulation of monotheistic religion as to make derivation from a single source a futile exercise indeed.[4] Rabbinic efforts to circumscribe the admissibility of such must be weighed against explicit pronouncements on the subject expressed in terms of popular faith, for example, by Maimonides.[5]

The thoroughly traditional character of Muslim polemic may be judged from the protests of mortality and disclaimers of miracles in the text of scripture itself.[6] What became, despite those assertions, the specifically Muhammadan miracle is alluded to in passages containing a demand not merely for credentials, but for written confirmation of the word of God, e.g. Q. 4: 153 يسئلك أهل الكتاب أن تنزل عليهم كتابا من السماء. That particular request is attributed to those already in possession of a scriptural revelation (*ahl al-kitāb*). Similar instances may logically be ascribed to the same quarter, even when not explicitly stated, e.g. Q. 17: 93, 21: 5, 43:

[1] Jāḥiẓ, *Kitāb Ḥujaj al-nubuwwa*, 145–6, but in a context in which the objective historicity of prophetical biographies is critically examined; Ibn Qutayba, *Ta'wīl*, 10.

[2] *Kashshāf* ii, 127: no prophet without a miracle; conversely, there could be no miracle without a prophet, cf. ʿAbd al-Jabbār, *Tanzīh al-Qur'ān*, 480 *ad Sūra* 105.

[3] 'Zur Muhammadlegende', 41–9; anticipated by Schreiner, 'Zur Geschichte', 593–5; apparently shared by Becker, 'Christliche Polemik', 437, and Wensinck, 'Propheten', 192–8. Conclusions drawn from the writings ascribed to John of Damascus are anyway questionable unless restricted, as they seldom are, to an assessment of polemical tactics, see my observations *BSOAS* xxxiii (1970) 391–3.

[4] Cf. Jeffery, 'Scripture', 132–3; Khoury, *Les Théologiens byzantins*, 89.

[5] *Iggeret Teman*, 56; cf. Gerhardsson, *Memory*, 178, 213.

[6] See above, p. 65; and I, pp. 6–7.

31, 47: 20, 74: 52. Collocation in scripture of 'prophethood and the book' (النبوة والكتاب Q. 29: 27, 57: 26) or 'the book, judgement/wisdom, and prophethood' (الكتاب والحكم والنبوة 3: 79, 6:89, 45: 16) refers exclusively to the Jews.[1] For verses of outspokenly polemical content, like Q. 35: 40 ام آتيناهم كتابا فهم على بينت منه (cf. 37: 157, 46:4), I am inclined to interpret *kitāb* as decree/authority (*sulṭān*, cf. 7: 71, 37: 156), rather than book (scripture), a conjecture supported by Zamakhsharī as well as by Quranic usage.[2] *Kitāb* as scripture is seldom differentiated in the Qur'ān, and exactly which scripture is meant can be elicited only from context.[3] The inherent ambiguity sensed by exegetes for many passages is reflected in Abū 'Ubayda's gloss of *dhālika 'l-kitāb* (that book) in Q. 2: 2 as *hādhā 'l-qur'ān* (this Qur'ān).[4]

Attempts at closer definition of *kitāb*, such as *naṣīb min al-kitāb* (a portion of the book, Q. 3: 23, 4: 44, 51, 7: 37), do not in fact eliminate the ambiguity, though in the exegetical tradition those passages were interpreted as allusions to the Torah.[5] On the other hand, *tafṣīl al-kitāb* (analysis/explication of the book) is once (Q. 10: 37) expressly predicated of the Qur'ān, while the term *tafṣīl* is elsewhere (6: 154, 7: 145, possibly 17: 12) a reference to the Mosaic revelation. The locution *kitāb allāh* (book of God), occurring nine times in Muslim scripture (five of which may well mean 'decree'), shared in the exegetical tradition a similar ambivalence. The alternative *kitāb allāh* and *qur'ān* in variant traditions of 'Umar's instructions to Abū Mūsā have been noticed.[6] A number of revealing anecdotes are related of the same caliph, e.g. that retailed by Ibn Ḥazm, according to which 'Umar was one day approached by the rabbi Ka'b carrying a book (*sifr*!), who said to him: Here is the Torah, read it! 'Umar replied: If you are certain that that is what God revealed to Moses, then I will read it night and day! The variant reply 'Then read it during the night and day', ill suited both to the preceding imperative in Ka'b's utterance and to the spirit of the story, reflects the dogmatic impulse responsible for another anecdote, in which Muhammad forbade 'Umar to read the Torah.[7] Just before the caliph's assassination the same rabbi informed him of his imminent death, indicating that he had found it predicted in the book of God, the Torah (أجده فى كتاب الله عز وجل التوراة).[8]

[1] Cf. Horovitz, *Untersuchungen*, 73: a conjectured calque of Hebrew tripartite scripture.

[2] *Kashshāf* iii, 617 *ad* Q. 35: 40, iv, 64 *ad* 37: 157; cf. Augapfel, 'Das "kitāb" im Qurān', 393.

[3] See Künstlinger, 'Kitāb', 238–47; id. 'Gottes-Schriften', 72–84.

[4] Wansbrough, 'Periphrastic exegesis', 250, 256.

[5] Cf. Künstlinger, 'Mathānī', 596–8.

[6] See above, p. 57.

[7] *Kitāb al-Fiṣal wal-milal* i, 217; Goldziher, 'Polemik', 345.

[8] Ṭabarī, *Annales* I/2722–3; cf. *BSOAS* xxxi (1968) 614–15, and below, IV pp. 189–90.

In a different context altogether, Ibn Ḥajar was constrained to observe that the locution *kitāb allāh* could refer to the Quranic codex (*muṣḥaf*).[1]

Collective designation of scripture(s) as *kutub allāh* (books of God) occurs in enumeration of the signs, as in Q. 2: 285 كل آمن بالله وملائكته وكتبه ورسله (cf. 4: 136, 66: 13, and the pair, 34: 44 and 68: 37, in which is stressed the plight of those not granted a scriptural revelation). In exegetical literature the total number of *kutub allāh* was given variously: 70, 104, 125, 163, the lowest figure being in all likelihood a reflex of 4 Ezra 14: 45–7.[2] 'Books' as prophetical credential is a notion widely attested in Judaeo-Christian literature, for which the paradigm was undoubtedly the Mosaic revelation.[3] In view of the central role played by the figure of Moses in both the scripture and prophetology of Islam, his relegation to the rank of sorcerer in Ibn Qutayba's typology of miracles is striking. So too, the dichotomy between the Arabian prophet of the *evangelium* and the recipient of God's final revelation, itself a miracle. Implicit in the typology is not merely the initial exchange of roles, but also precedence of the book over the prophet. It seems to me unlikely that such a development could have taken place outside the tradition of Rabbinic Judaism, in which Moses the leader of his people was succeeded by Moses the bearer of divine revelation. Translation of the word of God into a written record (scripture) was an essential element in the Mosaic tradition (Exodus 34: 27), perpetuated in the imagery of classical Hebrew prophecy (e.g. Isaiah 30: 8, Jeremiah 30: 2).[4]

Quranic reference to the word of God may also, and not unexpectedly, be allusion to scripture, e.g. Q. 4: 46 من الذين هادوا يحرّفون الكلم عن مواضعه (similarly 5: 13, 41), in which the action explicit in *taḥrīf* could only apply to the written word.[5] Conceptually related to *kalim* (words) in those verses is *qawl* (speech) in Q. 50: 29 ما يبدّل القول لدىّ, as well as *kalimāt* (words) in 6: 115 لا مبدّل لكلماته (similarly 10: 64) and *kalām* (speech) in 48: 15 يريدون أن يبدّلوا كلام الله (cf. 2: 75). In three of its four occurrences *kalim* requires to be understood as scripture (viz. Q. 4: 46, 5: 13, 41; the exception in 35: 10). Similarly all four occurrences of *kalām*, which appears only in construct with *allāh* (viz. Q. 2: 75, 9: 6, 48: 15, 7: 144, the last with an appropriate pronominal suffix). *Qawl* may be interpreted as scripture not only in Q. 50: 29, but also 23: 68

[1] *Apud* Suyūṭī, *Itqān* i, 221.

[2] See Abbott, *SALP* i, 54; Widengren, *Apostle of God*, 139–46; Eissfeldt, *Einleitung*, 773.

[3] Von Rad, *Theology* ii, 40–5.

[4] Cf. Jeffery, 'Scripture', 127.

[5] See below, IV pp. 188–92.

and 39: 18, though it more often renders 'word of God' in the sense of an expression of divine will (decree, e.g. 16: 40, 27: 82, 37: 31). In that dynamistic sense *kalimāt* is also employed, e.g. Q. 2: 37 (Adam) and 2: 124 (Abraham), but more common in that usage is the singular *kalima*, save for *amr* (utterance) the standard Quranic locution for God's decree, whether retributive (10: 33, 39: 19) or creative (7: 137, 37: 171).[1] Thus may be understood also those passages designated by O'Shaughnessy the 'Christological verses' (i.e. Q. 3: 39, 45, 4: 171).[2] It is only in the context of Quranic *kalima/amr* that one may speak of a reflex of the *logos* doctrine in Muslim theology, and that in a Philonic rather than Trinitarian sense.[3] A possible influence of the Christian doctrine might, however, be seen in sectarian phraseology, for example, interpretation of *kalimat al-faṣl* in Q. 42: 21 as ʿAlī b. Abī Ṭālib, or in the extreme formulations of the mystics on the creative power of the prophet Muhammad.[4] For the Ashʿarite doctrine on the eternity of the Qur'ān it is *kalām allāh* (scripture) which was the subject of controversy, and which may be distinguished from *kalima*, rather as in Christian theology *logos* and *rhema* refer respectively to Christ and scripture.[5] In Hebrew scripture the locution 'word of God' (דבר יהוה) is characteristic primarily of the prophetic oracle, and its *status constructus* may be judged comparable to that of Quranic *kalām allāh*.[6] The semantic range of the Hebrew formula includes scripture (e.g. Jeremiah 30: 2, 36: 1–2), but also the episodic expression of God's will (e.g. 1 Samuel 3: 7, 1 Chronicles 22: 8), which corresponds to Quranic *kalima/amr*. The specifically creative command of Psalm 33: 9 כי הוא אמר ויהי הוא צוה ויעמד may be compared with Q. 2: 117 وإذا قضى أمرا فإنما يقول له كن فيكون, or the retributive utterances of Isaiah 9: 7 and Amos 1: 2 with *waqaʿa 'l-qawl* (the word fell) in Q. 27: 82, 85. For the metaphorical *sefatai* of Psalm 89: 35 Saadya employed Arabic *qawlī* (my speech), not only to avoid the anthropomorphism but also as reflex of a Quranic term for command.[7]

The extraordinary position occupied by 'scripture' in Muslim prophetology requires to be examined in the light of two doctrines commonly interpreted as unique to the theology of Islam, namely, that the Qur'ān is inimitable and the word of God uncreated. Discussion of both turned upon the form and content of *kalām allāh*, which might seem to have taken on a dimension out of all proportion to its role as prophetical bona fides. While that role was never neglected, it would be more realistic to suppose

[1] But cf. Baljon, 'Amr of God', 7–18: equating *amr* with Biblical *ʿeṣah*.
[2] *Koranic Concept*, 19, 24 ff.
[3] *Pace* Bouman, *Conflit*, 15–16; cf. Speyer, *Erzählungen*, 24–5.
[4] Goldziher, *Richtungen*, 304; Andrae, *Person*, 333–57: *ḥaqīqa muḥammadiyya*.
[5] O'Shaughnessy, *Koranic Concept*, 62.
[6] Von Rad, *Theology* ii, 87–8.
[7] Galliner, *Saadja*, xxvi, 50 n. 18.

that the qualities of inimitability and eternity were formulated in the attempt to secure a position within the Muslim community for the document of revelation. The fact of canonicity, here postulated as sum of a long and uneven process of *Gemeindebildung*, meant acceptance of scripture not merely as evidence for the divine commission of one man, but also and more especially, recognition of its authority in the life of the community. Establishment of a historical connection between revelation and its recipient was, on the other hand, not simply a corollary of canonization.[1] In the preceding pages it has been argued that the historical portrait of the Arabian prophet conforms to a pattern composed partly of the Quranic data on prophethood, in character emphatically Mosaic, and partly of motifs drawn from a narrative tradition typically associated with men of God. The centrality of that portrait in the description of its origins formulated by the Muslim community lies in the role of the prophet as paradigm (*sunna*). The extent to which the specifically prophetical Sunna represented a refashioning of customary law and community practice is not easy to determine.[2] The tendency to subsume as much as possible of juridical precedent under the heading *sunnat al-nabī* was clear at the end of the second/eighth century. For a number of reasons, adduced at the end of the last chapter, the introduction of scripture as supplementary source of doctrine cannot have been earlier. The appearance of technical literature on the dogmas of its inimitability and eternity was even later. Now, from chronological indications alone it might seem that the document of revelation had achieved canonical status without being defined either as inimitable or as uncreated, but rather by virtue of its association with the prophet of Islam. I am inclined to interpret that link as one designed to support not merely the claim of Muhammad to prophethood (reflected in Quranic emphasis upon the Mosaic revelation), but also the claim of revelation to an effective role in the life of the community (already regulated by the prophetical Sunna). Of the three qualities predicated of Muslim scripture it was undoubtedly that of faithfully preserved prophetical *logia* which accounted for its acceptance as a source of doctrine. That the *logia*, once collected and canonized, might be granted enhanced status as the inimitable and uncreated word of God, would not appear to have been either logical or necessary. Both qualities, however, may be seen as reflexes of Rabbinic attitudes towards the Mosaic revelation, possibly adopted and modified in the course of Judaeo-Muslim polemic.

In the document of revelation itself that polemic is exhibited in those verses containing a demand for 'scripture' as sign, e.g. *kitāb*, *ṣuḥuf*, *sūra*, *qur'ān*. That such demands originated in a Jewish milieu is occasionally explicit (e.g. Q. 4: 153) and elsewhere a logical inference. If Christian, the

[1] See above, I pp. 47–52.

[2] Cf. Schacht, *Origins*, 180–9: legal maxims in traditions.

reference will none the less have been to Hebrew scripture, equally canonical and perhaps the only meaningful instance of specifically scriptural revelation for adherents of that faith.[1] Attempts in the exegetical tradition to ascribe those demands to the pagan Arabs of Mecca represent, in my opinion, elements of a *Nachdichtung* designed precisely to illustrate the Hijazi origins of Islam.[2] For that particular argument the exegetes were able to call into evidence an undisputed 'fact' of Arabian history in the seventh century, namely, the rhetorical accomplishment of the Arabs. Similarly I would submit that the concomitant challenge to produce an identical or superior scripture (or portion thereof), expressed five times in the Quranic text (the *taḥaddī* verses: Q. 2: 23, 10: 38, 11: 13, 17: 88, 52: 33–4), can be explained only within a context of Jewish polemic. In three of those verses (Q. 10: 38, 11: 13, 52: 33–4) the challenge: Then produce a *sūra*/ten *sūras*/a *ḥadīth* (!) like it, follows immediately upon an allegation of forgery (*yaqūlūn aftarāhu*/*taqawwalahu*), a charge which might be thought to come from those familiar with scriptural revelation. Further, the principal of the *taḥaddī* verses, Q. 17: 88 قل لئن اجتمعت الانس والجن على أن يأتوا بمثل هذا القرآن لا يأتون بمثله appears in a context introduced by a *locus classicus* for the celebrated 'rabbinical' test of prophethood (17: 85 And they ask you about the Spirit). Finally, a paraphrase of the challenge may be found in Q. 28: 49 قل فأتوا بكتاب من عند الله هو أهدى منهما where the quality of excellence is predicated alike of Qur'ān and Torah.

In what precisely the inimitability of Muslim scripture (*i'jāz al-qur'ān*) consists was the subject of long, ardent, and finally unresolved dispute.[3] Considered schematically, the material of controversy included arguments based upon: (*a*) divine prevention of the prophet's contemporaries and posterity from producing a successful counterfoil (*ṣarfa*: a position traditionally associated with the Mu'tazilī Naẓẓām); (*b*) the contents of the document, seen to include information about matters past, present, and future which could not possibly have come by natural means to the unlettered prophet (*akhbār al-ghayb*: thus the dogmatic emphasis upon Muhammad's illiteracy[4]); (*c*) its composition (*naẓm*/*ta'līf*), an area extended to include not merely linguistic form but artistic structure in the broadest terms possible, a consequence in part of rejection of the *ṣarfa* argument, seen by some to reduce the Qur'ān to the status of any phenomenon *contra naturam* (*khāriq lil-'āda*).

[1] Gerhardsson, *Memory*, 226.

[2] See above, pp. 58, 62, 72; I pp. 36–7; and below, IV pp. 122–6: the 'rabbinical' test of prophethood.

[3] A synoptic view in Suyūṭī, *Itqān*, *naw'* 64: iv, 3–23; cf. Schreiner, 'Zur Geschichte', 663–75; von Grunebaum, *EI*, s.v. I'djāz.

[4] See above, pp. 62–3; I p. 38.

From those three basic orientations elements were combined and varied with considerable ingenuity producing, save in the close rhetorical analysis of Jurjānī and, to a lesser degree, of Bāqillānī, a final synthesis characterized by subjective expression of the document's unimpeachable wisdom and clarity.[1] The slightly unrealistic and, in the end, unsatisfactory nature of the *ṣarfa* argument, whose very terms were self-defeating, followed from its precluding the test which itself would demonstrate the inimitability of the Qur'ān. Thus it was that references to content, with appropriate stress upon the *vaticinatio*, and to form may be seen to represent the dogma as distilled from the tradition. Assessment of the content of scripture tended to be ethical rather than aesthetic and expressed as wonder that one book could contain so much, indeed all that might be of utility to men. That its incomparable composition was not self-evident seems clear from the amount of literature produced to support the argument that it was. In this field attitudes ranged from a scrupulous desire to avoid the stigma of preciosity (*takalluf*) attaching to the Quranic style to the express intention of finding there the archetypes of all rhetorical device.[2] Views on the applicability of the rhetorical sciences to the problem of *iʿjāz* include the affirmation of Suyūṭī, that such could be apprehended only by means of those sciences (*maʿānī, bayān, badīʿ*), the denial of Ibn Ḥazm, that the word of God (*kalām allāh*) could in any manner be compared to human utterance (*kalām al-makhlūqīn*), and the carefully qualified statement of Bāqillānī, that while a variety of rhetorical embellishment was exhibited in scripture, such must be irrelevant to the fact of its inimitability.[3]

The significance of the *iʿjāz* controversy may, I think, be sought elsewhere than in its theological implications. In the course of those discussions it was, naturally, asked whether the Torah and Gospel(s), being the word of God, did not share with the Qur'ān the quality of inimitability. The reply, not surprisingly, was no: (*a*) though like the Qur'ān they did contain reports of the unknown (*akhbār al-ghayb*), there was nothing of the miraculous in their style (*naẓm*) or their structure (*ta'līf*); (*b*) this because God had not described them as such, nor had the challenge (*taḥaddī*) been referred to them, nor did the language(s) in which they were written contain anything of eloquence (*faṣāḥa*); (*c*) and finally, because no such claim had been made for those books by their sectaries.[4] A further point, attributed to Zarkashī and Zamakhsharī, stressed the Quranic

[1] See Weisweiler, 'Unnachahmlichkeit', 77–121; von Grunebaum, *Tenth-Century Document*; Bouman, *Conflit*; Suyūṭī, *Itqān* iv, 11–7.

[2] e.g. the dispute about *madhhab kalāmī*, see below, IV pp. 232–3; cf. von Grunebaum, *Tenth-century Document*, xv on the Venerable Bede.

[3] Suyūṭī, *Itqān* iv, 186; Ibn Ḥazm, *Kitāb al-Fiṣal* iii, 18–19; Bāqillānī, *I'jāz*, 107, 111–12; von Grunebaum, op. cit. 49, 54–5; Bouman, *Conflit*, 71.

[4] Bāqillānī, *I'jāz*, 31–2; Bouman, *Conflit*, 66.

arrangement (*tartīb*) in *sūras* according to divine plan, while such divisions in the texts of other scriptures were the work of their compilers.[1]

Of those arguments only one might be thought to contain some objective basis outside the immediate terms of the controversy, namely, the conviction that eloquence was peculiar to the Arabic language. Introduction of that element into what purported to be theological doctrine served a dual purpose: Muslim prophetology was enriched by the concept of a *lingua sacra*, and the elaboration of Islam characterized by its exclusively Arabian origins. Exegesis of the *taḥaddī* verses, in order to underline the complete failure to meet the challenge (*muʿāraḍa*: the absence of logic in that reasoning was never admitted), presupposed the specifically Arabic eloquence of all contestants.[2] When these failed, as indeed they must, how could the claim to inimitability be denied? Rather more important than the challenge which, paradoxically, must have been addressed to those familiar with scripture, was the notion that the word of God could be bound to a particular medium. For a number of reasons such a view was hardly possible for Christians, though evidence of an emphatically conservative attitude to the Biblical text was not wanting even there.[3] On the other hand, Rabbinic (and Targumic) designation of Biblical Hebrew as the *lingua sacra* (*leshon ha-qodesh*) might seem to have provided the immediate *Vorbild* for Muslim usage.[4] Now, there is admittedly no equivalent in Rabbinic theology to the dogma of *iʿjāz al-qurʾān*, and Jewish polemic concerned with that doctrine appears to have taken as point of departure, by calling into question, the Muslim premiss that the Quranic style was demonstrably superior to that of profane compositions in Arabic.[5] It might indeed be supposed that no other course was open to those whose notion of *lingua sacra* was not bound to Arabic: aesthetic assessment of the Quranic style was almost necessarily a preoccupation internal to the Muslim community. Two aspects of the dogma which, however, could have been devised to meet the needs of external polemic were the fact of a sacred language other than Hebrew, and its appropriate bestowal upon a people whose appreciation of rhetorical niceties was established.[6]

A third aspect of the *iʿjāz* controversy generated an independent series of dogmatic propositions. In retailing Muʿtazilī views on the inimitability of the Qurʾān Ashʿarī cited the insistence of Naẓẓām on the *ṣarfa* argument and added that both Hishām Fuwaṭī and ʿAbbād b. Sulaymān refused to

[1] *Apud* Suyūṭī, *Itqān* i, 186–7; cf. the opposition *munajjam*: *jumla* in discussions of the mode of revelation, above, I pp. 36–8.

[2] e.g. as in Ibn Qutayba, *Taʾwīl*, 17; Bouman, *Conflit*, 66–73, seems here to have missed the point of the argument.

[3] See Loewe, 'Latin Vulgate', in *CHB* ii, 106–7.

[4] Cf. Segal, *Mishnaic Hebrew*, 2–3.

[5] Cf. the fragments in Steinschneider, *Polemische Literatur*, 103, 314 n. 23.

[6] See below, III pp. 93–9.

acknowledge the Qur'ān either as witness to the existence of God or as credential for the prophet.[1] While the *ṣarfa* argument could be inverted to demonstrate the fact of Arab eloquence (in the absence of which divine prevention of an imitation would have been unnecessary!), the rejection of revelation as miracle provoked a different kind of rebuttal. The rejection was based upon an assertion that the word of God, hence the Qur'ān (*sic*), could only be described in relation to the existence of God as contingent (*ʿaraḍ*): the Muʿtazilī definition of God's unity (*tawḥīd*) precluded adducing contingencies as witness either to His being or to His actions. Now, it is generally assumed that the Muʿtazilī position represented a reaction to an earlier and more popularly held view that the word of God, hence the Qur'ān (*sic*), was neither contingent nor created but, rather, inseparable from the unqualified existence of its creator. But it is difficult indeed to discern from the expression of Muʿtazilī views, most of which are preserved only in the later works of their triumphant adversaries, whether they exhibit opposition to other views already expressed, or merely the articulation of conclusions derived from their own creed. Worthy of remark is that the three Muʿtazilī spokesmen cited by Ashʿarī all lived in the first half of the third/ninth century, and that the utterances ascribed to them were made with specific reference to the inimitability of the Qur'ān. It might be thought that acceptance (or rejection except on the condition of *ṣarfa*) of its inimitability somehow entailed definition of the Qur'ān as uncreated. As I have indicated, both qualities appear to have been formulated with less concern for the description of prophetical bona fides than for assertion of the document's canonical status within the community. It may of course be argued that the evidence for a connection of the two dogmas is too circumstantial to be of real value, and that, in any case, the relation between the two cannot be described as causal. Ashʿarī noted that most members of the Muʿtazila accepted the inimitability of the Qurʿān (defined in terms of its composition!) without, apparently, admitting that it was uncreated.[2] The converse could hardly have been postulated.

In *Fiqh Akbar I* there is, expectedly, no mention of the uncreated Qur'ān. In the *Waṣīyat Abī Ḥanīfa*, dated by Wensinck towards the middle of the third/ninth century, the dogma is set out in Article IX, but without mention of inimitability.[3] Those data accord with what seems to have been the chronological framework of the controversy, from which emerged an instructive *terminus ad quem;* c. 235/850.[4] The opinions of the dissenting Muʿtazila cited by Ashʿarī had been expressed at about that date. The harmony between these details and the chronology proposed for the pro-

[1] *Maqālāt al-Islāmiyyīn*, 225–6; cf. Bouman, *Conflit*, 19.

[2] *Maqālāt*, loc. cit.; an example was the Muʿtazilī ʿAbd al-Jabbār, cf. Bouman, 'Doctrine', 67–86.

[3] See above, I p. 44; Wensinck, *Creed*, 127, 149–51, 187.

[4] Cf. Watt, 'Early discussions', 29 n. 5, 33, 36.

cess of canonization ought not to be overlooked. Now, that process might be described as the collocation of several elements: a corpus of prophetical *logia*, the figure of a prophet, a sacred language, and an unequivocally divine sanction for all three. Reconstruction of the manner in which these elements were evolved and adjusted to produce a more or less final and satisfactory synthesis can only be conjectural. It may be clear from the preceding observations that I regard the acquisition within the community of these elements as having taken place in the sequence set out above. Their interaction might be envisaged as follows: attribution of several, partially overlapping, collections of *logia* (exhibiting a distinctly Mosaic imprint) to the image of a Biblical prophet (modified by the material of the Muhammadan *evangelium* into an Arabian man of God) with a traditional message of salvation (modified by the influence of Rabbinic Judaism into the unmediated and finally immutable word of God).

Achievement of the final stage in the process may be equated with the declaration that the Qur'ān was uncreated. Identification of the Qur'ān document with the word of God (*kalām allāh*) was derived from a traditional metaphor, e.g. Q. 9: 6 فأجره حتى يسمع كلام الله. A further identification of the Qur'ān document with the word of God as interpreted in the discussions of divine attributes (*ṣifāt*)[1] appears to entail a transition from metaphorical to veritable sense, which may be traced to the imagery of Q. 85: 21–2 بل هو قرآن مجيد فى لوح محفوظ. The concept of a celestial archetype evoked by this verse, which was crucial in the *ṣifāt* discussions,[2] belongs to an ancient and well-attested tradition, in which of course the referent was the word of God as injunction, law, even register, but not 'scripture' in the sense of record of revelation.[3] From the notion of 'law' inherent in the use of *lawḥ* (tablet) it is at least conceivable that *qur'ān* in Q. 85: 21–2 could be functionally equated with the Mosaic law, and more particularly with the Rabbinic concept of the pre-existent Torah as the immutable word of God.[4] That the ultimate authority of God's decree might thus be fixed provided a more or less satisfactory solution to the problem of scripture as normative in the life of the community. But theological difficulties provoked by the possible charge of dualism remained, and attempts to solve or to evade these are evident in the works of masoretic exegesis, e.g. Abū ʿUbayda's interpretation of Q. 85: 22 as *fī lūḥin maḥfūẓun*.[5] The

[1] e.g. Ashʿarī, *Maqālāt*, 582–607; cf. Goldziher, 'Fachr al-dīn al-Rāzī', 245–7.

[2] Cf. Ashʿarī, *Maqālāt*, 549 ff.

[3] Cf. Horovitz, *Untersuchungen*, 65–6; Jeffery, 'Scripture', 51–3; but also Widengren, *Apostle of God*, 115–61: for the equation Wisdom–Tablet–Book.

[4] e.g. Talm. Babl., Pesaḥim 54a, Nedarim 39b, and the Midrashic references in Speyer, *Erzählungen* 34 n. 2; see above, I pp. 35–6.

[5] Wansbrough, 'Periphrastic exegesis', 252 no. 29; cf. Zamakhsharī, *Kashshāf* iv, 733 ad loc.

reading 'preserved in an atmosphere' might be thought analogous to Saadya's theory of *awir sheni*, formulated to avoid the implications of a hypostasized word of God.[1] In contrast with the masoretes, Muslim theologians found satisfaction in distinguishing between the eternal word of of God as concept (*maʿnā*) and its reproduction (*dalīl/tanzīl*), an argument derived from a series of grammatical oppositions: *qirā'a–maqrū'*, *kitāba–maktūb*, *dhikr–madhkūr*. That formulation appears to have been the work of Naẓẓām (d. 231/846) or Ibn Kullāb (d. 240/854), incorporated finally into the theories of Bāqillānī (d. 403/1013). Its refutation by the late Muʿtazilī ʿAbd al-Jabbār (d. 416/1025) was unconvincing.[2]

Such problems, with their solutions, remained peripheral. Textual explication of Muslim scripture was able to accommodate variant, emendation, anomaly, ellipsis, pleonasm, in short all that might be described as characteristic of any literary record, irrespective of convictions about its source. The most interesting aspect by far of the application of literary criticism to the text of revelation was the extrapolation, from an allegedly profane tradition, of aesthetic criteria formulated to describe the substance and function of a sacred language. That was the product of masoretic exegesis.[3] The Muslim masoretes were above all grammarians, whose primary task was to relate the anomalies of a *lingua sacra* to the demands of a normative description of language. With analysis of that process the following chapter is concerned.

[1] Altmann, 'Theory', 20–4.
[2] Bouman, *Conflit*, 20–3, 37–8, 73–80; id. 'Doctrine', 74–84.
[3] See below, IV pp. 202–27.

III

ORIGINS OF CLASSICAL ARABIC

HISTORICAL descriptions of the Arabic language are reminiscent of a celebrated discussion among Renaissance humanists about the intrusion of Italian into areas allocated by tradition to classical Latin. Against the isolated conjecture that the literary (Latin) and vernacular (Italian) languages were coeval but functionally separate was ranged a series of arguments concerned to describe a developmental relation between *sermo urbanus* and *sermo plebeius*: the latter was the product either of barbarians' misuse of the former, or of local (indigenous) deformation; conversely, *sermo urbanus* might be described as a conscious (social and aesthetic) refinement of *sermo plebeius*.[1] The hypothesis of a functional dichotomy, to be qualified by the observation that usage varied not with social position but with the demands of a given linguistic situation, was both non-evolutionary and not very forcefully asserted. The three evolutionary concepts appeared, on the other hand, to make some sense of the historical data, and have survived as points of departure for those theories of linguistic genealogy which have not been entirely discredited.

Nowhere have such proved more durable than in studies of the position occupied by Classical Arabic in the historical development of Semitic languages. An inclination to see in Classical Arabic (CA) at least the phonological and morphological constituents of a hypothetical Proto-Semitic is both understandable and of some value for comparative and diachronic analyses. To draw from the same data conclusions about the origins and evolution of CA involves implicit acceptance of considerable non-linguistic material often and erroneously supposed to be 'historical fact'. I refer to such assumptions as that of the isolation of speakers/writers of Arabic within the Arabian peninsula up to the seventh century, or that of the existence of a *ne varietur* text of the Islamic revelation not later than the middle of the same century. Both the origin and the utility of those assumptions are patent. Evidence of abrasion (phonological/morphological) and of interference (syntactic/lexical) could be ascribed to the use of CA by foreigners or to widespread dislocation within the Arabic-speaking community, both being consequences of the expansion of Islam during the seventh century. Moreover, that CA could survive to serve as model (orthographic/grammatical) for a literary language could be explained by

[1] Vossler, *Einführung ins Vulgärlatein*, 48–52.

the fixed, sacred, and immutable text of the Qur'ān, representing the highest form of rhetorical achievement in Arabic. Provision of a geographical and chronological setting for the diachronic examination of CA enabled observers of the purely linguistic phenomena to interpret these as evidence of a more or less uninterrupted process of decline: movement away from a point of linguistic (and ethnic!) purity towards a situation characterized by fragmentation, dialect cleavage, unattainable ideals, and a permanent tension between theory and practice. The historical assumptions underlying such an interpretation of the data are, however, not merely unverifiable, but also internally inconsistent and, in some respects, demonstrably false.

Now, the marshalling of phonological evidence (consonantal range/vocalic quality and position) as well as of that pertaining to morphology and, in the strictest sense, to grammar (inflexion: case/mood) might be thought unexceptionable, so long as it is recognized that such material reflects the highly specialized and often idiosyncratic usage of rather meagre literary records preserved in comparatively late recensions.[1] Syntactical evidence has been interpreted as exhibiting the effects of a normative process, and thus as proof of some distance between CA and Proto-Semitic, whose proximity, on the other hand, had been inferred from the witness to phonology and morphology.[2] There is, of course, no compelling reason why any of that linguistic material should yield conclusions of a chronological, as opposed to structural, nature. In the context of evolutionary interpretation, the work of Vollers with reference to the consonantal range of CA as exhibiting, in relation to Proto-Semitic, not preservation, but rather, phonetic proliferation, and to the essentially euphonic and rhetorical significance of the *iʿrāb* phenomena, represented a reaction to traditional views, but required at the same time, in order to fit the geographical/chronological environment alleged to have produced the earliest Arabic literature, a very questionable reconstruction of the history of the Quranic text.[3] The concept of CA as a kind of linguistic (and literary) canon, apart from reflecting a well-attested and strongly entrenched tradition of rhetorical criticism, may owe something of its putative authority, at least for modern philological scholarship, to its role as confirmation *cum* source of Proto-Semitic reconstructions. For identification of actual specimens of CA, exponents of that scholarship have for the most part been content to accept the received tradition as found in works of rhetoric and exegesis, namely, that CA is exhibited in the corpus of poetry described as pre-Islamic and in the document of

[1] e.g. *GVG* i, 23–4, 120–1, 459–62, 554; Moscati, *Comparative Grammar*, 14, 52, 95–6, 134–5.

[2] e.g. Bergsträsser, *Einführung*, 134–5; Blau, 'Problems', 1.

[3] 'Arabisch und Semitisch', 165–217; id. Review: Nöldeke, *Zur Grammatik*, 125–39; id. *Volkssprache*, 55–175.

Islamic revelation. The only deduction possible was that, within the bounds imposed by available literary remains, CA stood at the beginning and not at the end of or at a point in the course of a long and varied linguistic evolution.[1] To interpret that evolution, which seems always to to have been identified with description of the vicissitudes of CA in a post-classical environment, two criteria in particular have emerged with an apparently reasonable claim both to utility and to objectivity.

The first of these may be described as a cluster of interpretative principles derived from the concept of *koine*, adduced to provide a *terminus ad quem* for the historical evolution of CA. *Koine* has been employed to designate: (1) the language of pre-Islamic poetry and Qur'ān, (2) a kind of bedouin lingua franca, and (3) the hypothetical source of modern sedentary vernaculars.[2] Despite the inadvisability of accepting one term for such varied phenomena, the several applications of *koine* reflect a certain unity of impulse, namely, to describe difference in terms of divergence from a single source, an intellectual principle commonly associated with genetic linguistics. Though the implications of *koine* taxonomy for the history of Arabic, particularly in respect of its second and third uses, have been questioned and eventually modified, the definition of CA as the language of poetry and of revelation has not been unseated.[3] The *koine* principle was also applied to the scanty and problematic evidence of dialect cleavage to produce a series of plausible if necessarily hypothetical polarities: e.g. regional (Nejd–Hijaz), economic (nomadic–sedentary), social (patrician–plebeian), ethnic (*ʿarab–ʿajam*). One result of the experiment was to demonstrate that, contrary to the assertions of Muslim philologists, CA was not and had never been identifiable with any single Arabian dialect.[4] By a somewhat eccentric application of logic, that negative argument confirmed the identification of CA with the ineptly formulated 'poetic *koine*'.

The second criterion adduced to describe the fortunes of CA includes several variations upon the theme of pseudo-correction. As a descriptive principle pseudo-correction presupposes the existence of an acknowledged standard of linguistic (or literary) excellence and witness, across a range of individual speakers/writers, to *incomplete* mastery of it.[5] Thus, the evidence of pseudo-correction cannot alone be employed to demonstrate

[1] Which did not, of course, preclude versions of a hypothetical pre-history, cf. Rabin, 'Beginnings', 35–6.

[2] Cf. Blachère, *Histoire* i, 79–82; Fück, *ʿArabīya*, 7; Nöldeke, 'Das klassische Arabisch und die arabischen Dialekte', *BSS*, 13; Ferguson, 'Arabic koine', 616–30.

[3] Cf. Cohen, 'Koinè', 119–44; Blau, *Emergence*, 10–18; *GVG* i, 23; Spitaler, Review: Fück, *ʿArabīya*, 145.

[4] e.g. Rabin, *West-Arabian*, 17–24; id. 'Beginnings', 32–4: the view that CA could be traced ultimately to a dialect was, incidentally, not the exclusive property of Muslim scholarship.

[5] See Blau, *Pseudo-corrections*, 11–22.

existence of a linguistic/literary standard, proof of which must already have been established. For the history of CA it need hardly be added that applications of this criterion will not be very helpful in determining just *when* that particular form of the language attained its status as standard.[1] But the usefulness of the principle is not thereby exhausted. Absence of pseudo-correct features may indicate either mastery of the standard or, alternatively, that the standard is not distinguishable from the *usus loquendi*. The two possibilities may, it seems to me, be regarded as mutually exclusive, evident from the composition of works in faultless CA by authors who could not conceivably have spoken that language. To insist that the absence of pseudo-correct features in the Qur'ān (accepting that such is the case) reflects not mastery of the literary idiom but rather the 'true vernacular of Mecca' involves an assumption based on non-linguistic evidence, namely, that at the time the Qur'ān was recorded in writing the literary and spoken languages were, at least in Mecca, indistinguishable.[2] Necessarily conjectural, that assertion would appear also to preclude an alternative possibility: that when the Qur'ān was recorded in writing the grammar of CA had been formulated and could be learned by someone whose mother tongue it was not. Chronological problems are, of course, not thereby solved, but neither are they prejudged by tacit acceptance of the 'Uthmanic recension traditions. The criterion of pseudo-correction, like that of the *koine* concept, has served illogically to confirm the position of CA in seventh-century Arabia by dependence upon it as a historical fact. As instruments of synchronic analysis both criteria are of indisputable value; for purposes of historical description they are at best convenient fictions.

For the diachronic study of CA linguists have naturally, if somewhat ingenuously, had recourse to the framework supplied by historians of the early centuries of Islam. In their construction of that framework historians, in turn, have relied largely upon a corpus of literature extant only in recensions dating from the beginnings of the third/ninth century. Exceptions to that circumstance are few, indeed, the major one being, in the consensus of Muslim and Orientalist scholarship, the text of the Islamic revelation itself. General assent to 'le fait coranique'[3] links in an extraordinary manner the most disparate and even contradictory interpretations of early Islamic history, a secondary consequence of which has been affirmation of the 'fact' by virtue of repeated assertion. In an essay which did not depart significantly from the traditional view of the Hijazi origins of Islam, the historian C. H. Becker proposed a distinction between the

[1] Consider the dates of the material so carefully analysed by Blau in his *Grammar of Christian Arabic*, 2–36; cf. *BSOAS* xxxi (1968) 610–13.

[2] Cf. Blau, *Pseudo-corrections*, 57–8 esp. n. 15.

[3] Blachère, *Histoire* ii, 230–41.

processes of Arabicization and Islamization, in his opinion separated by a period of from two to three centuries.[1] The former term was applied to the several religiously neutral factors thought to have effected the movement of the Arabs beyond the frontiers of the Arabian peninsula; the latter to the subsequent imposition of religious uniformity upon subject peoples by an Islamic power. While not at all concerned with the problems being examined here, Becker's work provided a valuable lesson in the typological differentiation of source materials, according to which 'le fait coranique' might indeed qualify as 'fact' but apparently only as one whose historical effect was (temporarily) suspended. On that particular point there is at least room for argument,[2] but the example is none the less instructive. I should like to propose a metaphorical extension of Becker's dichotomy by defining Arabicization as the expression of a centrifugal force and figure of expansion; conversely, Islamization could be interpreted as a centripetal force and figure of contraction. Materially the antithetical figures might be understood to represent, on the one hand, the spread of Arabic dialects at a pace approximately consonant with that of the Arab conquests, and on the other, the imposition of CA as a linguistic/literary standard. Symbolically the contrast would be one between natural, uninhibited diffusion and artificial, consciously directed restriction. Linguistically Arabicization is characterized by a concept of language as the most convenient means for meeting the demands of normal communication (*Mitteilungsbedürfnis*), and Islamization by a concept of language as an instrument of education (*Bildungsprinzip*). An example of the first was the introduction of Arabic as official language into the Umayyad chancery; *the* example of the second was, of course, the Qur'ān.

Now, it has for some time been assumed that both the chancery language in question and that of the Qur'ān represent CA, and further, that both reflect the 'poetic *koine*' asserted to have been the medium of pre-Islamic poetry. Since all three may be described as forms of literary expression, the equation is at least theoretically valid. And from the notion of continuity implicit there was born the concept of *koine* as descriptive principle in the historical analysis of CA. Whether or when the *koine* might have been even approximately similar to an Arabic vernacular is a problem still awaiting solution, or reformulation. Rather more important, in my opinion, is whether the equation is in practice justifiable. May one, in fact, identify the language of poetry with that of scripture and, in turn, both with that of the earliest chancery papyri? Further, what chronological conclusions can legitimately be drawn from the purely linguistic content of that material? Orthographic and morphological features common to all three permit a degree of synchronic comparison. Lexical, syntactic, and above all, stylistic requirements of each of the three genres might be

[1] 'Der Islam als Problem', 6–7.

[2] See above, I pp. 43–52.

thought to preclude a diachronic analysis. Assertions of linguistic continuity can here only be based upon non-linguistic data, and the first century of Islam can hardly be described as 'a period fully in the light of history'.[1]

From employment of the *koine* concept as an explicative mechanism to assertion of its historicity is, after all, a long and significant step. If it is to be attempted at all, the points of departure must be an examination of five kinds of linguistic material, each with some claim to be representative of the earliest form of CA:

1. Poetry (pre-Islamic and early Islamic).
2. Qur'ān.
3. *Ḥadīth* (subsuming *sīra–maghāzī* literature).
4. *Ayyām.*
5. Papyri.

With the exception of the papyri, use of these data is subject to three caveats of general nature as well as to a number of specific reservations for each category. First, the purpose of each may be described as essentially educative rather than merely communicative. Literary composition with an avowed aim must be evaluated in terms of the rhetorical schemata consciously employed to achieve that aim, whether aesthetic, cultic, juridical, or historical, and seldom if ever constitutes disinterested linguistic evidence.[2] Second, a curious quality of simultaneity characterizes the recensions in which this material has been preserved, as well as the commentary and other critical literature generated by it: all appears to have come into existence at the end of the second/eighth and beginning of the third/ninth centuries. A concomitant homogeneity of subject-matter is reflected in the overlapping of genres: poetry placed within a narrative frame, prose relieved by poetic insertions both as exegesis and *ornatus*, juridical and lexical problems solved by reference to scripture, scriptural problems solved by reference to jurisprudence and lexicography, all with approximately the same end in view: historical description of a situation two centuries earlier.[3] Third, practical application of the linguistic data preserved in that literature has tended to blur what might be thought a traditionally valid distinction between prose and poetry: freely variable syntax as a function of rhetoric. Formulation of grammatical rules from poetry, from the style of scripture, or from ornate prose is bound to result in a very specialized table of correct procedures, *not* in a generally useful description of language. Resort to such may produce a circumscribed and unrealistic image, which will thus become a decidedly unattainable ideal.

[1] As in Rabin, 'Beginnings', 29.
[2] See Wehr, Review: Fück, '*Arabīya,* 185.
[3] See Spitaler, 'Arabisch', 125.

From the point of view of the Arab grammarians that may not have been unintentional. Results are, after all, as much conditioned by method as by material.[1]

It might seem from these observations that the real value of this material lies in its relevance to literary and scholarly activities within the community of Islam at about the turn of the second/eighth and third/ninth centuries. Such, at least, would be my provisional conclusion, but it is worth noting that despite the limitations set out here and acknowledged elsewhere, acceptance of the sources at face value continues to find adherents.[2] Now, the single exception to a very strong possibility of *Nachdichtung* is the linguistic content of the chancery papyri. That has been assessed as exhibiting CA with some slight deviation of colloquial origin, or Middle Arabic admixture.[3] However that early chancery language may be described, it is clearly not the language either of poetry or of scripture. It could thus be allocated to the sphere of CA only by reference to a standard posterior in time to the composition of the documents themselves. Consideration of the resultant anachronism may have led Rabin to the hypothesis that the language of the papyri might be 'a Classical Arabic (*sic*!) not yet standardized by grammarians'.[4] In practice it is essential to distinguish between adaptations and translations from the Byzantine *epistolaris sermo* and free composition in what could be called sub-literary or 'business' Arabic, but also to observe that the chancery language as such eventually was, and in fact had to be, elaborated from both sources.[5] Consistent deviation from a hypothetical CA in the language of the papyri may only be interpreted as such by reference to a standard for which there are no extant *loci probantes*. Even the literary papyri studied by Abbott exhibit the same departures from 'classical' Arabic.[6] It might indeed be thought that these reservations contribute to undermine the unitary concept of a 'literary *koine*' and, more especially, of its development no later than the sixth century.

Lexical and syntactical disparities between the styles respectively of poetry, scripture, and chancery documents represent functional cleavages of a sort difficult to reconcile with the notion of a single source for CA. It can, in fact, be argued that neither poetry nor scripture could have, or ever did, become canons of actual linguistic usage, as opposed to sources

[1] Spitaler, 'Arabisch', 126; id. Review: Bloch, *Vers und Sprache*, 317–18; Ullmann, *Rağazpoesie*, 218–32.

[2] e.g. Rabin, 'Beginnings', 21–2; the same curious and quite illogical position seems to be that underlying Blachère's in many respects very useful *Histoire*.

[3] See e.g. Grohmann, *Einführung*, 103–7; Blau, *Emergence*, 123–32.

[4] *EI*, s.v. ʿArabiyya: I, 564.

[5] Consider the rhetorical components of classical *inshā*ʾ, as extrapolated from Qalqashandī by Björkman, *Staatskanzlei*, 87–92; but also the medieval European development of *ars dictaminis*, Curtius, *Europäische Literatur*, 83.

[6] e.g. *SALP* ii; my references in *BSOAS* xxxi (1968) 614–16.

of grammatical theory.[1] Assertions to the contrary exhibit theological orientations defined to accommodate two dogmas inextricably part of the traditional assessment of Islamic origins, namely, those of the inimitability of the Qur'ān and of the rhetorical potential of the Arabic language.[2] Both played considerable roles in the establishment of a chronological and geographical framework for the diachronic description of CA. On the other hand, the evolution suggested by an examination of the papyri displays what might appear to be a normal process of refinement: from the exigencies of administrative communication to the luxury of an elaborate *Kunstprosa* in the third/ninth century. For that development we have, at least, the requisite *loci probantes*: bilingual and monolingual chancery papyri, monolingual literary papyri, the prose parts of *sīra*, *maghāzī*, and *ayyām*, as well as the *ḥadīth* literature. Save as sources of stylistic embellishment (*iqtibās*) and lexical *exotica*, scripture and poetry will hardly have affected the elaboration of a CA prose style, whether discursive or narrative. In their earliest definitive forms these styles may be studied in recensions of the third/ninth century, indicating thus a chronological span which might be thought to correspond to the time-lag of two to three centuries postulated by Becker for the separate processes of Arabicization and Islamization. Neither religious orthodoxy nor linguistic standard could be imposed before each had achieved canonical status.

Administrative employment of Arabic symbolized the beginnings of acculturation. On the basis of the chancery papyri that event could be dated to about 86/705.[3] Against the ethnic composition of the Arab dominions at that time, the role of Arabic must be seen as primarily that of a practical instrument of communication (*Verkehrssprache*). Its subsequent development can be interpreted as the compound result of several non-linguistic factors: social and economic necessity, formation of urban centres of diffusion, and prestige of the ruling minority. Evidence of bilingualism (substrate phenomena) and of diglossia (dialectal phenomena) ought not to be assessed with reference to a normative CA, for which there are no contemporary source materials, but rather with a view to the requirements of the community served by that sub-literary language. It is important to remember that from the beginning of that evolution to its end the evidence is always that of a written language, whatever its pre-history may have been. The material is thus always witness to formal and/or formalized communication, for which emergence of a standard of excellence was not only its organizing principle but also its logical conclusion.[4] The evolution so projected does not, however, require the existence of a pre-Islamic *koine*, and especially not one whose linguistic description can

[1] See below, pp. 100–3.
[2] See above, II pp. 79–82.
[3] Becker, *Geschichte Ägyptens* i, 130–1; Blachère, *Histoire* iii, 718.
[4] Cf. Weinreich, *Languages in Contact*, 74–82, 83–110; Garbell, 'Remarks', 303–5.

only be elicited from a corpus of bedouin and courtly poetry.[1] The transformation of functional prose, of which the primary characteristic and criterion is efficiency, into artistic prose will naturally reflect the impingement of a rhetorical tradition. Communicative efficiency will be gradually superseded by a conscious striving for what is often called 'elevated language', of which the underlying motive is not *Mitteilungsbedürfnis* but *Bildungsprinzip*. It is then, and probably only then, that the rhetorical embellishment associated with poetry and scripture may be seen as operative in the formation of prose style. For the history of Classical Arabic, however, those two sources of rhetorical schemata were defined, preserved, and transmitted not as accessory to the basic task of communication, but as formative principles of linguistic description. The presuppositions were two: (1) that eloquence and clarity were properties exclusive to the Arabic language, and (2) that by virtue of divine election Arabic was also a sacred language, for which change could only mean corruption.

. . . . .

Any sampling of the Orientalist tradition will reveal the axiomatic quality of Arab eloquence,[2] an impression derived presumably from the writings of such celebrated scholars as Ibn Qutayba, Bāqillānī, and Suyūṭī, as well as from exegesis of the *taḥaddī* verses.[3] But the Muslim tradition, considerably older than the dates of those authors, exhibits in its earlier stages remarkable absence of unanimity on such questions as the presence in Arabic of foreign lexica, the grammatical and syntactical idiosyncrasies of poets, and the paradigmatic quality of Quranic style.[4] Predictably dogmatic positions on these questions were taken up in the fourth/tenth and fifth/eleventh centuries, culminating in the systematic and isagogic works of scholars like Ibn Fāris and Suyūṭī.[5] In a characteristic discussion of eloquence (*faṣāḥa*) as partaking of both diction and elocution, Suyūṭī adduced the by that time traditional pair of assertions that the most eloquent of men (*afṣaḥ al-khalq*) was the prophet Muhammad, and of the Arabs (*afṣaḥ al-ʿarab*) Quraysh.[6] The non-linguistic nature of the argument, which might ultimately be traced to a sanctuary tradition concerning Mecca, emerged clearly in the famous prophetical *ḥadīth* أنا أفصح العرب

[1] *Pace* Rabin, 'Beginnings', 29; cf. *BSOAS* xxxi (1968) 611.

[2] A random selection might include e.g. Schreiner, 'Zur Geschichte', 663; Fischer, 'Usaiịid usw.', 581 n. 2; Nöldeke, *NBSS*, 5, 22; Andrae, *Person*, 95–7; Blachère, *Histoire* iii, 719, 725, 730; accounting thus for approximately a century of European scholarship.

[3] Ibn Qutayba, *Ta'wīl*, 17; Bāqillānī, *I'jāz*, 24, 250; Suyūṭī, *Itqān* ii, 270, iv, 4, 16; id. *Muzhir* i, 209–10; see above, II p. 79.

[4] See Kopf, 'Religious influences', 33–59.

[5] See Goldziher, 'Sprachgelehrsamkeit' iii, 511–52.

[6] *Muzhir*, *nawʿ* 9: i, 184–213, esp. 209–10.

بيد أني من قريش.[1] Suppression of claims made on behalf of other tribal groups to the title *afṣaḥ al-ʿarab* is symbolized in the account ascribed to Farrā' of how the inhabitants of cosmopolitan (!) Mecca (i.e. Quraysh) were in a position to recognize and adopt the best ingredients from each of the bedouin dialects in Arabia.[2] Besides drawing attention to the role of Mecca as cultic and commercial centre, this tradition, like the ones it eventually replaced, served to identify the northern regions of the Arabian peninsula as the cradle of CA at a date prior to the proclamation of Islam. Worthy of note in Suyūṭī's treatment of Arab eloquence is regular use of the elatives *afṣaḥ*, *abyan*, *ablagh*, and *aʿrab* in adverbial constructions with *lisān* and *lugha* to signify clear and effective speech.[3] Their terminological antithesis is conveyed by *aʿjam*, glossed *lā yufṣiḥ*, and it seems more than likely that Quranic employment of the contrasting pair *aʿjamī–ʿarabī* was intended to express just such a distinction.[4] The semantic evolution of *ʿarabī/aʿrābī* is not unfamiliar: in the corresponding series *deutlich/deuten/deutsch* the formative element *diutisk* > *theodiscus* was, after all, a linguistic designation prior to becoming an ethnic and ultimately a geographical title.[5] But such an interpretation may not be adduced to demonstrate that the locution *afṣaḥ al-ʿarab* is merely a tautology; the reference was to bedouin Arabic speech.

A natural, though perhaps not quite logical, inference from discussion of Arab eloquence was that the language spoken by bedouin must be identical with that of the poetry called pre-Islamic (*Jāhilī*). Opinions of scholars about that equation range from the almost vehement affirmation of Nöldeke across the nicely qualified acceptance of Blau to the outright rejection of Wehr and Spitaler.[6] Even qualified assent will postulate a dual role for the bedouin in question: (1) as referees if not arbiters in linguistic disputes, and (2) as preservers and transmitters of *Jāhilī* poetry. Emphasis upon the first of these roles is symbolized in Muslim tradition by the claim of Basran grammarians to have got their linguistic information from none but authentic dwellers in the desert: نحن نأخذ اللغة من حرشة الضباب, a figure expanded to include the second role and made the object of not very subtle caricature in the fifth/eleventh century by Maʿarrī.[7] Though stories of the unreliability, venality, and even treachery of bedouin informants

[1] Cf. Mehren, *Rhetorik*, 120–1, but also Rabin, *West-Arabian*, 22–3.

[2] Suyūṭī, *Muzhir* i, 221; cf. Kahle, 'Readers', 70–1: the story was pressed into the service of a number of distinct but related causes; for the literary effect of similar traditions see also above, I pp. 42–3, II pp. 69–70.

[3] *Muzhir* i, 202, 209–10 and *passim*.

[4] See below, pp. 98–9.

[5] Cf. Weisberger, *Deutsch als Volksname*, 96, 252, 278–86; Kluge–Götze, *Wörterbuch*, 132–3.

[6] Nöldeke, *BSS*, 4–5 *vs.* Wetzstein, see below, p. 249; Blau, 'Bedouins', 42–51; Wehr, Review: Fück, 183–4; Spitaler, Review: Fück, 145–6.

[7] See Weil, *Schulen*, 41 n. 1; Maʿarrī, *Risālat al-ghufrān*, 168–9 on the name/sobriquet of the *mukhaḍramī* poet Aʿshā.

may reflect nothing more than school disputes, it would seem that these hardly functioned as disinterested referees.[1] It might be thought that the principle significance of the bedouin contribution, whether real or fabricated, to the formation of CA lay in the grammarians' concept of *iʿrāb*: as a term of linguistic description it may, after all, denote a self-conscious process of bedouinization.[2] As reference to a historical event *iʿrāb* is supported by evidence of a substantial *Völkerwanderung*.[3] For our purposes it is well to remember that the written record of transactions between bedouin and philologist dates only from the third/ninth century, and is thus coincident with the literary stabilization of both Quranic exegesis and Muslim historiography.

The reputation of bedouin as custodians of Arab eloquence rests upon the link connecting them with the creation, preservation, and transmission of *Jāhilī* poetry. For at least the second and third elements of that link Nöldeke's pessimistic assessment in 1864 was not materially modified by Blachère's cautiously optimistic account written nearly a century later.[4] Such factors as *variae lectiones*, infinitely variable line sequence, and a system of attribution which can only be described as irresponsible, do not inspire confidence in the philological tradition. On the other hand, disputes about the authenticity of the *Jāhilī* poetry seem to me almost entirely futile, so long as the evidence (*pro et contra*) is assessed in the light of traditional chronology. Two examples of this approach were the essay of Margoliouth and the retort of Bräunlich:[5] acceptance of the identity of scriptural with poetic language, of the historicity of the prophet's quarrel with the poets, and of the allegation that poetry was from the very first employed for scriptural exegesis (i.e. by ʿAbdallāh b. ʿAbbās), exhibits an unjustifiable and quite unnecessary acquiescence in the data of a normative tradition. It may be useful to distinguish between the content of the poetry and the use made of it by philologists. Assent to a putative bedouin environment requires analysis of both theme and imagery. Elements of either for which only bedouin origin is conceivable are very few indeed.[6] And even those will not support unequivocal conclusions about the date of composition of the verses in which they appear.

Such at least is the only legitimate inference from the contents of the anthology transmitted as the legacy of B. Hudhayl, thought to have been composed between 550 and 700.[7] Its value as historical source, for the

[1] Cf. Blachère, *Histoire* i, 117–27.

[2] Cf. Fleisch, *EI*, s.v. Iʿrāb; and see below, pp. 106–11.

[3] See Caskel, 'Zur Beduinisierung Arabiens', *28–36*.

[4] *Kenntnis der Poesie*, vi–xvii; Blachère, *Histoire* i, 83–186, esp. 166–79.

[5] 'Origins', 417–49; 'Frage der Echtheit', 825–33; cf. Shahid, 'Contribution', 564 n. 3. following Arberry and Gibb.

[6] See Blachère, *Histoire* ii, 368–453; Bräunlich, 'Versuch', esp. 222–38.

[7] Bräunlich, 'Versuch', 201–11.

origins both of CA and of Islam, must be accordingly modified. Bedouin poetry was not so much 'pre-Islamic' as it was 'un-Islamic', a distinction surely of some relevance to its use in solving chronological problems. Delineation of a *Jāhilī* ethos by reference to the binary opposition *muruwwa* (*virtus*, ἀρετή): *dīn* (religion, law) is subject to the same reservation.[1] Goldziher's conclusions on the nature of the conflict between Islam and paganism reflect an arbitrary chronology imposed upon rather than elicited from his source materials. Neither *muruwwa* as the embodiment of valour (*ḥamāsa*), nor *dīn* as essentially asceticism (*zuhd*) exhibits a chronological line of demarcation between Islam and *Jāhiliyya*. Bedouin rejection of religious prescription represents, after all, a constant in Islamic history, and can more profitably be interpreted as a reflex of social, economic, even regional dichotomies, and chronologically unlimited.[2] For the bulk of *Jāhilī* poetry information is more, not less, refractory than that pertinent to the Hudhalī *dīwān*: quite apart from the notorious lack of scruple attributed to transmitters (*ruwāt*), themselves often ambitious apprentice poets, biographical notices of *Jāhilī* authors are known to conform to a very few stereotypes extrapolated from the imagery of whatever verse might (fortuitously) have been ascribed to them.[3] That historiographical technique, by means of which metaphor generated reality, was the object of considerable parody in those passages of Maʿarrī's *R. Ghufrān* depicting the encounters of his protagonist Ibn al-Qāriḥ with a series of celebrated poets.[4] Easily the most famous example of aetiological exegesis is that of the *Muʿallaqāt* being 'suspended' in the Kaʿba: a combination of sanctuary tradition and witness to Arab eloquence was a temptation not easily resisted, even though only as an afterthought.[5]

It is, curiously, the religious imagery in *ḥaḍarī* (!) poetry, historically associated with the 'seeker of God' (*ḥanīf*) in Arabia, that appears to exhibit a link with the themes of Islamic revelation. Hirschberg's treatment of that material illustrated its ambivalent documentary value.[6] For each element there three distinct problems arise: relation of the verse in question to the Judaeo-Christian tradition (whether written or oral); relation of the verse to the Qur'ān; and finally, the authenticity of the verse. But solutions to the last tended to be subjective, and naturally based upon the traditional chronology of Islamic origins. Rejection of an intentional Muslim forgery of that poetry on the grounds that such would have undermined claims to originality made on behalf of the prophet of Islam is ingenuous: both the

[1] As in Goldziher, *Studien* i, 1–39.

[2] Cf. Bravmann, 'Background', 317–24, who regarded the concepts of *muruwwa* and *dīn* not as antithetical but as complementary.

[3] Blachère, *Histoire* i, 96–107, 161–6.

[4] Maʿarrī, *Risālat al-ghufrān*, 187 ff: ʿAdiy b. Zayd; 191: Abū Dhu'ayb.

[5] Blachère, *Histoire* i, 144–7, following Nöldeke, *Kenntnis*, xvii–xxiii.

[6] *Lehren*, 2–10.

content of scripture and of the exegetical tradition presuppose close association with Judaeo-Christian sources. On the other hand, the hypothesis of widespread forgery is unnecessary: isolated occurrence (however numerous the examples) of the schemata of revelation does not indicate imitation of the canonical text of scripture, or even that the canon existed. The recensions of source material for urban (Umayya b. Abī 'l-Ṣalt) and court poetry ('Adīy b. Zayd, Nābigha Dhubyānī, A'shā) are, after all, quite late.[1] It is not entirely insignificant that precisely this corpus of poetry was *not* accepted by (Muslim) philologists as evidence of Arabian *faṣāḥa*.[2] But literary analysis of the schemata of revelation must take account of the possibility at least of Arabic *Vorlagen*, and an Arabian tradition of monotheism might be thought, from the point of view of later Islamic orthodoxy, to have provided more appropriate reference than Arabic versions of Jewish and Christian materials. That such reservations were not, however, characteristic of the earliest Muslim exegesis is clear from examination of the haggadic literature.[3]

Whatever may have been the original motives for collecting and recording the ancient poetry of the Arabs,[4] the earliest evidence of such activity belongs, not unexpectedly, to the third/ninth century and the work of the classical philologists. The manner in which this material was manipulated by its collectors to support almost any argument appears never to have been very successfully concealed. The procedure, moreover, was common to all fields of scholarly activity: e.g. the early dating of a verse ascribed to the *mukhaḍramī* poet Nābigha Ja'dī in order to provide a pre-Islamic proof text for a common Quranic construction (finite verb form preceded by direct object),[5] Mubarrad's admitted invention of a *Jāhilī* verse as gloss to a lexical item in *ḥadīth*,[6] and Abū 'Amr b. 'Alā's candid admission that save for a single verse of 'Amr b. Kulthūm, knowledge of Yawm Khazāz would have been lost to posterity.[7] The three examples share at least one common motive: recognition of pre-Islamic poetry as authority in linguistic matters, even where such contained non-linguistic implications. Also common to all three is another, perhaps equally significant feature: Ibn Qutayba, who adduced the verse of Nābigha to explain/justify Quranic syntax, lived at the end of the third/ninth century, as did Mubarrad; Abū 'Amr, of whom no written works were preserved, lived in the second half of the second/eighth century, but this particular dictum was alluded

1 Hirschberg, *Lehren*, 14, 32–40.
2 Hirschberg, *Lehren*, 25–6, n. 3; see below, pp. 105–6.
3 See below, IV pp. 122–48.
4 A not very convincing enumeration in Blachère, *Histoire* i, 94–5.
5 Spitaler, Review: Bloch, 320.
6 Margoliouth, 'Origins', 431.
7 Ibn 'Abd Rabbih, *Al-'Iqd al-farīd* iii, 106–7; the problematic character of this particular one of the *ayyām al-'arab* may be guessed from its inclusion in Jāḥiẓ, *Kitāb al-Tarbī'*, 101.

to only in Jāḥiẓ (third/ninth century) and explicitly stated in Ibn ʿAbd Rabbih (fourth/tenth century). Now, that pre-Islamic poetry should have achieved a kind of status as linguistic canon some time in the third/ninth century may provoke no quarrel. That it had achieved any such status earlier must, I think, be demonstrated. The fact that it had not, in one field at least, can be shown: the absence of poetic *shawāhid* in the earliest form of scriptural exegesis might be thought to indicate that appeal to the authority of *Jāhilī* (and other) poetry was not standard practice before the third/ninth century.[1] Assertions to the contrary may be understood as witness to the extraordinary influence exercised by the concept of *faṣāḥat al-jāhiliyya*.

The utility of that concept is nowhere more apparent than in the interpretation of what otherwise might be held comparatively neutral references to language in the text of the Qur'ān. That Q. 14: 4 وما أرسلنا من رسول الا بلسان قومه could be made to bear diametrically opposed meanings has been noticed.[2] That generous view was, however, not shared by all exegetes, and Zamakhsharī was quite explicit on the point.[3] His cross-reference there to Q. 41: 44 ولو جعلناه قرآنا أعجميا لقالوا لولا فصّلت آياته ءأعجمى وعربىّ is significant because in that verse he interpreted *fuṣṣilat* as *buyyinat* (clarified) and the contrast between *aʿjamī* and *ʿarabī* as the absence and presence, respectively, of clarity.[4] The polarity reflects, of course, the terminology of arguments about (Arab) eloquence,[5] but for Q. 41: 44 produced, illogically, the meaning: is it an unclear (*qur'ān*) and an Arab (messenger)? The alternative: is it an unclear (*qur'ān*) and (yet) an eloquent (messenger), is not absolutely excluded, but Zamakhsharī's additional observation that *aʿjamī* might refer to barbarians (*ummat al-ʿajam*) makes the former interpretation rather more likely. Evidence of the transition from *aʿjam* as inarticulate to *aʿjam*/*ʿajam* as barbarian/non-Arab emerges from the literary references to *mawālī* in Islam assembled by Goldziher, especially where inferior social status was the consequence of both foreign blood and defective speech, e.g. *aʿjamu ṭimṭimiyyun*, *Ziyād al-aʿjam*, and *alḥān al-mawālī*.[6] I am inclined to interpret *aʿjam* as originally a term of linguistic description.

For a related verse, Q. 16: 103 ولقد نعلم أنهم يقولون انما يعلمه بشر لسان الذى يلحدون اليه أعجمى وهذا لسان عربىّ مبين Zamakhsharī defined *aʿjamī* as ineloquent (*ghayr bayyin*) and *ʿarabī mubīn* as clear (and) eloquent (*dhū bayān wa-faṣāḥa*).[7] It may be that collocation here of *mubīn* (clear/obvious)

[1] See below, IV pp. 216–18.
[2] See above, II p. 53.
[3] *Kashshāf* ii, 538–9 ad loc.
[4] *Kashshāf* iv, 202.
[5] See above, p. 93.
[6] *Studien* i, 101–46, esp. 103 n. 2, 118 n. 2, 120.
[7] *Kashshāf* ii, 635.

with *ʿarabī* facilitated this interpretation, but the same collocation in Q. 26: 194–5 على قلبك لتكون من المنذرين بلسان عربيّ مبين provoked the comment that *ʿarabī* must refer to the Arabic language because the heart of a prophet could only be affected by hearing his mother-tongue![1] Similarly, collocation of *ḥukm* with *ʿarabī* in Q. 13: 37 produced the explanation: an Arabic decision, translated into the language of the Arabs (حكمة عربية مترجمة بلسان العرب).[2] Collocation of *qur'ān* with *ʿarabī* (Q. 12: 2, 20: 113, 39: 28, 41: 3, 42: 7, 43: 3) did not invariably provoke the same response, and indeed for Q. 39: 28 the apposition *ghayra dhī ʿiwajin* (without distortion) might be thought anyway to have precluded such. Most occurrences of *lisān* in the text of scripture exhibit the use of 'tongue' as vocal organ rather than as language, and might appear to reflect the speech difficulties associated with the calling of Moses (cf. Exodus 4: 10–17). The locutions واحلل عقدة من لسانى (Q. 20: 27) and أفصح منّى لسانا (28: 34) refer of course to Moses, and it is worth recalling that the verses following upon Q. 14: 4 also take up the Mosaic narrative, in a manner indeed which suggests that the original function of verses 1–4 could have been to introduce that narrative. A similar instance was noted for the *isrā'* verse Q. 17: 1.[3] The imagery of Q. 19: 97 and 44: 58 فانما يسرناه بلسانك as well as of 54: 17, 22, 32, 40 (serving as refrain) ولقد يسرنا القرآن is more than merely reminiscent of Exodus 4: 15 ואנכי אהיה עם־פיך, and could support the hypothesis that linguistic allusions in the Qur'ān are not to the Arabic language but rather, to the task of prophetical communication.[4] That such eventually involved identification of the instrument by means of which the word of God was transmitted may seem not unreasonable, but the evidence of scripture itself yielded assistance only under duress.

. . . . .

The concept of *lingua sacra*, like that of the mythopoeic *faṣāḥat al-jāhiliyya*, belongs to a view of language as criterion of culture. The primary function of language so considered is not communication but edification. Its semantic spectrum is selective, its syntax stereotype and rhetorical, its style paraenetic. Whether specialized form is a consequence of specialized function, or vice versa, may be impossible to determine, at least as a generally valid proposition. What does seem clear is that linguistic data of that kind cannot be very profitably examined from the standpoint of 'the

[1] *Kashshāf* iii, 334–5.
[2] *Kashshāf* ii, 533; cf. also iv, 301 *ad* Q. 46: 12 and *lisān ʿarabī*.
[3] See above, II pp. 67–8.
[4] The traditional view is variously expressed in Horovitz, *Untersuchungen*, 75; Torrey, *Foundation*, 43–4; Obermann, 'Agada', 47–8; Widengren, *Apostle of God*, 151–2.

ordinary day-to-day requirements of a normal speech community'.[1] And yet, the derivation of normative grammar from scripture and poetry, if it ever meant more than merely theoretical accommodation of non-linguistic (e.g. theological) postulates, supposes just such a point of view. As a genre of narrative prose the scriptural style was examined by Auerbach in an essay designed to emphasize the contrast between Homer and the Elohist.[2] Of the nine factors adduced by the author as characteristic of Old Testament narrative, one in particular deserves mention here: the need for exegesis (*Deutungsbedürftigkeit*). This is not merely to say that the content of scripture is enhanced by commentary, or that it may be made to bear any number of (complementary and/or contradictory) interpretations, but that the scriptural style is itself incomplete without commentary. Reasons for that condition were partly syntactic (*Abgerissenheit, Stilmischung*), partly rhetorical (*Vielschichtigkeit, Hintergründigkeit*). The analysis can be extended to include at least one additional element, namely the symbolic quality inherent in scriptural diction. That quality may be regarded as one fundamentally semantic, enhanced by the crystallization of imagery which achieves an existence and application independent of its constituent elements, a distinction which might be covered by the contrast information *vs.* reference.[3] An example from Biblical literature was the Aramaic locution בר אנש.[4] For Muslim scripture those elements analysed here as schemata of revelation, appropriate to the theodicy and to prophetology, exhibit the metamorphosis of originally neutral notation conveying 'information' into significantly charged 'references'. The underlying change may be described as rhetorical, the references themselves as symbols (*Stichworte*) both requiring and producing exegesis. The interpretation thus generated spans a range limited to the spectrum of allusion contained in the imagery. For the Quranic revelation that range was preselected by the more or less unqualified employment of Biblical schemata. Analysis of the limits of interpretation is the subject of the following chapter; the question to be examined here is whether this particular example of *lingua sacra* could, or did, provide genuinely useful data for the grammar of Classical Arabic.

To what extent establishment and transmission of the text of scripture involved its grammatical analysis is a problem to which tentative solutions often reflect preconceptions elicited from non-linguistic data. For the Hebrew Masorah Bacher's view was that little, if any, grammatical description resulted from the activity of the Masoretes and then, as it were, only accidentally.[5] Later studies of the same phenomena reveal a

[1] Ullendorff, 'Is Biblical Hebrew a language?', 241. [2] *Mimesis*, 5–27.

[3] Barr, *Comparative Philology*, 118, 291–3; id. *Semantics*, 206–62; Vermes, *Scripture*, 11–66: on exegetical symbolism; see below, IV pp. 210–12.

[4] See Vermes, 'Jewish Aramaic'.

[5] 'Die Anfänge der hebräischen Grammatik', 8.

rather more generous assessment of Masoretic criteria, even if these had not produced descriptive terminology.[1] For the document of Islamic revelation acceptance of the ʿUthmanic recension traditions has entailed assent to a period of from 150 to 200 years between textual stabilization of the Qur'ān and analysis of its contents in the formulation of Arabic grammar. The implication must be that the text of scripture, like those of pre-Islamic poetry, was faithfully transmitted and intelligently read/recited and heard for a very long time indeed, without once provoking the questions about its meaning and its form with which the literature of the third/ninth century is filled. Logic alone might preclude serious consideration of this version of Islamic history. Examination, moreover, of the Quranic exegesis which I have called masoretic suggests that both the document of revelation and the corpus of pre-Islamic poetry were being there assembled, juxtaposed, and studied for the first time.[2]

Systematic collation of *loci probantes* from both sources, such as informs Zamakhsharī's *Mufaṣṣal* (sixth/twelfth century), represents the final stage of a long period of synthesis. The theological, as opposed to linguistic, nature of that dual source of grammar has been noticed.[3] It may further be observed that Zamakhsharī's concern with grammar in the most restricted sense of that term (i.e. morphology and juncture) permitted omission of the broader issues of syntax and even context, in consequence of which his *loci probantes* are stylistically neutral. As descriptive material they are also linguistically indifferent, consisting almost exclusively of deliberate and formalized utterances postulated as paradigms, from which deviation could only be regarded as corruption. The method is familiar, its results predictable. That these could, and occasionally did, provoke opposition seems clear from the formula attributed to Basran grammarians in their rejection of the Kufan practice of drawing grammatical analogies from scripture: فمجرد دعوى لا يقوم عليها دليل الا بوحى وتنزيل.[4] Such did not, of course, prevent the Basrans' adducing scripture where this supported their own arguments.[5] Unlike Zamakhsharī's normative grammar, Ibn Anbārī's description of grammatical dispute (also sixth/twelfth century) includes considerable discussion of syntax, though preponderantly of configurations generated by the use of tmesis, hyperbaton, chiasmus, etc. (*taqdīm wa-ta'khīr*), for which the styles of scripture and poetry might be thought appropriate arbiters. Neither work is, thus, free of concern with preciosity, whether grammatical or stylistic. In both, rhetorical ideals pass for linguistic

[1] Cf. Würthwein, *Text*, 11–22; Corré, 'Phonemic problems', 59–66; Gerhardsson, *Memory*, 43–55, esp. 52 n. 3 on the work of Kahle; Barr, *Comparative Philology*, 202–7, and 214–17 on Kahle.

[2] See below, IV pp. 202–27.

[3] Cf. also Vollers, Review: Nöldeke, 126–7; Kopf, 'Religious influences', 46–50.

[4] Ibn Anbārī, *Al-Inṣāf*, 137, cf. also 264, 392; Weil, *Schulen*, 80 n. 1.

[5] e.g. Ibn Anbārī, *Al-Inṣāf*, 47, 53, 61, 7 and *passim*.

description and the concept of grammar as a balance between analogy and anomaly with reference to an acceptable prose style is absent.

It is, however, necessary, even within this restricted framework, to ask whether the document of revelation ever became in any practical sense a model of linguistic usage. Probably the only recorded instance of agreement between Vollers and Nöldeke was about the character of Quranic syntax.[1] But while Nöldeke rightly concluded that such a collection of anacolutha must remain *sui generis*, Vollers shifted his ground just slightly, in order to bring into existence the hypothesis associated with his name since 1905: that the original (vernacular) text of the Qur'ān had been refashioned to meet the linguistic standard represented by pre-Islamic poetry, and so to produce what is known as CA (*'arabiyya*).[2] That view, which has found more or less unanimous dissent for reasons both sound and not so sound, involved a change of emphasis from syntax to accidence, more specifically to the properties of inflexion. The argument revealed a seductive, if in the event erroneous, logic, since it was only in the realm of inflective phenomena that Quranic usage might be seen to intersect that of *Jāhilī* poetry. The basic error lay in Vollers's adherence to an arbitrary and fictive chronology,[3] though that may have been less important than his contention that the refashioned language of scripture could be identified as the CA of the Arabic grammarians. Neither from the point of view of lexicon nor from that of syntax could the claim be justified.

An intrinsic feature of *lingua sacra* is its 'elevated style'. While there is undoubtedly something to be said for interpreting that characteristic as the impingement of poetic syntax upon prose, it may also be something more, or less, or quite different.[4] If it is true that Bloch's investigations resulted in a statement which tended to justify extrapolation of normative grammar from poetic texts, that was probably because his comparative material was drawn from what can most accurately be described as *Kunstprosa*.[5] His virtual omission of Quranic *shawāhid*, as well as of other examples of rhymed prose, may thus be seen as arbitrary, since their inclusion could hardly have altered his findings. On the other hand, the elevated style (*gehobene Sprache/Verheissungsstil*) associated with *Kunstprosa* need not have had its origins in poetry. The transformation of sub-literary, even vernacular, language into composition of sustained elevated style may be effected by nothing more than resort to an established rhetorical tradition.[6] An example was the creation of medieval Hebrew poetry, which, in addition to metrical features adapted from Arabic verse, depended for its

1 Vollers, op. cit. 127; Nöldeke, *NBSS*, 22–3.
2 *Volkssprache*, 175–85.
3 See above, p. 86.
4 See Bloch, *Vers und Sprache*, 30–1, 39; cf. Spitaler, Review, 320.
5 *Vers und Sprache*, 154–5: 'tabellarische Übersicht'.
6 Cf. Barr, *Comparative Philology*, 227–32: on 'restorations'; id. *Semantics*, 263–87.

aesthetic effect upon the incorporation of Biblical imagery, and hence Biblical syntax.[1] Such did not, of course, limit adaptation(s) from the Arabic poetic tradition, though the re-creation of these in Hebrew involved yet a further step in the mimetic process. But introduction of Biblical imagery, whether in Hebrew poetry or in Arabic scripture, may be regarded as the agent of an altered status for the language employed, and a reflex of style as *Bildungsprinzip*.[2] In the *lingua sacra* itself the principle of edification often took the form of linguistic archaism. A conscious resuscitation of past glory by recourse to language is symbolized for seventh-century Israel in the figure of Josiah and Deuteronomy (2 Kings 22–3).[3] In that and other examples of archaizing tendencies in literature the purpose was invariably paideutic (*Gemeindebildung*),[4] and often conceived as a panacea in conditions of social fragmentation. The linguistic tradition to which reformers and prophets, as well as poets, turn may be ancient. What it must be, is other than the current *usus loquendi*, and instances of that kind of archaization are abundant.[5]

The allegation of antiquity might seem a valuable corollary to the role of language in communal reformation. In Arabic philology the formative principle of language as sacred was applied also to that problem. Exegesis of Q. 2:31 وعلّم آدم الأسماء كلها ranged from the straightforward assertion that language was a divine creation, leaving the Quranic verse diametrically opposed to Genesis 2: 19–20, to the modified proposal that God enabled Adam to bestow the names أقدر آدم على أن واضع عليها, bringing thus the Quranic and Biblical notions somewhat closer.[6] A concept of purely rational revolution (*iṣṭilāḥ*) appears to have been displaced, or modified beyond recognition, by a number of pseudo-evolutionary theories linking the gift of pure speech with that of revelation (*tawqīf*), historically related to the period encompassed by Ishmael and Muhammad.[7] Implicit admission that pre-Ishmaelite Arabic (*sic*) was impure tended to be muddled by the assertion that the word of God (*kalām allāh*) was Arabic.[8] But the marginal development thus admitted had to cease with the revelation to Muhammad: فلا نعلم لغة من بعده حدثت.[9] The natural but not quite necessary transition

[1] See Goldziher, 'Bemerkungen zur neuhebräischen Poesie', 719–36; Mirsky, 'Biblical variants', 159–62; Gertner, 'Medieval Hebrew writing', 163–93.

[2] See Rabin, 'Qumran Hebrew', 144–61; Koch, *Growth*, 106–7; Seeligmann, 'Midraschexegese', 163.

[3] Cf. von Rad, *Theology* i, 77, and 81: on Lamentations 5: 21.

[4] See above, I pp. 51–2; II pp. 77–8, 82–4.

[5] Rabin, 'Qumran Hebrew', 159; id. *West-Arabian*, 17, references to Cantineau, Doughty, and Socin.

[6] Suyūṭī, *Muzhir* i, 8–11; cf. Geiger, *Was hat Mohammed*, 96–7; Kopf, 'Religious influences', 55–9.

[7] Suyūṭī, *Muzhir* i, 27–35.

[8] See above, II pp. 77, 83–4.

[9] Suyūṭī, *Muzhir* i, 9.

from word of God to language of God was not, of course, confined to Islam. Vaguely contradictory traditions achieved a remarkably comfortable co-existence: on the one hand, the seventy/seventy-two languages in which the Torah had been revealed/interpreted was reflected in the Pentecostal gift of tongues and in the Muslim version of the confusion at Babel;[1] on the other, the subsumption of indifferent Biblical designations of the Hebrew language under the Rabbinic concept of *leshon ha-qodesh*, reflected in Patristic assessments of both Septuagint Greek and Vulgate Latin,[2] and in the Muslim dogma of *tawqīf*. Scriptural references to the language of God, consisting for the most part either of metaphorical extensions of the 'word of God' or of allusions to the organ(s) of speech, could prove refractory. A passage like Ezekiel 3: 5 כי לא אל־עם עמקי שפה וכבדי לשון אתה שלוח אל בית ישראל may be thought typologically akin to Q. 14: 4 وما أرسلنا من رسول الا بلسان قومه: both exhibit the essentially ethnic orientation of the prophetical mission.[3] Neither verse restricted in the least theological inferences that identified the vehicle of revelation with the language of God.

If that language was Arabic internal variations had none the less to be isolated and eventually eliminated. The kind allocated to the period before Ishmael, like the varieties associated with Qaḥṭān and Jurhum, could be, and were, superseded by the fact of the Quranic revelation.[4] The at least theoretical identification of linguistic with confessional community which resulted from that argument (in so far as it ever achieved unanimous resolution) yielded a standard by which dialectical differences (*lughāt*) could be equated with heterodoxy and worse. A succinct statement of that procedure appears, unexpectedly, in Suyūṭī's discussion of the *imāla* and related phenomena, and in the form of a prophetical *ḥadīth*: اقرؤوا القرآن بلحون العرب وأصواتها واياكم وأصوات أهل الفسق وأهل الكتابين (Recite the Qur'ān with the rhythmic embellishment of the Arabs, and avoid that of sinners, Jews, and Christians).[5] Determination of the kind and degree of tendentiousness in that utterance will depend upon which of a multiplicity of interpretations is finally selected: I cannot but suspect that the hendiadys (?) *luḥūn wa-aṣwāt* is a reference to *iʿrāb*.[6] What does seem clear is the delimitation of yet a further dialect cleavage, here based on a confessional distinction: Muslims contrasted with infidels.[7] A version of the same *ḥadīth*, traced to the authority of Abū Hurayra and reported by Tustarī is more explicit: اقرؤوا القرآن بلحون العرب من غير تكلف لغيرها ولا

[1] Cf. Jeffery, 'Scripture', 130; Geiger, op. cit. 116; Suyūṭī, op. cit. i, 32.

[2] Bergsträsser, *Hebräische Grammatik* i, 9–10; Eissfeldt, *Einleitung*, 745–9; and see above, II pp. 81–2.

[3] See above, pp. 98–9; and II, pp. 53–4.

[4] Suyūṭī, *Muzhir* i, 30–5.

[5] *Itqān* i, 255.

[6] See below, pp. 110–11.

[7] See above, p. 87.

تقرؤوه بلحون أهل الكنائس والبيع وأهل الأهواء والبدع فإنى وأمتى الأتقياء براء من التكلف وانه سيأتى أقوام من بعدى يرجعون فيه أصواتهم تراجع القينات بالأغانى مفتونة قلوبهم فتانة القلب السامع اولئك هم الغافلون There the stigma was related specifically to the practice of synagogue and church (i.e. cantillation), which Tustarī in his commentary ascribed to 'diabolical possession' of the kind characteristic of the Jāhilī poets: حتى ملك إبليس قلوبهم كما ملك قلوب شعراء الجاهلية.[1] Now, reliable evidence of such dialect cleavage, apart from assertions derived from scattered and ambiguous testimony, hardly exists.[2] In his study of modern and contemporary materials exhibiting this kind of phenomenon, Blanc was sceptical of those few reports of earlier distinctions, and suggested that the later (!) major differentiation was probably a consequence of the bedouinization of Muslim sedentary dialects.[3]

From the prophetical tradition retailed by Tustarī and Suyūṭī it is, of course, impossible to draw specifically linguistic conclusions about varieties of spoken Arabic, either during the lifetime of the Arabian prophet or at whatever period this particular caveat may have been uttered. The statement is theological, not philological, but could be of some value in determining the function of *iʿrāb* and, further, the role of CA in the historical description of Islamic origins. Similarly, the story of ʿAbdallāh b. ʿAtīk's dispatch by the prophet on an especially delicate mission 'because he could talk like the Jews' (لانه كان يرطن باليهودية) may be understood as the historical projection of a polemical, and very likely much later, impulse: communal discrimination on the basis of an alleged difference in linguistic usage.[4] Severe comment on the 'Christian dialect' (*ʿibādiyya*) of the *Jāhilī* poet ʿAdīy b. Zayd might be thought to reflect the same impulse, here motivated by the Islamic appropriation of *Jāhilī* poetry as its rightful legacy.[5] Historical conclusions about the Christian origins of what became CA, derived from evidence of this type, are perhaps ingenuous.[6] On the other hand, the inverse conclusions invariably drawn from the data of 'pre-Islamic' poetry written by Jews are simplistic; that material is subject to the caveats applicable to the entire corpus of *Jāhilī* poetry (comprising not only Jewish, but also Christian and *ḥanīf* elements), the linguistic value of

[1] *Tafsīr*, 8–9.

[2] e.g. Goldziher, 'Literatur der muhammedanischen Mystik', 766 n. 5; id. 'Mélanges judéo-arabes', 14 n. 4; Lammens, *Arabie*, 81; Fück, *ʿArabīya*, 88; and in general, Torrey, *Foundation*, 17, 47–53.

[3] *Communal dialects in Baghdad*, 167–71, esp. 202 n. 180.

[4] Wāqidī, *Kitāb al-Maghāzī*, 392; cf. Fück, *ʿArabīya*, 88 n. 1; and *BSOAS* xxxi (1968) 149.

[5] See the caricature of those attitudes in Maʿarrī, *Risālat al-Ghufrān*, 192–3.

[6] e.g. Wellhausen, *Reste*, 232–3; Rabin, 'Beginnings', 27–8.

which cannot be separated from its theological significance.[1] The judgement of Fück, that the Christian poet Akhṭal could never have been recognized as 'classical' had his language (*sic*: *langue courante*) been different from that of non-Christians, may be cited as characteristic of that kind of argument.[2]

The later evidence of Middle Arabic, found largely in texts of Jewish and Christian provenance, belongs of course to a different sphere, and attests to a dichotomy between spoken and written Arabic even within the Muslim community.[3] It is none the less not impossible that the linguistic situation described as Middle Arabic and extensively analysed in Blau's studies was typical also of the earlier period, from which the emergence of CA might represent a substantial deviation.[4] Against such a background the prophetical *ḥadīth* adduced by Tustarī and Suyūṭī could acquire added meaning: Muslims were exhorted to use a language other than that associated with non-Muslims. Now, it may be that the language recommended was also the language of God, and of Quraysh, and of the Arabian prophet (for Quranic recitation or otherwise), but in this particular context it was the emblem of a religious community, serving as a badge of distinction. The functional value of that language could, indeed, have figured more than just marginally in its historical description.

. . . .

Those elements of Classical Arabic which have been of most use for studies in comparative Semitic philology are its inflective properties. From the orthography of CA it is difficult but possible to discern specific syntactic values for a range of phenomena traditionally accepted as evidence of the preservation in CA of Proto-Semitic case and mood.[5] To infer from this evidence that CA exhibits an archaic form of Semitic language, or that inflexion is indispensable for its communicative efficacy, is in my opinion unjustified. That interpretation rests, as I have in several contexts suggested, upon a chronological and geographical framework that is nebulous and anyway unverifiable. A typical example of that kind of inference is the description of CA orthography as uniformly 'pausal' proposed by Nöldeke, a consequence presumably of his understanding of the Quranic evidence.[6] More recently W. Fischer suggested that several instances of so-called 'pausal' forms which occur in the Qur'ān might, rather, be interpreted as

[1] See Nöldeke, *Kenntnis der Poesie*, 52–86.

[2] *'Arabīya*, 88.

[3] See Blau, *Emergence*, 1–18.

[4] Cf. my remarks on Blau, *Grammar of Christian Arabic*, in *BSOAS* xxxi (1968) 610–11.

[5] *GVG* i, 459–66, 554–9; Moscati, *Comparative Grammar*, 94–6, 134–6.

[6] *BSS*, 7; id. *NBSS*, 6: 'Aller Anfang ist eben schwer', etc.; also *GdQ* iii, 27; Birkeland, *Pausalformen*, 10.

exhibiting the syllabic structure characteristic of modern Arabic.[1] Irregularity of Quranic rhyme makes it refractory material upon which to construct phonetic analogies,[2] but Fischer's proposals relating to the behaviour of *tā marbūṭa* (i.e. exhibiting *-ā*→*ah*/st. const. *-at*), especially in *Sūra* 80, make more sense of that phenomenon than does the traditional description in terms of an opposition *at*: *ah*.[3] On the other hand, Fischer's investigations caused him to postulate an early date for the onset of Middle Arabic (i.e. '*neuarabisch*') morphological structures,[4] rather than a later date for establishment of the Quranic text. His reasons were the traditional ones, and turn upon the inflective properties of Quranic Arabic.

While it may be true that the text of the Qur'ān displays a linguistic situation in which syntactic values correspond for the most part to orthographic convention,[5] that fact does not of itself yield information towards dating establishment of the text. Moreover, the instances in which the consonantal text does not indicate syntactic relations far outnumber those in which it does. That such may be regarded as a fortuitous shortcoming of the Arabic alphabet cannot diminish in any way the importance of observing that the missing orthographic detail was supplied by resort to *textual exegesis*. The procedure to that end, as well as the substance itself, was called *iʿrāb*; the exegetical activity was the work of the Muslim masoretes and belongs to the third/ninth century.[6] According to a long and popular tradition, of which the most recent exponent was Fück, parts of the Qur'ān could not be understood without *iʿrāb*.[7] Assertions of that sort date back at least to Ibn Qutayba (d. 276/889), whose discussion at this point reveals a characteristic lack of concern for stress, pause, context, gesture, and other rhetorical factors normally the accompaniment of human utterance. Thus, the putative contrasts هذا قاتلٌ أخى/هذا قاتلُ أخى and لا يقتلْ/لا يقتلُ قرشى صبرا بعد اليوم were claimed to contain the same inherent ambivalence as Q. 36: 76 فلا يحزنك قولهم إنّا/أنّا نعلم ما يسرّون وما يعلنون.[8] Of that

[1] 'Silbenstruktur', esp. 45–53, 53–60; vaguely anticipated by A. Fischer, 'Arab. aysh', 816.

[2] See below, pp. 116–17.

[3] 'Silbenstruktur', 57–8; I am unable to follow the objection of Blau to this argument on the grounds that because the accusative was 'too different' it was adapted to the nominative/genitive for nouns of this category, see 'Linguistic setting', 11; id. 'L'Apparition', 199 n. 3; id. *Pseudo-corrections*, 57 n. 14; the contrast *thamānya*/*thamān*, cf. id. *Christian Arabic*, 57–8, is not in my opinion functionally analogous to the grammatical differentiation of nouns ending in *tā marbūṭa*; cf. also Birkeland, *Pausalformen*, 96–8, esp. 97 n. 1, rejected by Blau.

[4] 'Silbenstruktur', 59–60, but see Blau's cogent objections to that designation in the references cited in preceding note.

[5] See Nöldeke, *BSS*, 1–4; id. *NBSS*, 1–5.

[6] See above, pp. 95, 105; and below, IV pp. 219–27.

[7] *ʿArabīya*, 3.

[8] *Ta'wīl*, 11–12.

reasoning Zamakhsharī made curt dismissal, explaining the non-canonical *annā* as an elliptical form of *li-annā* (على حذف لام التعليل).[1] Similarly, the passages adduced by Fück, i.e. Q. 2: 124 واذ ابتلى ابراهيمَ ربُّه; Q. 9: 3 أن الله برئ من المشركين ورسولُه; and Q. 35: 28 إنما يخشى اللهَ من عباده العلماءُ could be, and were, analysed to show that any and all readings produced acceptable, and often identical, meanings.[2] A further impression of the manner in which this particular problem was approached by the exegetes may be gained from the subdivision of Suyūṭī's chapter on Quranic *iʿrāb* in which are set out twenty-five verses that could be read with all three case inflexions (ما قرئ بالتثليث من حروف القرآن).[3] Even the several much-discussed instances of orthographic deviation from the grammatical standard of inflexion, e.g. Q. 2: 177, 4: 162, 5: 69, 20: 63, could be accommodated by refining the boundaries between *casus rectus* and *casus obliquus*.[4] Of these the *locus classicus* was Q. 20: 63 إن هذان لساحران, to the various solutions of which a good share of masoretic method may be traced.[5] The traditional crux was the syntactic function of the accusative/adverbial case, interpreted to cover a quite extraordinary range of phenomena. For the Quranic text these included ambivalent value for the particle *iyyā*, represented by the variant اياك تُعبَد in Q. 1: 4 اياك نَعبُد;[6] by an optional nominative/accusative in constructions based on *ammā*, e.g. in Q. 41: 17 أما ثمودُ/ثمودَ فهديناهم;[7] and by considerable latitude in the formation of object pronominal suffixes with verbs terminating in *ūn/ūna*, e.g. Q. 15: 54 فبِمَ تبشرونَ/تبشرونِ and 39: 64 قل أفغير الله تأمروني/تأمرونني اعبد ايها الجاهلون.[8] The arbitrary, if not irresponsible, nature of this treatment was not limited to the grammar of scripture, and in other contexts provoked caustic observations on the activities of grammarians, e.g. in the celebrated *mas'ala zunbūriyya*,[9] and in the reaction of men like ʿAdīy b. Zayd, Nābigha Jaʿdī, and Farazdaq to

[1] *Kashshāf* iv, 29 *ad* Q. 36: 76.

[2] e.g. *Kashshāf* i, 183–4, ii, 245, iii, 610–1, respectively; cf. Spitaler, Review: Fück, 147 nn. 19, 22; Wehr, Review: Fück, 181; Fück's fourth example, Q. 4: 8, exhibiting orthographical evidence of case, was omitted from the French edition.

[3] *Itqān, nawʿ* 41: ii, 277–80.

[4] Cf. Vollers, *Volkssprache*, 163, including further examples derived from variant readings.

[5] See *GdQ* iii, 2–6; Wansbrough, 'Periphrastic exegesis', 264; and below, IV pp. 222–4.

[6] Ibn Hishām, *Mughnī 'l-labīb* i, 96: ascribed to Ḥasan Baṣrī; cf. Suyūṭī, *Itqān* i, 216: anonymous.

[7] Kofler, 'Reste', 255–6 (Part 3).

[8] Wansbrough, 'Periphrastic exegesis', 252 no. 27; Vollers, Review: Nöldeke, 134.

[9] Ibn Anbārī, *Al-Inṣāf* no. 99 (pp. 702–6); cf. Fischer, 'Zunbūrija', 150–6; Blau, 'Bedouins', 42–51.

philological interpretations of their poetry.[1] Anecdotes of that sort, whether or not apocryphal, might be thought to cast some doubt on the traditional description of CA.

It might also seem that the primary function of *iʿrāb* was not, or at least not exclusively, grammatical. If, indeed, syntactic relations could be adequately expressed by insertion of *iʿrāb*, it would hardly appear, even from the few examples given here, that they could not otherwise be expressed. Nöldeke's much-cited *pièce justificative* demonstrated that the constituents of *iʿrāb* were not unique in Semitic philology, but neither that their grammatical values were constant nor that they were intrinsically essential to the expression of syntax in CA.[2] Defence of the authenticity (*sic*), as opposed to the function, of *iʿrāb* had already been undertaken by Derenbourg in a transparent *argumentum ad hominem*.[3] A distinction between form and function was hardly adumbrated in the works of Muslim philologists. Suyūṭī's references, as well as his own observations, stressed the syntactic value of *iʿrāb* for both scripture and profanc litcrature.[4] From his treatment of the subject, however, one impression in particular emerges, namely, that insertion of the *iʿrāb* into any given locution required first knowing what it meant.[5] Not related perhaps to this paradoxical formulation, but none the less relevant, is Suyūṭī's distinction between the '*iʿrāb* of the grammarians' and the '*iʿrāb* whose recitation in the Qur'ān will be rewarded in heaven' (المراد بإعرابه معرفة معانى ألفاظه وليس المراد به الإعراب المصطلح عليه عند النحاة وهو ما يقابل اللحن لان القراءة مع فقده ليست قراءة ولا ثواب فيها).[6] Vollers interpreted this passage as question-begging, and understood the *iʿrāb* defined there to refer to 'die stilistischen und rhetorischen Feinheiten (die aus dem grammatischen Iʿrāb gefolgert werden)'.[7] Whatever that may mean, it was Vollers himself whose studies provided support for an earlier view that the function of *iʿrāb* was essentially that of rhythmic *ornatus*.[8] The point had been made by Wetzstein, with reference to bedouin practice, that poetry was intended to be sung and hence required an abundance of vowels: 'Alle diese Bestimmungen über den Wegfall oder die Verkümmerung der kurzen Vocale gelten für die Umgangssprache, nicht für die Poesie. Das Gedicht

[1] Maʿarrī, *Risālat al-Ghufrān*, 183 (for ʿAdīy's allegation that *hamz* was an Islamic innovation), 202–3; cf. Nöldeke, *Kenntnis der Poesie*, 31–2.

[2] *BSS*, 1–10; cf. Corriente, 'Functional yield', 20–50; and Blau, 'Synthetic character', 29–38.

[3] 'Quelques remarques', 210–11.

[4] *Itqān*, *nawʿ* 41: ii, 260–80; id. *Muzhir* i, 327–8; the preponderant role of syntax and the exclusion of much that was traditionally subsumed under morphology renders 'inflexion' an unsatisfactory translation of *iʿrāb*, cf. Fleisch, *EI*, s.v. Iʿrāb.

[5] *Itqān* ii, esp. 260–1, 269.

[6] *Itqān*, *nawʿ* 36: ii, 3.

[7] *Volkssprache*, 181.

[8] *Volkssprache*, 165–75, and see references above, pp. 86–7.

des Nomaden ist bestimmt gesungen zu werden und der Gesang liebt die Reibungen der Consonanten nicht, sondern braucht Vocale'.[1] Transfer of that axiom from bedouin poetry to Muhammad's recitation of the Qur'ān (*sic*) may be thought gratuitous; the source of *iʿrāb* was in any case 'bedouin' poetry. In this context it could be worth remarking that the only cogent argument adduced by Derenbourg in favour of *iʿrāb* was that without it Arabic poetry would no longer scan (*sic*): 'D'ailleurs, toutes les poésies arabes, dont une partie a été longtemps transmise seulement par tradition orale, perdraient le rythme qui leur est indispensable, si l'on ne reconnaissait pas l'authenticité de la déclinaison arabe'.[2]

Now, whether the scansion of Arabic verse ever depended exclusively upon regular variation of syllable length, and hence *iʿrāb*, is a question complicated by the predominantly theoretical character of Arabic prosody: that scansion was accentual as well as quantitative is more than likely.[3] But Wetzstein's observations on the avoidance of consonantal friction and the necessity of vowels are in either case, or both, apposite. In a discussion of optional modes of poetic recitation, Sībawayh contrasted employment of (*a*) *tarannum*, in which all final vowels were pronounced long (*madd al-ṣawt*), with (*b*) the (*Tamīmī*) practice of adding *-n* (presumably *tanwīn*) to all final short vowels irrespective of grammatical circumstances, and with (*c*) the omission of all final vowels (save *ā*), as in prosaic pausal position.[4] In the light of modern vernacular prosody, the attested antiquity of the third mode is not without interest. Similarly, in a late treatise (seventh/thirteenth century) on poetics Ḥāzim Qarṭājannī enumerated the devices employed in verse to achieve aesthetic effect, among which figured the *ḥurūf al-tarannum* and/or *ḥurūf muṣawwita*.[5] Affixed to certain class(es) of frequently occurring words, those vowels produced continuity of sound (*jarayān al-ṣawt*) and transition between words (*nuqla*), and served also to mark off (*farq*) separate themes and images. That here *iʿrāb* was meant seems clear, not merely from context but also from employment of the descriptive terms *lawāḥiq* and *niyāṭa* (affix/suffix). Though appended according to fixed prescription, the primary function of those vowels is not syntactic, save possibly as thematic markers (*furūq*), but, rather, rhetorical, and might be thought to correspond to that of Suyūṭī's non-grammatical *iʿrāb*.[6] That distinction, however, will hardly have been other than one of function, since *iʿrāb* vowels must have been formally identical, whether aesthetically or syntactically applied. It may be of some interest to note that in the examples assembled by Kofler of verse exhibiting attrition of

[1] 'Sprachliches aus den Zeltlagern', 193–4.

[2] 'Quelques remarques', 210–11.

[3] See Weil, *Grundriss und System*, 104–5, but also 86.

[4] Sībawayh, *Kitāb*, para. 507, cited Birkeland, *Pausalformen*, 10–18.

[5] *Minhāj al-bulaghā'*, 122–4: trans. Heinrichs, *Arabische Dichtung*, 252–5.

[6] See above, p. 109; and also his observation that *iʿrāb* in the sense of grammatical inflexion was a neologism, below, IV p. 155.

those vowels, the rhetorical (acoustical) effect of *iʿrāb* is not markedly diminished.[1]

Application of the term *tarannum* to Qur'ān recitation signified cantillation, and was thus related to *laḥn* in the sense not of defective speech, but of melody.[2] The expression *bi-luḥūni 'l-ʿarab wa-aṣwātihā* employed in the tradition adduced by Tustarī and Suyūṭī would seem, indeed, to convey an exhortation to employ *iʿrāb*, not because the language of Jews and Christians, and others disqualified from membership of the Muslim community, was ungrammatical, but because it was not that of Arab bedouin. Suyūṭī's use of the term *laḥn* is, however, not unequivocal: in the passage on non-grammatical *iʿrāb*, *laḥn* was adduced merely as theoretical antithesis of the grammatical variety of *iʿrāb*, while elsewhere he rejected the allegation that *laḥn* as *lapsus calami* (*khaṭa' al-kuttāb*) could be present in the text of scripture.[3] This usage is naturally not that of the prophetical tradition, for which it was proposed that *luḥūn wa-aṣwāt* is a hendiadys meaning rhythmic embellishment(s). Now, it may seem that discussions of Qur'ān recitation with and without *iʿrāb* could profit from attention to these several nuances. Apart from references to the practice of Muhammad, which complicate unnecessarily a diachronic description of CA, failure to consider differentiation of the *terminus technicus iʿrāb* has meant placing inordinate emphasis upon the evidence of both scripture and poetry for purposes of linguistic analysis. From Suyūṭī's interpretation of the traditions promising celestial reward for recitation with *iʿrāb* it emerges that such was not a matter of grammar: recitation without *iʿrāb* was, after all, to be rewarded by half that promised for recitation with (من قرأ القرآن فأعربه كان له بكل حرف عشرون حسنة ومن قرأه بغير إعراب كان له بكل حرف عشر حسنات).[4] The use of such material for serious philological argument seems somehow unjustified.[5]

. . . . .

Expression of syntactic relations in Arabic could not be, nor was it in practice, limited to or even dependent upon those devices collectively and symbolically designated *iʿrāb*. Both sequence (word order) and segmentation (conjunctive/disjunctive markers) bear a considerable portion, if not the whole, of that burden. Incorporation of these two principles in the styles of poetry and scripture, as well as of *Kunstprosa*, must and did result in a set of modifications most conveniently described as rhetorical.

1 'Reste' (Part 3), 26–30 (case), 235–40 (mood).

2 Cf. Fück, *ʿArabīya*, 196–8, esp. 197 n. 16; *GdQ* iii, 193–4, 232–3; Hirschfeld, *Researches*, 115.

3 *Itqān* ii, 3, and 269–75 on grammatical *iʿrāb*.

4 *Itqān* ii, 3: also a prophetical *ḥadīth*.

5 But cf. Kahle, 'Readers', 65–71; Wehr, Review: Fück, 181; Spitaler, Review: Fück, 146; Rabin, 'Beginnings', 25–6.

Bloch's analysis of those styles revealed a high degree of procedural uniformity which ought not to be confused with what is often called 'normal linguistic usage'.[1] Reference, explicit or implicit, to the latter for description of the Quranic style could seem almost insidious: if the only contemporary *loci probantes* are those found in *Jāhilī* poetry the argument is bound to be circular; if, however, it is conceded that the chancery papyri qualify as contemporary comparative material, their linguistic content cannot then fairly be judged inferior to the standard of CA. The problem can hardly be solved by deriving that standard from the data of poetry and scripture. It might seem superfluous to add, at this point, that in my judgement the notions of CA origins underlying Nöldeke's celebrated 'Sündenregister' of Quranic usage are very questionable indeed.[2] Extrapolated from his surprisingly uncritical acceptance of a pseudo-historical portrait of the Arabian prophet, opinions about the psychological relationship of Muhammad to his public (e.g. 'Unsicherheit', 'Unbeholfenheit', 'Verlegenheit', 'Wiederholung als Einschärfung', 'den Arabern war eben fast alles neu', 'aller Anfang ist schwer', etc.) became organizing principles of linguistic description. The result was a fairly systematic and thoroughly relentless critique of a personal and individual style.

But observed from the standpoint of rhetorical schemata and organic development, the uneven quality of scriptural style seems quite appropriate to a document recognized by a religious community as the literary expression of divine authority. Recurrence of formulaic phraseology, for example, might reflect conventional links between related but originally separate traditions, rather than one man's lack of rhetorical skill. Moreover, the recurrent formulae are functionally distinct, and their uses may thus be ascribed to different motives, e.g. apodictic, supplicatory, narrative.[3] Similarly, repetition of rhyme words in *sūra*s 25, 4, 19, and elsewhere may be interpreted as the same kind of linkage, extended occasionally to the dimension of a proper refrain.[4] Rhyme, as well as assonance and other paronomastic formations, operate conjunctively and disjunctively in the manner of conventional markers: resultant constructions like those based on epexegetic *min* and the juxtaposition of perfect and imperfect/past continuous can hardly be said to cause semantic distortion.[5] In the light of a plural *anhār*, the singular *nahar* in Q. 54: 54 could not have been preferred for the sake of rhyme, and was anyway interpreted by Zamakhsharī

[1] See above, pp. 91–2, 99–100, 102–3.

[2] *NBSS*, 5–23; cf. Spitaler, Review: Fück, 146.

[3] Nöldeke, *NBSS*, 8–9; the liturgical/cultic value of *qul* justifies many of its occurrences, cf. above, I pp. 13–15.

[4] *NBSS*, 9; see above, I pp. 13, 19, 26.

[5] See below, pp. 116–17; pace Nöldeke, *NBSS*, 9; cf. Reckendorf, *Arabische Syntax*, 256 para. 3a, but also 254 para. 2b for *min*, and 10–11 for 'präsentisch resultativ'; cf. *BSOAS* xxxi (1968) 612.

as generic.[1] Condemnation of disjunctive formulae like والله عزيز حكيم etc. as stylistic superfluities was consistent with adverse criticism in general of recurrent locutions, but reveals in my opinion a mistaken notion of the document's composition, and especially of its halakhic and narrative components.[2] As for the accusation of illogic in Q. 10: 43, 27: 80, and 30: 52, it seems abundantly clear from the context of these verses that the epithets 'blind' and 'deaf' were intended and understood figuratively, that is 'wilfully blind and deaf to the truth'.[3] I find unconvincing Nöldeke's bewilderment at the sudden changes of interlocutor (God, angels, *jinn*) in Q. 37: 164 ff. and 72: 15–16. Discontinuity of that kind is common in Muslim scripture and may be compared with other more fundamental lines of cleavage, such as the truncated structure of variant traditions.[4] In Q. 72: 15–16 the introductory particles are anyway not those employed for the preceding speech of the *jinn*, and might well signal a change of speaker.

Nöldeke's treatment of Quranic simile was stringent to the point of being quite unimaginative.[5] Much of the imagery there is admittedly primitive, but comparison of the lot of almsgivers to the increased fruits of the field blessed by God (Q. 2: 261, 265) and that of the mean to the produce of stony and barren soil (Q. 2: 264) is neither illogical nor entirely unsuccessful. Further, comparison of that which is spent in vanity with (the effect of) an icy wind (Q. 3: 117) is not at all inconsistent, especially in the light of that verse's ending: وما ظلمهم الله ولكن أنفسهم يظلمون. Nöldeke's objection to the formulation of a *secundum comparationis* as instrument rather than effect in Q. 3: 117, as in 10: 24 and 18: 45, appears to me to rest upon a very literal interpretation of metaphorical language. In Q. 2: 17–19 it is God's extinguishing of it, not the fire itself, which must be set against the storm producing darkness. Q. 47: 15, on the other hand, does exhibit some syntactical confusion, owing to what must be the lengthy interpolative gloss to *janna*, though it could be argued that the *primum comparationis* is not *janna* at all, but rather the *a-fa-man . . . ka-man* construction of the preceding verse. But there, and in the following example (Q. 9: 19) there is, indeed, disequilibrium between substantival constructions as first term and finite verbal/pronominal constructions as second term of the simile. Finally, for Q. 31: 28 I suspect that the locution *ka-nafsin wāḥidatin* is intended to convey *ka-shay'in wāḥidin* (as one thing/act).[6] It is almost possible to understand Zamakhsharī's commentary to that verse as at least

[1] *NBSS*, 9; *Kashshāf* iv, 442 ad loc.: *ism al-jins*, but it is more than likely that *jannāt*, here employed eschatologically, was understood as singular, see above, I pp. 27, 29.

[2] *NBSS*, 9–10.

[3] *NBSS*, 10; cf. Q. 2: 18–20, 7: 79, 11: 24, 47: 23; Isaiah 43: 8, Matthew 13: 10–17 alluding to Isaiah 6: 9–10.

[4] *NBSS*, 10; and see above, I pp. 20–7.

[5] *NBSS*, 10–11.

[6] *Pace* Sister, 'Metaphern', 130; that schematic compilation is, however, very useful; cf. also Buhl, 'Vergleichungen', 1–11; and below, IV pp. 239–42.

implicit support for this interpretation: أن لو شغله شأن عن شأن وفعل عن فعل.[1]

Inconcinnity like the parallelism of determined and undetermined substantives in Q. 42: 49 is of course not infrequent in the Qur'ān, though this particular example appears to have been a consequence of the necessary pausal/rhyme form, and is perhaps conspicuous only because of occurrence in the next verse of a related locution, both members of which are undetermined.[2] Q. 27: 1 offers a less felicitous target for criticism (read anyway آيات القرآن و كتاب مبين), since the scriptural designations *qur'ān* and *kitāb* may refer to portions of or to the whole of revelation, a distinction often expressed by absence and presence, respectively, of the definite article.[3] To attribute some repetition to affection for the *figura etymologica* is sound enough,[4] but Q. 4: 136 contains a fixed formula of address (يا ايها الذين آمنوا) which can hardly be said anywhere in the Qur'ān to influence, or to be influenced by, the expression which follows. Similarly, the particle *ka-dhālika* in Q. 2: 113, 118 may be understood as presentative 'thus' and quite without influence upon the following locution (for Q. 2: 118 read من قبلهم).[5] Q. 6: 161 إننى هدانى ربّى الى صراط مستقيم دينا قيما ملة ابراهيم حنيفا وما كان من المشركين is indeed awkward, its clumsy syntax in my opinion a result of distinctly theological patchwork. Abraham's role in Islamic prophetology and the doctrinal nature of the epithets *ḥanīf* and *milla*, rather than an aesthetic failing, might be thought to account for this very curious construction.[6] The phrase الا قليلا مما تأكلون in Q. 12: 47, 48 is an appositional relative clause and may be idiomatic.[7] Similarly, the locution فهو جزاؤه which must be read in the whole context of Q. 12: 74–5, might qualify not merely as idiomatic but as a fair example of *erlebte Rede*.[8] Nor do I find illogical the pronominal construction in Q. 35: 11, in which it is a question of one man's life being either lengthened or shortened. Moreover, Q. 17: 74, which contains a straightforward concessive construction, appears to make perfect sense without Nöldeke's paraphrastic translation.[9] Confusion of function between the concessive particles *wa-in* and *wa-law* is a matter of degree rather than of kind, and thus difficult to insist upon.[10] That Q. 12: 17 وما أنت بمؤمن لنا ولو كنّا صادقين would be logically improved by substitution

[1] *Kashshāf* iii, 502 *ad* Q. 31: 28.
[2] *NBSS*, 11.
[3] See above, II pp. 74–6.
[4] *NBSS*, 11.
[5] Cf. Hebrew *lakhen*; see above, I pp. 12–13.
[6] *NBSS*, 11; cf. Q. 3: 66, 16: 20, and above, II p. 54.
[7] *Pace* Nöldeke, *NBSS*, 12; cf. Reckendorf, *Arabische Syntax*, 435–6.
[8] *Pace* Nöldeke, *NBSS*, 12; cf. Reckendorf, op. cit. 286.
[9] *NBSS*, 12; cf. Reckendorf, op. cit. 495.
[10] *NBSS*, 12, 21; cf. Reckendorf, op. cit. 494, 513.

of *wa-in* for *wa-law* is just possible, though I am inclined, in view of the predominantly vernacular context of *Sūrat Yūsuf*, to see here the trace of popular idiom. It may be of some interest to record that whereas Kalbī inserted *wa-in* without comment, Zamakhsharī resorted to paraphrase: 'even though (*wa-law*) we were in your opinion men of truth and reliability'.[1]

Two categories of Nöldeke's 'stilistische Eigentümlichkeiten' are recognized types of exegetical problem, for treatment of which specific rules were formulated by the masoretes: change of number and change of person.[2] The phenomena adduced here became early on part of the established masorah, and provided the evidence from which the principle of *majāz/taqdīr* was derived.[3] Nowhere perhaps, does the impression of mechanically linked prophetical *logia* emerge more clearly than from observation of this discrete syntax, e.g. reference to God alternately in first and third person.[4] The likelihood of textual mutilation as consequence of pre-ʿUthmanic methods of preservation seems to be remote,[5] and could hardly explain the consistent lack of logical structure in the document. Capricious syntax would appear to reflect not the Arabian prophet's imperfect grasp of CA, but, rather, that mechanical linkage. Nöldeke's detailed discussion of ellipsis would be even more persuasive read in the way I have suggested, especially the 'pendant' narrative formulae.[6] Incidentally, linking *wa-rusulan* and *rusulan* in Q. 4: 164–5 with *innā awḥaynā* of the preceding verse is not quite so far-fetched as Nöldeke appeared to believe, though that lengthy enumeration probably owes its existence to a series of arbitrary connections.[7] It may be that many instances of pleonasm, as of ellipsis, were the result of separate *logia* traditions roughly co-ordinated. Pleonastic negation, on the other hand, often exhibits vernacular idiom, as surely in Q. 6: 109 وما يشعركم أنها اذا جاءت لا يؤمنون.[8] The references to anacolutha could be infinitely expanded,[9] e.g. Q. 7: 2 كتاب أنزل اليك فلا يكن فى صدرك حرج منه لتنذر به وذكرى للمؤمنين a formulation upon which conscientious and grammatically minded exegetes spent many words indeed. However one might interpret the stylistic aberrations of Muslim scripture, Nöldeke's conclusion that the work was, and must remain, *sui generis* can hardly be challenged: 'Der

[1] *Tafsir*, MS Ayasofya 118, 129r ad loc.; *Kashshāf* ii, 451.
[2] *NBSS*, 12–13, and 13–14, respectively.
[3] See Wansbrough, 'Periphrastic exegesis', 254–9; and below, IV pp. 219–27.
[4] See above, I p. 28.
[5] *NBSS*, 14, 16 n. 1.
[6] *NBSS*, 15–19.
[7] *NBSS*, 15–16; see above, I pp. 34–5 on *waḥy/irsāl*.
[8] *NBSS*, 19; the examples cited there, and in *Zur Gramm.*, 91, present fewer problems if *wa-lā* is read 'or', as in vernacular Arabic; for extension of pleonastic negation see Blau, *Christian Arabic*, 313–15; also *BSOAS* xxxi (1968) 613.
[9] *NBSS*, 22.

Koran bildet eine Literatur für sich, er war ohne wirklichen Vorgänger und konnte auch keine Nachfolger haben'.[1]

Whatever one could respond to the question of possible precursors, it is very doubtful whether Quranic style ever had an effect upon the subsequent course of Arabic literature, save as source of aphoristic citation. Its curious system of periodization (*fawāṣil*) made relation to the literary genre known as rhymed prose (*saj'*) unavoidable. The effect of that system upon Quranic syntax did not of course escape Nöldeke, and was more recently the subject of a special study in which morphology and lexicon were also included.[2] Terminological dispute about whether Qur'ān and *saj'* could even be mentioned in the same breath found a kind of resolution in the expression *mutamāthilat al-maqāṭi'* (homoioteleuton).[3] Arguments against the obvious were mostly of a theological or *ad hominem* character: e.g. if the Qur'ān were nothing but traditional (*sic*) rhymed prose, how could it be miraculous/inimitable (*mu'jiz*)? or, in *saj'* meaning was made to fit the rhyme, while in the Qur'ān verse endings may enhance but do not inform the communication, etc. Resort to *termini technici* provided the useful *fāṣila*, by which Quranic rhyme could be distinguished from that of poetry (*qāfiya*) and of *saj'* (*qarīna*). In the analysis of forty kinds of grammatical and other mutation (*aḥkām*) both characteristic of and affected by the Quranic *fāṣila*, Suyūṭī adduced material sufficient to support the contention that Quranic syntax, as well as certain of its morphological and lexical features, owed something of their eccentricity to its periodization.[4] But relation of the *fāṣila* to other forms of rhyme (i.e. *qāfiya* and *qarīna*) was never suppressed: a shared descriptive terminology derived from the vocabulary of rhetorical *ornatus* (*badī'*) was offset by the assertion that the rules of application for the *fāṣila* were other than those which obtained for poetry, e.g. *taḍmīn* (enjambment) and *īṭā'* (repetition of rhyme word), condemned in verse, were recommended in prose.[5]

Even a rough statistical survey of Quranic rhyme indicates predominance of forms containing long vowel plus consonant (usually *ī/ū* with *-n*, or *ī/ū* and *ā* with *-n* or another consonant), followed in order of frequency by vocalic rhymes (*ah/ā/iya*) and, finally, forms containing short vowel plus consonant.[6] That the dominant rhyme pattern (long vowel/diphthong plus consonant) should also carry stress might be inferred from the pausal pronunciation of those syllables, whose primary characteristic is the long

[1] *NBSS*, 22.

[2] *NBSS*, 6, 9, 10, 22; and Müller, *Reimprosa*, for which see *BSOAS* xxxiii (1970) 389–91.

[3] Suyūṭī, *Itqān*, *naw'* 59: iii, 290–315, esp. 292–5; cf. Norden, *Antike Kunstprosa*, 909–60 on *clausula/cursus*; Lausberg, *Handbuch*, paras. 985 ff, 1052.

[4] *Itqān* iii, 296–301, citing Ibn al-Ṣā'igh.

[5] See especially *Itqān* iii, 302–15.

[6] See *GdQ* i, 36–44; Vollers, *Volkssprache*, 55–80; feminine rhyme is rare; Fischer, 'Silbenstruktur', 54–5: short vowel plus two consonants is rare; Birkeland, *Pausalformen*, 18–21.

vowel/diphthong, rather than the accompanying consonant. Segmentation may be said, in other words, to depend as much upon assonance as upon rhyme. A number, though not all, of Müller's morphological and lexical phenomena exhibit substitution of iambic for other measures, e.g. *fiʿʿāl*, *tafʿīl*, *ifʿāl*, and especially *faʿīl*.[1] The effect of such is of course greater in contexts where the rhyme/stress/pausal forms are not too widely spaced, less where the sound-echo is heard only at great intervals. In passages of the latter kind, predominant in the longer *sūra*s, periodization is achieved by insertion of fixed formulae, e.g. *wa-llāhu ʿazīzun ḥakīm*, *wa-huwa 'l-ʿalīmu 'l-raḥīm*, etc. Employment of formulaic systems may possibly not account for all the phenomena adduced by Müller, for example, such lexical items as the proper names *Ilyāsīn* and *Ṭūr Sīnīn*.[2] On the other hand, a document which, like the Qur'ān, exhibits so much of traditional imagery and of rhetorical schemata, deserves description in those terms, rather than as a series of deviations from 'normal linguistic usage'. Most, if not quite all, of the Quranic passages exhibiting post-position of *faʿīl* forms contain scarcely varying predications of God.[3] While post-position may be contrasted with pre-position in non-pausal contexts, that contrast seems to me less important than the over-all impression of formulaic phraseology, for which normal word order is in fact post-positional. Similarly, locutions like *huwa yuḥyī wa-yumīt* and *wa-ilayhi turjaʿūn* might well represent crystallized formulae of cultic origin and thus not the most appropriate evidence of irregular syntax. For the same reasons the Quranic material hardly lends itself to assertions about misuse of tempora.[4] Employment in scripture of the perfect 'tense' as optative or apodictic reflects ancient tradition, however inconvenient to the formulation of normative grammar, e.g. Genesis 17: 20 הנה ברכתי אתו והפריתי אתו והרביתי אתו.[5]

How much of Quranic periodization may be attributed to the use of cultic formulae and how much to conscious adaptation of the *usus loquendi* to such formulae, is probably impossible to determine. That the document owes its undeniable stylistic homogeneity to repetition has been proposed.[6] Even rudimentary data of quantification might be thought to support this view. Of a total 78,000 words the Qur'ān contains approximately 1,850 separate lexical entries, of which about 455 are *hapax legomena* (*nomina propria* are not included in either count). The resultant ratios, 40: 1 and 4: 1 respectively, are those found for the corresponding phenomena in Hebrew scripture.[7] A cursory examination of any Quranic concordance will show that it is not merely separate lexica which occur repeatedly, but also fixed images and the rhetorical conventions associated with these. To

[1] *Reimprosa*, 41–59, 112–28. [2] *Reimprosa*, 136–7. [3] *Reimprosa*, 112–28.
[4] *Reimprosa*, 128–30; see Reuschel, '*Wa-kāna llāhu ʿalīman*', 147–53.
[5] Cf. Koch, *Growth*, 211–12. [6] See above, I pp. 46–7.
[7] Cf. Ullendorff, 'Biblical Hebrew', 243.

the question of frequency and distribution ratios the reply may be formulated in terms of 'typical structures', or entire segments of recurring pattern. To this end my description of the document in terms of schemata of revelation was conceived.[1] Thematic treatment (retribution, sign, exile, covenant) and variant traditions (prophetical mission and eschatological promise), as well as the entire range of assimilated imagery (the vanished nations and the battles of God, angelology and resurrection), depend for literary expression upon a set of hardly varying phrases. The relationship of these to the rules of normative grammar is consistently anomalous. That relationship is exhibited also in the scriptural lexicon. Surprisingly few of the *hapax legomena* are from the point of view of literary Arabic rare words, e.g. substantives like *abābīl*, *ṣamad*, *ṭāmma*, *ʿilliyūn*, etc. Most represent familiar and practical notions, like *baḥath*, *tabassam*, *majālis*, *jawf*, *sakat*, *ramz*, *lafẓ*, *ḥarrak*, *ḥaṣṣal*, etc. One is hardly justified in assuming that these latter did not figure in common usage during the period of the Qur'ān's composition. There is of course no reason to expect in that document only a reflection of the common usage, or to suppose that notions not expressed there did not exist. Those semantic sectors, and there are many, not represented in the Qur'ān may be thought indifferent, *sub specie aeternitatis*.[2]

But even as *lingua sacra* scripture must be analysed as a unit of literary production. Guided by the subject matter itself, one has not far to seek for the archetypes of Quranic imagery. For that the search is not less arduous. The incorporation of Biblical concepts and imagery entailed an important stylistic concomitant, namely, the *Deutungsbedürftigkeit* characteristic of sacred language.[3] From the moment of its utterance the word of God required exegesis. Once it had achieved canonical status, scripture produced systematic interpretation. The forms generated by that process and the hermeneutical principles from which they were derived varied with the needs of the community. Both constitute the subject of the following chapter.

[1] See above, I pp. 1–33.

[2] Cf. Barr, *Comparative Philology*, 223–37.

[3] See above, pp. 99–100.

IV

PRINCIPLES OF EXEGESIS

THE elaboration of Islam may be seen as co-ordination of three generically distinct factors: canon, prophet, and sacred language. A useful index to the relative significance of each in that elaboration emerges from examination of the kinds of exegetical literature in existence at various points of its course. Even apart from the interpretative material included within the text of the canon, the exegetical literature can hardly be described as homogeneous, and several criteria have been employed in its description: the type of scriptural material treated, argument of the author, date of composition, etc. I propose here to experiment with two different criteria of classification, the one stylistic, the other functional, which seem to me to be mutually corroborative in producing the following exegetical typology:

1. Haggadic.
2. Halakhic.
3. Masoretic.
4. Rhetorical.
5. Allegorical

From the point of view of function, by which I mean the role of each in the formulation of its history by a self-conscious religious community, these exegetical types exhibit only a minimum of overlapping and, save for the last-named, might almost be chronologically plotted in the above sequence. The increasing sophistication discernible in the treatment of scripture corresponded to a demand, at least among the exegetes themselves, for finer and subtler terms of clarification and of dispute. Allegorical exegesis represented a reaction to the generous manner in which that demand had been met.

From the point of view of style, however, the types proposed here display a degree of uniformity which could be misleading. Common to all is the presence, wholly or in part, of the canonical text of revelation. One of the problems to be examined is the precise relationship of that text in each type of exegesis to the accompanying commentary, qualified by the observation that redactional processes have contributed inevitably to an over-simplified picture of that relationship. A second cause of uniformity is posed by the recurrence in each type of technical terms whose usage seems at first sight to be constant, thus providing apparent, but in fact deceptive, evidence of methodological similarity. An example was application of the term *majāz* to two quite different exegetical procedures.[1] Finally, the identity of explanations, whether lexical, grammatical, or rhetorical, throughout the literature of scriptural interpretation provokes an understandable impression of uniformity. Here, too, the evidence can be deceptive. The value, indeed the sense, of any such explanation can, it seems to me, be elicited only from the total context of the commentary in which it appears. Thus, glossing *alladhīna kafarū* (those who reject/disbelieve) in Q. 25: 32 as *yahūd* (Jews) will not have meant to Zamakhsharī (d. 538/1143) what it did to ʿAbdallāh b. ʿAbbās (d. 68/687).[2] Similarly, the 'extrapolation' technique recommended by a number of scholars in the attempt to recover from the works of later exegetes those of the early authorities (e.g. Mujāhid from Ṭabarī, al-Aṣamm from Thaʿlabī) can have but limited success, quite apart from the presence of defective chains of transmission and of conflicting judgements based on a single authority (perfectly illustrated by the profusion of dicta ascribed to Ibn ʿAbbās).[3] It will be useful to remember that no writer merely transmits, and that even a compilation reveals principles both of selection and of arrangement.

As corrective to this impression of uniformity I propose for the stylistic analysis of exegetical literature a distinction between the elements of explication and the framework in which they appear. Both may be described as containing a measure of characteristic form, the relation between them being always one of tension, often of opposition. Tension may be said to exist when explicative elements that are minimal and to some extent basic units of interpretation (e.g. *hākadhā* for *kadhālika*, *wallāhi* for *tallāhi*) occur in a typical context, which is their original framework or point of literary origin. Such elements, always recognizable and seldom productive, are freely borrowed by writers employing the same exegetical framework. Opposition may be said to exist when these and more elaborate explicative elements figure in atypical contexts. An example is the appearance in Farrā' (d. 207/822) *ad* Q. 17: 1 of the story of Muhammad and the caravan belonging to Quraysh on the road from Jerusalem, an instance of prophetical thaumaturgy quite out of place in a masoretic context.[4] Less conspicuous but no less important examples of opposition between element and framework are found in late exegetical works where dissenting or minority opinions were introduced by such locutions as *wa-qīla* (and it has been said) and *wa-quri'a* (and it has been read). For example, in the *variae lectiones kalimāt/kalima* for Q. 7: 158 the non-canonical singular was adduced reluctantly by both Zamakhsharī and Bayḍāwī (d. 691/1292)

[1] See Wansbrough, 'Periphrastic exegesis', 254–9, 265–6; and below, pp. 227–32.

[2] *Kashshāf* iii, 278 ad loc.; Suyūṭī, *Itqān* i, 122; see above, I pp. 36–8.

[3] Cf. Birkeland, *The Lord guideth*, 20–1, 62–3; Horst, 'Zur Überlieferung', 290–307; see below, pp. 139–40.

[4] *Maʿānī 'l-Qur'ān* ii, 115–16; see above, II pp. 69–70.

and the dogmatic equivalent *kalima*:*logos* included only as a final option.[1]

Now, it is the ascertainable quantity of explicative elements in a typical context or habitual framework which constitutes an exegetical type. Such a type exhibits a structure sufficiently consistent for intrusions of the kinds alluded to above to be noticeable, and I have indicated five which in my judgement provide a typology of Islamic exegetical literature. The total number of elements will of course vary according to definition, which for the following analysis will be as broad as possible. I have selected twelve kinds of procedural device, each of which is potentially variable but not beyond recognition, irrespective of the combinations in which it is employed:

1. *Variae lectiones.*
2. Poetic *loci probantes.*
3. Lexical explanation.
4. Grammatical explanation.
5. Rhetorical explanation.
6. Periphrasis.
7. Analogy.
8. Abrogation.
9. Circumstances of revelation.
10. Identification.
11. Prophetical tradition.
12. Anecdote.

Study of the distribution of these phenomena across the range of exegetical literature ought to produce a means of isolating the essentially separate activities which preceded the appearance of classical Islamic *tafsīr*. That is a conventional term whose origin appears to have been rhetorical rather than exegetical and the result of a preoccupation with profane rather than with sacred literature.[2] It may have been the monumental work of Ṭabarī (d. 311/923) which contributed to an almost permanent eclipse of some interesting controversy on the subject of exegetical nomenclature. It is not at all impossible that the arguments of his younger contemporary Māturīdī (d. 333/944) were calculated to establish a fixed semantic value for the term *tafsīr*, not merely to postulate the eventually inconclusive distinction *tafsīr—ta'wīl*.[3] But whatever its technical designation, Quranic exegesis would seem to have found its earliest expression within a basically narrative framework which may conveniently be described as haggadic.

[1] Cf. *BSOAS* xxxiii (1970) 392, on the misinterpretation of that method in Khoury, *Les Théologiens byzantins*, 21 n. 13; see above, II pp. 76–7.
[2] See Wansbrough, 'Qur'ānic exegesis', 469–85.
[3] See Götz, 'Māturīdī', esp. 31–8; and below, pp. 154–8.

I. HAGGADIC EXEGESIS

In an exegetical work ascribed to Muqātil b. Sulaymān (d. 150/767) and entitled *Tafsīr*, the author related the following story *ad* Q. 18: 9.[1]

Abū Jahl said to Quraysh: Send someone to the Jews of Yathrib to ask them whether this man (Muhammad) is a prophet or a liar—that would be a solution. So they sent five, among whom were Naḍr b. Ḥārith and ʿUqba b. Abī Muʿayṭ. When these reached the city they said to the Jews: We have come to you about something which happened to us recently and which is getting worse. We fear that it may cause confusion and upset the *status quo*. This man—humble, poor, and an orphan—prays to Raḥmān. Now the only Raḥmān we know is Musaylima the false prophet who, as you also know, never caused anything but destruction and slaughter. But he (Muhammad) claims to be informed by Gabriel, who is an enemy of yours, so tell us whether you find any mention of him in your scriptures. The Jews replied: We do find him described as you say. The men of Quraysh interrupted: Among his own clan those nobler and richer than he do not believe him. The Jews answered: We find that his own people are those most violently opposed to him, and yet this is the time in which he is to appear. The men of Quraysh countered: But Musaylima the false prophet is his teacher, so tell us something that we can ask him about, that Musaylima cannot teach him, and that only a prophet can know. So the Jews said: There are three things—if he knows them he is a prophet, if not he is a liar. Ask him about the Men in the Cave, and Dhū 'l-Qarnayn, and the Spirit. And they told the men of Quraysh the stories of the first two and added, with regard to the third: If he says either little or much about that, he is a liar. Delighted, the men of Quraysh returned to Mecca, and Abū Jahl said to the prophet (*sic*): Son of ʿAbd al-Muṭallib, we are going to ask you about three things—if you know them, you are telling the truth, and if not, you are a liar. The prophet replied: What is it? Ask me what you like. So Abū Jahl replied: We ask you about the Men in the Cave, so tell us about them. And Dhū 'l-Qarnayn, so tell us about him. And the Spirit, so tell us what that is. If you know what they are, you are vindicated, but if you do not, you are deluded and bewitched. And the prophet answered: Come back tomorrow and I will tell you. But he did not say: God willing! He waited three days, then Gabriel came to him, and the prophet said: Gabriel, the people are asking me about three things. The latter replied: For that very reason I have come to you.

Somewhat abridged and following upon an elaborate description of attempts by Quraysh to seduce Muhammad with promises of money, power, and even medical attention, the same story appears in the biography of the Arabian prophet composed by Ibn Isḥāq (d. 151/768), in the recension of Ibn Hishām (d. 218/834).[2] In that account Quraysh sent only two men (those actually named in Muqātil's version); the three minor motifs—connection of Raḥmān with Musaylima, Gabriel as enemy of the Jews,

[1] *GAS* i, 36–7; MS H. Hüsnü 17, 167ᵛ–168ʳ.
[2] *GAS* i, 288–90, 297–9; *Sīra* i, 300–2.

and prediction of Muhammad in Jewish scripture—were omitted; the three components of the 'test' were designated Youths (*fitya*), Wanderer (*rajul ṭawwāf*), and Spirit (*rūḥ*); and Muhammad waited fifteen days for Gabriel.

In both works the story provided a narrative framework for lengthy commentary on *Sūrat al-Kahf*. Examination of the means by which that was achieved ought to throw some light on the structural consistency of haggadic exegesis. Central to both versions is the part played by the rabbis of Yathrib (Medina) in the formulation of its strategy by Meccan opposition to Muhammad. As such, it is one of many but typical of all literary devices which implied a historical link between two sources of resistance to the Arabian prophet.[1] Employment of this particular framework, which figures also as an immediate cause of revelation (*sabab al-nuzūl*), compels the reader to accept the Qur'ān document as a source for the life of Muhammad and thus for conditions in the Hijaz during the seventh century. With regard to the integrity of the Quranic tcxt, Muqātil's use of the narrative appears at least to be the more rigorous of the two: the entire content of *Sūrat al-Kahf* (one or two parts but tacitly) was related to the story of Abū Jahl and the rabbis. The author achieved that end by resort to two somewhat mechanical devices. *Ad* Q. 18: 1 the word *'iwajan* was glossed *mukhtalifan* and the meaning 'variation/irregularity' applied not to the content of scripture but to its mode of revelation.[2] Evocation of the terminology pertinent to that dispute will have been intentional, since Muqātil added immediately a prophetical anecdote containing an admonition addressed to the Jews by Muhammad on the certain consequences of their ignoring the message from God. Moreover, the prolepsis so characteristic of Muqātil's style is exhibited here by conjoining to the prophetical anecdote the claim of four Medinese Jews (named) that 'Uzayr (Ezra) was the son of God. The *locus classicus* for discussion of that allegation is Q. 9: 30, where it may be combined with anti-Christian polemic, as well as with the idolatry of Quraysh.[3] Muqātil interpreted Q. 18: 4 exclusively as reference to the Jews, while Ibn Isḥāq mentioned only Quraysh: الذين قالوا اتخذ الله ولدا يعنى قريشا فى قولهم إنا نعبد الملائكة وهى بنات الله a formulation which, however unlikely the utterance ascribed to the prophet's Meccan opponents, did service to the cause of the exegetical tradition which emphasized the Hijazi background to Islam. As such, the *Sīra* passage could be thought to exhibit traces of editorial intervention, while Muqātil's treatment, in

[1] See above, I pp. 16–17, 18, 36, II pp. 62, 72–3, 78–80; and Hirschfeld, 'Controversies', 100–16.

[2] See above, I, pp. 36–8.

[3] e.g. Zamakhsharī, *Kashshāf* ii, 263 ad loc.

contrast, is almost certainly a reflex of Rabbinic and/or apocryphal traditions concerning Ezra.[1]

Thus, in Muqātil's version verses 4–8 of *Sūra* 18 were anticipated and the narrative, replete with allusion to the fate of earlier heedless peoples (*umam khāliya*),[2] brought up to the account of Abū Jahl. Two of the three episodes representing the components of the 'rabbinical' test of prophethood, contained in verses 9–26 and 83–98, are commented at some length, and the third accommodated by reference at verses 108–10 to yet another facet of the Jewish opposition to Muhammad:[3] خالدين فيها/لا يموتون/لا يبغون عنها حولا/يعنى متحولا الى غيرها وذلك أن اليهود قالوا للنبى تزعم أنك أوتيت الحكمة والحكمة العلم كله وتزعم أنه لا علم لك بالروح وتزعم أن الروح من أمر ربّى فكيف يكون هذا فقال الله تعالى ذكره لنبيه إنّك أوتيت علما وعلمك فى علم الله قليل فقال سبحانه لليهود/قل لو كان البحر مدادا لكلمات ربّى لنفد البحر قبل أن تنفد كلمات ربّى. This passage (obliques separate canonical text from commentary) illustrates several aspects of Muqātil's method: zero connective between *khālidīn fīhā* and *lā yamūtūn* may signal paraphrase; the connective *yaʿnī* between *ḥiwalan* and *mutaḥawwilan* may introduce either an interpretation or, as here, a gloss; *wa-dhālika an/anna* generally indicates the 'occasion' of revelation; *fa-qāla subḥānahu* signals resumption of the canonical text, often accompanied, as here, by a 'stage direction' indicating the person(s) addressed. Now, in this instance Jews were adduced expressly to complete the narrative: by including the third component of the test of prophethood, namely, knowledge of the Spirit. But rather than cite the relevant Quranic passage (17: 85), Muqātil paraphrased it in terms of a Jewish allegation, Muhammad's assertion, and God's confirmation of His prophet, in the course of which scriptural syntax suffered not a little. The stylistic advantages of this procedure become apparent when compared with the method of Mutātil's contemporary, Ibn Isḥāq.

There, a longer and more intricate prelude to the revelation of *Sūrat al-Kahf* necessitated a correspondingly complex interpretation, in the course of which fragments of ten Quranic *sūra*s were treated (in the following sequence: 19: 64, 18: 1–8, 18: 9–26, 18: 83–98, 17: 85, 31: 27, 13: 31, 25: 7–10, 20, 17: 90–3, 13: 30, 96: 9–19, 34: 47, 41: 26, 74: 31, 17: 110), being adduced as the revelations brought to Muhammad in consequence of his encounters with the combined forces of Arabian Jewry

[1] *Tafsir*, MS H. Hüsnü 17, 167^{r}, *Sīra* i, 302; see below, p. 127; Geiger, *Was hat Mohammed*, 191–2; Horovitz, *Untersuchungen*, 127–8, 167; Speyer, *Erzählungen*, 413; and cf. Künstlinger's speculation on the messianic content of 4 Ezra 7: 28–9, ''Uzair', 381–3, though attribution to Muhammad of a 'mistaken interpretation' seems far-fetched.

[2] See above, I pp. 2–5.

[3] *Tafsir*, MS H. Hüsnü 17, 167^{v}–9^{r}, 172^{r}–3^{r}, 173^{r-v}, respectively.

and Quraysh.[1] Ibn Isḥāq's treatment is characterized by the strictest economy. The three episodes central to the theme of the Medinese rabbis occupy six pages, and the scriptural passages (18: 9–26, 18: 83–98, 17: 85) are compactly and explicitly presented.[2] Narrative precedes and follows but does not interrupt. Interpretation consists primarily of gloss and paraphrase, the only connectives employed being *ay* and zero. *Ad* Q. 17: 85 Jews and Quraysh were brought together in the following manner: قال ابن اسحاق وحدثت عن ابن عباس أنه قال لما قدم رسول الله المدينة قالت أحبار يهود يا محمد أرأيت قولك/وما أوتيتم من العلم الا قليلا/ ايانا تريد أم قومك قال كلا قالوا فانك تتلو فيما جاءك انا قد أوتينا التوراة فيها بيان كل شئ فقال رسول الله انها فى علم الله قليل وعندكم فى ذلك ما يكفيكم لو أقمتموه. There the rabbis (*aḥbār yahūd*) confronted Muhammad in Medina with an alleged utterance of his confirming the omniscience of the Torah (formulated as revelation: *tatlū fīmā jā'aka*) and citing (correctly) Q. 17: 85, to which Muhammad retorted that it referred to both Quraysh and Jews: and of knowledge you have been granted but little. Thus the story of Abū Jahl and the rabbis was completed and confirmed by a later event. In Ibn Isḥāq, moreover, the denouement was logical and consistent. In Muqātil the Jews reproached Muhammad for claiming to have knowledge from his Lord and yet professing to know nothing of the Spirit, thus revealing their treachery, since it was that very ignorance which was to be proof of Muhammad's divine calling.[3]

The 'rabbinical' test of prophethood employed with varying skill by the exegetes is clearly remote from Jewish doctrine, and reflects a very primitive level of polemical discourse.[4] But its function here might be thought stylistic rather than merely polemical, a suspicion corroborated if not confirmed by the transparent adaptation of an *ayyām* motif: the offer of three courses of action (*thalāth khiṣāl*) to the protagonist, as a means of both stimulating and limiting movement within the narrative framework.[5] The motif was consistently related to Jewish, if not always to Meccan, resistance to Muhammad, as can be seen from a version adduced by Suyūṭī: قال سمع عبد الله بن سلام بمقدم رسول الله فأتاه فقال إنى سائلك عن ثلاث لا يعلمهن الا نبى: ما أول أشراط الساعة وما أول طعام أهل الجنة وما ينزع الولد الى أبيه أو الى أمه قال أخبرنى بهن جبريل آنفا قال جبريل قال

[1] *Sīra* i, 294–302 and 302–14.
[2] *Sīra* i, 303–8.
[3] Cf. Geiger, *Was hat Mohammed*, 38 *ad* Q. 25: 4.
[4] See above, II pp. 70–1, 74; and cf. Vajda, 'Juifs et Musulmans', 99–108 for the versions in Aḥmad b. Ḥanbal.
[5] See Caskel, 'Aijām al-'Arab', 49–52; Widengren, 'Oral tradition', 232–43; Sellheim, 'Die Muhammad-Biographie', 70, 84–5; Stetter, *Topoi und Schemata*, 36–9; cf. the same device in 1 Chronicles 21: 10–13.

(Q. 2: 97) نعم قال ذلك عدو اليهود من الملائكة فقرأ هذه الآية. There the interrogation took place in Medina and the three components of the test were different, but the minor motif depicting Gabriel as enemy of the Jews was included, with the expected reference to Q. 2: 97.[1] Elsewhere Suyūṭī adduced a part of the Muqātil/Ibn Isḥāq version of the test, including only Q. 17: 85 and the question of the Spirit, with a choice of Medinese or Meccan setting, and with characteristic logic opted for the latter since that was where Q. 17: 85 had been revealed.[2]

The observation of Nöldeke–Schwally: 'das Ganze ist höchst fabelhaft, so dass wir nicht viel darauf zu geben haben', is also characteristic of the arbitrary 'historical' method which for a century has dominated the course of Islamic and particularly of Quranic studies. There are, in fact, very few verses of the text of revelation which were not 'bald nach Mekka, bald nach Medina verlegt', abundantly clear from even a cursory reading of the first fifteen chapters of Suyūṭī's *Itqān*.[3] Despite Nöldeke's confident assertion: 'Wir haben vor ihnen allen aber doch namentlich eins voraus: die Unbefangenheit gegenüber dem religiösen Vorurteil. Und dazu sind wir in der Schule der wissenschaftlichen Kritik aufgewachsen', his historical evaluation of traditional data did not bring him much beyond the position established and occupied by Suyūṭī 400 years earlier.[4] Modifications of Nöldeke–Schwally by Bell and Blachère, respectively, exhibit refinement of detail but no critical assessment of the principle involved, namely, whether a chronology/topography of revelation is even feasible.[5] Nor is the historical analysis of six *sūra*s undertaken by Birkeland free of the implications of that principle, which can, after all, only be a matter of conjecture.[6] An example is his interpretation of Q. 93: 6–8 in terms of exegetical alterations inflicted upon the data of the prophet's 'orthodox' biography.[7] A literary analysis would at least require consideration of traditional cultic formulae, e.g. Psalms 10: 12–18, 22: 24 on the 'orphan's lot'.[8] Suyūṭī's argument for Q. 17: 85 was anyway of minimal

[1] *Itqān* i, 97: citing Bukhārī on the authority of Anas; see above, II pp. 62–3.

[2] *Itqān* i, pp. 93–4.

[3] *GdQ* i, 139: but both rejection and acceptance of these conflicting reports presuppose criteria of assessment at worst pernicious, at best subjective, see above, I pp. 38–41, and below, pp. 177–81.

[4] *NBSS*, 5–6.

[5] Cf. Bell, *Bell's Introduction*, esp. 108–20; Watt, 'Richard Bell's theories', 46–56; Blachère, *Introduction*, esp. 182–98, 240–63; but also Torrey, *Foundation*, 91–8.

[6] *The Lord Guideth*, *sūra*s 93, 94, 108, 105, 106; id. 'Sūrah 107', 13–29.

[7] *The Lord Guideth*, 23–37.

[8] Such is the method attempted here, particularly in ch. I (theodicy) and ch. II (prophetology). A valuable and detailed exposition of the snares inherent in literary analysis may be studied in the recent work of Richter, *Exegese als Literaturwissenschaft*, esp. 27–48. For the Quranic revelation a systematic theology, such as Stieglecker, *Die Glaubenslehren des Islam*, or a comparative one, such as Masson, *Le Coran et la révélation judéo-chrétienne*, dispenses with the historical dimension and thus also with a makeshift psychoanalysis of prophetical experience, see above, II pp. 56–8.

significance for the narrative value of the prophetical 'test'; concern with the precise dating and location of separate revelations was a serious occupation only at the halakhic level of scriptural exegesis.

For Muqātil and Ibn Isḥāq it was the story that mattered. Indeed, it may be said of the former that the scriptural text was subordinate, conceptually and syntactically, to the *narratio*. That this is less true of Ibn Isḥāq's work could be a result of its having been drastically edited by a scholar fully conversant with the methods and principles of masoretic exegesis. To anticipate with a single illustration my discussion of that exegetical type: in the *Sīra* lexical problems, e.g. *bākhiʿun nafsaka* (Q. 18: 6), *al-raqīm* (18: 9), *shaṭaṭan* (18: 14), are elucidated by reference to *loci probantes* from poetry, not, however, by the author of the work but by its editor (signalled *qāla Ibn Hishām*).[1] When glossing a scriptural locution, e.g. *sulṭān bayyin* (Q. 18: 15), Ibn Isḥāq merely declared: that is, an eloquent proof (*ay bi-ḥujja bāligha*), without adducing external evidence.[2] Muqātil, on the other hand, limited his comparative material for lexica to scriptural *shawāhid*, introduced by the expressions *wa-naẓīruha* (analogous to that) and *mithla qawlihi taʿālā* (as in scripture), which became technical terms in the masorah.[3] Now, the intrusion of such editorial elements into Ibn Isḥāq's biography of the prophet is only the beginning of an answer to the question: how did the author of the *Sīra* deal with scriptural material? From my analysis of the story of Jaʿfar b. Abī Ṭālib and the Najāshī it will be clear that I regard the *narratio* as paramount and the isolation of scriptural texts in canonical form an afterthought.[4] The fairly tidy separation of scripture from *narratio* in the story of *Sūrat al-Kahf* I am tempted to ascribe to editorial revision of the kind in which poetic *shawāhid* for scriptural lexica would also be characteristic. In other words, the *Sīra* exhibits evidence of both halakhic and masoretic reformulation: of the former in its attention to *asbāb al-nuzūl*, nowhere more clearly illustrated than in the proliferation of Quranic passages appended to the story of Abū Jahl and the rabbis of Medina; and of the latter in the employment of poetry to explain Quranic lexica. None the less, the structural similarity between the works of Ibn Isḥāq and Muqātil seems to me almost beyond dispute, and if the terms *sīra* and *tafsīr* later became designations of distinct literary genres, their basic identity for the earlier period may, I think, be conceded.[5]

The narrative style is best observed in Muqātil. There, separation of scripture from commentary is difficult, frequently impossible. The author achieved that unity of presentation by resort to several devices: prolepsis, repetition (subsumption), presence/absence of connectives, stage directions,

[1] *Sīra* i, 302–4; see below, pp. 216–18.
[2] *Sīra* i, 304.
[3] See below, pp. 208–15.
[4] See above, I pp. 38–43.
[5] Cf. *BSOAS* xxxi (1968) 148–9.

supercommentary, and interpolation (paraphrase). Prolepsis is the means by which the *narratio* was maintained intact, and I have described the manner in which the first eight verses of *Sūrat al-Kahf* were rendered introductory to the tale of Abū Jahl, with subsequent accommodation of verses 9–26 (the Men in the Cave), verses 83–98 (Dhū 'l-Qarnayn), and inclusion of the third component of the test (the Spirit) by reference at verse 109 to a confrontation of Muhammad with the Jews of Medina, in which Q. 17: 85 was paraphrased (equation of *kalimāt rabbī* in 18: 109 with *'ilm* in 17: 85). Intervening segments of the *sūra* were related to the narration (*Leitmotiv*) by a system of cross-reference. For example, the parable of the two gardens, verses 32–44, was connected with the Men in the Cave by giving the name of one of them, Yamlīkhā (who was sent by the others into a near-by village to buy food and thus brought about their discovery), to that one of the (two) gardeners who found favour with God. Now, the (two) gardeners were members of B. Isrā'īl and so too, according to Muqātil, were the Mūsā and Khiḍr of the journey related in verses 60–82. Identification of the latter was important, since it appears to have been a matter of dispute and intimately linked to the role of Moses in Muslim prophetology.[1] It may also be noted that in the anecdote introducing the journey that particular Moses was instructed by Gabriel, despite his hostility to the Jews (!), on how to reach the Fountain of Life (*'ayn al-ḥayāt*).[2] Of some interest, too, is the dialogue preceding the initial quest of Mūsā for Khiḍr, in which the former was reproached by God (a non-Quranic revelation introduced by *fa-awḥā 'llāhu ilayhi*) for thinking himself the most intelligent of men. That theme was resumed in the ensuing conversation between Mūsā and Khiḍr, in which the former's knowledge of God was compared with the amount of food which a bird could with its beak collect from the sea.[3] The specifically marine imagery of that passage (*'ilm*:*baḥr*) anticipated the phraseology of verse 109 which, as I have shown, was Muqātil's method of introducing Muhammad's knowledge of the Spirit into his commentary on *Sūrat al-Kahf*.

Continuity was also achieved by frequent repetition of scriptural passages occasionally paraphrased and/or anticipated by paraphrase, as in the anecdote introducing the journey of Mūsā and Khiḍr, where the locution *fa-awā ilā 'l-ṣakhra* anticipates verse 63. Smooth transition from commentary to text could result in omission, e.g. of the anaphoric *fanṭalaqā ḥattā idhā* of verse 71 (cf. verses 74, 77), sacrificed in the interests of a

[1] *Tafsīr*, MS H. Hüsnü 17, 169v–70r, 171r–2r; see above, II pp. 56–7, 76; and Goldziher, *Studien* ii, 163: citing Bukhārī, *Ṣaḥīḥ* iii, *Kitāb al-Tafsīr*, 277–82.

[2] Cf. above, II pp. 62–3; Geiger, *Was hat Mohammed*, 168, 187–8; Zunz, *Vorträge*, 137–9, esp. 138 n. (a): for Elijah and R. Joshua b. Levi; but also Horovitz, *Untersuchungen*, 141–3; *GdQ* i, 141–2; Speyer, *Erzählungen*, 238–9; Schwarzbaum, 'Theodicy legends', 119–69.

[3] *Tafsīr*, MS H. Hüsnü 17, 171r–v.

racy dialogue between Khiḍr and the ship's captain; or at verse 47, where the gloss *fa-lam yabqa minhum aḥad* appears without the corresponding text.[1] Inconsistent employment of connectives (mostly *yaʿnī*, occasionally *yaqūl*, rarely *ay*) produces the impression that such were used not so much or at least not exclusively to separate text from commentary, but rather as punctuation, the equivalent of pause in oral delivery. This usage is especially remarkable where *yaʿnī* signals a gloss not of a scriptural term but of one in the commentary, e.g. *wa-lakinna ʿuzayr ʿabd allāh dākhir yaʿnī ṣaghīran*, anticipating verse 4, or *jazāʾan karīman yaʿnī ʾl-janna*, glossing *ajran ḥasanan* of verse 2.[2] Supercommentary of that kind, for example, *ad* verse 54: *ṣarrafnā yaʿnī lawwannā yaʿnī waṣafnā*, and *passim*, would seem to indicate oral delivery.[3] Zero connective, on the other hand, e.g. *ad* verses 108–9: *khālidīn fīhā/lā yamūtūn*, and verse 31: *asāwir min dhahab/wa-asāwir min luʾluʾ*, provokes a different kind of problem, namely; whether the explicative element is to be understood as gloss or as interpolation or, indeed, as part of scripture.[4] The phenomenon is not limited to Muqātil: in Ibn Isḥāq *ad* Q. 18: 2 the intrusive phrase *wa-ʿadhāban alīman fī ʾl-ākhira* is glossed as though it were scripture.[5] Even more arresting are revelations not now part of the canonical text introduced by formulae such as *wa-qāla subḥānahu* and the like, usually reserved by Muqātil to signal resumption of the canonical text in combination with a 'stage direction', e.g. *qāla likuffār makka*, *lil-yahūd*, *lil-naṣārā*. For instance, the passage *ad* verse 45 يقول سبحانه مثل الدنيا كمثل النبت بينما هو أخضر اذ هو قد يبس وهلك فكذلك تهلك الدنيا اذا جاءت الآخرة could be a gloss, possibly a paraphrase of Q. 6: 99, though I am inclined to understand it as an independent utterance,[6] like that included in a prophetical *ḥadīth* at the end of *Sūrat al-Kahf*:[7] يقول الله أنا خير شريك من أشركنى فى عمل جعلت العمل كله لشريكى ولا أقبل الا ما كان لى خالصا. Subsumed by traditional scholarship under the heading *ḥadīth qudsī*, dicta of this sort may owe their origin to haggadic exegesis.[7]

Muqātil's style is characterized by recurrence of certain minimal units of explication whose distribution was naturally determined by the text of scripture, but which may be regarded as constants in the over-all structure. Examples are *dhālika* glossed *hādhā*, *kadhālika*:*hākadhā*, *ladun*:*ʿinda*, *lawlā*:*hallā*, *khayr*:*afḍal*, *mathal*:*shabah*, etc. Such units, in so far as they were seldom if ever points of departure for extended interpretation, were non-productive and applied with considerable freedom throughout works belonging to the haggadic type. At the levels of halakhic and masoretic

1 *Tafsīr*, 171ʳ, 171ᵛ, 170ʳ, respectively; the third example may be merely a *lapsus calami*.
2 *Tafsīr*, 167ʳ.
3 *Tafsīr*, 170ᵛ.
4 *Tafsīr*, 173ʳ, 169ᵛ.
5 *Sīra* i, 302.
6 *Tafsīr*, 170ʳ.
7 *Tafsīr*, 173ᵛ.
8 See Tahānawī, *Iṣṭilāḥāt*, 280–1; *GdQ* i, 256–8.

exegesis these minimal units might become productive and even crucial to a solution of a juridical or textual problem, but within the haggadic framework their cumulative effect cannot be said to disturb the central position of the *narratio*. Thus, examination of the exegetical work of Muqātil's contemporary, Muḥammad Kalbī (d. 146/763),[1] turns up a similar range of minimal units of explication, e.g. *dhālika* glossed *hādhā*, *kadhālika*: *hākadhā*, *ladā*: *ʿinda*, *in*: *mā*, *laʿalla*: *likay*, *wa-in*: *wa-qad*, *atā*: *aʿṭā*, *tallāhi*: *wallāhi*, *khayr*: *afḍal*, etc. In neither writer are these syntactical and lexical equivalents accompanied by *loci probantes*, scriptural or profane, or any other argument of justification.

This manner of glossing generated in the works of both writers two characteristic and related techniques: serial repetition and circular explication. An example of the first is found in Muqātil *ad* Q. 18: 85, 89, 92, where the refrain *fa-atbaʿ sababan* (so he pursued a course) is glossed at each appearance: *yaʿnī ʿilm asbāb manāzili ʾl-arḍ wa-ṭuruqihā* (that is, knowledge of the structure of the world and its ways).[2] In Kalbī *ad* Q. 12: 25–8 the verb *qadda* (cut, tear) is glossed four times by the synonymous *shaqqa*, and the locution *min dubur* (from behind) twice by the synonym *min khalf*.[3] Again, *ad* Q. 12: 28 *kayd* (wile) is glossed twice *makr wa-ṣanīʿ* (deceit and deed), and immediately thereafter, *ad* verses 33–4 by *makr* (deceit) alone; earlier, in verse 5, *kayd* is glossed by another synonym: *ḥīla*.[4] *Ad* Q. 12: 85 *qālū* (they said) is provided with the 'stage direction' *wulduhu wa-wuld wuldihi* (his children and grandchildren), repeated for verses 95 and 97 and varied for verse 96 with the synonymous *li-banīhi wa-banī banīhi*.[5] Now, such repetition without appreciable interval seems quite unnecessary, and must not be confused with genuinely helpful explanation like the gloss of *aktharu ʾl-nās* (most of the people) everywhere in *Sūrat Yūsuf* (12: 21, 38, 40, 68) as *ahl miṣr* (Egyptians), except at verse 103, where the admonition is transferred from a typological to an aetiological plane and the locution glossed *ahl makka* (Meccans).[6] Moreover, in the last example the intervals between occurrence of the phrase in scripture might seem to justify repetition.

The second glossing technique shared by the two exegetes, and which I have called circular explication, may be seen in Muqātil *ad* Q. 18: 104–5. There *ḍalla* (errant) is glossed *ḥabiṭat* (in vain), while in the very next verse *ḥabiṭat* in the text of scripture is glossed with the synonym *baṭalat*.[7] In Kalbī *ad* Q. 12: 31, 51 *ḥāsha lillāh* (God forbid!) is glossed each time with the synonymous *maʿādh allāh*, while in verses 23 and 79, where the

[1] *GAS* i, 34–5; MS Ayasofya 118.

[2] *Tafsīr*, MS H. Hüsnü 17, 172v; at verse 85 the scriptural text itself is omitted, probably owing to homoioteleuton with the preceding verse, but the gloss is there.

[3] *Tafsīr*, MS Ayasofya 118, 130r.

[4] *Tafsīr*, 130v, 128v.

[5] *Tafsīr*, 134v, 135r–v.

[6] *Tafsīr*, 129v, 131r–v, 133v, 135v.

[7] *Tafsīr*, MS H. Hüsnü 17, 173r.

latter expression is scriptural, it is glossed both times *aʿūdhu billāh* (I take refuge with God).[1] This circular, or perhaps more accurately, sliding explication was applied also to those glosses which I have designated minimal units, e.g. *laʿalla* (perhaps) is throughout *Sūrat Yūsuf* explained by Kalbī as equivalent to *likay* (in order to), but in verse 83 the word *ʿasā* (perhaps) is gratuitously glossed *laʿalla*.[2] The semantic principle that words have uses, not merely meanings, is clearly one with which both Muqātil and Kalbī were familiar. On the other hand, the exaggerated manner in which those simplistic lexical equivalents were adduced provokes a question at least as to their purpose. Here I suspect that the answer can be more profitably sought in the authors' concern with ease of delivery, less in their concern to elucidate scripture.[3]

Like Muqātil's, Kalbī's work has traditionally been entitled *Tafsīr*, though it is unlikely that either author called his work by that name. In addition to the stylistic devices common to both and already mentioned, there are other similarities but also differences. To illustrate Kalbī's method I have selected his presentation of *Sūrat Yūsuf*, an effort at sustained narrative commentary which could thus dispense with imposition of the haggadic framework (*narratio*) noted in Muqātil's treatment of *Sūrat al-Kahf*. But Quranic narrative is nothing if not elliptic, often unintelligible without exegetical complement. This structure applies without reservation to the Quranic story of Joseph, 'the most beautiful of tales revealed in that book' (cf. Q. 12: 3). An idiosyncratic and very conspicuous feature of Kalbī's style may be seen in the distribution of commentary in relation to scriptural text. Words, occasionally phrases, even clauses, but never sentences or entire verses, were glossed in sequence at a ratio of approximately 1:1, resulting in a highly segmented composition. This is accentuated by employment of zero connective with 'envelopment' of the (preceding) text, so that separation of text from commentary by means of obliques produces the following, very typical, pattern for Q. 12: 56–7.[4] وكذلك مكنّا ليوسف/هكذا ملكنا يوسف/فى الأرض/أرض مصر/يتبوأ منها/ينزل فيها/حيث يشاء/يريد/نصيب برحمتنا/نحضر برحمتنا النبوة والإسلام/من نشاء/من كان أهلا لذلك/ولا نضيع/لا نبطل/أجر المحسنين/ثواب المؤمنين المحسنين بالقول والفعل/ولأجر الآخرة/ثواب الآخرة/خير/من ثواب الدنيا/للذين آمنوا/بالله وجملة الكتب والرسل/وكانوا يتقون/الكفر والشرك والفواحش. Curiously, segmentation did not necessarily entail fragmentation, and it may be that the overlapping effected here by recourse to zero connective and retroflexive envelopment was devised by the author to ensure continuity. Though zero connective is of highest frequency by far in Kalbī, he

[1] *Tafsīr*, MS Ayasofya 118, 130ᵛ, 132ᵛ, 130ʳ, 134ʳ.
[2] *Tafsīr*, 134ᵛ.
[3] See below, pp. 144–8.
[4] *Tafsīr*, MS Ayasofya 118, 132ᵛ–133ʳ.

employed occasionally and indifferently *yaqūl*, as well as its variation *yaʿnī*, the latter especially and for obvious reasons following *qāla/qālū* (he/they said), a convenient device in a *sūra* consisting almost entirely of dialogue, e.g. *ad* verse 44: *qālū yaʿnī ʾl-ʿarrāfīn wal-kahana wal-saḥara* (they said, i.e. the seers, the soothsayers, and the sorcerers), or verse 74: *qālū yaʿnī fatā yūsuf* (they said, i.e. Joseph's men).[1] The connective *ay* may also occur, not as a means of joining comment to scriptures, but rather, of adding supercommentary, e.g. *ad* verse 6:[2] وكذلك/هكذا/يجتبيك ربّك/ يصطفيك ربّك بالنبوة/ويعلمك من تأويل الأحاديث/من تعبير الرويا/ويتمّ نعمته عليك/بالنبوة والإسلام أى يميتك على ذلك/وعلى آل يعقوب/بك أى ويتم أيضا نعمته على أولاد يعقوب بك/ كما أتمّها/ نعمته بالنبوة والإسلام/على أبويك من قبل/من قبل ابراهيم واسحاق/إن ربّك عليم/ بنعمته/حكيم/بإتمامها. It may be noted that the imagery of the two passages cited here, with particular emphasis upon prophethood (*nubuwwa*) and its soteriological fulfilment (*islām*), is identical, and thus anticipated Kalbī's concluding observations on this *sūra*, concerned specifically with Muhammad and the Quranic revelation,[3] very similar to Muqātil's paraenesis at the end of *Sūrat al-Kahf*.[4]

Despite the essentially narrative structure of *Sūrat Yūsuf*, Kalbī's treatment cannot be called anecdotal in quite the sense that the epithet may be applied to Muqātil's work. There are at least two reasons for the difference of quality between the two styles. The first is the presence in Kalbī of two features virtually absent in his contemporary, namely, *variae lectiones* and alternative glosses for a single locution. Both figure in such quantity with Kalbī as to be characteristic of his work as preserved and, like the presence in the *Sīra* of *asbāb al-nuzūl* and poetic *shawāhid*, may be regarded as evidence of editorial reformulation. Features such as these, though not typical of haggadic exegesis, may exist there even in quantity without altering the typological structure. All four devices, together with a few others yet to be mentioned, are appropriate to halakhic and masoretic exegesis and thus, within the haggadic framework, represent intrusions. That intrusive quality is clear not only from the breach in the narrative caused by the presence of, say, a *varia lectio*, but also from the nature of the element itself. To anticipate again my discussion of masoretic exegesis with a single example from Kalbī's work: at Q. 12: 63 the author observed فارسل معنا اخانا/بن يامين/نكتل/ يشترى لنفسه حملا ويقال نشترى له حملا إن قرأت بالنون a useful illustration of method, since it includes a haggadic element (our brother: Benjamin), a gloss depending upon an implied textual variant (he obtains measure/

1 *Tafsīr*, 132^{r}, 134^{r}.
2 *Tafsīr*, 128^{v}.
3 *Tafsīr*, 136^{r-v} *ad* verses 109–11.
4 *Tafsīr*, MS H. Hüsnü 17, 173^{r-v}.

we obtain measure), and an alternative (introduced 'and it is said') based on the other of the two transmitted readings.[1] But the passage is elliptic and the key to the argument missing, namely the reading *yaktal* (he obtains/will obtain measure). For the discussion in complete and rather more logical form, one may turn to Farrā':[2] قوله فأرسل معنا أخا نا نكتل قرأ أصحاب عبد الله يكتل وسائر الناس نكتل كلاهما صواب من قال نكتل جعله معهم فى الكيل ومن قال يكتل يصيبه كيل لنفسه فجعل الفعل له خاصة لانهم يزادون به كيل بعير. There the source of both readings is stated together with the judgement of Farrā' that both were correct (!), depending upon whether the amount of grain obtained by Jacob's sons in Egypt was merely that promised by Joseph if they were accompanied by Benjamin, or to be increased by a special allocation to the youngest brother. Now, almost without exception the textual variants adduced by Kalbī are of elliptic and referential character, and appear to me to presuppose acquaintance with the masoretic activities of scholars like Farrā'. The implications of this hypothesis, which touch upon matters of redaction, will be examined in due course.[3] It may suffice here to suggest, despite absence of explicit editorial revision of the kind available for the *Sīra*, that Kalbī's work as preserved exhibits a considerably modified form of haggadic exegesis.

The second cause of difference between the commentaries of Kalbī and Muqātil is the absence in the former of a narrative device much favoured by Muqātil: the prophetical tradition (*ḥadīth*). In a work which, like Kalbī's, was claimed to have been transmitted exclusively from the authority of ʿAbdallāh b. ʿAbbās, one might expect a profusion of such dicta, as well as of *ḥadīth qudsī*, also remarked in Muqātil's work. In the latter the prophetical *ḥadīth* could be didactic, as for Q. 18: 46:[4]

And the Prophet said: The enduring good works are [utterance of the prayers] 'Glory to God', 'Praise be to God', 'There is no god but God', and 'God is great'.

Or it might be merely anecdotal, an entertaining digression, as for Q. 18: 96:[5]

And a man said to the Prophet: I have seen the barrier of Yājūj and Mājūj. So the Prophet said: Describe it to me then, And he replied: It is like striped cloth—black and red. The Prophet said: Yes, you have seen it.

The absence of this kind of material in Kalbī is difficult to explain. In contrast to the unhurried, almost chatty style of Muqātil, Kalbī is terse, humourless, matter-of-fact. That austere manner may have been intentional, but comparison of the two authors together with the significant

[1] *Tafsīr*, MS Ayasofya 118, 135ʳ.
[2] *Maʿānī 'l-Qur'ān* ii, 49 ad loc.
[3] See below, pp. 138–44.
[4] *Tafsīr*, MS H. Hüsnü 17, 170ʳ.
[5] *Tafsīr*, 172ᵛ.

fact that both preceded by nearly two generations that stage of exegetical scholarship in which the basic problems, doctrinal and textual, were to be examined in exhaustive detail, provokes a question at least about the redaction of Kalbī's commentary.

The *narratio* was not, however, entirely obscured. The Quranic story of Joseph requires, to escape the stigma of *non sequitur*, a minimum of supplementary material. Such was provided by Kalbī, and in a proleptic form reminiscent of Muqātil's method. For example, *ad* Q. 12: 36 the dreams of Pharaoh's cupbearer and baker, only alluded to in the text of scipture, were set out in considerable detail and also interpreted by Joseph, thus anticipating verse 41. Moreover, the interpretation contains several refinements not found in Genesis 40: 9–19, e.g. the symbolic values of the vineyard and of the vine, as well as that of the three branches.[1] Again, at 12: 43 Pharaoh's dream was embellished to accord with Joseph's interpretation of it at verse 49, and twice provided with the interpolation 'emerging from the river' (خرجن من نهر cf. Genesis 41: 2 מן היאר עלת).[2] At 12: 59 Joseph's peremptory demand: Bring me a brother of yours from your father, was supplemented by the (very necessary) 'as you have just said that you have a brother at home with your father', an interpolation expanded without comment at verses 69–70: '(Joseph's) brother, from the same father and mother'.[3] At 12: 93: Take this shirt of mine, was glossed 'and his shirt was of heavenly origin', a reflex of Rabbinic descriptions of the כתנת פסים (Genesis 37: 3).[4]

The obvious source for most, if not all, of that material is Rabbinic literature, which has been culled and collated by a number of scholars, among whom the most knowledgeable and sophisticated were Horovitz and Speyer.[5] For the document of revelation itself, the latter's work might be described as exhaustive, but an examination of Muslim exegetical literature would have revealed additional and equally interesting parallels, and prevented at the same time one or two false impressions. To declare, for example, of the locution *qāla kabīruhum* in Q. 12: 80 that 'Es sprach der grösste von ihnen, wobei mit kabīr hier sicherlich der älteste, also Ruben, gemeint ist' may be logical (cf. Genesis 42: 22) but is quite unnecessary:

[1] *Tafsīr*, MS Ayasofya 118, 131^{r}. [2] *Tafsīr*, 131^{v}–2^{r}. [3] *Tafsīr*, 133^{r-v}.

[4] *Tafsīr*, 135^{r}; and cf. Speyer, *Erzählungen*, 219–20.

[5] e.g. Geiger, *Was hat Mohammed*; Grünbaum, *Sagenkunde*; Schapiro, *Elemente*; Sidersky, *Légendes*; Katsch, *Judaism*; cf. Heller, 'Récits', 113–36 (on Basset); id. 'Légende', 1–18 (on Ahrens, Torrey, and Künstlinger, but especially Sidersky); for the problematic assumption of 'emprunts' see Moubarac, *Abraham*, 163–75; my concern here is less with Biblical and Rabbinic elements in the Quranic text than with the materials and methods employed in the elaboration of Quranic exegesis: haggadic material from later exegetical works (post-Ṭabarī) was adduced by several of these scholars, often working independently, of which the widest selection may be found in Grünbaum, *Sagenkunde* (e.g. Ya'qūbī, Ṭabarī, Mas'ūdī, Zamakhsharī, Bayḍāwī, Ibn Athīr, Abū 'l-Fīda, Qazwīnī).

Kalbī, as well as most of his successors, knew that it was Judah, 'the foremost of them in intelligence' (cf. Genesis 44: 18–34).[1]

Thus the gaps in the Quranic narrative were filled from a very familiar mine of Biblical lore. But only at Q. 12: 36 and 43, those verses having to do with interpretation of dreams, does Kalbī's commentary exceed in length the portion of scripture being interpreted. Though it could be argued that the laconic and somewhat monotonous style is witness to the author's conviction that his public required no further amplification of the well-known story, such is not really supported by the available evidence. I have mentioned the identification of Judah at Q. 12: 80. He it was also, who at 12: 10 counselled his brothers not to kill but to sell Joseph, and who at 12: 96 brought the news of Joseph's existence in Egypt to Jacob.[2] At 12: 8 and 63–76 the brother was of course Benjamin; at 12: 4 Joseph's parents were identified as Rachel and Jacob; at 12: 19 the scene of the crime was Dūshān (Dothan); at 12: 21 Joseph's buyer in Egypt and his wife were named Qūẓifar (Potiphar) and Zulaykha; at 12: 36 the two 'servants of the king' imprisoned with Joseph were specified vintner and chef, later cupbearer and baker; and at 12: 93 the number of Joseph's family sent for from Palestine was put at about 'seventy persons'.[3] Now, save for Zulaykha and placing Dothan between Midian and Egypt, this material is unexceptionable. There was some further embellishment: at 12: 19 the man who rescued Joseph from the well and sold him in Egypt was called Mālik b. Daghr, an Arab (bedouin) from Midian; at 12: 30 and 50 the women responsible for Joseph's humiliation and imprisonment (four in number) were identified by their husbands' respective ranks in Pharaoh's service; and at 12: 94 the caravan bearing Jacob and his family to Joseph departed from al-ʿArīsh, a village between Egypt and Canaan.[4]

The technique was early established and must have had its origins in haggadic exegesis.[5] Kalbī was moderate, if not quite restrained; in Muqātil's commentary to *Sūrat al Kahf* no one and nothing remained anonymous. I have adduced one example of the latter's employment of the device (*taʿyīn/tasmiya*): to link two otherwise unrelated narratives by naming the protagonist of each Yamlīkhā.[6] It would appear from the primitive treatment of vague and anonymous references in scripture that these were

[1] Speyer, *Erzählungen*, 217; Kalbī, *Tafsīr*, MS Ayasofya 118, 134^v; cf. Zamakhsharī, *Kashshāf* ii, 494 ad loc., who also mentioned Reuben and Shimeon as possibilities; see Schapiro, *Elemente*, 64–7.

[2] *Tafsīr*, 128^v, 135^r; the Quranic conflation of the roles of Reuben and Judah is reflected in Kalbī's exegesis, cf. Genesis 37: 21–2, 26–7.

[3] *Tafsīr*, 128^v, 133^{r-v}, 128^v, 129^r, 129^v, 130^v, 135^r, respectively.

[4] *Tafsīr*, 129^r, 130^r, 132^v, 132^v, 135^r, respectively.

[5] See Goldziher, *Richtungen*, 289–98.

[6] See above, p. 128; that name achieved a degree of general usefulness in the interpretation of Quranic narrative, cf. Suyūṭī, *Itqān* iv, 86–7: variant Tamlīkhā; and Zamakhsharī, *Kashshāf* ii, 720: the reference is Q. 37: 51.

regarded initially as lapses, or at least as inadequacies requiring the simple corrective measure of amplification. With the elaboration of exegetical method such vagueness of reference (*mubham*) was seen not only to be intentional but also evidence of rhetorically sophisticated prose. That much is clear from Suyūṭī's synoptic description of the subject, in which he set out seven reasons for that phenomenon in scripture: identification (*ta'yīn*) was unnecessary if the matter in question had been elucidated elsewhere in the Qur'ān, if it was too generally known to require such, or if there was no particular value in closer specification; identification was undesirable if the purpose of the *mubham* had been to attract attention by (partial) concealment, or to emphasize general by excluding specific application, or to achieve the effect of praise or of contempt by allusion rather than direct designation.[1] Now, Muqātil and Kalbī were hardly concerned with such nice distinctions, nor could it be said that their respective applications of *ta'yīn* clarify in any way the scriptural passages so treated. But the quality of the narrative was enhanced thereby and particularly, I suspect, for the purpose of oral delivery.

Several elements in Kalbī's supplementary material to the Joseph story derive not from the text of Genesis but from the Biblical tradition in a wider sense. For example, *ad* Q. 12: 24 three interpretations were offered:[2] لولا أن رأى برهان ربّه/عذاب ربه على نفسه لازم ويقال رأى صورة أبيه ويقال لولا أن رأى برهان ربه لهمّ لها. The first and third of these, which merely paraphrase the Quranic locution, may be regarded as symbolic of the author's concern to offer, wherever possible, more than one explanation. The second: 'he saw the image of his father', draws upon an older and well-attested tradition (cf. Genesis Rabba 87, 9 איקונין של אביו ראה) and is the only one that actually interprets the scriptural term *burhān* by adducing the gloss *ṣūra*, and thus isolating the notion of 'manifestation'.[3] *Ad* 12: 67 Kalbī explained Jacob's advice to his sons to enter Egypt not by one but by several gates as the father's fear that their striking beauty could attract the evil eye: وكان خاف عليهم يعقوب من العين, with which may be compared Genesis Rabba 91, 2 אל תכנסו בפתח אחד ואל תעמדו כולכם במקום אחד מפני העין.[4] That kind of haggadic accretion, which must be distinguished from material of strictly Biblical origin, was not limited to the writings of exegetes like Kalbī and Muqātil, suspect in the judgement of later generations for their undisciplined employment of Jewish material.[5]

[1] *Itqān, naw'* 70: *mubhamāt al-Qur'ān* iv, 79–100.
[2] *Tafsīr*, MS Ayasofya 118, 130r.
[3] See Speyer, *Erzählungen*, 201–3; Geiger, *Was hat Mohammed*, 139–40; Schapiro, *Elemente*, 40–1; Rabin, *Qumran*, 113 n. 5; the standard explanation was *burhān*:*āyāt*, see Suyūṭī, *Itqān* i, 115.
[4] See Speyer, op. cit. 214; Geiger, op. cit. 144–5.
[5] See Suyūṭī, *Itqān* iv, 207–9; Goldziher, *Richtungen*, 58–60, 87, 112.

It is also found in the work of their contemporary, Sufyān Thawrī, to whom that stigma did not attach.

The Quranic exegesis of Sufyān (d. 161/778), parts of which have for many years been known from citations in later writers, is extant in a unique manuscript at Rampur.[1] The work, contained in eighteen folios, consists of somewhat disjointed observations on forty-nine *sūra*s (from *Baqara* to *Ṭūr*, missing out *Dukhān* and *Muḥammad*) in the order of the canonical text, though the internal sequence of verses is not that of the canon. The fragmentary and uneven character of the work may be no more than an accident and the compilation merely an aggregate of Sufyān's opinions extracted from later works. That assessment will not, however, explain the internal order of comment nor the quality of the explicative elements themselves. It is those which, in the absence of a narrative framework of the sort encountered in Muqātil, Ibn Isḥāq, and Kalbī, require particular scrutiny. In *Sūrat Yūsuf*, for example, the symbolism of Joseph's dream (Q. 12: 4) was interpreted 'his parents and his brothers' and, alternatively, 'his father, his brothers, and his aunt', taking into account Rachel's death before that event.[2] Although Kalbī had not made explicit his knowledge of this fact until he reached verse 99, it would, I think, be an error to assume that Rachel's earlier death was not generally known to the exegetes as well as to the narrators of both the Quranic and Biblical versions of the story.[3] At Q. 12: 24 *burhān* was interpreted by Sufyān as the figure of Jacob; at 12: 67 it was Jacob's fear of the evil eye which prompted the warning to his sons; and at 12: 88 the locution *biḍāʿa muzjāt* was glossed both 'little money' and 'butter, wool' (*sic*), reflecting the much more detailed inventory of commodities adduced by Kalbī to make up the gifts brought to Egypt by Joseph's brothers on their third (*sic*) visit, a description very likely inspired by that of Genesis 43: 11–12 and one that became a stock item of the exegetical tradition.[4] Very occasionally Sufyān is more informative than Kalbī, as at Q. 12: 77, where the cryptic 'if he has stolen then a brother of his stole before him' was interpreted 'Joseph had stolen their gods', exhibiting a confusion between Joseph and Rachel which with very few exceptions persisted in Muslim exegesis to this verse. Kalbī has merely an inconclusive reference to Joseph, from which it is impossible to say whether the coat of many colours or Laban's idols were intended.[5]

[1] *GAS* i, 518–19; ed. Imtiyāz ʿAlī ʿArshī.

[2] *Tafsīr*, 95–107; the editor has rearranged the material in canonical order and indicated the manuscript sequence in his numbering of the separate entries.

[3] Sufyān, *Tafsīr*, 95; Kalbī, *Tafsīr*, 135v; *pace* Speyer, op. cit. 194 with reference to Genesis 37: 10 and 44: 20; cf. Geiger, op. cit. 147–8.

[4] Sufyān, *Tafsīr*, 98 (adducing two traditions), 102, 104, respectively; Kalbī, *Tafsīr*, 135r; Zamakhsharī, *Kashshāf* ii, 500 *ad* Q. 12: 88.

[5] *Tafsīr*, 103; Kalbī, *Tafsīr*, 134r; cf. Speyer, *Erzählungen*, 215–16; Geiger, *Was hat Mohammed*, 145.

It will be clear from these few examples that both the range and the quality of Sufyān's glosses may justifiably be compared with those of Kalbī. There is a shared tendency to transmit more than one interpretation of a Quranic locution and, similarly, a concern with *variae lectiones*. For example, *ad* Q. 12: 31 Kalbī commented واعتدت لهن متكا/ وسايد يتكين عليها إن قرأت مشددة وإن قرأت مخففة يقول الأترج leaving open the option between cushion and citrus (*etrog*: some manuscripts read *utrunj*), whereas Sufyān, also adducing a variant, restricted the choice to one between foodstuffs حدثنا سفين عن منصور عن مجاهد قال من قرأها متكا ونونها قال الطعام ومن لم ينونها قال الأترنج.[1] Since the entertainment provided by Potiphar's wife clearly drew upon Rabbinic tradition, it may reasonably be suggested that Sufyān's represents the earlier choice of interpretations, and that the proposal to read 'cushions' (*muttaka'an*: *wasāyid*) exhibits yet another instance of redactional intervention in the transmission of Kalbī's commentary.[2] To Muqātil's glosses, too, those of Sufyān may be compared, as for instance *ad* Q. 18: 46 and 19: 76 *al-bāqiyāt al-ṣāliḥāt* were interpreted as the five (ritual) prayers, that is, as *ṣalāt* rather than as *duʿā*, but the equivalence works: prayers is a common ground.[3] Thus, from this sampling of its ingredients the exegesis of Sufyān can be described as belonging to the haggadic type. There are none the less some conspicuous lacunae: not only is *Sūrat al-Kahf* shorn of its traditional narrative framework, passages normally pegs for extensive and varied anecdote, like the opening verses of *sūras* 17 and 30, are here given no attention whatever. Omissions such as these, like absence of comment for *Dukhān* and *Muḥammad* in the Rampur manuscript, are difficult to explain, even if that document were to be no more than an extrapolation of Sufyān's utterances from later writers (e.g. ʿAbd al-Razzāq, Ṭabarī, Rāzī), rather than the fragment of an independent work. External evidence, such as it is, appears to lend support to the latter alternative, though I am unable to accept without reservation the remark of Ibn Abī Ḥāṭim that Sufyān disapproved of those who, like Kalbī, commented on the entire text of a *sūra* even where there were no problems to be solved.[4] Sufyān's glosses are of the quality characteristic of an original narrative framework and are virtually interchangeable with those of his contemporaries, here designated haggadic. But it may be recalled that for posterity the reputation of Sufyān, unlike those of Muqātil, Kalbī, and Ibn Isḥāq, remained unblemished.

Problems of transmission and redaction history are notoriously complex.

[1] Kalbī, *Tafsīr*, 130ᵛ; Sufyān, *Tafsīr*, 100.
[2] Cf. Speyer, op. cit. 205–6; Geiger, op. cit. 140–2; and see above, pp. 132–3.
[3] *Tafsīr*, 136, 147; cf. above, p. 133, for Muqātil, *Tafsīr*, 170ʳ *ad* Q. 18: 46.
[4] Editor's introduction, 33–8; *Taqdima*, 79, cited in introduction, 16.

A parallel to the relationship between the Rampur manuscript and those dicta ascribed in later works to Sufyān (as set out in the editor's detailed apparatus) could probably be found in a comparison of opinions attributed to Mujāhid b. Jabr (d. 104/722) and adduced by Ṭabarī (d. 311/923) with the Cairo manuscript of Mujāhid's *Tafsīr*.[1] Remarkable indeed is the use by Ṭabarī of Mujāhid to support what Goldziher described as 'rationalistische Koranauslegung'.[2] In the light of that argument it would be of considerable value to examine Mujāhid's methods in the context of his own work. An obstacle to the kind of comparison suggested is posed by the practice, widespread in later exegetical writings, of introducing minority, dissenting, and unpopular interpretations anonymously.[3] The technique may be illustrated with reference to Q. 12: 31, noticed above in a comparison of Kalbī with Sufyān: now, Zamakhsharī (d. 538/1143) offered for the enigmatic *muttakan/muttaka'an* the following possibilities: place in which to recline (literal), place in which to eat (metaphorical), food whole or sliced (metonymical), and citrus (calque of Hebrew *etrog*) in that sequence and with several orthographical variants, some attributed others introduced *wa-qīla/wa-quri'a*. Out of context as it were, and anonymous, the *etrog* etymology neither served the same purpose nor produced the same effect as when situated within the haggadic framework.[4] Zamakhsharī's work presupposed both methods and results of the haggadic, halakhic, and masoretic types. Quranic interpretation had long since achieved the status of normative discipline and the exegete was free to select from the tradition those elements best suited to his purpose and, moreover, to arrange them according to one of a large number of priorities. The original aim and/or significance of a gloss might be accidentally overlooked or intentionally discarded, its typical context thus ultimately forgotten.

Drawing upon these elementary observations I would submit that the attempt to extrapolate from later works those of earlier authorities is bound to produce both incomplete and inaccurate results. It was, not surprisingly, Wellhausen who first applied the (Pentateuchal) *Urkundenhypothese* to Arabic literature. The end of that exercise, available in both his *Skizzen und Vorarbeiten* VI (1899) and *Das arabische Reich und sein Sturz* (1902), was to isolate regional and partisan tendencies in Ṭabarī's monumental history of the Islamic world. While it would be ungracious not to acknowledge that this was an interesting and valuable experiment, one will be chary of concluding from it that Ṭabarī's primary sources have been or can be recovered in a form at all close to their original state. To assert the contrary would imply that Ṭabarī's work is merely a compilation, exhibiting little

[1] *GAS* i, 29; see Horst, 'Zur Überlieferung', 295–8, 307.

[2] *Richtungen*, 88, 107–10.

[3] See above, pp. 120–1 for an example *ad* Q. 7: 158.

[4] *Kashshāf* ii, 462–4 ad loc.

or no trace of the writer's craft. Such I find impossible to accept and in illustration mention the artfully composed account of Ibn Ashʿath's revolt, allegedly transmitted from Abū Mikhnaf (d. 157/774) and consisting almost entirely of *ayyām* motifs constructed round a fluctuating employment of first-person narrative.[1] For application of the *Urkundenhypothese*, and of other principles of Biblical literary (documentary) criticism, it is well to distinguish between questions about origins (*chronologische Ansetzung*) and those designed to isolate parallel, divergent, and conflicting strands within the literary tradition (*Herausschälung der Fäden*).[2]

From the point of view of chronology, the development of Muslim exegetical literature envisaged here required a span of approximately a century and a half, from Muqātil (d. 150/767) to Ibn Qutayba (d. 276/889). Within that period the principles of exegesis were evolved and perfected, and it would not be too much to say that thereafter few, if any, methodological innovations were introduced. For isolation and description of its components the selection of criteria is a matter requiring the greatest care. In his analysis of Ṭabarī's history Wellhausen employed exclusively the factor of ascription, a choice rendered deceptively attractive by Ṭabarī's fairly consistent use of chains of transmission. But even when supported by a highly differentiated nomenclature for the modalities of transmission, ascription can be remarkably unstable.[3] It is on the one hand vitiated by internal contradiction (as in dicta attributed to authorities like Ibn ʿAbbās and the prophet), and on the other attenuated by anonymity (*wa-qīla/wa-quri'a*). Ascription is also arbitrary: biographical information on the exegetes is found exclusively in literature composed to impugn or to vindicate (*jarḥ wa-taʿdīl*) or to assess relative merit (*ṭabaqāt*), and as such constitutes merely a pseudo-historical projection of the acceptance or dismissal of their views. For these reasons I have thought it best to ignore, or at least to discount, ascription and, by concentrating on the elements of explication both in and out of context, to isolate and identify methodological devices which can be recognized without resort to biographical data.

In the four examples of exegetical writing so far considered I have underlined the centrality of the *narratio*, which is normally accompanied by or appears itself to generate a number of typical devices. Many of

[1] *Annales* ii, 1064–77; cf. *BSOAS* xxxiii (1970) 616; on Ṭabarī's manipulation of tradition cf. Birkeland, *The Lord Guideth*, 9, 10, 16, 22, 29, 40–1; and Widengren, 'Oral tradition', 244–58.

[2] See Eissfeldt, *Einleitung*, 185–216; and above, I pp. 16–17 on Wellhausen's *Reste*; for the tyranny of the 'literary critical' method see also the observations of Mowinckel, 'Psalm criticism', 13–33, and Richter, *Exegese*, 66–7, 120–2, 145–52.

[3] e.g. Abbott, *SALP* i, 5–31, ii, 5–83, 106–13; Sezgin, *GAS* i, 53–84, 237–56; despite careful and often illuminating analysis of technical terminology, the studies of both authors suffer, in my opinion, from an ingenuous acceptance of the *isnād* apparatus, but represent at the same time a not altogether unexpected reaction to the work of Goldziher and Schacht.

those are means of sustaining continuity: prolepsis and cross-reference, repetition/subsumption, variable connectives, interpolation and paraphrase. Others, like segmentation, supercommentary, apostrophe/parenthesis, and recurrence of the minimal units, would seem to, but in fact do not, interrupt the narrative flow. In addition to those stylistic devices, narrative elements such as anecdote, prophetical tradition, identification of the vague and ambiguous (*taʿyīn al-mubham*), and description of the occasions of revelation (*asbāb al-nuzūl*) are present in varying quantity, always sufficient to identify the haggadic type. Even where the *narratio* itself is absent, as in the Rampur manuscript of Sufyān's exegesis, the presence of a number of these elements makes possible identification of the type. Of the twelve explicative elements proposed as criteria for a descriptive analysis of exegetical literature, three at least may be regarded as typically haggadic: anecdote, prophetical tradition, and identification. Others of them are also found there, but in a relation to the type which I should call accidental rather than essential. Some, like poetic *loci probantes* and *variae lectiones* (and the related alternative explanation), are clearly intrusive, not least owing to their disruptive effect upon the *narratio*.

A special case is description of the occasion of revelation, characteristic of halakhic exegesis but present in underdeveloped form in the haggadic type.[1] By that I mean merely that the essential function of the *sabab al-nuzūl* (or *tanzīl*), which was to establish a chronology of revelation, is not evident in haggadic exegesis. There the value of the device is exclusively anecdotal, and may provide the narrative framework for an extended interpretation, either of a whole *sūra* as in Muqātil or of fragments of many *sūra*s as in Ibn Isḥāq. In that sense of course it could be argued that the entire *narratio* functions as *tanzīl*. The formulae usually employed to introduce the device are *nazalat* (*hādhihi 'l-āya*) *fī fulān* and *wa-dhālika ḥīna/annahu qāla fulān*, often accompanied by an anecdote to provide background or local colour. But almost never in haggadic exegesis is the *tanzīl* qualified by alternative explanations of the circumstances of its revelation or followed by a discussion of its juridical significance. Even where interpretation was adapted to an over-all narrative structure, as in Muqātil's treatment of *Sūrat al-Kahf*, separate occasions of revelation may be adduced. An example may be seen *ad* Q. 18: 28, where 'you desire the vanity of this world' was said to have been revealed in reproach of the extreme vanity of ʿUyayna b. Ḥiṣn during an interview with Muhammad, into the account of which was inserted an allusion to the social inequality obtaining between Arab and *mawlā*. Since ʿUyayna's vanity was proverbial, it may well have been not that but the social motif which prompted inclusion of this particular *tanzīl*.[2] An occasion of revelation may be

[1] See below, pp. 177–9. [2] *Tafsīr*, 169r.

gratuitously specified, as in Kalbī *ad* Q. 12: 7, where the passage 'there are lessons for those who ask' is followed by 'this verse was revealed with reference to a story of the Jews'. The purpose of that disclosure in a context exclusively Israelite is not immediately clear, but since it is the only example of *tanzīl* in Kalbī's treatment of *Sūrat Yūsuf*, I am tempted to regard it as merely formal acknowledgement of a methodological principle incorporated into a later redaction and foreign to the original version of Kalbī's exegesis.[1] The frequency of *tanzīl* in haggadic exegesis varies, and in Sufyān is concentrated in *sūra*s containing in fact a high degree of halakhic content. But even there it is sporadic and unpredictable, and its value merely anecdotal, e.g. *ad* Q. 2: 125, 2: 164, and 2: 186. Exceptions are seldom, as at Q. 2: 143–4, where the change of *qibla* from Jerusalem to Mecca was dated.[2] For later theorists the expression 'this verse was revealed about . . .' contained a significant ambiguity, by means of which it became possible to distinguish between a cause (*sabab*) of revelation and a report (*khabar*) about it. According to that distinction *tanzīl* of the sort found in haggadic exegesis could be relegated to the status of *khabar*.[3]

The most flagrantly intrusive of the explicative elements found in haggadic exegesis is poetry adduced to explain Quranic lexica. It is not present in Muqātil, Kalbī, or Sufyān, and instances in the *Sīra* may be attributed to the editorial intervention of Ibn Hishām. That method of interpretation belonged to the masorah and was intimately related to the contemporary development of techniques for the transmission of poetic texts.[4] Solutions to lexical problems were sought by the haggadists within the vocabulary of scripture itself, by recourse to a crude but apparently effective kind of textual analogy. For that device Muqātil employed the term *naẓīr*, but also *mithl* and *shabah*, and occasionally the particle *ka*. With the exception of *naẓīr*, these terms designating analogue appear also, though less frequently, in the work of Kalbī and Sufyān. Together with the term *wajh* ('reference' as contrasted with 'information'), these formed a technical vocabulary for the distributional analysis of meaning in scripture.[5] Closely related thereto is a series of concepts attaching to the terms *mushtabih* and *mutashābih* which, with *wujūh* and *naẓā'ir*, were not fully developed before elaboration of the masorah.[6] I have therefore deferred discussion of them, though it may be observed that as with *tanzīl*, concern with recurrent and even crucial terms in scripture is found in its earliest stage of development in the haggadic literature.

Another kind of lexical treatment was that accorded *hapax legomena* and words conceded to be of foreign origin, as when Muqātil *ad* Q. 18: 31 explained *istabraq* as a Persian word (*lughat fāris*) for brocade, or *ad* 18:

[1] *Tafsir*, 128ᵛ.
[2] *Tafsīr*, 9, 14, 17, 11, respectively.
[3] Cf. Suyūṭī, *Itqān* i, 90; see above, I pp. 41–2, and below, pp. 177–8.
[4] See above, III pp. 94–8; cf. *BSOAS* xxxiii (1970) 390, 616.
[5] See above, III pp. 99–100.
[6] See below, pp. 208–16.

107 *firdaws* as Latin/Greek (*lughat al-rūm*) for walled garden.[1] That procedure, found also in Sufyān, e.g. for *qisṭās* in Q. 17: 35,[2] but not in Kalbī, may be of some value in dating efforts to derive the scriptural lexicon from exclusively Arabic origins, a process which, though associated with the name of Ibn ʿAbbās, was almost certainly the product of masoretic exegesis.[3] Like the variants (both textual and explicative) found in the work of Kalbī and Sufyān (but not in that of Muqātil and Ibn Isḥāq), concern with the lexicon might be thought to presuppose a standard if not quite *ne varietur* text. The earliest method for dealing with basic (crucial) words/notions appears to have been simple paraphrase, as in Kalbī *ad* Q. 12: 87 ولا تيأسوا من روح الله/من رحمة الله.[4]

The elements here briefly described and characterized as intrusive within the haggadic type belong, with one exception, to the interpretative paraphernalia of the masoretes. The exception, mention of the occasion of revelation, is essentially halakhic. Now, isolation of these devices at the haggadic level is difficult, owing to the virtual absence of fixed technical terminology. Save for *naẓīr* (analogue), Muqātil employed in his *Tafsīr* only two other terms which could be described as of more or less rigorous technical application: *istiʾnāf* (juncture) and *taqdīm* (hyperbaton). Even that minimal evidence of technical vocabulary cannot be found in the works of his contemporaries, and it is not quite impossible that these terms, too, could be regarded as intrusive. While there is not for Muqātil evidence of redactional activity of the kind available for Ibn Ishāq, the following entry *ad* Q. 18: 22 deserves notice:[5] وإنما صاروا بالواو لانه انقطع الكلام قال أبو العباس ثعلب قال الفراء هذه الواو واو الحال كان المعنى وهذه حالهم عند ذكر الكلب. It may first of all be remarked that this kind of close philological treatment is not at all typical of Muqātil's exegesis. Insertion of a conjunction into the last only of a series of distributive enumerations was not the sort of problem which interested the author of that work, and one is thus not surprised, apart from the anachronism, to find cited the grammarians Farrā' (d. 207/822) and Thaʿlab (d. 291/904). Curiously, the explanation is not found in the commentary of Farrā', for which Thaʿlab was principal *rāwī*, despite concern there with grammatical niceties.[6] Nor do the several examples of hyperbaton adduced by Muqātil for *Sūrat al-Kahf* (i.e. *ad* verses 6, 10, 21, 25, 31: all instances of an indefinite accusative/adverbial, shifted from a logical to a pausal position) figure in Farrā's treatment of those verses, though these were admittedly not referred to the later authority. Now, the recension in which Muqātil's exegesis was

[1] *Tafsīr*, 169ᵛ, 173ʳ. [2] *Tafsīr*, 131. [3] See below, pp. 218–19.
[4] *Tafsīr*, 135ʳ. [5] *Tafsīr*, 168ᵛ.
[6] *Maʿānī 'l-Qurʾān* ii, 138 top, ad loc.; *GAL* i, 116, Suppl. i, 178 (Farrā'); *GAL* i, 118, Suppl. i, 181 (Thaʿlab).

transmitted is that of Hudhayl b. Ḥabīb, who can hardly have been responsible for mention of Thaʿlab and probably not even of Farrāʾ.[1] But external evidence of that kind is after all secondary, since the intrusive character of the commentary to Q. 18: 22 can be established on structural grounds.

Similarly, structural analysis of Kalbī's exegesis provokes some doubt about the authenticity of *variae lectiones* attributed to the author.[2] There the elliptic phraseology might seem to presuppose the detailed discussions of textual variants found in masoretic authorities, e.g. Farrāʾ. Because of its fragmentary state Sufyān's exegesis is more difficult to assess. As in other examples of haggadic commentary the explicative elements there consist mostly of paraphrastic equivalents, but shorn of an over-all narrative structure which could have provided stylistic uniformity. References in the body of the *Tafsīr* to Sufyān's *rāwī*, Abū Ḥudhayfa (d. 240/854), e.g. at Q. 2: 297 and 36: 12, supply a date which might explain the occasional appearance there of masoretic (*varia lectio*) and halakhic (*tanzīl*) elements.[3] It must, I think, be recognized that extant recensions of exegetical writing here designated haggadic, despite biographical information on its putative authors, are not earlier than the date proposed to mark the beginnings of Arabic literature, namely 200/815. For the relationship between (canonical) text and commentary the implications of that acknowledgement will be obvious: original distinctions have been blurred by redactional activity. The fact itself of literary transmission, moreover, will have contributed to a degree of stylistic and methodological uniformity throughout the range of exegetical literature that makes difficult, if not quite impossible, description of the *Sitz im Leben* of any of its types.

At the beginning of *Sūrat al-Rūm*, Muqātil told the story of a wager between Abū Bakr and Quraysh on the number of years to pass before a Byzantine victory over the Persians would wipe out the humiliation of their defeat by the latter mentioned in scripture. Besides emphasizing the reading *ghulibat* and glossing consistently the scriptural *muʾminūn* as *muslimūn*, the story combines an example of Quranic prognostication (*akhbār al-ghayb*) with a neat connection between events in the Hijaz and the wider world.[4] The primary motif, a natural alliance between Muhammad's followers and the Byzantines (both being 'people of the book') against his opponents and the Persians (both being idolaters), became a constant in Quranic exegesis and a 'fact' of oriental history.[5] The circular argumentation underlying that process is graphically illustrated by the manner in which Ahrens drew upon Wellhausen's assertion (itself apparently an inference from the haggadic interpretation of Q. 30: 1–4)

[1] *GAS* i, 37: 'der noch 190/805 lebte'.
[2] See above, pp. 132–3.
[3] *Tafsīr*, 22, 208; *GAS* i, 41, but cf. the editor's introduction, *Tafsīr*, 38, adducing the dates 220/835 and 226/841.
[4] *Tafsīr*, 230v *ad* Q. 30: 1–4; see above, II pp. 69–70.
[5] e.g. Ibn Saʿd, *Ṭabaqāt* ii, 24; and references in Kister, 'Al-Ḥīra', 144 nn. 2–3.

that the Jews in Arabia (hence opponents of Muhammad) had traditionally (!) sided with Persia against Byzantium, to prove, conversely, that Islam was influenced in its development by the prophet's sympathetic attitude to Christianity.[1] I have mentioned the absence of comment to this passage in the Rampur manuscript of Sufyān; Kalbī alluded to the wager and, like Muqātil, linked the eventual Byzantine victory with the Muslim one at Badr. Thus, what for the exegetes could only be regarded as *vaticinatio ex eventu* furnished anecdotal material both entertaining and edifying.[2]

Narrative ingredients such as that may be described as pseudo-historical digressions.[3] Other kinds are also found, e.g. the prophetical *ḥadīth* adduced by Muqātil in which was described the barrier erected against the depredations of God and Magog, or by Sufyān, where three gentlemen, physically ample but intellectually feeble, discussed in an ingenuous way the kind of conversation God might be expected to overhear.[4] Each story provides a very literal, almost tactile, realization of the verse in question. Related to these features is the apostrophe (parenthesis), in which the exegete addressed his audience by paraphrasing and amplifying a scriptural locution, as in Muqātil *ad* Q. 18: 69 قال ستجدنى إن شاء الله صابرا/قال مقاتل فلم يصبر موسى ولم يأثر بقوله,[5] or Kalbi, *ad* Q. 12: 99 وقال ادخلوا مصر إن شاء الله آمنين/وقد شاء الله آمنين من العدو والسوء.[6] Like most of the haggadic techniques examined here, of which the primary example is the *narratio* itself, digressions such as those do not so much explain scripture as render it familiar. No device could, after all, have been more appropriate to the task of making familiar than provision of names (*taʿyīn*) for the anonymous.[7] The situation into which such procedures could be insinuated might be thought a very informal one indeed.

I have suggested that regular expression of connectives and employment of supercommentary could indicate oral delivery; similarly, 'stage directions' following *qāla*, as well as serial repetition and circular explication, would seem unnecessary in a text designed to be read rather than heard.[8] That the evidence both of style and of content should point to the popular sermon as *Sitz im Leben* of haggadic exegesis is hardly surprising.[9] For the

[1] 'Christliches im Qoran', 148; *Reste*, 236; what may have been the source of this alignment is attested in the history of Palestinian Jewry, see Mann, *Fatimid Caliphs* i, 42 citing Graetz.

[2] See above, p. 138; *Tafsīr*, 228r–v; worthy of remark is the unquestioning acceptance by the haggadists of the reading *ghulibat*, cf. *GdQ* i, 149–50; Goldziher, *Richtungen*, 18–19.

[3] The example is not isolated, cf. Goldziher, *Richtungen*, 58–61, especially on Muqātil *ad* Q. 17: 60.

[4] See above, p. 133; *Tafsīr*, 226–7 *ad* Q. 41: 22.

[5] *Tafsīr*, MS H. Hüsnü 17, 171v.

[6] *Tafsīr*, MS Ayasofya 118, 135v.

[7] See above, pp. 135–6.

[8] See above, pp. 128–31.

[9] See above, I pp. 46–52, esp. pp. 48–9.

history of Arabic literature a long period of oral composition and transmission, or possibly of oral delivery from notes, is commonly supposed to have preceded the redaction of more or less fixed texts. It is the chronology of that process which eludes satisfactory description. Two points in this respect deserve some attention. First, literature exhibiting the haggadic type is preserved only in recensions dating from the third/ninth century. The presence there of what I have described as intrusive elements, though indicative of an incipient sophistication of exegetical method, is not of such dimension as to distort the basic character of the type, which remained recognizable and continued presumably to perform some useful function in the community. Second, it seems clear from the manner in which textual problems were treated, or ignored, that development of the haggadic type preceded in time the refinement of method characteristic of masoretic exegesis. An alternative would be to suppose that the two types developed in mutual isolation and perhaps simultaneously. That view could derive some support from scattered attempts to perpetuate the haggadic type, for example, by Dīnawarī (d. 308/920) or Qummī (d. 309/921).[1] The former work, a nearly verbatim reproduction of Kalbī's commentary and like the latter transmitted on the authority of Ibn ʿAbbās, is hardly conceivable at a time when the writings certainly of Ibn Qutayba (d. 276/889) and probably of Ṭabarī (d. 311/923) were available. It may be that Dīnawarī considered the work of his contemporaries (quite correctly) inappropriate to the pulpit, but if that were so the work of Kalbī himself or of Muqātil could have been used. Qummī's *Tafsīr* (here the title could be authentic), on the other hand, may have been composed to meet a different need. Purportedly derived from the authority of Jaʿfar al-Ṣādiq and of his father, the commentary consists entirely of haggadic elements applied to sectarian theology and displays, curiously, very little in common with the allegorical exegesis contained in writing attributed to Jaʿfar.[2] Lexical explanation is based on paraphrastic equivalence, textual emendation on ʿAlid symbolism, poetic *shawāhid* are minimal, and the use of *narratio* abundant and in conformity with haggadic practice. An interesting variation, in his account of the 'rabbinical' test of prophethood, was location of the rabbis at Najrān.[3] Perpetuation of the haggadic type might thus be ascribed to the survival of its traditional function within the Muslim community; it can hardly be explained within the framework of literary history. Formally haggadic elements in the exegesis of Ṭabarī and his successors were functionally of another order, and had been adapted to a different set of priorities.

Source materials for the popular sermon and other forms of public

[1] *GAS* i, 42 (Dīnawarī), MS Ayasofya 221–2; *GAS* i, 45–6 (Qummī).

[2] Cf. *GdQ* ii, 180; Goldziher, *Richtungen*, 279 ff; *GAS* i, 528–31 (Jaʿfar), and see below, pp. 245–6.

[3] Qummī, *Tafsīr* ii, 31–2 *ad* Q. 18: 9.

oratory are remarkably unstable. An apposite illustration is the *khuṭba* ascribed by Jāḥiẓ to ʿAbdallāh b. Masʿūd, adduced verbatim by Wāqidī, who attributed it to the prophet during his expedition to Tabūk.[1] Literary form can be of assistance in determining date if not always authenticity. It is perhaps not without interest to observe that the parallel employment of elative constructions in that *khuṭba* is found also in the *laudatio* of Umm Maʿbad, allegedly composed during the prophet's *hijra*, and in the address to Quraysh by Naḍr. b. Ḥārith on the appearance in their midst of Muhammad.[2] The earliest examples of oratory seem to have been characterized by synonymous or synthetic parallelism (*muṭābaqa*) rather than by rhymed prose (*sajʿ*), a conclusion supported by the form of speeches in the *ayyām* literature.[3] It is, on the other hand, quite impossible on the basis of such material to date the appearance of rhymed prose or, more important, to infer reasons for abstention from that particular form.[4] Now, a historical development described in terms of evolution from pre-Islamic *khaṭīb* to Islamic *qāṣṣ* might be thought to reflect the argument in favour of *faṣāḥat al-jāhiliyya*, were it not invariably accompanied by a portrait of the popular preacher as degenerate and irresponsible purveyor of fable.[5] That the designation *qāṣṣ* became an epithet of abuse may have been a consequence in part of the fact that he remained a 'popular preacher' on the periphery of the religious establishment. Opprobrium might thus reflect as much functional eccentricity as doctrinal irregularity.[6]

Much if not all of his material, however, is found in the writings of the haggadic exegetes. It may not be irrelevant to note that the Quranic scrolls from Damascus, composed certainly for the purpose of private and possibly communal devotion, contain almost exclusively scriptural passages which could, and did, generate haggadic material, e.g. prophetology, eschatology, and paraenesis.[7] To perceive in the origins of Arabic literary prose a combination of public oratory and elaboration of 'prédication coranique' is undoubtedly sound.[8] Elaboration must of course be understood as interpretation, of which in this context the typical variety was that represented by the aetiological legend, like those related of Abraha's elephant and Muhammad's nocturnal journey.[9] The *narratio* was both didactic and

[1] Jāḥiẓ, *Al-Bayān wal-tabyīn* ii, 52; Wāqidī, *Kitāb al-Maghāzī*, 1016.

[2] See Fischer, 'Umm Maʿbad-Legende', 318–27; Ibn Hishām, *Sīra* I, 299–300; cf. also Stetter, *Topoi und Schemata*, 42, 45–6.

[3] See Caskel, 'Aijām al-ʿArab', 45–6.

[4] *Pace* Goldhizer, *Abhandlungen* i, 57–76, esp. 67–8; cf. Fischer, 'Umm Maʿbad-Legende', 318 n. 1; *BSOAS* xxxiii (1970) 390; and see above, III pp. 116–17.

[5] See above, III pp. 93–9; cf. Goldziher, *Studien* ii, 161–70; id. *Richtungen*, 58–61; id. 'Chaṭīb', 97–102; id. 'Neue Materialien', esp. 478–9.

[6] See Pedersen, 'Islamic Preacher', 226–51; id. 'Criticism', 215–31.

[7] See Ory, 'Un nouveau type', 87–149, esp. 144–9.

[8] See Blachère, *Histoire* iii, 717–36, 737–803, though I am unable to accept the author's proposed chronology.

[9] See above, I pp. 42–3, II pp. 67–70.

entertaining, and anecdotal accreta appended to scriptural texts conformed admirably to the pre-halakhic concept of pious and edifying tradition, symbolized in the formula حديث ضعيف ولكن يستأنس به (poorly accredited but of therapeutic value).[1] To the long and many-faceted process of *Gemeindebildung* which culminated in the canonical text of Muslim scripture, the sermon (*khuṭba*) must have been central, as the instrument of both transmission and explication of the prophetical *logia*. The role of Haggadah was described by Zunz as that which most easily and naturally met similar needs in the post-Exilic Jewish community.[2] The manner in which the popular sermon and the popular preacher were eventually incorporated into, or eliminated from, the orthodox establishment belongs to the internal history of the religious community. The strictures of halakhic and masoretic exegesis did not of course preclude oral delivery, but probably limited such to the lecture room. The requirements of a wider public were not for that reason neglected.

2. DEUTUNGSBEDÜRFTIGKEIT

Concern with both hermeneutical value and grammatical form of revelation could be justified by recourse to scripture itself, whose *Deutungsbedürftigkeit* was in more than one passage explicitly stated.[3] The related but distinct processes of hermeneutical derivation and textual adjustment, neither of which figured more than marginally (or intrusively) in the work of the haggadists, were conveniently described by Vermes as 'applied' and 'pure' exegesis respectively.[4] Those labels are eminently practical, and indicate functional value rather than methodological content of the exegetical types. Related to the formation of the Islamic community, and measured against the data of Arabic literary history, both kinds of exegetical activity (or rather, hermeneutics and exegesis proper) represent phenomena typologically distinct from the haggadic expression analysed in the preceding pages. These phenomena consist principally in the elaboration of analogical method and in the concomitant acquisition of a technical vocabulary. While elements of the latter can often be traced to scriptural usage, the further semantic development of exegetical terminology usually followed paths divergent from, and even contrary to, the rudimentary associations of scriptural context. That such is so for the vocabulary of Biblical exegesis was stated recently by Loewe and is amply demonstrated in Bacher's lexicon.[5] If the elaboration of Rabbinic, and sectarian, exegesis

[1] Goldziher, *Studien* ii, 154; cf. *BSOAS* xxxi (1968) 615.

[2] *Vorträge*, 342–441, esp. 354–73; and Grünbaum, *Sagenkunde*, 1–54; cf. Elbogen, *Gottesdienst*, 194–8; Seeligmann, 'Midraschexegese', esp. 176–81; Vermes, *Scripture*, 1–10, 67–126.

[3] See above, III pp. 99–102.

[4] 'Bible and Midrash', in *CHB* i, 199–231.

[5] 'The "plain" meaning', 154; Bacher, *Terminologie* i–ii, *passim*.

can be shown to reflect the impingement of Hellenistic rhetorical tradition,[1] the corresponding evolution of Muslim exegetical terminology, closely associated with the Jewish tradition, was even more complex. The emergence, at the end of the third/ninth century, of rhetorical criticism apparently derived from and certainly directed to works of profane literature may be, and indeed has been, interpreted as evidence of Hellenistic influence upon the Arabic science of rhetoric.[2] That particular view is of course only one of several possible. But whatever the ultimate source of any given procedure or device, it is quite impossible to separate the development of profane rhetoric from that of scriptural exegesis, at least in any but the haggadic sense of that expression. However contrived and exclusively theoretical the relation of Arabic eloquence to the word of God might seem, the tendency to seek in scripture authority for the principles of rhetoric was very real.[3]

Symbolic of the alliance between the two disciplines was the use made of Q. 3: 7 هو الذى أنزل عليك الكتاب منه آيات محكمات هن أم الكتاب وأخر متشابهات فأما الذين فى قلوبهم زيغ فيتبعون ما تشابه منه ابتغاء الفتنة وابتغاء تأويله وما يعلم تأويله الا الله والراسخون فى العلم يقولون آمنّا به كل من عند ربّنا وما يذّكّر الا أولوا الألباب. Commentary on this passage, unanimously agreed to represent the point of departure for all scriptural exegesis, itself exhibits a historical and typological spectrum of interpretative method. The operative terms in the verse were seen to be three: *muḥkam*, *mutashābih*, and *umm al-kitāb*, each of which came to be assigned a distinguished if uneven semantic history. Concern at the haggadic level was naturally with unitary definitions, and for Muqātil the *āyāt muḥkamāt* were those verses whose prescriptions were to be implemented, further specified (or exemplified) as Q. 6: 151–3. Such were designated mother/source of the book (*umm al-kitāb*:*aṣl al-kitāb*) since they were not only preserved with God (*fi'l-lawḥi 'l-maḥfūẓ*: *sic*, cf. Q. 85: 21–2) but also in the scriptures of all peoples (*sic*).[4] Kalbī's view was not dissimilar, but included the additional qualification that these verses set out permission and prohibition and were ones which had not been abrogated (*mubayyināt bil-ḥalāl wal-ḥarām lam tunsakh*).[5] For both exegetes the *āyāt mutashābihāt* were the four initial *sigla* آلم والمص والمر والر found in thirteen *sūra*s, and here of numerical and apocalyptic value, related to the taunts

[1] Cf. Loewe, op. cit., 140–54; Daube, 'Rabbinic methods', 239–64; Gertner, 'Terms' 1–27; id. 'Pharisaioi', 245–68.

[2] See Ṭāhā Ḥusayn, 'La Rhétorique arabe', 3–24; Heinrichs, *Arabische Dichtung*, 11–18, 105–70, with reference to von Grunebaum, 'Die aesthetischen Grundlagen der arabischen Literatur', *Kritik*, 130–50.

[3] See above, II pp. 79–80, and below, pp. 232–9.

[4] *Tafsīr*, MS H. Hüsnü 17, 35ᵛ.

[5] *Tafsīr*, MS Ayasofya 118, 29ʳ.

of Muhammad's Jewish opposition.[1] That this kind of interpretation served a useful, if limited, purpose may be clear from the preceding observations on haggadic method. It could not, and did not, survive the more exacting demands of halakhists and masoretes. Kalbī's reference for *muḥkam* to the principle of abrogation (*naskh*) necessitated a correlation *mutashābih*: *mansūkh*, implicitly ascribed to Ibn ʿAbbās and extending considerably application of the term *mutashābih*. In rather more detail, and with explicit ascription to Ibn ʿAbbās, was the introductory statement of Abū ʿUbayd (d. 224/838) in his treatise on abrogation, for which Q. 3: 7 must have seemed to the author an appropriate peg: المحكمات ناسخه وحلاله وحرامه وفرائضه ومما يؤمن به ويعمل به والمتشابهات منسوخه ومقدمه ومؤخره وأمثاله وأقسامه وما يؤمن به ولا يعمل به.[2] By means of that aphoristic formulation, which did not add appreciatively to delimitation of a technical vocabulary, scriptural material not of regulative content, in the opinion at least of Abū ʿUbayd, was relegated to the status of *mutashābih*: 'the object of belief but not of conduct'. That functional cleavage could hardly be of use for the masorah, and it is thus curious to find repeated by Farrā' the information in Muqātil and Kalbī, including the allusion of the latter to abrogation.[3] The same material was also adduced ad loc. by Zajjāj (d. 311/923) who, however, proposed a further contrast: *muḥkam* verses were immediately meaningful owing to their straightforward/obvious expression (*ẓāhir bayyin*), while *mutashābih* verses in order to be understood required insight (*naẓr*) and reflection (*tadabbur*/*tadbīr*). Examples of the first category were the stories of the prophets and of creation (*sic*), of the second the claims for the fact of resurrection.[4] Explicit reference to the 'plain meaning' of scripture might seem arbitrary, if not quite insidious, in a work where the *muḥkamāt* were also subjected to exegesis. Even a theoretical postulate that the *muḥkamāt* were immediately clear (*wāḍiḥ mubīn*) was rejected by Māturīdī (d. 333/944) in his detailed survey of the several traditions relating to Q. 3: 7.[5] A series of contrasting pairs was set out: the meaning of *muḥkamāt* could be rationally apprehended (*fil-ʿaql bayānuhu*), that of *mutashābihāt* only by recourse to authoritative tradition (*bi-maʿrifat al-samʿ*); *muḥkamāt* were verses of regulative content (*aḥkām*), while knowledge of the *mutashābihāt* was not even necessary (*laysa bil-nās ḥāja ilā 'l-ʿilm bihi*); *muḥkamāt* were abrogating, *mutashābihāt* abrogated; *muḥkamāt* could be understood

[1] Cf. *GdQ* ii, 68–78; and above, II p. 64; Muqātil and Kalbī are too allusive: the entire anecdote on the expected duration of Muhammad's power is retailed in Suyūṭī, *Itqān* iii, 25–6.

[2] *GAS* i, 48; MS Ahmet III 143, 3ʳ.

[3] *Maʿānī 'l-Qur'ān*, MS Nurosmaniye 459, 29ᵛ ad loc.

[4] *GAS* i, 49; MS Nurosmaniye 115, 67ᵛ: entitled *ʿIrāb*/*Maʿānī 'l-Qur'ān*.

[5] *GAS* i, 49, 604–6; *Ta'wīlāt al-Qur'ān*, MS Medine 179, 116ᵛ–7ʳ.

by meditation (*tafakkur/ta'ammul/naẓr*), *mutashābihāt* by research (*ṭalab/baḥth*); *muḥkamāt* could be known, *mutashābihāt* not at all. Finally, *mutashābihāt* might be explained by reference to *muḥkamāt*: وقيل يجوز أن يوقف على المتشابه بمعرفة المحكم, a rational postulate which might be thought to eliminate the contradictions inherent in the preceding series. For Māturīdī, it may be noted, the antithesis *ẓāhir*: *bāṭin* meant not the 'literal' as opposed to the 'concealed' significance of the verse in question, but rather the 'apparent' as contrasted with the 'real' meaning, a distinction which became the point of departure for his methodological application of *ta'wīl*.[1]

It was the explicit relating of *mutashābihāt* to *muḥkamāt*, the latter in the role of exegetical *point d'appui*, that provided a foundation for both halakhic and masoretic exegesis. Jaṣṣāṣ (d. 370/981) considered that relation central to the task of exegesis, but admitted that not every possible meaning (*ma'nā*) or aspect (*wajh*) of the *mutashābihāt* could thus be discovered: فثبت بذلك أن المراد بالمتشابه المذكور فى هذه الآية هو اللفظ المحتمل للمعانى الذى يجب ردّه الى المحكم وحمل على معناه.[2] The procedure of referring *mutashābihāt* to *muḥkamāt* might entail reasoning (*'aql*) or recourse to authority (*sam'*), though the former could not be the undisciplined application of independent reason, but rather the rational employment of scholarly tradition.[3] Juxtaposition of *muḥkamāt* and *mutashābihāt* involved explicit recognition of analogy as an exegetical principle, whether textual or doctrinal, and this became the cornerstone of scriptural interpretation.[4] That the initial impetus in the application of analogical deduction to scripture was halakhic, rather than masoretic, might be thought corroborated by the ascription to Shāfi'ī (d. 204/820) of the earliest work entitled *Aḥkām al-Qur'ān*.[5] More systematically formulated even than the work of Jaṣṣāṣ was the *Aḥkām al-Qur'ān* of Ibn 'Arabī (d. 543/1148) who, in his commentary to the *Ṣaḥīḥ* of Tirmidhī reiterated the relation of analogy obtaining between *muḥkamāt* and *mutashābihāt* and drew attention to the spiritual valuc of the exegetical activity which must result from inclusion in scripture of the two kinds of verse.[6] On the necessity of that differentiation Ibn Qutayba had been even more explicit: ولو كان القرآن كله ظاهرا مكشوفا حتى يستوى فى معرفته العالم والجاهل لبطل التفاضل بين الناس وسقطت المحنة وماتت الخواطر.[7]

[1] See below, pp. 154–8.
[2] *GAS* i, 444–5; *Aḥkām al-Qur'ān* ii, 3.
[3] *Aḥkām* ii, 5–6.
[4] See below, pp. 166–70.
[5] *GAS* i, 484–90, esp. 489–90 no. VII; the recension is that of Bayhaqī (d. 458/1066), from which it may be necessary to conclude that only the organizing principle, not its application/illustration, can be dated as early as the end of the second/eighth century.
[6] *GAL* i, 412–13, Suppl. I, 632, 663, 732; on the margin of Tirmidhī, *Ṣaḥīḥ* xi, 114–20.
[7] *Ta'wīl*, 62.

This view of scriptural exegesis as a divinely imposed task inherent in the very structure of the document of revelation exhibited considerable advance towards the scientific formulation of interpretative method and away from the haggadic division of God's word into prescription, narrative, and paraenesis. The obligation to study, to immerse oneself in religious science (*rāsikh fil-ʿilm*), could be and was derived from the much-disputed segmentation of Q. 3: 7, namely, whether interpretation (*ta'wīl*) of the *mutashābihāt* was limited to God alone or to God and to those firmly rooted in religious knowledge. Ibn Qutayba argued that since the prophet must have known the meaning of those verses (!), such was necessarily transmitted to his companions and thus made accessible to the community.[1] The question of juncture (*isti'nāf/ibtidā'*) in Q. 3: 7, between *allāh* and *wal-rāsikhūn*, may be understood to symbolize all argument about the limits of exegetical activity. Insistence upon a disjunctive syntactical value for the particle *waw*, as articulated by Suyūṭī,[2] was neutralized by the admission that not every facet of their manifold significance could anyway be wrung from the *mutashābihāt*.[3] That something of the mystery of revelation should be reserved to its author could be accepted without encroaching unduly upon the domain of the exegetes: والى أن بعض المتشابه مختصّ بالله تعالى.[4] Their unceasing effort to understand was not thereby circumscribed, concisely expressed by Zamakhsharī *ad* Q. 3: 7.[5] That the ultimately prevailing point of view should be identical with the attitude of Rabbinic Judaism towards the study of scripture will, in view of all that has so far been adduced, hardly surprise. Authority was after all provided by scripture itself, e.g. Ezra 7: 10, Nehemiah 8: 7, where the basic ingredients of a technical vocabulary were also found.[6] Isolated attempts, already remarked, in Muslim exegetical literature to equate *muḥkam* with *ẓāhir* (obvious, in the sense of unambiguous: *maʿnā wāḥid*) represent a polemical tendency, if not specific school disputes, and may be compared with such disarming statements as דברה תורה כלשון בני אדם or אין מקרא יוצא מידי פשוטו.[7] It is at least not beyond reasonable doubt whether the terms *peshaṭ/peshuṭ* signified the 'obvious' or 'literal' meaning of scripture, though in the context of dispute they might tendentiously be so used: more realistic are Loewe's proposals 'familiar' in the sense of widespread, and 'authoritative' in the sense of interpretation sanctified by tradition.[8] Save in the polarity *ẓāhir*:*bāṭin* employed for allegorical exegesis, Muslim

[1] *Ta'wīl*, 72–4.
[2] *Itqān* iii, 5–6, also i, 253.
[3] e.g. Jaṣṣāṣ, *Aḥkām al-Qur'ān* ii, 3.
[4] Suyūṭī, *Itqān* iii, 9.
[5] *Kashshāf* i, 337–8; translated in Goldziher, *Richtungen*, 127–9.
[6] See Zunz, *Vorträge*, 13–36; Elbogen, *Gottesdienst*, 194–8.
[7] Bacher, *Terminologie* i, 98, ii, 103, 173.
[8] 'The "plain" meaning', 158–9, 167, 176–82; cf. Bacher, op. cit. ii. 172–3.

use of the term *ẓāhir* signified 'obvious' only in the sense that one's own argument was felt to be more compelling than that of one's adversary.[1]

Identification in Q. 3: 7 of the *muḥkamāt* with *umm al-kitāb* was uniformly understood to refer to the divine archetype of scripture, i.e. its nucleus (*aṣl al-kitāb*), analogically deduced from the two other Quranic occurrences of the phrase *umm al-kitāb*: 13: 39 الله . . . وعنده أم الكتاب and 43: 4 وانه فى أم الكتاب لدينا. Though it may be objected that the deduction was facile and hardly substantiated by the respective contexts of the locution, the only modification ever proposed was that the *muḥkamāt*, containing as they did divine prescription, enjoyed priority of rank over verses which were not regulative, and in that sense could be designated 'mother of the book', a phrase often and for quite different reasons applied to *Sūrat al-Fātiḥa*.[2] Only in Q. 3: 7, where it could be an interpolation, may *umm al-kitāb* refer not to scriptural archetype, but rather to exegetical *point d'appui*. Such of course would have been more satisfactorily expressed by a construction **umm lil-kitāb* exhibited in the Rabbinic precepts יש אם למקרא/למסורת. Horowitz was probably right to reject the equivalence on the grounds that phraseological similarity was belied by their quite different applications.[3] On the other hand, that view of the *muḥkamāt* as reference (*maradd*) for interpretation of the *mutashābihāt* might well be thought comparable to the Rabbinic notion of *em* as 'authority'.[4]

Allusion to the ultimate necessity of exegesis is contained also in Q. 75: 19 ثم إنّ علينا بيانه. The two other Quranic occurrences of *bayān*, in 3: 138 and 55: 4, as well as the single instance of *tibyān* in 16: 89, designate 'sign', revealed as guidance and mercy.[5] Such also is the function of the exclusively substantival *bayyina/bayyināt*, while the participle *mubīn* is in scripture employed only as attribute (as also adjectival *bayyin* in 18: 15 and *bayyina* in 2: 211 and 29: 35). In Q. 75: 19 *bayān* was understood by exegetes to signify not merely 'clarity' but also 'clarification', that is, equivalent to *tabyīn*.[6] In that verse the agency was divine, as in all occurrences of the transitive finite forms, which have as object the word 'signs' (*āyāt*; e.g. Q. 24: 18, 58, 59, 61) or a noun clause (e.g. 16: 44, 64). *Bayān* as exegesis was thus sanctioned by scriptural usage, though the Quranic locution had not quite the paideutic sense of Biblical *hebin*, e.g. Nehemiah 8: 7–9, Daniel 11: 33.[7] Synonymous with Quranic *bayān* is the term *tafṣīl*, also 'clarification' and restricted to the agency of God: either the

[1] See below, pp. 242–3.

[2] e.g. Māturīdī, *Ta'wīlāt*, MS Medine 179, 117r; Suyūṭī, *Itqān* iii, 9–10.

[3] *Untersuchungen*, 65; Torczyner's conjecture, *apud* Augapfel, '"Kitāb"', 387, presupposed in any case a misunderstanding.

[4] See Zunz, *Vorträge*, 338 n. (b); Bacher, *Terminologie*, i, 119–21.

[5] See above, I pp. 5–6.

[6] e.g. Zamakhsharī, *Kashshāf* iv, 661 ad loc.

[7] Cf. Gertner, 'Terms', 21 n. 3.

book makes all things clear (Q. 6: 154) or is itself made clear (6: 114) by the act of revelation. The notion of being made distinct by separation/demarcation (cf. Q. 11: 1, 41:3) provided a technical term for Quranic periodization.[1] Interpretation of *faṣṣala/tafṣīl* as separation and hence specification is reminiscent of Rabbinic and Qumranic *peresh*:[2] the Muslim term was employed predominantly in halakhic exegesis.

The generic designation of Quranic exegesis is in scripture itself a *hapax legomenon*: Q. 25: 33 ولا يأتونك بمثل الا جئناك بالحق وأحسن تفسيرا. The subject of *ya'tūnaka* is 'those who reject/disbelieve' (*alladhīna kafarū* in the preceding verse), and the entire passage an assurance that opposition to God's messenger will be countered by divine assistance. The unique context of the term *tafsīr* is thus polemic, of a kind frequently alluded to in the exegetical tradition.[3] Zamakhsharī's gloss *takshīf* referred to the 'uncovering' of a (maliciously) concealed truth, and represents a standard charge in sectarian dispute.[4] A similar, but rather more academic, lexical exercise is contained in the etymology by metathesis (*tafsīr*:*tasfīr*—'unveiling') proposed in a commentary to Māturīdī's *Ta'wīlāt*.[5] But it seems more than doubtful that for the technical term *tafsīr* either the Quranic verse 25: 33 or the metathesis exhibits an authentic *Sitz im Leben*.[6] It may further be doubted whether *tafsīr* ever meant, or could really mean, uncovering, in the sense of bringing to light a concealed significance. The hermeneutical process involved in *tafsīr* becomes clearer from examination of what became the standard binary opposition *tafsīr*:*ta'wīl*. There the several attempts to define the contrast were based on primarily epistemological considerations. In a synthesis of pertinent arguments Suyūṭī established a dichotomy of exegetical modes in which *tafsīr* was defined as the transmission of authoritative witness, *scil.* to the occasions of revelation (*riwāya/samā'/shahāda*), and *ta'wīl* as the product of research and expertise, *scil.* in the analysis of scripture (*dirāya/istinbāṭ*).[7] The polarity had found diagrammatic expression in the work of Māturīdī: *tafsīr* belongs to the companions of the prophet, *ta'wīl* to those learned in doctrine (التفسير للصحابة والتأويل للفقهاء).[8] Now, it is hardly possible that these comparatively formal

[1] See above, III pp. 116–17; *fāṣila/fawāṣil*.

[2] e.g. *Kashshāf* IV, 184 *ad* Q. 41: 3 (with formal but unnecessary reference to a reading without *tashdīd*); cf. Gertner, 'Pharisaioi', 254–5.

[3] See above, pp. 122–7; and I, pp. 36–8.

[4] *Kashshāf* iii, 279 ad loc.; for *kitmān/taḥrīf/tabdīl*, see below, pp. 189–90.

[5] Samarqandī (*ca.* 540/1145); see Götz, 'Māturīdī', 35–6; adduced anonymously by Suyūṭī, *Itqān* iv, 167.

[6] See below, pp. 233–5; Wieder's relating Karaite (?) *mashpirim* to Arabic *tasfīr* might be linguistically sound, but it may be noted that the Arabic word was never an exegetical term, and further, that in Arabic lexicology this kind of etymology (metathesis) need not be taken seriously, see Wieder, *Scrolls*, 59 n. 4.

[7] *Itqān, naw'* 77: iv, 167–73; *Kitāb al-Mabānī*, ch. VII, 172–82.

[8] *Ta'wīlāt*, MS Medine 180, 1v; cf. Götz, 'Māturīdī', 31–8.

definitions antedate by much the generation of Ṭabarī and Māturīdī (end of the third/ninth century). But the antithesis *tafsīr*:*ta'wīl* appears in inverted form in a rudimentary classification of exegesis at the beginning of Muqātil's *Tafsīr* where, on the authority of Ibn 'Abbās, it was stated that *tafsīr* is what was known by scholars (*'ulamā'*) and *ta'wīl* by God alone.[1] To the problems attending the recension of Muqātil's *Tafsīr*, it may be added that the same tradition from Ibn 'Abbās was adduced by Suyūṭī, but contains the term *tafsīr* throughout.[2] It is perhaps not without interest that in his exposition of the *tafsīr*:*ta'wīl* polarity Suyūṭī employed as generic designation of exegesis the terms *bayān* and *i'rāb*, explaining that the use of *i'rāb* in the sense of grammatical sign (*ḥukm naḥwī*) was in fact a neologism.[3] That *i'rāb* could, in the light of philologists' use of *a'rab* and of Quranic *'arabī*, signify 'clarification' is not at all unreasonable, and that usage was embodied in the titles of the commentaries ascribed to Farrā' and Zajjāj.[4]

In addition to the almost purely formal criteria represented by the *riwāya*:*dirāya* contrast, a substantial distinction between *tafsīr* and *ta'wīl* was also formulated. *Tafsīr* was methodologically limited to scriptural passages bearing but a single interpretation, *ta'wīl* to those bearing more than one: فالتفسير ذا (*sic*) وجه والتأويل ذا وجوه.[5] The operative terms were *wajh*/*wujūh* (aspect) and *rājiḥ*/*marjūḥ* (prevailing/preferred), used respectively to designate the range of options and of those the optimum. As with most technical terminology ultimately associated with a particular discipline, the locution *dhū wujūh* retained its earlier and general significance, and could refer simply to the many facets of the Quranic message, e.g. القرآن ذلول ذو وجوه or القرآن حمّال ذو وجوه.[6] The proximity of *wujūh* to the Tannaitic *panim* was pointed out by Goldziher, in respect of which it may be noted that both terms were employed in halakhic as in other types of exegesis.[7] It could be argued that the distinction between *tafsīr* and *ta'wīl* remained a theoretical one; Abū 'Ubayd, whose interest in the text of scripture was primarily halakhic, had asserted that

[1] *Tafsīr*, MS H. Hüsnü 17, 2r.

[2] See above, pp. 143–4: the introduction is full of technical terms which seldom or never appear in the body of the work; *Itqān* iv, 188: i.e., some *tafsīr* can be known to men, other *tafsīr* only to God.

[3] *Itqān* iv, 172–3; *iṣṭilāḥ ḥadīth*; see above, III pp. 109–11.

[4] See above, III pp. 93–4, 98–9; e.g. MS Nurosmaniye 459 and 115, respectively; cf. *GAS* i, 48–9.

[5] Māturīdī, *Ta'wīlāt*, MS Medine 180, 1v; Suyūṭī, *Itqān* iv, 167.

[6] Suyūṭī, *Itqān* iv, 184; *Nahj al-balāgha*, cited Goldziher, *Vorlesungen*, 41, 74, n. 4; cf. also Abbott, *SALP* ii, 100 n. 48.

[7] *Richtungen*, 84–5; cf. Bacher, *Terminologie* ii, 157, and on *panim* as synonym of *ṭe'amim*, i, 151; for the locution *mā 'l-wajh*, as calque of *mah ha-ṭa'am*, an example may be found in Zamakhsharī, *Kashshāf* i, 519–20 *ad* Q. 4: 48.

they were one and the same.[1] The difficulty lay in determining which Quranic verses might be characterized as containing more than one aspect (*wajh*) and hence suceptible of interpretation by *ta'wīl*. From Q. 3: 7 it was clear that *ta'wīl* was applicable only to the *mutashābihāt*, identification of which was, as noted, remarkably unstable. The analogical relationship seen by Māturīdī and Jaṣṣāṣ to obtain between *muḥkam* and *mutashābih* meant that in practice the latter could be explained by reference to the former, even though not every aspect of the *mutashābihāt* could be so illuminated. The methodological difference between *tafsīr* and *ta'wīl* might seem thus at least blurred, if not entirely effaced, by the admitted interdependence of *muḥkamāt* and *mutashābihāt*. The formal difference could, however, be maintained: in contrast to *ta'wīl*, which involved investigation and research, *tafsīr* depended upon tradition. The same solution to a scriptural problem might, in other words, be reached by different methods: its acceptability was often no more than a matter of presentation, that is, with or without the requisite witness (*shahāda*/*riwāya*). It seems clear that the *tafsīr*: *ta'wīl* dichotomy symbolized a dispute rather more fundamental than one merely of method or terminology, namely, the exegetical relationship between canonical and non-canonical material in the witness to revelation preserved and transmitted by the Muslim community.

The necessity of resort to tradition as interpretative complement to scripture was the crux of sectarian dispute between and within the Jewish and Christian communities. The extent to which tradition could be regarded as dispensable depended upon the successful elaboration of exegetical techniques which might be seen to elucidate scripture, as it were, from within. Without stressing unduly the essential futility of steps taken to that end, it is worth observing that there is about them a considerable measure of uniformity. The 'Torah-centricity' of such groups as the Qumran sectaries, the Apostolic Christians, and the Karaites generated a series of interpretative principles which might have been, and in some instances actually were, freely exchanged.[2] One such common element was the division of scripture into 'manifest' and 'concealed' parts, the latter epithet employed not in the sense of esoteric but of ambiguous or equivocal, in short, *deutungsbedürftig*. It would, in my opinion, not be unjustified to see in the antithesis *muḥkamāt*: *mutashābihāt* a reflex of *niglot*: *nistarot*, and in particular of the contention that in each pair the second element might be elucidated by reference to the first.[3]

In Muslim practice that process of analogical deduction presupposed

[1] *Apud* Suyūṭī, *Itqān* iv, 167.

[2] See Gerhardsson, *Memory*, 172–3, 233, 284–7; Wieder, *Scrolls*, 53–62; Rabin, *Qumran*, 95–111.

[3] Wieder, *Scrolls*, 76–7; Rabin, *Qumran*, 99.

the self-sufficiency of the Qur'ān, and as such must be regarded as polemical in character. The dispute was articulated, if never quite satisfactorily resolved, in the elaboration of halakhic exegesis.[1] The notion of ambiguity in the term *mutashābih*, as partaking of more than one semantic aspect, was reinforced by identification with *mushtabih*, possibly an allusion to the parallel passages Q. 6: 99 and 6: 141, or others, e.g. Q. 2: 25 and 2: 118,[2] but more probably engendered by its antithetical relation to *muḥkam*. The synonymity of *mutashābih* and *mushtabih* is explicit in Zamakhsharī *ad* Q. 3: 7, and had much earlier become axiomatic for masoretic exegesis.[3] It would be misleading, depite the centrality of Māturīdī in its formulation, to suggest that scriptural exegesis which dispensed with tradition was invariably designated *ta'wīl*. In scripture itself the term occurs seventeen times and, save for *Sūrat Yūsuf* (Q. 12: 6, 21, 36, 37, 44, 45, 100, 101) where it could only be rendered 'dream-interpretation' (*taʿbīr al-ru'yā*), it was consistently glossed 'outcome'/'sequel' (*ʿāqiba*), thus lending the term a distinctly eschatological flavour which accorded nicely with the haggadic definition of *mutashābihāt* as four of the cryptic Quranic *sigla*.[4] It seems to me that this eschatological, or at least prognostic, sense fits rather better than 'interpretation' the use of *ta'wīl* in the much-cited verse of ʿAbdallāh b. Rawāḥa: نحن قتلناكم على تأويله   كما قتلناكم على تنزيله.[5] It was partly owing to that application that the term *ta'wīl* achieved enduring status in allegorical exegesis, which was largely though not exclusively sectarian.[6]

Function as generic designation of scriptural exegesis devolved thus upon *tafsīr*, eventually employed for most if not quite all varieties of that exercise. That its *Sitz im Leben* was almost certainly the lexicon of profane rhetoric does not of course exclude influence from other quarters.[7] Whether the literary activity of the haggadists was actually described by its authors as *tafsīr* is, owing to redactional complications, not easily answered. In his historical survey of exegetical method Goldziher described that 'primitive' interpretation as the nucleus of what became traditionist *tafsīr* (*tafsīr manqūl*) and as secondary to establishment of the text of scripture (*Textgestaltung*).[8] That view of the anterior existence of a *ne varietur* text gradually subjected to interpretation reflects of course the ʿUthmanic recension traditions with all their very familiar implications. A complementary feature of this traditional view of Islamic origins is the assertion that early attempts to interpret the text of scripture were frustrated by an

[1] See below, pp. 175–7, 188, 201–2.
[2] Cf. Ibn Qutayba, *Ta'wīl*, 74.
[3] See below, pp. 212–15; *Kashshāf* i, 337–8.
[4] See above, p. 149.
[5] Ṭabarī, *Annales* I/1595; cf. Goldziher, *Studien* ii, 112 n. 5; id. *Abhandlungen* i, 60 n. 2; id. *Richtungen*, 278.
[6] See below, pp. 243–6.
[7] See below, pp. 233–5.
[8] *Richtungen*, 55–85 and 1–54, respectively.

official prohibition, or at least restriction, of exegetical activity.[1] Reason for the official measures, invariably associated with the figure of ʿUmar b. Khaṭṭāb, was seen to be an expression of extreme piety. Modifications of this view have subsequently appeared, notably those of Birkeland and Abbott.[2] Birkeland recognized that the alleged opposition was a late formulation exhibiting school disputes about the *form* in which *tafsīr* ought to be transmitted, a contention often and misleadingly expressed in terms of the opposition *tafsīr bil-ʿilm*: *tafsīr bil-raʾy*.[3] Abbott's insistence upon the historicity of the story of ʿUmar and Ṣabīgh seems to me to have missed the point entirely, as do her simplistic references to *mutashābihāt* and *tafsīr al-nabī*.[4]

The figure of ʿAbdallāh b. ʿAbbās (d. 68/687) as *tarjumān al-Qurʾān* might be thought to pose something of a problem. Birkeland's relegation of that figure to a personification of consensus (*ijmāʿ*), symbolized in particular by the *isnād* Ibn Saʿd–Ibn ʿAbbās, is a reasonable hypothesis indeed, especially if qualified by an admission that the historical process reflected in *tafsīr* cannot be reconstructed before the beginning of the third/ninth century.[5] References in the *ṭabaqāt* literature to earlier authorities, almost without exception disciples of Ibn ʿAbbās transmitting on his authority, can hardly be said to represent more than the proliferation of companion *isnād*s shown to be characteristic of legal traditions. Impetus for the production of both legal and *tafsīr* traditions was halakhic, and objections to '*tafsīr*' are in my opinion to be understood only secondarily as disapproval of independent reasoning (*raʾy*) as opposed to traditional science (*ʿilm*). The primary dispute was about the sources of doctrine (*uṣūl al-fiqh*) and reflected in the respective claims to priority put forward by advocates, on the one hand, of canonical revelation, and on the other, of non-canonical revelation.[6] The role of ʿUmar in the anti-*tafsīr* traditions might be compared to that of ʿUthmān in the canonization traditions: an explanatory mechanism designed to attest the earliest possible origins for the components of Islam.[7] The absence of scriptural interpretation before the generation of haggadists does not require an explanation so contrived and internally inconsistent.

That during the second/eighth century halakhic disputes were essentially ones about principles as opposed to methods may be thought corroborated

[1] *Richtungen*, 55–64.

[2] *Muslim Opposition*; and *SALP* ii, 106–13.

[3] *Muslim Opposition*, 28–32.

[4] *SALP* ii, 106–13; that the story of ʿUmar and Ṣābigh constituted proverbial illustration of tiresome interrogation, not only about the *mutashābihāt*, but also halakhic material in scripture, seems clear from Mālik's reference in a discussion of the spoils of war, *Muwaṭṭaʾ*, 455: *Kitāb al-Jihād* no. 19.

[5] *Muslim Opposition*, 32–42; I am not quite certain, however, whether Birkeland would accept that qualification.

[6] See above, I pp. 51–2; and below, pp. 161–3, 188.

[7] See *BSOAS* xxxi (1968) 613–16.

by the witness of two documents often adduced as milestones in the juridical and political development of Islam. The first of these is the *Risāla fil-ṣaḥāba* of Ibn Muqaffaʿ (d. 142/759).[1] The standpoint of the author in matters pertaining to the practical administration of justice was characterized by Schacht as a recommendation of procedural uniformity, to be imposed by the government (*sic*) upon a situation of juridical chaos.[2] The elements of confusion could be identified as regional dispute, about the priority of *sunna* (as *ius consuetudinis*) and *ra'y* (as practical inference), overlaid by the legacy of Umayyad administrative practice. It may well be that Ibn Muqaffaʿ's proposals were derived from Persian models, but the notion of charismatic leadership underlying his emphasis upon the position of the caliph hardly required foreign inspiration.[3] My interest here lies exclusively in the role of scripture in Ibn Muqaffaʿ's suggestions for organizing the Islamic community. As a source of caliphal authority the Qur'ān (designated *kitāb*) received but scant attention, usually in tandem: *al-kitāb wal-sunna*, and was only once cited, as 'revelation' (*tanzīl*), i.e. Q. 7: 43 وما كنّا لنهتدى لولا أن هدانا الله in a context which recommended, appropriately, recourse to sound reasoning.[4] Arbitrary employment of reason was condemned, but also arguments based upon *sunna* which could not be derived from the prophet or from one of his rightly guided successors (!) على عهد رسول الله أو ائمة الهدى من بعده.[5] Sound reasoning consisted in the caliphal application of analogy (*tadbīr wa-qiyās*), and in matters of dispute the caliph was to employ that instrument: فينظر فيه الى أحق الفريقين بالتصديق وأشبه الأمرين بالعدل.[6] A reference to the significance of *ahl al-fiqh wal-sunna wal-siyar wal-naṣīḥa* leaves a distinct impression that the function of scholarship was to enhance the caliphal authority.[7]

Now, the tenor of this official communication might be thought to corroborate a good deal of similar evidence that at mid second/eighth century revelation had yet to achieve status as recognized authority for doctrine or for policy within the Muslim community.[8] The appeal to analogical reasoning reflects a stage of doctrinal development prior to the onset of formalized transmission of authoritative opinion, and a period in which the celebrated instructions to the *qāḍī* of ʿUmar b. Khaṭṭāb might well have been composed.[9] Further evidence of Ibn Muqaffaʿ's attitude to Muslim

[1] *GAL* i, 138, 151, Suppl. I, 210, 236; in M. Kurd ʿAlī, *Rasā'il al-bulaghā'*, 117–34.
[2] *Origins*, 58–9, 95, 102–3, 137.
[3] Schacht, *Origins*, 95; cf. Goitein, 'Turning point', *Studies*, 149–67, esp. 163–4, where the theory of a Persian model is modified.
[4] *Risāla fil-Ṣaḥāba*, 121, 123, 122.
[5] *Risāla*, 126.
[6] *Risāla*, 127.
[7] *Risāla* 127.
[8] See above, I p. 44.
[9] See above, II pp. 56–7; and below, pp. 166–7.

scripture might possibly be elicited from the refutation of arguments ascribed to him by the Zaydī *imām* Qāsim b. Ibrāhīm (d. 246/860).[1] Attribution of the work being refuted was rightly considered by Guidi to be very questionable indeed.[2] So little of that ascribed to its putative author is preserved in the refutation that it is quite impossible to say more of Qāsim's adversary than had he not existed he would have had to be invented. References to the document of revelation consist exclusively of ingenuously literal interpretations of Quranic phraseology, e.g. descriptions of God as wager of war, as destroyer of the *umam khāliya*, as seated upon His throne, etc.,[3] each deftly and in turn thrown out of court by Qāsim, whose display of expertise in the metaphorical exegesis of anthropomorphic expression was faultless. That the author of the *Risāla fil-ṣaḥāba*, a work both formally pious and substantially sophisticated, could have been responsible for the trivial argumentation attributed to him by Qāsim is unlikely. At several points the latter found occasion to criticize severely his opponent's knowledge of Arabic, and accused him of having composed a barbarous book (*aʿjam al-bayān*).[4] Childishly inept humour like the alleged beginning of the book: 'In the name of the merciful and beneficent light' (*bismi 'l-nūri 'l-raḥmāni 'l-raḥīm*) can be taken seriously only as caricature and point, not so much to a *muʿāraḍa* of the Qur'ān (traditionally ascribed to Ibn Muqaffaʿ), as to an ideal target for the vituperative criticism of the Muʿtazilī Qāsim.[5] The major portion of the refutation, thus presumably also of its *fons et origo*, consists of polemic about the principles of divine creation and of God's justice and retribution, suspiciously appropriate, it might seem, to a Muʿtazilī *tour de force*.

Significant in a way quite different from the *Risāla fil-ṣaḥāba* of Ibn Muqaffaʿ is the work entitled *Risāla fil-qadar* and ascribed to Ḥasan Baṣrī (d. 110/728).[6] Its authenticity and ascription were accepted by Ritter and by Obermann; and its authenticity, if not ascription, by Schacht.[7] The argument of the tract, essentially dogmatic and in fact little more than identification of Satan as agent and repository of Evil, was found offensive by Shahrastānī (d. 538/1143), who was thus willing to ascribe it to Wāṣil b. ʿAṭā' but not to Ḥasan.[8] Schacht remarked the exclusive employment of Quranic *shawāhid* in the work and a concomitant absence of

[1] *GAS* i, 561–3; *Kitāb al-radd ʿalā 'l-zindīq*, in Guidi, *La Lotta*, arabic pagination 3–55.

[2] *La Lotta*, viii–xi, though he judged it to be a typical product of the period in which Ibn Muqaffaʿ lived, cf. xxi–xxiii; also, Nyberg, 'Zum Kampf', 425–41, esp. 431–2.

[3] *La Lotta*, arabic pagination 17–26, 29–31, 35.

[4] *La Lotta*, arabic pagination 8, 10, 31, 33, 39–40, 43.

[5] *La Lotta*, arabic pagination 8; cf. Goldziher, Studien ii, 401.

[6] *GAS* i, 591–4, esp. 592 no. 3; MS Köprülü 1589, Ayasofya 3998; in Ritter, 'Frömmigkeit', 67–82; for an analysis of its contents, see Schwarz, 'Letter', 15–30.

[7] Ritter, 'Frömmigkeit', 62–4; Obermann, 'Political theology', 138–62, esp. 154–8; Schacht, *Origins*, 74, 141, 229.

[8] *Kitāb al-milal wal-niḥal*, on the margin of Ibn Ḥazm, *Kitāb al-fiṣal* i, 59.

traditions from companions or prophet, arguing *e silentio* for composition at the beginning of the second/eighth century, chronologically consonant with the scholarly activities of Ḥasan.[1] There are, indeed, ninety-five verses and parts of verses adduced (five of them twice), from thirty-nine well-spaced *sūra*s of the canonical text of revelation, a few passages consisting of nothing more than a concatenation of scriptural *loci*.[2] None of the scriptural material may be described as regulative, but rather, as admonitory and paraenetic, drawn from eschatological contexts stressing the ethical implications of the Quranic theodicy. The over-all structure of the *risāla* is polemical rather than halakhic, formulated as epistolary address and regularly punctuated by imperatives beginning 'O commander of the faithful', with one passage based on sustained employment of the apostrophic 'And if you were to say . . .' (*wa-law qulta*).[3] The main body of the treatise contains a series of allegedly disputed points in scripture, thirteen in all and introduced 'There is dispute about His word' (*fa-yujādilūn/yunāziʿūn fī qawlihi*), in which the author disposes in a tidy though facile manner of his anonymous adversaries.[4] Those disputes could have no basis in fact, since scripture (*kitāb allāh* generally; *qur'ān* occasionally) contained neither inconsistency nor contradiction unless it had been tampered with (*wa-ḥarrafūhu*).[5] Reference to the reliability and omniscience of scripture is sufficiently recurrent and emphatic as to provoke the question of the author's real purpose. It might seem that the very absence of all but scriptural *shawāhid* and the express insistence that all answers were to be found therein could suggest an *uṣūl* controversy, in which the 'plain meaning' of scripture was being asserted in the face of analogical reasoning and of tradition, whether from companions or prophet.

Some support for this conjecture is found in what may be designated the 'framework' of the *risāla*. The request of the caliph ʿAbdalmalik for information on the problem of *qadar* (*liberum arbitrium*) was constructed round his wish to know whether Ḥasan's knowledge had been derived from tradition(s) from companions of the prophet, his own opinion/reasoning, or from an argument confirmed in scripture: أعن رواية من أحد من أصحاب رسول الله أم عن رأى رأيته أم عن أمر يعرف تصديقه فى القرآن.[6] The reply was interestingly circumstantial: he (Ḥasan) had learned from his predecessors who lived according to the word of God and transmitted His wisdom, who followed the *sunna* of the prophet (*sic*), who knew right from wrong, and who did not assert other than that which God had Himself expressed for the benefit of mankind in His book: أدركنا يا أمير المؤمنين أصلحك الله من السلف الذين عملوا بأمر الله ورووا حكمته واستنوا

[1] *Origins*, 229.
[2] Ritter, 'Frömmigkeit', 71, 73, 82.
[3] Ritter, 75.
[4] Ritter, 72–80.
[5] Ritter, 70 line 15–71 line 2.
[6] Ritter, 67 lines 8–9.

بسنة رسول الله وكانوا لا ينكرون حقا ولا يحقون باطلا ولا يلحقون بالربّ الا ما ألحق الربّ بنفسه ولا يحتجون الا بما احتج الله به على خلقه فى كتابه.[1] Similarly, in the 'covering letter' from Ḥajjāj to the caliph recommending Ḥasan's treatise, the Quranic sources of Ḥasan's views were stressed by means of a paraphrastic conflation of the caliph's own inquiry.[2] Thus, prophetical Sunna and companion traditions were included there as respectable sources of knowledge, though inferior to scripture: ويعرف تصديقه فى كتاب الله وسنة رسول الله . . . . . واعلم انه لم يبق ممن أخذ عن السلف الماضى من أصحاب رسول الله أحد هو أعلم بالله تعالى وأفقه فى دين الله وأقرأ لكتاب الله من الحسن. Protestations like 'Any argument not based on scriptural proof is fallacious' (فكل قول ليس عليه برهان من كتاب الله فهو ضلالة)[3] or 'Thus does scripture speak, O commander of the faithful' (هذا يا أمير المؤمنين كتاب الله ينطق)[4] might seem to indicate a more than merely casual concern for *uṣūl* priorities. Reference to the deformation (*taḥrīf*) of scripture is not infrequent,[5] as also to arbitrary or otherwise unsatisfactory exegesis,[6] twice specified as interpretation by personal opinion/reasoning: فيتأوّلون ذلك برأيهم and فيفسّرون ذلك برأيهم.[7] That particular charge can hardly be taken seriously, since it was the method employed by the author himself throughout the treatise, and the epithet may have been nothing more than a tag for opinions from which he dissented. His own exegesis consisted in the ingenuous assertion of scripture's 'plain meaning', easily apprehended by the unprejudiced eye and a basic knowledge of Arabic. Though quite unconcerned with linguistic or rhetorical analysis, he adduced in two instances examples from the *usus loquendi* (*kalām al-ʿarab*): *ad* Q. 19: 59 أى عذابا أليما وقد تقول العرب لقى فلان اليوم غيا أى ضربه الأمير ضربا شديدا وعذبه عذابا أليما,[8] and 3: 178, where a line of poetry was offered and the locution *qur'ān ʿarabī* apostrophically (and predictably) explained as a concomitant of Arabic

[1] Ritter, 68 lines 3–6.

[2] Ritter, 80–1: note (MS Ayasofya 3998).

[3] Ritter, 68 lines 13–14; cf. Schacht, *Origins*, 141.

[4] Ritter, 69 line 13; curiously, the parallel construction in Q. 45: 29 was not adduced by the author of the *risāla*, i.e. *hādhā kitābunā yanṭiq ʿalaykum bil-ḥaqq*; while in the *risāla* reference to scripture is unmistakable, it could be of interest to note that Qummī, *Tafsīr* ii, 295, emended *kitābunā* to *bi-kitābinā*, thus making the prophet, not the book, the spokesman of God, probably a reflex of Imāmī apologetics, similar to the emendation *umma*: *a'imma* in Q. 2: 143 and 3: 110, *Tafsīr* i, 63 and 110, respectively; cf. Goldziher, *Richtungen*, 281–2.

[5] Ritter, 68 line 11, 69 line 19, 70 line 16; see below, pp. 189–90.

[6] Ritter, 69 lines 19–20, 75 line 2 (*ta'wīl*); 74 line 2, 78 line 16 (*ta'awwul*).

[7] Ritter, 74 line 6, 78 line 5: *ta'awwala* and *fassara* synonymous.

[8] Ritter, 79 lines 8–9.

eloquence والقرآن يا أمير المؤمنين عربى أنزله الله الى قوم عرب خاطبهم بكلامهم الذى يعرفون معناه.[1]

Method and style in the *risāla*, unblemished by textual and semantic problems or scholarly apparatus, are not unlike those of the haggadists, characterized by straightforward equations and absence of authorities. Occasional employment of the connectives *ay* and *yaʿnī*, even *yaqūl*,[2] may be thought to attest to that similarity, corroborated by a simplistic interpretation of the Khiḍr verses (Q. 18: 60–82) in order to demonstrate the compatibility of free will with divine foreknowledge.[3] In the light of explicit reference to companion tradition, prophetical Sunna, with which may be contrasted mention of *sunnat allāh* in Q. 40: 85,[4] and exegetical *ra'y*, it could be argued that the exclusive employment of Quranic *loci* was neither fortuitous nor a consequence of the early composition of the *risāla*.[5] I am inclined to assign the treatise to the end of the second/eighth century, after the development of haggadic exegesis and during the period of *uṣūl* disputes represented by, at least, the conflict between traditionists and Muʿtazila. Ascription of this hortatory and edifying work to a figure like Ḥasan Baṣrī hardly requires explanation, and may be compared to a similar tendency serving the reputation of ʿAbdallāh b. ʿAbbās.

One point in the *risāla* deserves further mention. The author's assertion that the text of scripture was free of inconsistencies and/or contradictions rested upon two assumptions: first, that such as might be found must be the result of (malicious) alteration, second, that the meaning of *mutashābih* was 'analogous', in the sense of mutually corroborative (as in Q. 39: 23): ولقد خالف القوم يا أمير المؤمنين كتاب الله وحرّفوه وما كان قول الله ليكذّب [بعضه] بعضا بل هو كما وصف أحسن الحديث كتابا متشابها يشبه بعضه بعضا ولا يخالف بعضه بعضا.[6] Thus, the antithesis *muḥkam*:*mutashābih* could, once formulated, be adduced in justification not only of 'applied' but also of 'pure' exegesis.[7] Preoccupation with apparently contradictory statements in scripture generated two separate but interdependent views within whose terms a very carefully delimited typology of contradiction (*ikhtilāf*/*tanāquḍ*) could exist side by side with what might be called a recognized set of 'standard puzzles'. What must be the earliest version of the latter is found in the form of an appendix to Muqātil's *Tafsīr al-khamsimi'at āya*.[8] The relation of the appendix, contained in folios 100ᵛ to

[1] Ritter, 76 line 20–77 line 3.
[2] Ritter, e.g. 79 line 8, 68 line 15, 67 line 12.
[3] Ritter, 77 lines 12–19; see above, p. 128.
[4] Ritter, 79 lines 3–4.
[5] *Pace* Schacht, *Origins*, 74, 141, 229; in this connection the observation of Obermann, 'Political theology', 142 n. 11, that these technical terms here make a remarkably early appearance, gains fresh and certainly unintended significance.
[6] Ritter, 70 line 15–71 line 2.
[7] See above, p. 148.
[8] *GAS* i, 37 no. 1; MS British Museum Or. 6333; Abbott, *SALP* ii, 96; cf. *BSOAS* xxxi (1968) 614.

103[r], to the body of the work is something of a problem. For the copyist of this manuscript (an *unicum*, dated 4 Jumādā I 792/20 April 1390) the appendix clearly belonged to the main text (same paper, ink, hand, etc.), but was separated therefrom by a fresh *basmala* and two abrupt changes of subject. The style is haggadic and almost certainly that of Muqātil (or of the works traditionally ascribed to him), beginning with a *taʿyīn* of Q. 18: 60–82 identical to that of his major *tafsīr*: اسم الذى كان يأخذ كل سفينة غصبا ابن جلندا.[1] Once the dramatis personae of the Mūsā–Khiḍr story were identified, a new *isnād* introduced the topic of scriptural contradiction (*ikhtilāf al-Qurʾān*), related on the authority of Ibn ʿAbbās, and illustrated by the following nine problems:[2]

1. Whether on the day of Judgement there shall be communication between those being tried: Q. 23: 101 vs. 37: 27 (37: 50, 52: 25).
2. Whether on that day polytheists will or can avail themselves of the services of their deities: Q. 6: 22 vs. 6: 23.
3. Whether God created heaven or earth first: Q. 79: 27–30 vs. 41: 9–11.
4. Whether the grammatical value of *kāna* in Q. 4: 23, 4: 134, etc. reflects a permanent or a temporary quality.
5. Whether the promise in Q. 20: 124 (he who ignores my admonition shall live in penury) is confirmed or belied by experience.
6. Whether the promise in Q. 16: 97 (goodness shall be rewarded) is confirmed or belied by experience.
7. Whether on the day of Judgement those being tried shall be asked about their misdeeds: Q. 55 : 39 vs. 15 : 92–3.
8. What is the precise meaning of 'guidance' (*hudan*) in God's warning to Adam and Eve: Q. 20: 123?
9. What is the precise meaning of 'before him' (*amāmahu*) in Q. 75: 5 (but man desires to sin before him)?

The solutions proposed by Ibn ʿAbbās to these problems were unequivocal and unsophisticated, and evoked a primitive level of popular discourse.[3] The exegetical principle involved in the elimination of apparent contradictions was that which distinguished between different contexts (*mawāṭin*) despite similar or identical phraseology. Thus, nos. 1, 2, 3, and 7 did not contain 'real' contradictions because the opposing verses referred to quite different situations, or to different aspects of the same situation. Nos. 5 and 6 were, on the other hand, allusions to eschatological fulfilment or, alternatively, virtue as its own reward. To the lexical problems in nos. 4, 8, and 9 solutions were evaded by resort to theology: *kāna* predicated of God must signify an eternal attribute;[4] 'guidance' was the Qurʾān; 'before him' indicated progression in disobedience (*quduman fil-maʿāṣī*).

[1] *Tafsir*, MS. H. Hüsnü 17, 171[v]–2[r]; see above, pp. 128, 135–6.
[2] *Tafsīr*, MS BM Or. 6333, 100[v]–1[r].
[3] *Tafsīr*, 101[r]–2[r].
[4] Cf. Reuschel, '*Wa-kāna llāhu ʿalīman*', 147–53.

A schematic and slightly more sophisticated version of what eventually became the standard (!) scriptural puzzles was attributed to Muqātil and included in his *Kitāb al-tanbīh wal-radd* by Abū Ḥusayn Malaṭī (d. 377/987).[1] The extracts from Muqātil, adduced by Malaṭī without supporting reference to Ibn ʿAbbās, are two:[2] on Quranic contradictions, and on semantic and phraseological correlations, of which the first seems to be a systematic expansion of the material described above from BM Or. 6333. I have found no other work of Muqātil in which this material appears, or in this form could appear, except as appendix or as some other variety of formal intrusion.[3] In Malaṭī's version,[4] the number of scriptural contradictions was increased to twenty-five, including four examples from BM Or. 6333 (nos. 1, 2, 3, 7). The principles of harmonization remained the same, but were enhanced by differentiated and normative expression. Each solution was, for example, introduced by the formula فهذا عند من يجهل التفسير ينقض بعضه بعضا وليس بمنتقض ولكنهما فى تفسير كذا and the reason for the apparent discord specified as different contexts (*mawāṭin mukhtalifa*), similar phraseology in analogous circumstances (*ṣilāt al-kalām mushtabiha/wujūh al-ḥālāt mushtabiha/ikhtilāf al-ḥālāt mushtabih*), temporally separate aspects of the same situation (*wujūh taqdīm al-kalām mushtabiha*), etc. That in exegetical usage *mushtabih* and *mutashābih* were functionally synonymous has been noted.[5]

The manner in which this kind of problem, together with its attendant *loci probantes*, became a constant in the literature of scriptural exegesis may be elicited from Suyūṭī's chapter on the subject in his *Itqān*, where the notion of 'contradiction' was appropriately described as irresponsible fantasy and beneath the dignity of God's word والمراد به ما يوهم التعارض بين الآيات وكلامه تعالى منزه عن ذلك, and illustrated by four standard examples from Ibn ʿAbbās (nos. 1–4 in BM Or. 6333).[6] But for Suyūṭī these were merely a point of departure for a survey of elaborate rhetorical techniques designed to prove what had been unequivocally asserted, namely, that the text of revelation contained neither contradiction nor inconsistency. So stated, that position was manifestly indefensible, in tacit recognition of which recourse was had to more sophisticated terminology. Ibn Qutayba was able, for example, to distinguish between contradiction proper (*ikhtilāf taḍādd*) not found in the Qur'ān save in cases of regulative abrogation,

[1] *GAS* i, 607; in Dedering, Bibliotheca Islamica IX.

[2] *Kitāb al-Tanbīh*, 44–56 and 56–63, respectively; see below, p. 210.

[3] *Pace* Abbott, *SALP* ii, 96; manuscripts have so far been discovered for three, not four, separate works of Muqātil, cf. *GAS* i, 37; the extracts from Malaṭī were published separately, and earlier, by Massignon, *Recueil*, 194–210.

[4] *Kitāb al-Tanbīh*, 44–56.

[5] See above, p. 157.

[6] *Itqān*, *nawʿ* 48: iii, 79–89.

and difference by variation (*ikhtilāf taghāyur*) of which an example was the word *umma* in Q. 12: 45, expressing both period (*ḥīn*) and forgetting (*nisyān*).[1] This argument did not, however, prevent his adducing a simplistic harmonization of the by that time traditional instance of contradiction: in the question of conversation on the day of Judgement.[2] For Ibn Taymiyya the distinction lay between contradiction proper (*ikhtilāf taḍādd*) and variation (here *ikhtilāf tanawwuʿ*) of which only the latter could be found in scripture.[3] For Kirmānī the antithesis was expressed as concepts mutually exclusive (*tanāquḍ*) not present in the Qur'ān, and relational difference (*ikhtilāf talāzum*), found in scripture as multiple variations upon a single theme.[4] That proliferation of technical vocabulary is witness to an abiding concern with textual consistency. It was one form of exegetical activity in which no serious scholar ever adduced in support of his argument the 'plain meaning' of scripture.

The concept of *ikhtilāf* as variation, and not simply as flagrant contradiction, presupposed or at least implied some degree of both textual integrity and conceptual unity in the document of revelation. The manner in which those were perceived or, perhaps more accurately, were created, emerges from examination of the work of halakhists and masoretes. Their primary, and indispensable, instrument was *analogy*. Under that general title was subsumed a number of related but methodologically distinct procedures. The basic distinctions were two: between deductive and inductive establishment of an analogical relation, and between halakhic and masoretic application of the instrument. While a general impression that the Arabic term *qiyās* denotes an exegetical procedure both inductive and halakhic is not altogether unjustified, it is also an over-simplification. An example can be seen in Bergsträsser's selection of *qal wa-ḥomer* as illustrative of *qiyās* method: 'da sie nicht wie die anderen die Interpretation eines normativen Textes, sondern die Gewinnung einer neuen Bestimmung aus einer vorhandenen regeln soll'.[5] In fact, *qiyās* was employed both for extrapolation of fresh principles from existing premisses and for interpretation, as well as for establishment, of the scriptural text, though the appearance of fixed and consistent terminology was admittedly later than the phenomena themselves.[6]

What must be the earliest, or almost the earliest, reference to recourse to analogy for halakhah occurs in the *Risāla fil-ṣaḥāba* of Ibn Muqaffaʿ: فينظر فيه الى أحق الفريقين بالتصديق وأشبه الأمرين بالعدل.[7] The locution

[1] *Ta'wīl*, 31.

[2] *Ta'wīl*, 47 *ad* Q. 77: 35 vs. 39: 31, one of several sets of contradictory verses on that subject, e.g. BM Or. 6333 no. 1, *Kitāb al-Tanbīh*, 44.

[3] *Apud* Suyūṭī, *Itqān* iv, 176–7.

[4] *Apud* Suyūṭī, *Itqān* iii, 89.

[5] Bergsträsser, 'Anfänge', 81.

[6] See Tahānawī, *Iṣṭilāḥāt*, 1189–96: *qiyās lughawī* and *qiyās sharʿī*.

[7] *Risāla fil-Ṣaḥāba*, 127; see above, pp. 158–60.

ashbah al-amrayn bil-ʿadl can only refer to 'equitable comparison of two cases', in the sense that their respective merits and demerits were to be juxtaposed. In that particular context it was the reasoning of the caliph which was evoked to produce a solution. Possibly contemporary with, but probably later than that passage is the recommendation ascribed to ʿUmar b. Khaṭṭāb in his instructions to Abū Mūsā: مما ليس فيه قرآن ولا سنة واعرف الأشباه والأمثال ثم قس الأمور بعد ذلك.[1] That the imperative *qis* here signified 'juxtapose' was recognized by Margoliouth, who related that usage to Talmudic *hiqqish*.[2] Of similar importance in the recommendation are the terms *ashbāh* and *amthāl* (probably hendiadys), referring to those common elements in (two) propositions which may be juxtaposed (*scil.* for the purpose of comparison). The explicit condition 'in those matters for which there is neither *qur'ān* nor *sunna*' suggests, in my opinion at least, a date later than the corresponding passage in Ibn Muqaffaʿ, which reads 'in halakhic dispute (*ikhtilāf al-aḥkām*) either about a matter transmitted from the ancients (*ma'thūr ʿan al-salaf*) . . . or about a case of arbitrary reasoning (*ra'y ajrāhu ahluhu ʿalā 'l-qiyās*)'.[3] The use of *shabbaha* for analogical juxtaposition is attested elsewhere, e.g. in Mālik[4] and in Bukhārī.[5] Whatever the linguistic relation of Arabic *qās* to Hebrew *hiqqish*, it may seem that *shabbaha* was equally appropriate as notional equivalent to the Hebrew term.

In the contexts adduced above the terms *ashbah/ashbāh/shabbaha* can hardly refer to juxtaposition based on identical or even similar phraseology. Introduction of a *tertium comparationis* is at least implicit in Bukhārī's discussion of the legatee's obligation to fulfil a pilgrimage vow derived from a duty to pay the outstanding debts of the deceased.[6] Employment of Talmudic *hiqqish* was characterized by the same latitude: some but by no means all of the examples assembled by Bacher depend upon a recurring locution or even textual juxtaposition in scripture.[7] Methodological distinction in reasoning by analogy with and without a third term became evident only with the refinement of technical terminology, of which a valuable illustration is afforded by the evolution of Talmudic *gezerah shawah*. That that term came to, but did not originally or consistently, designate analogy based on occurrence of the same word has been often and convincingly demonstrated.[8] In halakhic argument the principle of

[1] Margoliouth, 'Omar's instructions', 309, 320; Goldziher, *Ẓāhiriten*, 9.
[2] Margoliouth, loc. cit.; see also Schacht, *Origins*, 99.
[3] *Risāla fil-Ṣaḥāba*, 127.
[4] *Mudawwana* ii, 94, cited Schacht, *Origins*, 117: 'to assimilate'.
[5] *Ṣaḥīḥ*, 'Kitāb al-Iʿtiṣām', no. 12, cited Goldziher, *Ẓāhiriten*, 107.
[6] Goldziher, loc. cit.
[7] *Terminologie* i, 44–6, ii, 57–8.
[8] See Bacher, op. cit., i, 13–16; Gertner, 'Terms', 24–5; Loewe, 'The "plain" meaning', 164–5; and cf. the Pauline application in Romans 4: 3–9, which did depend upon an identical word, Gerhardsson, *Memory*, 287–8.

inductive analogy, by which I mean those varieties involving a *tertium comparationis* or *ratio*, is likely to have antedated insistence that the analogue be an identical phrase. It must, on the other hand, be admitted that contexts held to be analogous could in the first instance have been so related by reference to common phraseology. The complementary principle of deductive analogy may be thought to have had its origin in masoretic rather than halakhic argument.[1] In Muslim juridical literature the appearance of argument based on inductive analogy preceded by about a century systematic use of the technical term *ʿilla* for *ratio*, a notion for which Shāfiʿī employed *aṣl* (root/base/basis) and *maʿnā* (meaning/sense).[2] With the development of (fundamentalist) opposition to inductive analogy (called *taʿlīl*), differentiation crystallized in the antithesis *taʿlīl*:*manṣūṣ*, the latter term being employed, at least by sectaries of the Ẓāhirī school, for analogy based on a textual similarity.[3] The generic term itself for analogy, *qiyās*, came increasingly to be modified by such epithets as were found necessary to describe the relation to one another of its components, e.g. *jalīy*/*ẓāhir* (explicit), *khafīy* (implicit), and even by phrases which effaced the opposition *taʿlīl*:*manṣūṣ*, such as *ʿilla manṣūṣa* and *qiyās maʿqūl al-naṣṣ*.[4] Much of that proliferation of technical terms reflected (often necessary) steps to circumscribe the range of analogical argument, frequently undisciplined and far-fetched.[5]

Masoretic analogy was, on the other hand and by its very nature, mostly deductive. Though designated *qiyās* and defined in terms identical to those employed for its halakhic counterpart, e.g. by Ibn Anbārī ولا بد لكل قياس من أربعة أشياء: أصل وفرع وعلة وحكم,[6] the role of a *tertium comparationis* (*ʿilla*) was largely formal. That consisted often in the articulation of a grammatical 'rule', not adduced as justification for the analogy in question, but rather deduced from its first and second terms and seldom of general prescriptive value. The restricted usefulness of that kind of reasoning was enshrined in the Basran dictum cited earlier: فمجرد دعوى لا يقوم عليها دليل الا بوحى وتنزيل.[7] The analogical foundations of (all) grammar were not thereby shaken, though it is worth noting that those had, in the face of pious objections that the word of God was unique, from time to time to be reasserted: ... اعلم أن إنكار القياس فى النحو لا يتحقق لان النحو كله قياس فمن أنكر القياس فقد أنكر النحو ولا يعلم أحد من العلماء أنكره.[8] In its

[1] See below, pp. 208–12.
[2] Schacht, *Origins*, 110, 117, 125.
[3] Goldziher, *Ẓāhiriten*, 11–12, 41–3, 56, 91–3: Dāwūd al-Ẓāhirī, d. 270/884.
[4] Cf. Tahānawī, *Iṣṭilāḥāt*, 1192–5; Tyan, 'Méthodologie', 79–109, esp. 92 ff.
[5] For similar tendencies in the application of Talmudic *middot*, see Loewe, 'The "plain" meaning', 152–4, and Bacher, *Terminologie* i, 110–11.
[6] Weil, *Schulen*, 19 n. 3.
[7] See above, III p. 101.
[8] Ibn Anbārī, cited Weil, *Schulen*, 29 n. 1.

masoretic form grammatical analogy consisted essentially in the process of textual restoration/emendation called ultimately *taqdīr*, but in earlier stages also *majāz*.[1] The manner in which potentially arbitrary application of *majāz/taqdīr* was restricted by the formulation of grammatical norms illustrates perfectly the emergence of masoretic analogy and its conformity with halakhic standards.[2] But that conformity was always relative, and reflected as much of bewilderment at scriptural grammar as of piety before the word of God. Both sentiments found expression in the comment of Ibn Munayyir on Zamakhsharī *ad* Q. 6: 137, that scriptural data were to be given preference over the grammatical norms.[3] Formal protest against the use of analogy in scriptural exegesis is thus not unexpected, but an example of such adduced by Suyūṭī from the specialized material of Quranic readings and attributed to Dānī (d. 444/1053) may be thought vitiated by the latter's employment of analogy (*qiyās*) in his own work.[4]

A type of analogical reasoning found in both halakhic and masoretic exegesis is that based upon the relation between general and particular statements (*khāṣṣ*:*ʿāmm* or *khuṣūṣ* :*ʿumūm*). Made theoretically complex by dispute about whether all propositions were primarily/exclusively of general or of particular significance, application of the principle was in practice easy.[5] Apparently general statements in scripture like 'I am the first of the Muslims' (Q. 6: 163) and 'I am the first of the Believers' (Q. 7: 143) were interpreted by Ibn Qutayba as particular, on the grounds that 'first' was of temporal value (*al-awwal fī zamanihi*).[6] The argument was of course doctrinal (there had been Muslims and believers from the very beginning of time), but the same reasoning could be applied to textual problems, such as the often wayward treatment of number and concord in scriptural grammar.[7] The corresponding Talmudic precept (*kelal*: *peraṭ*) was of similar application.[8] More often than not, analogies based on this principle depended upon recurrence of the same word or phrase. Thus Suyūṭī, in an argument for the general applicability of particular Quranic verses, adduced as proof the prophet's juxtaposition of Q. 6: 82 ولم يلبسوا أيمانهم بظلم and 31: 13 إنّ الشرك لظلم عظيم.[9] Their common element, the word *ẓulm* (wrong/sin), was designated *naẓīr* (analogue): it is that term which, together with *shabah*, characterized the masoretic as

[1] Wansbrough, 'Periphrastic exegesis', 247, nn. 1–2.

[2] See below, pp. 219–24.

[3] *Kashshāf* ii, 69–70 (commentary); see below, pp. 223–4.

[4] *Itqān* i, 211; Dānī, *Taysīr*, 21, 22, 34, 128, etc. in the question of phonological assimilation (*idghām*), without *tertium comparationis*, for which however cf. *Itqān* i, 214–15, and *GdQ* iii, 154.

[5] See Goldziher, *Ẓāhiriten*, 120–4; Schacht, *Origins*, 56, 125.

[6] *Ta'wīl*, 217.

[7] Wansbrough, 'Periphrastic exegesis', 261 nn. 51–2.

[8] Bacher, *Terminologie* i, 79–82, 152–3, ii, 83–5, 161–2.

[9] *Itqān* i, 86.

contrasted with the halakhic use of analogy. The utility of *naẓīr/shabah* was most apparent in the solution of textual and grammatical problems by recourse to the many techniques of restoration and emendation (*majāz/taqdīr*), but was of course not restricted to such. An example of its application to what became a point of doctrine may be seen in the standard interpretation of *umm al-kitāb* in Q. 3: 7.[1] Descriptions like 'basis' or 'nucleus' (*aṣl*) or 'that which is common to all divine revelations' required, as link to the 'preserved tablet' of Q. 85: 21–2, the corroboration allegedly found in the two other Quranic occurrences of *umm al-kitāb* (13: 39 and 43: 4). Now, that kind of analogy (*naẓīr*) could founder on contextual dissimilarity, and that such did not go unnoticed may be inferred from the several exceptions to the standard interpretation which identified *umm* with 'precept' and 'authority'. Those were the *muḥkamāt*, in reference to which all exegesis was justified.

3. HALAKHIC EXEGESIS

Among the several topics treated by Muqātil b. Sulaymān in his *Tafsīr al-khamsimi'at āya* was the obligation to wage war on God's behalf against His enemies.[2] That section consists of eighteen Quranic passages (containing twenty-nine verses) related in the following pattern to six themes:

1. Divinely imposed obligation to fight (*qitāl*): Q. 2: 216, 22: 39–40, 9: 29, 49: 9–10
2. Reward for fighting on behalf of God: Q. 61: 4, 10–13, 4: 95–6
3. Observing God's covenant (*'ahd*): Q. 9: 111, 4: 74, 3: 200
4. Martyrdom and its reward: Q. 2: 154, 3: 169–70
5. Divine aid against the enemy: Q. 8: 15–16, 65–6, 3: 155, 9: 25
6. Division of spoils: Q. 8: 41, 3: 161–3

A degree of thematic overlapping, eliminated from this diagrammatic exposition, put Q. 3: 200 after 3: 169–70, and Q. 9: 29 and 49: 9–10 at the end of the section, where the introductory theme was appropriately given final mention. Muqātil's method can hardly be described as systematic or thorough: omitted were not only juridical questions traditionally associated with the subject of Holy War (*jihād*), e.g. safe conduct (*amān*), but also a number of Quranic *loci* pertinent to the themes which he did adduce, e.g. covenantal obligations.[3] It may none the less be inferred from his organization of the material that the halakhic theme had priority over the scriptural evidence marshalled in its support. Selection, and especially assessment, of the latter were to some extent arbitrary. Introduced by a *tanzīl* formula, the decree sanctioning war was expressed in terms stressing contrast with its earlier prohibition, chronologically separated by the Hijra

[1] See above, pp. 153.
[2] See above, pp. 163–4; MS BM Or. 6333, 93v–8r.
[3] See above, I pp. 8–12.

فنزلت كتب عليكم يعنى فرض عليكم القتال وأذن لهم بعد ما كان نهاهم عنه.[1] That same context provided an opportunity to fix *tawḥīd* (profession of faith), *ṣalāt* (ritual prayer), and *zakāt* (voluntary almsgiving: *ghayr muwaqqat*) as duties imposed upon Muslims during the Meccan (!) period. The graduated and contrasting rewards for those who participated in Holy War (*mujāhidūn*) and those who did not (*qāʿidūn*) were modified by a distinction, not further specified, between non-participants who were excused/exempted (*maʿdhūr*) and those who were not.[2] The passage setting out the rewards for martyrdom was inserted into the framework of a threefold address from God to the recipients of His favour, culminating in the familiar story of their desire to return to the world in order to be killed anew.[3] Verses attesting to divine assistance in battle and, conversely, to its withdrawal, e.g. Q. 8: 65–6 and 3: 155, were related anecdotally to the battles of Badr and Uḥud, and Q. 9: 25 of course (textually) to Ḥunayn.[4] In the passage describing division of spoils the rule for allocation of the prophet's fifth after his death was not only enhanced by, but also seen to derive from, an amicable interview between ʿĀ'isha and ʿAlī b. Abī Ṭālib.[5] The style of the whole is unmistakably haggadic, characterized by the serial repetition of explicative elements and by a profusion of anecdote. Both devices serve to create an atmosphere of *narratio*, so far as such was possible in the thematic arrangement of material, and the result may be compared with the style of the *Sīra* in the story of Jaʿfar b. Abī Ṭālib and the Najāshī.[6]

Muqātil's use of scriptural *shawāhid* gains significance by juxtaposition with the treatment of Holy War in the nearly contemporary *Muwaṭṭa'* of Mālik b. Anas (d. 179/795).[7] There, the relevant section ('K. Jihād') contains twenty-one chapters related to four themes:

1. Desire (*targhīb*) to wage Holy War: chapters 1, 17–19: Q. 99: 7–8, 3: 200
2. Conduct in Holy War: chapters 2–5
3. Division of spoils: chapters 6–13, 20, 21: Q. 16: 8, 8: 60
4. Martyrdom and its reward: chapters 14–16, 21

The four Quranic passages (containing five verses) appear here not in the role of organizing principle, but as an almost superfluous embellishment. Q. 99: 7–8 is paraenetic, quite unrelated to the subject, and was adduced by means of a prophetical *ḥadīth* beginning: Nothing else was revealed to me on that matter (*scil.* instilling a desire to wage Holy War) save for the general admonition (*āya jāmiʿa fādhdha*) 'Whoever does an

[1] See above, pp. 141–2; Tafsīr, 93ᵛ.
[2] *Tafsīr*, 94ᵛ.
[3] *Tafsīr*, 95ʳ; see Wensinck, *Handbook*, 148 for references in the *ḥadīth* literature; see above, p. 125.
[4] *Tafsīr*, 96ʳ⁻ᵛ.
[5] *Tafsīr*, 97ʳ.
[6] See above, pp. 129–30, 133–4; and I pp. 38–43.
[7] *GAS* i, 457–64; *Muwaṭṭa'*, 443–71: 'Kitāb al-Jihād'.

atom's weight of good shall see it, and whoever does an atom's weight of evil shall see it'.[1] In the same chapter, Q. 3: 200, which recommends perseverance, is rather more appropriate to conditions of battle, and was adduced for the same purpose by Muqātil.[2] In chapter 12, on the division of spoils according to men and mounts, Q. 8: 60 is but generally pertinent, while 16: 8 was employed to support a halakhic subtlety: whether in the allocation of plunder donkeys, mules, pack animals, and nags qualified as mounts.[3] In addition to these four passages, only one of which can be regarded as serving a juridical purpose, Mālik referred twice to 'revelation' as a source of authority: in chapter 10, Ibn ʿAbbās refused to specify further the *anfāl* 'mentioned by God in His book' (presumably the *hapax legomenon* at Q. 8: 1); and in chapter 14, the prophet supported his own view in a discussion about the rewards of martyrdom by asserting: And thus I was told by Gabriel.[4] In neither case was a serious appeal made to the text of scripture. Moreover, in chapter 10, where the battle of Ḥunayn was adduced as precedent, no mention was made of its only Quranic occurrence (9: 25), employed by Muqātil for another purpose.[5] In chapter 4, two utterances of Mālik on the honouring of safe conduct (*amān*) did not include reference to what became the *locus classicus* (Q. 9: 6).[6] Now, it might be argued that neither Q. 9: 25 nor 9: 6 is strictly relevant to the juridical points argued by Mālik, but consideration of the entire section on *jihād* tends to strengthen an impression that the role of scripture as witness to correct procedure was indeed minimal. The tendency towards 'Islamization' discerned in the *Muwaṭṭa'* by both Bergsträsser and Schacht can only refer to an effort to situate as early as possible the constituents of *sunna*, not to find corroboration thereto in the text of scripture.[7] The earliest evidence of the latter is to be found not in the *Muwaṭṭa'*, but rather in the *Tafsīr al-khamsimi'at āya* attributed to Muqātil.

The only extant recension of that work is ascribed to Hudhayl b. Ḥabīb (d. after 190/805), responsible also for the only version preserved of Muqātil's major *Tafsīr*.[8] In an introduction typically haggadic the essential components (*arkān*) of Islam were summarized by means of a parable related on the authority of Muqātil himself: قال مقاتل إن على جسر جهنم سبع قناطر محاسن يسال العبد عند أولهن عن الإيمان بالله عز وجل فإنْ جابه تاما مخلصا جاز الى الثانى فيسل عن الصلوة وإنْ جابه تاما جاز الى الثالث فيسل عن الزكوة فإنْ جابه تاما جاز الى الرابع فيسل عن الصيام فإنْ جابه

[1] *Muwaṭṭa'*, 445. [2] *Muwaṭṭa'*, 446. [3] *Muwaṭṭa'*, 447.
[4] *Muwaṭṭa'*, 455 and 461, respectively.
[5] *Muwaṭṭa'*, 454–5; cf. Schacht, *Origins*, 70–1, 286. [6] *Muwaṭṭa'*, 448–9.
[7] Bergsträsser, 'Anfänge', 76–80; Schacht, *Origins*, 283–7, 311–14.
[8] See above, p. 144; the *isnād* of MS BM Or. 6333 (1v) consists of the last five links in the chain of transmission for MS H. Hüsnü 17 (1v).

تاما جاز الى الخامس فيسل عن الحج فإنْ جابه تاما جاز الى السادس فيسل عن العمرة فإنْ جابه تاما جاز الى السابع فيسل عن المظالم فإنْ لم يكن يظلم أحدا جاز الى الجنة.[1] The imagery generated by the concept of a purgatorial bridge (here *jisr* and *qanṭara*, but elsewhere also *ṣirāṭ*), separating each soul from its destiny by a series of trials (traditionally seven), was somewhat unstable.[2] In Muqātil's seven stages: (1) Faith, (2) Prayer, (3) Almsgiving, (4) Fasting, (5) Pilgrimage, (6) Lesser Pilgrimage (*'umra*), (7) Wrongs (*maẓālim*), it may be that the sixth exhibits contamination with the preceding one and might well, in the context of the whole work, have been instead Holy War (*jihād*). In any case, the subsequent literary history of this cautionary tale was such that its employment here deserves notice.[3]

The treatise covers in fact rather more than the material of the seven rubrics contained in the introductory parable, though these were given first places:

Faith (fols. 1^{v}–2^{v}), Prayer (fols. 2^{v}–12^{v}), Almsgiving (fols. 13^{r}–21^{v}: including *zakāt* and *ṣadaqa*), Fasting (fols. 21^{v}–25^{r}), Pilgrimage (fols. 25^{r}–33^{v}: including *ḥajj* but not *'umra*), Wrongs (fols. 34^{r}–41^{r}), Testaments (fols. 41^{r}–44^{v}), Miscellaneous (fols. 45^{r}–49^{v}: including prohibition of usury and of wine), Marriage (fols. 50^{r}–59^{v}), Divorce (fols. 60^{r}–72^{r}), Adultery (fols. 72^{v}–77^{v}), Miscellaneous (fols. 77^{v}–93^{r}: including thefts, debts, contracts/treaties, sacrifice), Holy War (fols. 93^{v}–98^{r}), Miscellaneous (fols. 98^{r}–103^{r}: including informal prayer and 'contradictions' in scripture, the latter as an appendix).[4]

Treatment of each topic conforms with that described above for Holy War: concepts which are essentially, or even potentially, juridical are presented as ethical categories, exemplary and hortatory, but rarely prescriptive. The scriptural *loci probantes* are tentative and experimental: forming the principle by which material appears to have been included, but not that by which its halakhic validity was demonstrated.

Muqātil's ethical categories are rudimentary: *ḥalāl wa-ḥarām*, glossed by the parable of the purgatorial bridge. The antithesis is itself found in scripture, formulated negatively (Q. 10, 59, 16: 116), but in the exegetical tradition positively, e.g. as two of the seven *aḥruf* (here modes),[5] and in the earliest literature as gloss to *muḥkamāt*.[6] The five legal categories of classical jurisprudence were later, and do not appear to represent merely elaboration

[1] *Tafsīr*, MS BM Or. 6333, 1^{v}.

[2] Cf. references in Wensinck, *Handbook*, 40; id. *Creed*, 232–3.

[3] See Asín Palacios, *Escatología*, 180–91, esp. 181, 183 (where according to Ibn 'Arabī the sixth bridge was neither *'umra* nor *jihād*, but *wuḍū'*: ablutions), and 568–9; Cerulli, *Libro della Scala*, 202–5 (paras. 192–3), 299 (paras. 208–9), 530–2.

[4] See above, pp. 164–5.

[5] i.e. as two of the seven 'types' of material included in revelation: 'permission' and 'prohibition'; cf. Ibn Qutayba, *Ta'wīl*, 26; Suyūṭī, *Itqān* i, 136; Goldziher, *Richtungen*, 37.

[6] See above, pp. 149–51.

of the basic opposition *ḥalāl*:*ḥarām*, which did not as such achieve hermeneutical status.[1] As ethical categories *ḥalāl wa-ḥarām* may be compared to Talmudic מותר and אסור, or to the related Pauline τύπος διδαχῆς.[2] Their value for the earliest Muslim exegesis lay in the facility with which they could be directly and unambiguously applied to the text of scripture, a procedure which in its most unsophisticated form can be observed in Muqātil's treatise.

Comparison of the author's method with that of Mālik reveals a difference which eventually became an opposition, namely, Sunna *vs.* Qur'ān as source of law. The dates of Mālik, of Muqātil's *rāwī* Hudhayl b. Ḥabīb, and of Shāfi'ī, with whom the opposed tendencies found polemical expression, make the end of the second/eighth century a likely chronological focus for the dispute. It was the merit of Schacht to demonstrate the crucial role of Shāfi'ī in that dispute, though I am most reluctant to accept that the *ahl al-kalām* 'had a precursor in the author of the dogmatic treatise ascribed to Ḥasan Baṣrī', or that the evidence of 'problems which were based from the beginning on the Koran' proves beyond reasonable doubt existence of the canonical text of revelation.[3] On the other hand, Schacht's description of 'Koranic legislation' (*sic*) as 'the essentially ethical and only incidentally legal body of maxims contained in the Koran' is in my opinion especially felicitous, as is his observation that 'Even as regards his questions which presuppose the rules given in the Koran, we notice that anything which goes beyond the most perfunctory attention given to the Koranic norms and the most elementary conclusions drawn from them, belongs almost invariably to a secondary stage in the development of doctrine'.[4] In the light of those statements it would not, I think, be unjustified to interpret references to the 'Koran' throughout his book as of essentially polemical connotation, employed, as they for the most part are, in contexts describing Shāfi'ī's quarrels with his contemporaries and predecessors.[5] In Shāfi'ī allusions to the Qur'ān tend to be perfunctory and usually in tandem (*fil-qur'ān wal-sunna*), which suggests a formal hendiadys alluding to a single source of law, *scil.* revelation (consisting of both Qur'ān and Sunna).[6] The *sunna* elevated to the status of revelation was of course the prophetical Sunna, not the 'living tradition', and one might be par-

[1] Cf. Schacht, *Origins*, 133: post-Shāfi'ī; id. *Introduction*, 120–3: designated 'religious qualifications'.

[2] See Gerhardsson, *Memory*, 303–5: for Romans 6: 17, and 309, 313; cf. references in Jastrow, *Dictionary*, 98, 349, 946.

[3] *Origins*, 224–5, esp. 224 n. 2; see above, pp. 160–3, and I, pp. 44–5.

[4] *Origins*, 224–7, 191: examples are found on 193–8, 204, 208, 210–13, 215, 218, 250–1, 276–8, 279–80.

[5] The references to Qur'ān, *Origins*, 2, seem to me to be ambiguous.

[6] Schacht, *Origins*, 12, 14, 18, 19, e.g. 16: *ḥikma* as *sunna*, 135: 'the two sources' (*aṣlān*) and Shāfi'ī's 'lip-service to the overruling authority of the Koran, which he did not recognize in practice'; and cf. Shāfi'ī, *Risāla*, 106–46, tr. Semaan, 'Al-Nāsikh', 11–29.

doned for asking just what evidence there is for supposing that prior to Shāfiʿī 'revelation' meant exclusively the canonical text of scripture.[1]

Opposition to Shāfiʿī was heterogeneous and widespread, and an important, but by no means the only, element drew its arguments from the text of scripture.[2] Aphoristically formulated arguments like 'the book explains everything' (e.g. Q. 6: 154, 12: 111, 16: 89, 17: 12), or 'thus speaks scripture' and 'any argument not based on scriptural proof is fallacious', belong to the imagery of polemic and are not likely to have been uttered from positions unchallenged, or unless pleading a special case.[3] What seems to be a merely formal recognition of scripture as source of authority: 'what is and/or is not found in Qur'ān and Sunna', was characteristic not only of Shāfiʿī but also of his predecessors, e.g. Abū Yūsuf, and the same formula was employed to justify recourse to analogy![4] At that stage in the development of halakhah resort to strictly textual exegesis was rare indeed, e.g. a *varia lectio ad* Q. 65: 6.[5] The use of scriptural passages like 'There is a fine example (*uswa ḥasana*) for you in the Messenger of God' (Q. 33: 21) may be understood as nothing more than the obverse of 'scripture explains everything' argumentation, both of which exhibit dispute about sources, not merely methods.[6]

Now, it has more than once been found convenient to distinguish between the textual relation of law to scripture and their historical relation to one another. In studies of the Judaic tradition such distinction permitted the assertion that 'In many cases it is quite certain that the Halakhah antedates the scriptural proof by which it is propped up'.[7] In the Muslim tradition a parallel distinction was often and intentionally obliterated by secondary and pseudo-historical conclusions of the kind noticed above in Muqātil's dating of the divine decrees respectively for Holy War, the Profession of Faith, Ritual Prayer, and Almsgiving.[8] This version of the matter, dependent upon a chronology generated by the story of the prophet's exile (*hijra*) from Mecca, reflected a working premiss not unlike that expressed in the Talmudic formula הלכה למשה מסיני.[9] But while the paideutic function of that and related premisses recommended their employment in the description of Islamic origins, the haggadic version proved ultimately something of an embarrassment. The reactions of the

[1] Schacht, *Origins*, 58–81, 149: Shāfiʿī's ignorance of that particular tradition equating Sunna and Qur'ān is hardly relevant, save possibly as evidence that connection of both with the prophet required still to be articulated; see above, I pp. 51–2, II pp. 56–7.

[2] Schacht, *Origins*, 224, 258–9, but also 40–52: for several significant sources of 'non-Quranic' opposition.

[3] See above, p. 162.

[4] Schacht, *Origins*, 28–30, 101–6, 119, 122; and see above, pp. 166–7.

[5] Schacht, *Origins*, 225, 231–2.

[6] Schacht, *Origins*, 34, 53, 253–4.

[7] Strack, *Introduction*, 10; cf. also Gerhardsson, *Memory*, 83 and the references nn. 1–2.

[8] See above, pp. 170–1: *Tafsīr*, MS BM Or. 6333, 93ᵛ.

[9] Bacher, *Terminologie* i, 42, ii, 54–5; see above, II pp. 56–7.

halakhists were summarized by Suyūṭī in the form of two complementary principles: material of which the regulative content was effective prior to its revelation (ما تأخر نزوله عن حكمه) and material revealed prior to its becoming effective (ما تأخر حكمه عن نزوله).[1] The halakhic relevance of the latter principle was secondary to its historical function in establishing a chronology of revelation, by means of which the arbitrary assignment of Quranic verses respectively to Mecca and to Medina might be lent a degree of consistency, if not always of plausibility. Thus, the scriptural props for decrees relating to Almsgiving, Fasting, Holy War, and Ritual Prayer were regarded as belonging to the earliest stages of Muhammad's prophetical experience (*scil.* Meccan), though their regulative content (*ḥukm*) was not enforced until the Muslim community had been founded at Medina. Revelation (*nuzūl*) of that sort was described as containing a divine promise (*waʿd*), and may be compared to evidence of the prophetical *vaticinatio* in the Muhammadan *evangelium*, e.g. Q. 30: 1–4.[2]

Rather more important for juridical purposes was the first principle, according to which ordinances already established and effective were ratified by revelation. Examples adduced by Suyūṭī were Ablutions and Almsgiving, both of which were known and practised before their Quranic attestation: فقد يكون مصرفها قبل ذلك معلوما ولم يكن فيه (الزكوة) قرآن متلو كما كان الوضوء معلوما قبل نزول الآية ثم نزلت تلاوة القرآن تأكيدا له.[3] The operative terms are *maʿlūm*, *matlūw*/*tilāwa*, and *taʾkīd*, which appear respectively to signify: promulgated/published (made known), articulated/articulation in scripture, and corroboration/ratification. Not specified here are the source and mode of legislation prior to articulation in and ratification by scripture. Of such material the greater quantity by far never was articulated in scripture (*waḥy matlūw*), but was none the less regarded as revelation (*waḥy ghayr matlūw*/*waḥy marwīy*). The distinction between Quranic and non-Quranic revelation is one to which I have several times alluded: both were the word of God (*kalām allāh*) and, hence, of identical authority.[4] The distinguishing element itself was purely formal: *tilāwa* is a synonym of *qurʾān*, in the generic sense of recitation.[5] The term might be used of recitation in prayer, as mode of delivery, and by antonomasia of the canonical revelation. For the halakhists there was and could be no material difference between that which was recited as *qurʾān* and that which was transmitted as *sunna* of the prophet. *Tilāwa* was in fact a reference to 'status as scripture', that which with the canonization of revelation could in fact be found in the document, and may not be interpreted as indication

[1] *Itqān, nawʿ* 12: i, 104–6.
[2] See above, pp. 144–5, and II pp. 69–70.
[3] *Itqān* i, 106 citing Ibn Ḥiṣār.
[4] Suyūṭī, *Itqān* i, 127–8, iv, 174.
[5] See *GdQ* i, 258, iii, 144 n. 5.

of contrasting modes of transmission (oral and written) analogous to Rabbinic terminology.[1] The significant parallel between the Judaic and Muslim traditions was insistence upon a single source of legislation, which was divine.

Verses of regulative content, but not including the many non-prescriptive passages which might be adduced as *loci probantes* by the halakhists, make up approximately one-sixth of the Qur'ān. More than half of these are found in *sūras* 2–9, though material of potentially legal application is scattered throughout the book in no discernible pattern of distribution. Explicit reference to the commandments of God (*ḥudūd allāh*) is rare and unsystematic, e.g. Q. 2: 187 (fasting), 2: 229–30 (divorce), 4: 13–14 (verses 1–12 concern testamentary matters), 9: 97 (on the treachery of bedouin in contractual obligations), 9: 112 (paraenesis, but related to the foregoing), 58: 4 (verses 1–4: divorce), 65: 1 (divorce). The technical term *ḥadd* in penal law is thus only symbolically related to the scriptural *ḥudūd*.[2] More important than *ḥudūd*, and not restricted to penal law, was the hermeneutical concept *muḥkam*, related from the time of Muqātil to the general prescriptions in Q. 6: 151–3 and by Māturīdī to both Q. 6: 151–3 and 17: 22–39.[3] Designation of these two passages as the Quranic 'Decalogue'[4] is thus not quite so fanciful as Obermann appears to have believed, though a verse-by-verse correspondence is not really justified.[5] But if the principle contained in *muḥkam* offered a theoretical point of departure for both halakhic and masoretic exegesis, the finding of specific and useful juridical material (*ḥukm/aḥkām*) in the text of scripture was in practice frustrated by the absence of an unambiguous and uncontradictory historical framework. Solutions to the problems resulting from that condition were sought, and for the most part found, by imposing upon the document of revelation a chronological stencil. Historical order could thus be introduced into what was essentially literary chaos.

To that end the primary device employed was description of the circumstances of revelation (*asbāb al-nuzūl*, but also *mawāṭin*, *awqāt*, *wāqi'āt*, *akhbār*). I have touched upon the incidence of its haggadic application, in which concern for the *narratio* was paramount.[6] Elaboration and refinement of the technique were the work of the halakhists. An instructive

[1] See Goldziher, *Studien* ii, 194–202; in Rabbinic terminology stress was anyway on mode of delivery rather than of transmission, see Strack, *Introduction*, 12–20.

[2] Cf. Schacht, *Origins*, 126, 191, 208–10.

[3] Muqātil, *Tafsīr*, MS H. Hüsnü 17, 35ᵛ; see above, p. 149; Māturīdī, MS Medine 179, 116ᵛ–77ᵛ.

[4] e.g. Hirschfeld, *Researches*, 81–2; Speyer, *Erzählungen*, 305–10; Goitein, 'Birth-hour', in *Studies*, 132; Katsch, *Judaism*, 152.

[5] Obermann, 'Agada', 38 n. 2; to contend that the only Quranic occurrence of covenant (*mīthāq*) with allusion to B. Israel is Q. 2: 83 is arbitrary and irrelevant: the Mosaic context of both Q. 6: 151–3 and 17: 22–39 is quite clear.

[6] See above, pp. 141–2, and I pp. 38, 41.

summary of that process may be read in Suyūṭī.[1] A considerable portion of the discussion was devoted to the precision of temporal and spatial occasions of revelation, from which emerges an unmistakable impression of arbitrary, if not irresponsible, assignment.[2] For most of the *loci probantes* there adduced, non-regulative and hence halakhically neutral, the epithets 'Meccan' and 'Medinan' were not even mutually exclusive. For regulative material the contrast specific: general (*khāṣṣ*: *'āmm*) proved of some value in distinguishing just which of many possible verses represented the first and particular enactment of a decree (*awā'il makhṣūṣa*), e.g. for Holy War (*qitāl*), dietary laws, prohibition of wine, etc.[3] And further differentiation was available. Quranic revelation was alleged to be of two kinds: spontaneous (*ibtidā'an*), or in response to an event or a query (*'aqiba wāqi'a aw su'āl*). Application and reference of the latter were not, however, limited to the particular event or query which had inspired them: the operative distinction was found to lie between particularity of cause (*khuṣūṣ al-sabab*) and generality of expression (*'umūm al-lafẓ*).[4] But the arbitrary character even of this ruling becomes apparent in a discussion of the elative *al-atqā* in Q. 92: 17 'He who is (the) most pious shall be spared'. Desire to restrict that reference to Abū Bakr provoked some very dogmatic observations on the grammatical function of the definite article.[5] The agreed general chronology of revelation (twenty to twenty-five years divided approximately between Mecca and Medina) generated yet a further distinction between 'cause of' revelation (*sabab*) and 'report about' revelation (*khabar*): an example was *Sūra* 105 and the story of God's protection of the Meccan sanctuary.[6] Even that technique, which could be applied to all Quranic data on God's earlier interventions in history, was susceptible of modification: the reported miracle must be seen to have a cause, which was God's bestowal of His word upon His prophet, whether or not the latter was identified. The *khabar* was thus also a *sabab*.[7] Moreover, a single verse might have had several causes/occasions of revelation, e.g. both Q. 9: 113 and 16: 126 could each be traced to three separate events, well spaced in the career of Muhammad and hence both Meccan and Medinan: فنجمع بين هذه الأحاديث بتعدد النزول. Recognition of that possibility was naturally exploited to explain the phenomenon of repetition (*takrār*) in the document of revelation.[8]

Now, it ought to be clear from this summary of methods pertinent to

[1] *Itqān, anwā'* 1–15: i, 22–115, drawing extensively upon the classical work of Wāḥidī (d. 468/1076), *GAL* i, 411–12, Suppl. I, 730–1, *Kitāb Asbāb al-nuzūl*.
[2] *Itqān, anwā'* 1–8: i, 22–81; see above, pp. 126–7.
[3] *Itqān* i, 74–6.
[4] *Itqān* i, 82, 85.
[5] *Itqān* i, 87.
[6] *Itqān* i, 90; see above, I pp. 42–3.
[7] See 'Abd al-Jabbār, *Tanzīh al-Qur'ān*, 480; and above, II pp. 73–4.
[8] *Itqān* i, 95–6, 102–3.

A.U.B. LIBRARY BOOK REQUEST (Type or print)

ORDER No AR01 — 331

DEALER Bumpus

ORDERED 8 SEP 1978

LIST PRICE ~~£ 16.00~~ $34.95

RECEIVED 12 DEC 1978

BIND	WAIT L.C.	CAT

A U B ○
ON ORDER ○ cat. ✓
REC'D ○
BNB
CBI ✓ Sept. 1977 no. 8
BIBLIO
BIP
BBIP
NUC ○ K.S.

SPECIAL REMARKS

L. C. CARD No. X

FUND 18-2001-

CALL No.

AUTHOR (LAST NAME FIRST) WANSBROUGH, JOHN

TITLE QURANIC STUDIES: SCOURCES AND METHODS OF SCRIPTURAL INTERPRETATION

EDITION

PLACE OXFORD

PUBLISHER OXFORD UNIVERSITY PRESS, LONDON

DATE 1977

SERIES (London. University. School of Oriental and (P.T.O)

ISBN/SBN (0-19-713588-9)

REQUESTED BY

No OF VOLS One

No. OF COPIES One

CHARGE TO 18-2001

APPROVED BY [signature]

WHERE CITED ?

NOTIFICATION

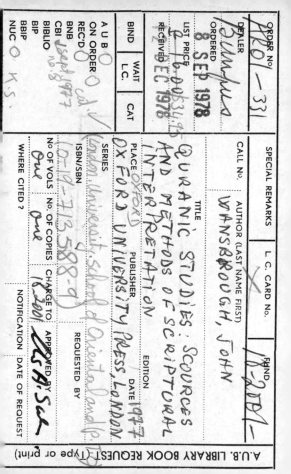

DATE OF REQUEST

African Studies. London Oriental
ser. V 3)

8 SEP 1978

Quranic chronology that the historical value of such material is restricted. A single criterion, articulated by Wāḥidī, found general acceptance: valid reports about the occasions of revelation must be based upon eye-witness accounts.[1] With that statement the entire subject was subsumed under the general rubric Tradition, and its expression can be assessed only by reference to the standards generally obtaining for evaluation of *ḥadīth* literature. Production of that literature rested upon two convictions: that the reliability (*thiqa*) of a witness could be known, and that for such continuity of transmission (*isnād*) could be established. The manner in which that was accomplished in the field of legal traditions was described by Schacht.[2] That so-called 'historical' traditions came into existence in precisely the same way as legal ones is clear from examples like those pertaining to the marriage of the prophet to Maymūna.[3] It seems at least doubtful whether for exegetical (*tafsīr*) traditions a different origin can be claimed. That these exhibited a reaction to the undisciplined employment of subjective criteria in scriptural interpretation was proposed by Goldziher.[4] From a purely formal point of view there is something to be said for that proposal, but from the point of view of substance, it may be observed that exegesis provided with formal *isnād*s can rarely be distinguished from that without. The supplying of *isnād*s, whether traced to the prophet, to his companions, or to their successors, may be understood as an exclusively formal innovation and cannot be dated much before 200/815. That Shāfiʿī's stringent standards with regard to prophetical *ḥadīth*s were not applied in the fields of history and exegesis is an impression derived from a wholly artificial classification of their contents. The substance of history, of exegesis, and of law was identical: its degree of attestation depended upon the particular use being made of it. And the quality of *isnād* (*marfūʿ*, *muttaṣil*, *mursal*, *maqṭūʿ*, etc.), too, varied for the same material according to its employment.[5] The frequently adduced view that the text of revelation was easily understood by those who had witnessed its first utterance, as well as by their immediate successors, but by later generations could not be, is in my opinion not merely ingenuous, but belied by the many stories of early efforts towards the interpretation of scripture associated with the figures of ʿUmar b. Khaṭṭāb and ʿAbdallāh b. ʿAbbās. Whatever the reasons for production of those stories, it seems hardly possible that at the beginning of the third/ninth century the Muslim community had to be reminded of what it had once known. *Tafsīr* traditions, like traditions in every other field, reflect a single impulse: to demonstrate the Hijazi origins of Islam.

The earliest extant work on the circumstances of the Quranic revelation

[1] *Apud* Suyūṭī, *Itqān* i, 89.
[2] *Origins*, 36–9, 163–75.
[3] *Origins*, 138–40, 153.
[4] *Richtungen*, 61–5: *tafsīr manqūl* (*bil-ʿilm*) as against *tafsīr bil-raʾy*.
[5] *Pace* Horst, 'Zur Überlieferung', 305–7; and cf. Birkeland, *Muslim Opposition*, 28–42.

is ascribed to Ibn Shihāb Zuhrī (d. 124/742) and entitled *Tanzīl al-Qur'ān*.[1] The ascription is arbitrary, but need not mislead: the recension is that of the Ṣūfī exegete Sulamī (d. 412/1021)[2] and in complete accord with the later accepted tradition on the chronological order of *sūra*s, shorn of the subtleties appropriate to scholastic discussion of the subject, and even of recognition that a single *sūra* might contain material of both Meccan and Medinan origin. On that particular point the author was revealingly explicit: وكان إذا نزلت سورة بمكة كُتبت بمكة.[3] The number of *sūra*s assigned to Mecca is 85 and to Medina 29,[4] and the internal order corresponds to that of Suyūṭī's third list.[5] For the history of Quranic exegesis this bald statement of fact circulated in the name of Zuhrī is quite without value. The *isnād* is anyway defective and the last authority but Zuhrī, one Walīd b. Muḥammad Muqarī, was considered *matrūk al-ḥadīth*.[6]

More important for the study of both *tafsīr* traditions and *asbāb al-nuzūl* is the 'Kitāb Tafsīr', included as chapter 54 in the *Ṣaḥīḥ* of Muslim (d. 261/875).[7] That very brief treatise consists entirely of witness to the occasions of revelation for sixteen Quranic verses, traced to the authority of 'Ā'isha, 'Umar, Abū Hurayra, and Ibn 'Abbās, with general mention of *sūra*s 8, 9, 59, and of the prohibition of wine. Reference to abrogation (*naskh*), the only reason for halakhic interest in the chronological order of revelation, is explicit: Ibn 'Abbās declared that Q. 4: 93 ومن يقتل مؤمناً متعمداً فجزاؤه جهنم was the last to have been revealed and had thus not been abrogated: لقد أنزلت آخر ما أنزل ثم ما نسخها شيء.[8] In a discussion of whether Q. 5: 3 (dietary laws) had been revealed about the Jews, 'Umar asserted his authority on the grounds that he knew all of the *asbāb al-nuzūl*.[9] Ibn Mas'ūd dated the revelation of Q. 57: 16 by reference to his own conversion four years earlier.[10] Muslim's material contains the premisses but not the arguments of halakhic exegesis: the chapter is fragmentary and badly organized, and may owe its very existence to the author's recognition that in a collection of traditions a few on the subject of scriptural exegesis would not be out of place. From that admittedly conjectural reading of the evidence one might conclude that for traditionists, even after the canonical text of revelation had been established, the Qur'ān was merely one topic among many requiring the formal embel-

[1] *GAS* i, 283. [2] *GAS* i, 671–4. [3] Zuhrī, *Tanzīl al-Qur'ān*, 32.

[4] Duplication of *Sūra* 7 and absence of *Sūra* 33, copyist's errors, are remarked by the editor, 30 n. 1.

[5] *Itqān* i, 26–7; reproduced *GdQ* i, 59–60. [6] Cf. Goldziher, *Studien* ii, 144.

[7] *GAS* i, 136–43; *Ṣaḥīḥ* viii, 237–46.

[8] Muslim, *Ṣaḥīḥ* viii, 241; adduced by Suyūṭī, *Itqān* i, 80, among a number of equally well-attested candidates for that honour.

[9] Muslim, 238.

[10] Muslim, 243.

lishment of *ḥadīth*. The hypothesis might be thought corroborated by the treatment of *tafsīr* in other collections of traditions.

In the *Ṣaḥīḥ* of Bukhārī (d. 256/870) the 'Kitāb Tafsīr' (chapter 65) occupies a prominent position.[1] In the corpus of 475 traditions every Quranic *sūra* received some attention from the author, if only in the form of a simple lexical identification on the authority of Mujāhid or Ibn 'Abbās, of one of the latter's disciples, or occasionally without citation of any authority at all.[2] Bukhārī's lexicology could be described either as decidedly primitive or as presupposing a long tradition in the course of which standard solutions to major problems had crystallized and no longer required authentication. Whichever of the alternatives is more likely, the presence of such material in a collection assembled to demonstrate the importance of traditional authority does not inspire confidence.[3] A popular etymology for the name Gabriel, adduced from 'Ikrima *ad* Q. 2: 97, deserves notice: جبرَ وميكَ وسراف عبدٌ إيل الله.[4] This was followed by a tradition from Anas on the 'rabbinical test of prophethood', here put to Muhammad by 'Abdallāh b. Salām.[5] Q. 2: 31 became a peg for asserting, by means of a Purgatory motif, the rank in heaven of Muhammad above all other prophets.[6] *Ad* Q. 2: 136 Abū Hurayra was cited for the prophet's prescription on the proper conduct of Muslims towards Jews.[7] *Ad* Q. 2: 183 a *ḥadīth* from 'Abdallāh b. 'Umar announced the substitution of Ramaḍān for the earlier pagan Arab fast (*sic*) of 'Ashūrā'.[8] *Ad* Q. 17: 85 definition of the Spirit (*rūḥ*) was related to the Jews.[9] The entire passage on *Sūrat al-Kahf* was devoted to the story of Mūsā and Khiḍr (Q. 18: 60–82), with special concern for the identity of Mūsā.[10] Bukhārī's exegetical method was, in brief, predominantly haggadic, and the absence of anecdotal material for such popular passages as Q. 30: 1–4, 85: 21–2, and *Sūra* 105, must be regarded as fortuitous. The essential difference between Bukhārī and the haggadists is the insertion of appropriate *isnād*s, many of which, however, were carried no further than to a successor (e.g. Mujāhid). The occasional intrusion of an element specifically halakhic or masoretic may be noted: e.g. whether the 'compensation clause' with regard to fasting in Q. 2: 184 (*fidya ṭa'ām miskīn*) had or had not been abrogated; whether the waiting period (*'idda*) for divorced and/or widowed women was regulated by Q. 2: 234 or by 2: 232; the relative merits of the variants *an yaṭṭawwaf* and *allā yaṭṭawwaf* in Q. 2: 158; explanation of *lākinnā* in Q. 18: 38 as *lākin anā*, produced by a combination of elision (*ḥadhf*) and assimilation (*idghām*).[11] Observations

1 *GAS* i, 115–34; ed. iii, 193–390.
2 Cf. Birkeland, *The Lord guideth*, 40.
3 See below, pp. 216–19.
4 Bukhārī, *Ṣaḥīḥ* iii, 196.
5 See above, pp. 122–6.
6 Bukhārī, 194–5; see above, pp. 172–3.
7 Bukhārī, 197.
8 Bukhārī, 201–2 (variant: Quraysh).
9 Bukhārī, 275; see above, pp. 125, 128.
10 Bukhārī, 277–82; see above, pp. 128.
11 Bukhārī, 202, 207, 200, 276, respectively.

on the occasions of revelation are circumstantial only, and never explicit as in Muslim's *Ṣaḥīḥ*.

What must be regarded as the *raison d'être* of *tafsīr* traditions in the major collections was most clearly formulated in the 'Kitāb Tafsīr' of Tirmidhī (d. 279/892), as chapter 44 of his *Ṣaḥīḥ*.[1] While the material itself is haggadic and for the most part identical to that adduced by Bukhārī, the chains of transmission are not only more complete, but each provided with comment on its degree of acceptability (e.g. *ṣaḥīḥ*, *ḥasan*, *gharīb*). Explicit reference to the purpose of that exercise was set out in an introductory paragraph, in which is stressed the danger of subjective exegesis (*tafsīr bil-ra'y*) and, conversely, the necessity of authoritative tradition (*'ilm*).[2] Coverage of the text of scripture is not complete (unlike Bukhārī), though adequate up to *Sūra* 75 (a total of twenty-one *sūra*s was not provided with comment). For verses containing a *crux interpretum*, e.g. Q. 3: 7, alternative *isnād*s were adduced.[3] Verses traditionally employed as pegs for anecdote, like Q. 17: 1, 18: 60–82, 30: 1–4, were treated as in Bukhārī, perhaps even more generously.[4] References to the *asbāb al-nuzūl* are, as in the latter, merely implicit and circumstantial. Allusion to the instrument of abrogation is explicit for the *qibla* controversy, e.g. Q. 2: 115 and 134.[5] Of textual exegesis there is virtually none, save for the variants *an* and *allā ad* Q. 2: 158.[5] Lexical explanation resembles that of Bukhārī, but is sporadic and not, as in the latter, adduced in concentration at the beginnings of *sūra*s. Chapters on *thawāb al-Qur'ān* and *qirā'āt* in Tirmidhī (nos. 42, 43), like the chapter on *faḍā'il al-Qur'ān* in Bukhārī (no. 66), attest to a view of scriptural studies somewhat more sophisticated than that displayed by their contemporary Muslim, but at the same time exhibit rather more of cliché and stereotype formulation.

The rhetorical analysis of *ḥadīth* literature, as contrasted with its exploitation for legal, historical, and sociological purposes, has attracted very little scholarly attention. Two studies in particular deserve mention: Vajda, 'Juifs et Musulmans selon le ḥadīṯ' (1937); and Stetter, *Topoi und Schemata im Ḥadīṯ* (1965). The most significant feature of that literature, signalled by both Vajda and Stetter, is its schematic formulation. Employment of much circumstantial and 'naturalistic' detail, judged also by Schacht as indicative of fictive situations,[7] tends to fall into recognizable and even predictable patterns. For example, emphasis upon the pastoral simplicity of Jāhiliyya and early Islam, accompanied by unsubtle humour at the expense of bedouin manners, attention to every aspect of the prophet's personality, and recurrent use of expressions implying intimate

[1] *GAS* i, 154–9; ed. xi, 67–xii, 264.
[2] Tirmidhī, *Ṣaḥīḥ* xi, 67–8.
[3] Tirmidhī, xi, 114–20; see above, pp. 149–53.
[4] Tirmidhī, xi, 290–3, xii, 2–13, 66–72, respectively.
[5] Tirmidhī, xi, 79–88, esp. 80.
[6] Tirmidhī, xi, 90.
[7] Schacht, *Origins*, 156.

recollection (e.g. كأنى أنظر and فيما يخال الىّ) are of such regularity as to suggest a common pool of narrative ingredients.[1] That circumstantial description might also contain elements of halakhic value, in particular references (explicit and implicit) to time and place, must be acknowledged. But the very ubiquity of both motif and formula is significant. The *ḥadīth* literature reflects both form and substance not only of juridical concern with the actions and utterances of the prophet of Islam and with the contents of the Quranic revelation, but also of its haggadic (narrative and historical) expression in *sīra*, *maghāzī*, and *ayyām*. The presence of *isnād*s as halakhic embellishment is, from the point of view of literary criticism, a superfluity. The substance of Bukhārī, Muslim, and Tirmidhī is that of Muqātil, Ibn Isḥāq, Sufyān, and Kalbī. It is also that of the entire exegetical tradition, excluding the masoretic literature, up to and including Suyūṭī.

A single illustration in place of many: a flagrant tendency discerned by Vajda in the *ḥadīth* literature was the transposition of anti-Jewish elements of Islamic prescription into the category of superseded Jāhilī custom. One example was designation of 'Ashūrā' not as a Jewish, but as an ancient Arabian practice.[2] Others were abolition of the custom of public lamentation at funeral processions and of abstention from sexual intercourse during menstruation, both identified with pagan Arab practice.[3] The incidence in haggadic exegesis of that kind of transposition, by which the roles of Arabian Jewry and Quraysh were exchanged or combined or otherwise blended, has been described.[4] The ultimate value of the technique was doctrinal; its origin, however, was polemic, not quite effaced from the memory of the Muslim community even in the third/ninth century.

The several ways in which the halakhists employed *tafsīr* traditions may be seen in three kinds of exegetical literature: *aḥkām* (prescription), *ikhtilāf* (dispute), and *naskh* (abrogation). While the scope of each extended beyond exclusively midrashic exploitation of the text of scripture, it is with that procedure in particular that I am concerned. The extrapolation of law from revelation was, in the Muslim community as in others organized on similar theocratic principles, a tortuous and interminable process.[5] Exceptions to the accord and harmony symbolized in the notion of consensus secured recognition in the complementary notion of permitted areas of dispute. For very few problems was there ever a final solution or even a set of agreed scriptural references. Prescriptions relating to Holy War are a case in point. For Jaṣṣāṣ the obligation to fight in the way of God was derived

1 Stetter, *Topoi und Schemata*, 4–34.
2 Vajda, 'Juifs et Musulmans', 122–3; Bukhārī, *Ṣaḥīḥ* iii, 201–2; see above, p. 181.
3 Vajda, 'Juifs et Musulmans', 78 n. 1 and 69–75, respectively.
4 See above, pp. 122–7, and II pp. 62–3, 70–3.
5 e.g. Rabin, *Qumran*, 82–94, 95–111.

not from Q. 2: 216 (as for Muqātil) but from Q. 2: 190 وقاتلوا فى سبيل الله الذين يقاتلونكم ولا تعتدوا إنّ الله لا يحب المعتدين in which was stressed the exclusively defensive character of combat imposed upon Muslims.[1] Precluded by its terms were thus non-combatants, such as women, children, and hermits/monks (*ruhbān/aṣḥāb al-ṣawāmi'*). A different qualification was that made between infidels (*mushrikūn*) and scriptuaries (*ahl al-kitāb*) as liable, by divine decree, to attack by believers. Of the four verses (Q. 2: 191 and 4: 91, 4: 89 and 9: 5) adduced to support the progression from defensive to offensive warfare and from selected targets to a general declaration of hostility to non-Muslims, Q. 9: 5 became the scriptural prop of a formulation designed to cover any and all situations which might arise between the Muslim community and its enemies, and included lingering compunctions about clauses attaching to the sacred months (*ashhur ḥurum*) and the sanctuary at Mecca (*masjid ḥarām*). Called in the exegetical tradition the sword-verse (*āyat al-sayf*), Q. 9: 5 فإذا انسلخ الأسهر الحرم فاقتلوا المشركين حيث وجدتموهم وخذوهم واحصروهم واقعدوا لهم كل مرصد فإن تابوا وأقاموا الصلوة وءاتوا الزكوة فخلّوا سبيلهم إن الله غفور رحيم achieved a quite extraordinary status in the elaboration of Islamic jurisprudence, as the alleged abrogant of 124 Quranic verses.[2] These included all passages in scripture which could be interpreted as recommending leniency (*ṣafḥ wa-'afw*; cf. Q. 2: 109, 5: 13) towards unbelievers. The range and variety of such were equally extraordinary, at least as set out in what became the classical work on Quranic abrogation, the *Kitāb al-nāsikh wal-mansūkh* of Hibatallāh (d. 410/1019).[3] The ubiquity of the abrogant *āyat al-sayf* in that treatise suggests that it was not the law of Holy War at all, but the presence of legislative repeal in the text of scripture which was being argued.[4] But Hibatallāh represented the final stage of halakhic exegesis, in which general conclusions could be advanced without authorities and shorn of scholastic justification. A century earlier Naḥḥās (d. 338/950)[5] had observed that *āyat al-sayf*, at least with regard to the treatment of prisoners of war, was itself abrogated by Q. 47: 4, the view of Ḥasan Baṣrī and others.[6] Some, on the other hand, held that the opposite was true: the leniency of Q. 47: 4 had been abrogated by Q. 9: 5. Naḥḥās himself argued that neither had been repealed, that both verses were *muḥkamāt* (*sic*, cf. Q. 22: 52) since they were not mutually exclusive, and that decision on the treatment of prisoners lay with the *imām*. That view was supported by several traditions on the action of the prophet during the

[1] *Aḥkām al-Qur'ān* i, 256–63: 'Bāb Farḍ al-Jihād'; see above, p. 170.
[2] e.g. Ibn 'Arabī, *apud* Suyūṭī, *Itqān* iii, 69.
[3] *GAS* i, 47–8.
[4] Hibatallāh, *Kitāb al-nāsikh wal-mansūkh*, 29, 37, 38, 51, and *passim*, esp. 53–88 for *sūras* 11–54, most of which could boast only one verse abrogated; see below, pp. 196–7.
[5] *GAS* i, 49.
[6] Naḥḥās, *Kitāb al-nāsikh wal-mansūkh*, 165–6.

conquest of Mecca. Much later Ibn ʿArabī, in whose discussion the general status of *āyat al-sayf* as abrogant attributed to him by Suyūṭī is in fact not found, employed the instrument of *khāṣṣ/ʿāmm* to demonstrate that although the specific reference of Q. 9: 5 was to pagan Arab idolaters (*ʿabīd lil-wathan*), the verse was generally valid for all who rejected God's message, whether during the sacred months or within the Meccan sanctuary.[1]

The employment of *tafsīr* traditions in the *aḥkām* literature was not limited to precision of juridical niceties. For Q. 3: 200 يايها الذين آمنوا اصبروا وصابروا ورابطوا واتقوا الله لعلكم تفلحون, adduced by both Muqātil and Mālik in the spirit of general paraenesis, Jaṣṣāṣ adduced two utterances of the prophet equating *ribāṭ* for the sake of God with the virtue deriving from fasting and prayer.[2] But the primary purpose of such traditions was halakhic: to render explicit that which was seldom more than implicit in the text of scripture, by establishing a specific historical context for the revelation in question. In the much-disputed problem of reference in Q. 5: 33 إنما جزاء الذين يحاربون الله ورسوله ويسعون فى الأرض فسادا أن يقتّلوا أو يصلّبوا أو تقطع أيديهم وأرجلهم من خلاف أو ينفوا من الأرض ذلك لهم خزى فى الدنيا ولهم فى الآخرة عذاب عظيم Jaṣṣāṣ provided two *ḥadīth*s: one from Ibn ʿAbbās applying the verse to polytheists (*mushrikūn*), and another from Ibn ʿUmar identifying 'those hostile to God and His prophet' as the clan of B. ʿUrayna (ʿUraniyyūn).[3] Summing up the evidence (there are several additional *ḥadīth*s from Ibn ʿAbbās, conflicting and with different *isnād*s) as offering a choice between polytheists and apostates, Jaṣṣāṣ found himself constrained to reject both on the grounds that whatever the occasion of the revelation, its semantic content was clear: reference was to all transgressors of God's law. The principle thus enunciated was that juridical application could not be based upon an 'occasion' (presumably a historical accident) but only upon the general validity of the scriptural expression: لان لا حكم للسبب عندنا وإنما الحكم عندنا لعموم اللفظ.[4] The manner in which this kind of argument cut across earlier exegetical method based on the chronological arrangement of scripture emerges from a comparison of Jaṣṣāṣ with Abū ʿUbayd, who reported that the incident involving B. ʿUrayna had taken place in the early years of Islam (*fī awwal al-islām*) before the revelation of these prescriptions (*qabla an tunazzal al-ḥudūd*), and that according to Ibn ʿAbbās (!)

[1] Ibn ʿArabī, *Aḥkām al-Qurʾān* i, 369–70.

[2] *Aḥkām al-Qurʾān* ii, 45: the metaphorical extension of that concept, from *ribāṭ al-khayl* to *ribāṭ al-nafs*, generated some interesting pseudo-history in medieval North Africa, see Norris, 'Origins of the Almoravid movement', 255–68, esp. 263–5.

[3] *Aḥkām al-Qurʾān* ii, 406–8.

[4] Jaṣṣāṣ, loc. cit.; see above, p. 178.

the contents of Q. 5: 33 left the precise punishment of transgressors to the discretion of the *imām*.[1] Now, the chronological relationship between that particular event and the revelation repealing the prophetical *Sunna* based upon it is anything but obvious. Undated in the *Sīra* and fixed at Shawwāl 6/February–March 628 by Wāqidī, the affair of B. ʿUrayna appears to have been one of several movable feasts in the early Islamic calendar.[2] Its assignment to the earliest period of prophetical activity by Abū ʿUbayd and to a much later date by Wāqidī was evidence of concern not with its historical truth, but with its juridical value.

The implications of Q. 5: 33 were never unanimously clarified, though that could hardly have been for want of effort. As an appendix to the sections on *jihād* and *jizya* in his *Ikhtilāf al-fuqahā'*, Ṭabarī adduced in his treatment of the subject a degree of consensus on identification of the *muḥārib* as sinner (*fāsiq*) rather than as infidel (*kāfir*), but added that the protected non-Muslim (*dhimmī*) was also liable to the *aḥkām al-muḥāribīn*, since transgression was tantamount to violation of a treaty.[3] It was further stipulated that the affair of B. ʿUrayna had taken place before revelation of Q. 5: 33, and that that was juridically relevant. The sophisticated logic of Jaṣṣāṣ's argument had presumably not yet been formulated.[4] The *aḥkām al-muḥāribīn* are the subject also of a short treatise tentatively, but incorrectly, ascribed to ʿAṭā Khurasānī (d. 136/757).[5] In fact the work, contained in seven folios inserted at the beginning of MS Ahmet III, 310,[6] represents a post-Ṭabarī stage of *ikhtilāf*. Considerable attention was devoted to the circumstances in which Q. 5: 33–4 had been revealed, and a series of traditions adduced, claiming 'some group of *ahl al-kitāb* who had broken their covenant with the prophet' (*sic*), of B. Qurayẓa when they had planned to assassinate the prophet, or (unspecified) infidels, or finally, B. ʿUrayna.[7] Whether the scriptural passage could be held to have abrogated the prophetical *sunna* explicit in the B. ʿUrayna tradition depended upon the identification of *muḥārib* (enemy) with *murtadd* (apostate), an equation for which corroboration might be found in the reference to *tawba* (contrition) in Q. 5: 34. For the author of that treatise *consensus doctorum* seemed to support the identification, and the remainder of the text is

[1] See above, p. 150: *Kitāb al-nāsikh wal-mansūkh*, MS Ahmet III, 143, 94^{v}–6^{r}.

[2] Cf. Jones, 'Chronology', 253, 279.

[3] Ṭabarī, *Kitāb Ikhtilāf al-fuqahā'*, 242–9: an example of analogy by *taʿlīl*, see above, pp. 167–8.

[4] That the proper concern of the lawgiver was with general principles rather than with specific circumstances (inferable, after all, by analogy and other hermeutic devices), had been articulated in both Hellenistic and Rabbinic legal literature, see Daube, 'Rabbinic methods', 247–51.

[5] *GAS* i, 33; MS Ahmet III, 310, 1–7.

[6] One of many copies of Qāḍī 'Iyād, *Kitāb al-Shifā'*: no. 2733 in Karatay, *Topkapı Sarayı Müzesi Kütüphanesi Arapça Yazmalar Kataloğu*, ii, under which entry this insertion with separate pagination is not mentioned.

[7] MS Ahmet III, 310, 2^{r-v}.

devoted to defining transgression of the divine law (*ḥudūd allāh*) as consisting primarily in murder (*qatl*), theft (*saraqa*), and banditry (*qaṭʿ al-ṭarīq*).

Two technical terms employed in Ahmet III, 310, and elsewhere in the *aḥkām/ikhtilāf* literature(s), deserve notice. In discussion of the punishment which could be imposed upon the *muḥārib*, a problem was created by the options set out in Q. 5: 33: he was to be killed, or crucified, or have his hands and feet severed, or be banished. The choice might be left to the discretion of the *imām* or based upon a precise definition of the culprit's offence. Ṭabarī was stated to have preferred (*murajjiḥ*) the latter, and that view was preferable (*rājiḥ*) since it conformed to the text of scripture (*huwa naṣṣ al-āya*).[1] On the manner of crucifixion where such was deemed appropriate, the view of Shāfiʿī was that the offender should be crucified alive and then killed on the cross, that being explicit in scripture (*huwa 'l-aẓhar min al-āya*) which recommended an exemplary punishment.[2] Now, in neither instance does connection of *rājiḥ* or *aẓhar* with the text of the verse in question indicate an obvious interpretation derived from the 'plain meaning' of scripture.[3] From the syntax of Q. 5: 33 it was not quite possible to insist that the series of proposed punishments exhibited gradation according to the nature of the offence, or that the notion of 'exemplary' punishment (*mathula*) was dominant. Limitation or exclusion of the *imām*'s discretion and interpretation of *jazā'* (recompense) as deterrent reflect substantial and sophisticated additions to the wording of scripture, and may be traced to the story of the prophet's action in the affair of B. ʿUrayna. Employment of the term *aẓhar* (or *ẓāhir*) was emotive, of *rājiḥ* (or *arjaḥ/marjūḥ*) subjective or at best conjectural.[4] Halakhic use of *tarjīḥ* for 'preference of one of several options' was a process justifiable only by resort to the abiding distinction between *muḥkam* and *mutashābih*, itself postulated as an integral characteristic of scripture.[5] In more general exegetic usage *tarjīḥ* was required to conform to the normative standards of analogy based upon juxtaposition of identical and similar passages.[6] In Ahmet III, 310 the terms *ẓāhir* and *rājiḥ* are synonymous and interchangeable and, save for the very special usage of the Ẓāhirī *madhhab*, such remained the practice in Muslim exegetical literature: فالظاهر فى الحقيقة هو الاحتمال الراجح.[7] Worthy of mention is Maimonides' use of *ẓāhir*, with appeal to the text of scripture (*naṣṣ*), in an exegetical context

[1] MS Ahmet III, 310, 3ʳ, 4ʳ.
[2] MS Ahmet III, 310, 3ᵛ.
[3] See above, pp. 150–1, 152–3.
[4] A point insisted upon by Fakhr al-dīn Rāzī, *apud* Suyūṭī, *Itqān* iii, 12.
[5] *Itqān* iii, 31–2, also citing Rāzī; see above, pp. 151–2.
[6] Particularly for the masorah, see Suyūṭī, *Itqān* i, 31, 58, 93–4, 229, and ii, 264, where a distinction between *marjūḥ* and *ẓāhir* may be thought scarcely discernible.
[7] Goldziher, *Ẓāhiriten*, 24 n. 4 citing Juwaynī.

requiring even more imagination than the allocation of penalties in Q. 5: 33, namely, the messianic symbolism of Daniel 7–8: והדה אמור תטהר מן מגרד אלנץ.[1] The concept of 'plain meaning' was indeed a generous one.

Whatever the linguistic and logical assertions made about the *ipsissima verba* of scripture, halakhic exegesis turned upon the assumption of a chronological, and hence causal, relation between Qur'ān and (prophetical) Sunna. The question of priority, though hedged with qualification, was generally answered in favour of the latter. Jaṣṣāṣ, who had elsewhere dismissed the occasion of revelation as irrelevant to interpretation of the Quranic text (in the case of B. 'Urayna and Q. 5: 33), admitted that in juridical matters the specific meaning (*takhṣīṣ*) of the Qur'ān could be determined by reference to a prophetical tradition, provided such was widely (*min ṭarīq al-tawātur*) not sparsely attested (*bi-akhbār al-āḥād*).[2] The particular context of that declaration was the abrogation (*naskh*) of Q. 7: 3 اتبعوا ما أنزل اليكم من ربّكم by 59: 7 وما آتاكم الرسول فخذوه وما نهاكم عنه فانتهوا. Resort to Sunna was thus justified by Qur'ān, and the conclusion drawn that for halakhah the prophet was of the same authority as the text of scripture: فانه فى إيجاب الحكم بمنزلة القرآن. The locution 'of a status with (= like) Qur'ān' could be misleading: it is quite clear from the context that it was scripture being subjected to interpretation, an operation for which the hermeneutical instrument was tradition, in the form of words and deeds attributed to the prophet. These were preserved and transmitted with the care prescribed for canonical revelation.[3] References to the contrast *litteratim* transmission (*riwāya/naql bil-lafẓ*): paraphrastic transmission (*riwāya/naql bil-ma'nā*) may not be understood as allusion to mutually exclusive modes, but, rather, to a polemically formulated concern for the authority of the Quranic text.[4] Paraphrastic transmission was anyway, in the view of the halakhists, limited to utterances from the companions of the prophet (*al-ṣaḥāba*), an attitude which may indeed have had its origins with, but was not restricted to, the Ẓāhirī *madhhab*.[5] An indication of stringency in the transmission of Sunna may be seen in Abū 'Ubayd's discussion of the prophet's action in the affair of B. 'Urayna: the phrase 'he put out their eyes with spikes (iron)' was preserved in two versions exhibiting the purely phonological contrast *samala*:*samara*, to which the author remarked 'in our opinion the correct version is *samala*' (المحفوظ عندنا اللام).[6]

[1] *Iggeret Teman*, 80 lines 15–16.

[2] Jaṣṣāṣ, *Aḥkām al-Qur'ān* iii, 28–9.

[3] e.g. Goldziher, *Richtungen*, 30.

[4] *Pace* Goldziher, op. cit. 34; id., *Studien* ii, 201, 242–3; and Blachère, *Histoire* iii, 798 n. 1; see above, pp. 176–7, I pp. 51–2.

[5] Goldziher, *Ẓāhiriten*, 33–4: on consensus (*ijmā'*).

[6] *Kitab al-nāsikh wal-mansūkh*, MS Ahmet III, 143, 95r.

For Ibn ʿArabī the problems relating to transmission of Sunna were clearly of polemical character.[1] His point of departure was the familiar charge against the Jews that they had altered God's word, e.g. in Q. 2: 59 فبدّل الذين ظلموا قولا غير الذى قيل لهم, referring specifically to *ḥiṭṭa* in the preceding verse (and Q. 7: 161), a much-disputed term thought to exhibit the malicious alteration of חטאה (sin) into חטה (wheat; Arabic *ḥinṭa*).[2] Whatever the historical background to that charge may have been, it was interpreted in the Muslim exegetical tradition as proving wilful distortion of a divine command. Ibn ʿArabī's argument was that if an act of worship (*taʿabbud*) depended upon the actual expression (*lafẓ*) employed, there could then be no question of paraphrastic transmission. The latter was in any case an indulgence limited to the companions of the prophet, and only for non-liturgical formulations. Now, Q. 2: 59 (like 7: 162) is one of many Quranic passages assumed by exegetes to refer to a conscious and malicious distortion of the word of God.[3] The three technical terms *tabdīl*, *taḥrīf*, and *kitmān*, employed to describe that procedure are amply attested in scripture, each in a variety of contexts permitting association of the act with written texts, and thus tantamount to forgery (e.g. Q. 10: 15, 4: 46, 2: 174, respectively). Haggadic embellishment of the charge turned mostly upon the absence from Hebrew scripture of proof-texts announcing the mission of Muhammad, symbolized by the many stories connected with the Jewish convert to Islam Kaʿb al-Aḥbār.[4] No one in Medina was more familiar with the Torah than Kaʿb, and in one account he specified ten Quranic verses (six of them concerned Abraham) which the Jews had allegedly erased from their scripture because they contained predictions of the advent of Islam: طلسمتها (?طلستها) اليهود وأمحتها لكى لا يشتهر أمرها.[5]

For the halakhists recourse to tactics such as those was hardly adequate, and the accusation of forgery was gradually elaborated to include both textual alteration and exegetical error, the latter in the sense of intentionally false interpretation. Intermediate and combined positions were also possible, and each had its origin in Judaeo-Muslim polemic.[6] The implications for Quranic exegesis were articulated by Jaṣṣāṣ: the concept *taḥrīf* in Q. 5: 13 يحرّفون الكلم عن مواضعه was limited to interpretation (*taʾwīl*) of the kind which necessarily resulted from lack of or from arbitrary method,

[1] *Aḥkām al-Qurʾān* i, 10.
[2] See Hirschfeld, *Researches*, 107; Speyer, *Erzählungen*, 337–8; and the discussion in Paret, *Der Koran*, 19–20 ad loc.
[3] See above, pp. 154–5; II pp. 63, 76.
[4] See above, II pp. 75–6; and Rabin, *Qumran*, 116, 118, 123–4.
[5] Perlmann, 'Another Kaʿb al-Aḥbār story', 48–58.
[6] See Steinschneider, *Polemische Literatur*, 320–2, 392; Goldziher, 'Polemik', 345, 364–72; Schreiner, 'Zur Geschichte', 599–601, 613–14, 626–8, 634–5, 640–7; Hirschfeld, 'Mohammedan criticism', 222–40.

e.g. elucidation of the *mutashābihāt* without reference to the *muḥkamāt*. *Taḥrīf* in the specific sense of alteration (*taghyīr/taghayyur*) could not be applied to any text whose attestation and transmission were derived from widespread authority (*istifāḍa/tawātur*), since that would diminish and even cancel the value of all tradition.[1] The semantic position thus defined for *taḥrīf* was rather more constructive than one from which merely abusive assaults on the integrity of Hebrew scripture could be made and, not unexpectedly, generated a more sophisticated polemic. For charges of maliciously false interpretation (!) levelled at one another by communities sharing a set of scriptures were a commonplace of sectarian strife.[2] That the quality of invective elaborated there might serve as model for dispute about the content of another scripture seems not unreasonable: the language of polemic is remarkably uniform. But in a primarily consonantal text interpretation might easily involve argument about variants in the received tradition, for which of course *taḥrīf* as textual 'alteration' could prove a convenient tag. It will, however, be useful to remember that the existence of textual variants presupposed rather than prefigured divergent interpretations.[3]

The actual condition of the *textus receptus* could always be justified, and even turned to advantage. For example, absence of the *basmala* at the beginning of *Sūrat al-Barā'a* caused Ibn 'Arabī to observe not only that the unity of subject-matter in *Sūra*s 8 and 9 had naturally (and logically) precluded insertion of the formula, but also that such was proof of the divine origin of analogy.[4] His argument was that the similarity (*tashbīh*) of the two *sūra*s had, in the absence of specific textual indication (*'inda 'adm al-naṣṣ*), caused the companions of the prophet (!) to resort to analogical juxtaposition (*qiyās al-shabah*) of the two originally separate revelations. That solution is less far-fetched than Nöldeke–Schwally appeared to believe, as ought to be clear from the use made of verses from both *sūra*s in discussion of the prescriptions for Holy War.[5] Not only analogy, but all other methods of demonstrative proof (*sā'ir ḍurūb al-istidlāl*) could, in the opinion of Jaṣṣāṣ, be derived from the text of scripture.[6] Designation of the book as 'clarification of all things' (*tibyān li-kull shay'*) constituted an invitation to the exercise of logic, permissible in the absence of explicit answers in Qur'ān and Sunna, or of *consensus*: إذا لم نجد للحادثة حكما منصوصا فى الكتاب ولا فى السنة ولا فى الإجماع وقد أخبر الله ان فى الكتاب

[1] *Aḥkām al-Qur'ān* ii, 398–9.

[2] For Qumran and the Karaites, see Wieder, *Scrolls*, 135–53, 161–3; and cf. e.g. Jeremiah 23: 36.

[3] See below, pp. 202–8.

[4] *Aḥkām al-Qur'ān* i, 366 ad loc.; cf. *GdQ* ii, 79–81.

[5] e.g. in Ṭabarī, *Kitāb Ikhtilāf al-fuqahā'*, *passim*.

[6] *Aḥkām al-Qur'ān* iii, 189–90 *ad* Q. 16: 89.

تبيان كل شئ من أمور الدين ثبت ان طريقه النظر والاستدلال بالقياس على حكمه

For Jaṣṣāṣ *consensus* represented the uninterrupted transmission of community opinion from the time of the prophet, the term *umma* (nation) in Q. 2: 143 being interpreted as a general (*ʿāmm*) not a specific (*khāṣṣ*) epithet for 'witness'.[1]

Instances of incompatibility or of conflict between scriptural passages containing juridical material were resolved by the halakhists with the aid of three related but distinct hermeneutical devices: *takhṣīṣ* (specification), *tafsīr* (here corroboration), and *naskh* (abrogation). *Takhṣīṣ* provided a means of linking a general statement to a particular situation, and was generously employed in identifying the *mushrikūn* of Q. 9: 5 and the *muḥāribūn* of Q. 5: 33.[2] Application of *takhṣīṣ* presupposed a very flexible standard of generality against which particularity was measured: it was thus found that the adjective *kull* (all/each) as well as the various relative pronouns, the definite article, and even indefinite predication, could be both general and particular.[3] The option in any given instance entailed almost invariably acknowledgement or rejection of a point of doctrine hardly adumbrated in the scriptural passage itself. Halakhic *takhṣīṣ*, in brief, depended upon the kind of analogy called *taʿlīl*, or inference from a *tertium comparationis*.[4] An example was the 'specification' of Q. 5: 3 (prohibition of carrion) by Q. 5: 96 (extension to carrion from the sea) and by 6: 145 (extension to flowing, as opposed to coagulated blood), in which the *ratio* (*ʿilla*) was contained in the opposition *ḥarām*: *ḥalāl*.[5] Another case was specification of Q. 24: 2 (punishment for fornication) by Q. 4: 25 (extension to the betrothed), by reference to the (general) fact of punishment.[6] More often than not it was Sunna to which appeal was made for specification of Qur'ān, a procedure defended by both Shāfiʿī and Jaṣṣāṣ, and of which an example was specification of Q. 2: 275 (prohibition of usury) by traditions extending the sanction to similar transactions, e.g. *ʿarāyā*.[7] Exclusion of the slave from inheritance by application of *takhṣīṣ* to Q. 4: 11–12 and 2: 180 belongs to the same category, though there the procedure was probably a device to conceal the priority of an established legal maxim.[8]

Like *takhṣīṣ*, the technical term *tafsīr* in halakhic usage exhibits a formula of harmonization designed to restrict the sphere of abrogation (*naskh*), itself the final court of appeal in the more general effort to demonstrate a scriptural source of authority for all Islamic law. An essential advantage of both *takhṣīṣ* and *tafsīr*, and to a considerable extent the difference between them and *naskh*, was that Quranic verses so treated remained effective

1 *Aḥkām al-Qur'ān* i, 88–90 ad loc.
2 See above, pp. 185–7.
3 Cf. Suyūṭī, *Itqān*, *nawʿ* 45: iii, 43–51, esp. 43–5.
4 See above, pp. 166–8.
5 Suyūṭī, *Itqān* iii, 44, 47.
6 *Itqān* iii, 48.
7 *Itqān*, loc. cit.; see above, pp. 175, 188.
8 *Pace* Suyūṭī, *Itqān* iii, 48, who considered it specification by consensus; see Schacht, *Origins*, 184–5.

(*muḥkamāt*). An example of *tafsīr*, though the term was not used, was the argument of Naḥḥās about the relevance of Q. 9: 5 (*āyat al-sayf*) and 47: 4 (recommending leniency) to the treatment of prisoners of war: the two verses were not mutually exclusive but corroborative, and the option lay with the *imām*.[1] The secondary role of scripture in that argument is, incidentally, illustrated by its appeal to prophetical traditions pertinent to the conquest of Mecca. Similar reasoning was adduced by Abū ʿUbayd, on the authority of Ibn ʿAbbās, in a discussion of the *lex talionis* (*qiṣāṣ*), for which Q. 5: 45 was held by some to abrogate the stricter ruling of 2: 178.[2] With regard, however, to the distinction between free men and slaves in Q. 2: 178, Abū ʿUbayd argued that the locution 'a life for a life' in 5: 45 was not the abrogant but, rather, the corroboration of equality within the separate categories of retaliation: فيما نرى الى فى الآية التى فى المائدة النفس بالنفس ليست بناسخة للتى فى البقرة الحرّ بالحرّ والعبد بالعبد ولا هى فى خلافها ولكنهما جميعا محكمات الا انه رأى ان التى فى المائدة كالمفسرة للتى فى البقرة فتأول ان قوله النفس بالنفس إنما هو على ان أنفس الأحرار متساوية فيما بينهم دون العبيد. The use of *ta'awwala* in this passage for 'interpretation' might be thought to confirm the specialized meaning of *mufassira* as 'corroboration', antithetically juxtaposed to *nāsikha* (abrogant).

That the hermeneutical principle of abrogation (*naskh*) did not refer to supersession of earlier divinely revealed statutes (*sharāʾiʿ al-anbiyāʾ*) by Muhammad's law (*sharīʿat muḥammad*) was expressly articulated by Jaṣṣāṣ.[3] It was, rather, the instrument by means of which particular statements (*khāṣṣ*) could be distinguished from general ones (*ʿāmm*), and polyvalent utterances (*mutashābih*) referred to univalent ones (*muḥkam*). In that formulation *takhṣīṣ* (specification) was subsumed under the general rubric *naskh*, but though certain of the phenomena which regularly appeared in discussions of scriptural abrogation were sometimes designated *takhṣīṣ*, it is both convenient and realistic to distinguish the two. The concept of Islam as the supersession of earlier dispensations was of course not alien to the Muslim exegetical tradition, and might even derive some support from scripture, namely Q. 5: 50 أفحكم الجاهلية يبغون ومن أحسن من الله حكما لقوم يوقنون. Explicit reference to a 'pagan dispensation' (*ḥukm al-jāhiliyya*) was interpreted by Goitein as signalling the commencement of a specifically Muhammadan legislation derived from material up to that point diffuse and only paraenetically expressed.[4] Acceptance of Jāhiliyya as a temporal rather than psychological or sociological concept and acquiescence in the utility of dating the contents of the Qur'ān reflect a

[1] See above, pp. 184–5.
[2] *Kitāb al-nāsikh wal-mansūkh*, MS Ahmet III, 143, 93^{r-v}.
[3] *Aḥkām al-Qur'ān* i, 58–60.
[4] Goitein, 'Birth-hour', 132–3.

view of Islamic origins which can hardly profit from modification of details. The context of the entire passage Q. 5: 42–51 is polemic and was so acknowledged by Muslim exegetes, whose view of the prophet's jurisdiction can only with difficulty be related to pagan practice in the process of replacement by divine decree. The historical circumstances envisaged by, and if not invented then certainly elaborated within, the exegetical literature were those surrounding Muhammad's celebrated confrontation *in foro externo* with the rabbis of Medina. The essential truth elicited from that story was, it may be recalled, that the role of the Muslim prophet lay not in abrogation or supersession of the Mosaic Law (!), but in its restoration and fulfilment.[1]

Now, in his monograph on the phenomena of abrogation, which apart from the *Risāla* of Shāfiʿī must be the earliest treatment of that subject,[2] Abū ʿUbayd found it convenient to link discussion of the penalty for fornication with that of Muslim jurisdiction among non-Muslims.[3] In the first section the author argued that both Q. 4: 15–16 and 65: 1 (on those justly charged with fornication) had been repealed by 24: 2 (which specified the punishment as 100 lashes) and the stoning penalty. In one of the two traditions adduced, both traced to Ibn ʿAbbās, stoning was reserved for those offenders who were *muḥṣan* (i.e. chaste, betrothed, possibly married, free, Muslim, etc.).[4] Though the stoning part of the penalty was there specified as Sunna, two versions of a tradition from ʿUbāda b. Ṣāmit immediately following leave no doubt that, Sunna or not, the stoning penalty had been revealed to the prophet: قال رسول الله خذوا عنى قد جعل الله لهنّ سبيلا البكر بالبكر والثيب بالثيب البكر يجلد وينفى والثيب يجلد ويرجم.[5] Thereafter, the author turned his attention to the problem of punishments (*ḥudūd*) to be inflicted upon *dhimmīs*, and the question of the abrogation of Q. 5: 42 by 5: 48. That the particular case envisaged was fornication is clear from the gloss of *bi-mā anzala 'llāh* in Q. 5: 48 as *al-rajm* (stoning), thus characterized again as 'revelation', though that point was followed by discussions of the *lex talionis* and the *muḥāribūn*.[6] In the second section the abrogation of Q. 5: 42 فإنْ جاؤوك فاحكم بينهم أو أعرض عنهم by 5: 48 فاحكم بينهم بما أنزل الله was also illustrated by the stoning penalty, this time specified as the prophet's stoning of the two Jews رجم النبى اليهودى

[1] See above, II pp. 70–1.

[2] See above, p. 175.

[3] *Kitāb al-nāsikh wal-mansūkh*, MS Ahmet III, 143: 'Bāb al-ḥudūd', 88ᵛ–97ʳ, and 'Al-Ḥukm bayna ahl al-dhimma', 172ʳ–4ʳ.

[4] Cf. Ibn Qutayba, *Ta'wīl*, 391.

[5] Abū ʿUbayd, op. cit. 89ᵛ and 90ʳ: variant prefaced by a naturalistic description of the prophet in a state of 'reception', widely employed in the *ḥadīth* literature, e.g. Bukhārī, *Ṣaḥīḥ*, 'Kitāb al-Shahādāt' 2, 15; and references Wensinck, *Handbook*, 162–3.

[6] Abū ʿUbayd, 90ᵛ–1ʳ; see above, pp. 192 and 186, respectively.

واليهودية.[1] In the opinion of the Iraqi jurists that incident had established the precedent for dealing with litigations among *dhimmī*s, while the Hijazis argued that it had taken place before imposition of poll-tax (*jizya*) and thus did not afford a precedent for the later period, when administrative procedure tended towards judicial autonomy within *dhimmī* communities. Abū ʿUbayd rejected the latter position on two grounds: first, that traditions did not in fact state that the stoning incident had taken place before the imposition of *jizya*; second, that even had that been so it would not preclude dealing with litigation among *dhimmī*s after imposition of the tax. Prior to that condition in fact, they would not have been *dhimmī*s but merely in treaty relationship (*hudna*/*muwādaʿa*) with Islam like other infidel nations (*umam al-shirk*). The question of jurisdiction would not even have arisen.[2] But once established, the contract between the Muslim community and the newly recognized *dhimmī*s enabled the latter to resort to Islamic jurisdiction. The implication was that Q. 5: 48 abrogated not only the circumstances described in 5: 42, but also those of 5: 50.[3] In the light of that argument it must, I think, be conceded that *ḥukm al-jāhiliyya* (Q. 5: 50) referred to, or at least included, Jewish practice prior to the prophet's intervention in that much-disputed litigation.

Though Abū ʿUbayd did not specify *āyat al-rajm* (stoning 'verse'), it is clear from his presentation of the traditions from ʿUbāda b. Ṣāmit that the stoning 'penalty' was of revealed status, that is Sunna but not Qur'ān. The movement exhibited in the transposition of stoning penalty into stoning verse[4] may be understood to reflect elevation of the Quranic text to canonical status: a source of legislative authority. The role of *āyat al-rajm* was henceforth (beginning of the third/ninth century) intimately connected not merely with the historical description of Judaeo-Muslim polemic, but also with the principle of legislative repeal in scripture. As a piece of historical evidence *āyat al-rajm* may be assessed by its haggadic projection, and especially within the narrative framework of the Muhammadan *evangelium*. As witness to a hermeneutical principle, it may be judged by its halakhic value in establishing, in the context of *disputatio fori*, that scripture was the ultimate source of all legislation.

The literary forms generated by Muhammad's confrontation with the rabbis of Medina were signalled by Goldziher in a study of Jewish practices as described in Muslim literature.[5] That those represent variations upon the archetypal theme informing the account of Jesus with the Pharisees was not mentioned by Goldziher. The conclusion of Vajda that there must be a nucleus of historical truth in the story cannot of course be ruled out,

[1] Abū ʿUbayd, 172ʳ–4ʳ, esp. 173ʳ.
[2] Abū ʿUbayd, 173ᵛ.
[3] Abū ʿUbayd, 174ʳ: *suḥt* is glossed 'bribe' (*rishwa*).
[4] Variants of the latter were assembled by Suyūṭī, *Itqān* iii, 72–3, 75–7; cf. *GdQ* i, 248–52.
[5] See above, II p. 71: reference n. 1.

but neither can it be demonstrated.[1] The entire literary complex belongs to a cycle of 'tests of true prophethood' widely distributed in Muslim exegetical literature, and hardly susceptible of positivist interpretation, such as Muhammad's being forced by circumstances to abandon a harsher penalty for adultery in favour of Rabbinic leniency, or as posterior justification of 'Umar's conduct in stoning for adultery.[2] In his impressive, if not entirely convincing, *mise en scène* of the adulteress pericope (John 7: 53–8: 11) Derrett stressed the qualification of witnesses, rather than the nature of the punishment or its scriptural sanction, The assumption must be that Jesus was approached not as a prophet (like Muhammad), but as a rabbi especially competent in the laws of evidence. Such was undoubtedly the significance of a link between the pericope and the story of Susanna and the elders, but not, I think, of its inclusion in the Muhammadan *evangelium*.[3] For the slightly modified Muslim version, the observation of Ibn al-Jawzī that the 'Torah passage' adduced by the rabbis contained the (Quranic) stipulation on the necessity of four (!) witnesses to the act of fornication (Q. 24: 4), might be thought sufficient indication of the polemical purpose for which the account of Muhammad's triumph had been devised, namely, the maliciously concealed coincidence of Muslim and Jewish scripture: אדׄא שהד ארבעהׄ אנהם ראוה ידכׄלה פיהא כמא ידכׄל אלמׄיל פי אלמכחלהׄ רגם.[4] Reference in the same report to Jewish abandonment of the scriptural (*ḥadd*) penalties after destruction of the Second Temple (*idh kān al-mulk lanā*) served as motive to Muhammad's restoration (*iḥyā'*) of the Mosaic Law, and may be exegetically related to *ḥukm al-jāhiliyya* in Q. 5: 50.

Halakhic elaboration of the story had as point of departure the interesting circumstance that neither stoning penalty nor stoning verse was included in the canon. That such gave less cause for alarm than might be supposed will be clear if it is understood that the principle of abrogation, as well as the development of *aḥkām* (halakhot), concerned the entire, very flexible, corpus of revelation, of which the Qur'ān was only part. Efforts to relate the phenomena of abrogation to the canonical text exhibit not a necessity but merely a tendency to seek scriptural support for positions already occupied and for the most part consolidated. Neither the principle of abrogation nor the formulation of *aḥkām* required support in scripture until scripture itself came into being as a result of external pressure in polemic. For *āyat al-rajm* Burton put the case well: 'The "process" here promised was later "appointed" in the revelation of the stoning penalty. The stoning penalty, and not the Qur'ān, was thus the historical source of

[1] Vajda, 'Juifs et Musulmans', 93–9.

[2] See Vajda, loc. cit.: Hirschfeld, *Researches*, 103, 137.

[3] *Law in the New Testament*, 156–88.

[4] Goldziher, 'Usages juifs', 326: for the description of consummation cf. Talm. Babl. Makkot 7a.

the "stoning verse".'[1] 'Later appointed' is a reference to a variant reading in Q. 2: 106 ما ننسخ من آية أو ننسها (ننسأها) نات بخير منها أو مثلها, which became the *locus classicus* for the doctrine of abrogation. The variant itself, 'we defer' as opposed to 'we cause to forget', drew upon that category of *asbāb al-nuzūl* which included the concepts of promise and ratification, by whose means the arbitrary data on Quranic chronology could be conveniently neutralized.[2] For Jaṣṣāṣ,[3] a variant reading was unnecessary: the verb *ansā* might signify either forgetting (*nisyān*)[4] or deferment (*ta'khīr*), both in the sense of exchange (*tabdīl*) for the public weal (*maṣlaḥa*: *ius propter utilitatem publicam*).[5] Examples were the exchange of *qibla* (Mecca for Jerusalem) and the repeal of Q. 8: 65 by 8: 66 (*takhfīf*), which together illustrated the principle that Qur'ān could abrogate Sunna and Qur'ān, the term *āya* in Q. 2: 106 being a reference not to the *ipsissima verba* of scripture (*tilāwa*) but to the precept contained or implied therein (*ḥukm*). That particular view of the range of abrogation was only one of five, set out by Naḥḥās:[6] Qur'ān could abrogate Qur'ān and Sunna (the argument of the Kufans); Qur'ān, but not Sunna, could abrogate Qur'ān (of Shāfi'ī, whose concern with Qur'ān was anyway peripheral);[7] Sunna could abrogate Qur'ān and Sunna (anonymous); Sunna, but not Qur'ān, could abrogate Sunna (also anonymous); these categories were not mutually exclusive and each case had to be judged on its merits (ascribed to Muḥammad b. Shujā'). In practice only the last could survive as a working principle, and few if any cases were ever decided by an actual appeal to the priority of one over another kind of revelation.

Of four major works devoted to the phenomena of abrogation, two were concerned primarily to demonstrate the presence of such in the text of scripture: those of Naḥḥās and of Hibatallāh. Each introduced his work with the story of 'Alī b. Abī Ṭālib and the preacher in Kufa who was banished from the mosque for not knowing his principles of abrogation.[8] That level of discourse was hardly modified throughout the treatise of Hibatallāh, who defined *naskh* as removal/cancellation (فى كلام العرب رفع

[1] Burton, 'Cranes', 261. [2] See above, pp. 175–7.

[3] *Aḥkām al-Qur'ān* i, 58–60.

[4] On the problems provoked by the interpretation *nisyān*, see Burton, 'Cranes', 260–3; to which might be added the observation that in the Quranic lexicon *ansā* is not infrequently connected with satanic agency (e.g. Q. 6: 68, 12: 42, 18: 63, 58: 19), and may have been employed as metaphorical counterpoint to the verb *alqā* (e.g. Q. 4: 171). The conjecture is in no way weakened by explicit reference to divine agency in Q. 2: 106 and 59: 19, and to satanic agency with *alqā* in 20: 87 and 22: 52–3, and could be related to the neutral concept 'inspiration' by mediation, characteristic of Muslim prophetology; see above, II pp. 58–61.

[5] See Goldziher, 'Istiṣḥāb', 229–30.

[6] Naḥḥās, *Kitāb al-nāsikh wal-mansūkh*, 6–7.

[7] Cf. Schacht, *Origins*, 15: tacit correction of Goldziher, *Studien* ii, 20.

[8] Naḥḥās, op. cit. 5–6; Hibatallāh, *Kitāb al-nāsikh wal-mansūkh*, 3–5.

(الشئ) and limited its incidence in the Qur'ān to explicit command and prohibition (*amr wa-nahy*) or to reports (*akhbār*) containing or implying such. Of these he found 239 instances in 71 *sūras*, a consequence of massive and undifferentiated assertion, rather than of subtle and reasoned analysis: 107 occurred in *Sūras* 2–9 and Q. 9: 5 (*āyat al-sayf*) figured as abrogant 124 times.[1] For Naḥḥās the problem was less simple. The term *naskh* might mean cessation (*izāla*) or transfer (*naql*), and the Quranic principle of abrogation was based upon the latter.[2] He also found expedient a distinction between *naskh* and *badā'*: the former might apply only to command and prohibition, the latter to instances of contradiction or inconsistency (apparent!) in reports, to which one could attach a limitation in terms of altered time or place, e.g. the changing circumstances of narrative, as in the stories of the prophets.[3] Of abrogation according to his own definition Naḥḥās found 137 instances in 48 *sūras*, of which 75 appeared in *Sūras* 2–9.

Common to Hibatallāh and Naḥḥās was a typology of the modes of abrogation attested in scripture.[4] These were three (the authors employed different terminology, and Naḥḥās, perhaps for the sake of lexical tidiness, included a fourth which identified *naskh* in the sense of 'copy'); abrogation of both wording and ruling (نسخ خطه وحكمه/نسخ الحكم والتلاوة); abrogation of wording but not of ruling (نسخ خطه وبقى حكمه/نسخ التلاوة دون الحكم); abrogation of ruling but not of wording (نسخ الحكم دون التلاوة/نسخ حكمه وبقى خطه). That these formal distinctions contained, and were also very likely meant to conceal, essentially irreconcilable views on the constituent parts of Muslim law was indicated by Burton.[5] For my purpose here it is sufficient to state that the modes of abrogation set out by Naḥḥās and Hibatallāh reflect a concerted effort to identify *naskh* as an originally Quranic phenomenon. Once seen to enjoy scriptural sanction, the principle of abrogation could in theory and with impunity be applied across the entire range of source materials for the formulation of Muslim law.

A favourite example of *naskh* in the Quranic text was the alleged repeal of Q. 8: 65 by 8: 66, where the number of enemy which Muslims were expected successfully to oppose in combat was reduced (*takhfīf*: lightened) from a ratio of 10: 1 to 2: 1, e.g. in Ṭabarī: فخفّف الله عنهم فنسخها بالآية الأخرى.[6] Belonging to the third mode (above), that instance of abrogation was typical of nearly all those adduced by Naḥḥās and Hibatallāh, pride of

[1] See above, pp. 183–5.
[2] Naḥḥās, 8.
[3] Naḥḥās, 10–11; see Goldziher, *EI*, s.v. Badā'.
[4] Hibatallāh, 5–6; Naḥḥās, 8–9.
[5] 'Cranes', 258–64, and discussed in detail in the study referred to there, 249 n. 4.
[6] *Tafsīr* x, 27 ad loc.

place going of course to *āyat al-sayf*. To illustrate the first mode (above), the much-discussed 'satanic verses' alleged originally to have been at Q. 53: 19–22 and abrogated by 22: 52 were invariably adduced, and the several motives which led to that assertion were analysed at length in Burton's study.[1] It was to demonstrate the second mode (above) of abrogation that *āyat al-rajm* was commonly introduced into halakhic controversy, namely, as an example of a valid ruling whose wording had been removed from the text of scripture. Now, that the origin of the stoning verse lay in the account of the stoning penalty has been proposed. That the origin of the stoning penalty may be sought in the haggadic *topoi* traditionally employed to illustrate the test(s) of 'true prophethood' seems more than likely. Juridical appropriation of that particular *topos*, however transparent the motive, was the inevitable consequence of pressure compelling recognition of the Qur'ān as a source of legislation equal to the Sunna. The adjustment exhibited in the transposition: stoning penalty→stoning verse was only necessary after establishment of the canonical text of revelation. Acceptance of the transposition, or even of the second mode of abrogation, was not universal: Naḥḥās, for example, recognized the *isnād* of *āyat al-rajm* as sound but insisted upon regarding it as Sunna, and thus not as evidence of Quranic abrogation.[2]

Two other works dealing with *naskh* were less concerned with the specifically Quranic data and rather more with the principle of abrogation as a valid juridical premiss. From what has been said of Abū 'Ubayd's treatise on *nāsikh wa-mansūkh* it ought to be clear that status as Qur'ān or Sunna was hardly operative in his formulation of the rules. Arrangement of the material is topical, rather than by Quranic division, and most, if not quite all, chapters bear the subtitle 'that which abrogates and is abrogated in both Qur'ān (*kitāb*) and Sunna'. The twenty-seven chapters contain the conventional range of *aḥkām*, e.g. Prayer (fols. 8ᵛ–13ᵛ), Almsgiving (fols. 14ʳ–19ᵛ), Fasting (fols. 20ʳ–46ʳ), Marriage (fols. 46ʳ–74ʳ), Divorce (fols. 74ʳ–88ʳ), etc.[3] Whether Abū 'Ubayd (d. 223/838) was the first scholar to treat monographically (!) the subject of abrogation can probably best be answered with reference to the chronological development of Quranic studies, rather than to reports of earlier written works. One such is the ascription to Zuhrī (d. 124/742) of a book entitled *Nāsikh wa-mansūkh fil-Qur'ān*.[4] Like the quite worthless *Tanzīl al-Qur'ān* attributed to the same author,[5] the work on abrogation is preserved in the recension of the Ṣūfī

[1] Burton, 'Cranes': to the 'historical' (Orientalist) references mentioned there, 246–9, may be added Andrae, *Person*, 129–32.

[2] *Kitāb al-nāsikh wal-mansūkh*, 9; cf. the dissenting opinions recorded in Suyūṭī, *Itqān* iii, 72–7; and the anonymous *ikhtilāf* in Ash'arī, *Maqālāt*, 607–11.

[3] *Kitāb al-nāsikh wal-mansūkh*, MS Ahmet III 143; cf. the arrangement in Muqātil's halakhic treatise, MS BM Or. 6333, above pp. 173–4.

[4] *GAS* i, 283 no. 4; MS Beyazit 445.

[5] See above, pp. 179–80.

exegete Sulamī (d. 412/1021) and will, even if it exists, hardly contribute to the history of *naskh* theories prior to Abū ʿUbayd. However that may be, the manuscript Beyazit 445 is not the work of Zuhrī–Sulamī, but of ʿAbdalqāhir Baghdādī (d. 429/1038).[1] The significance of Baghdādī's position in the study of *naskh* is that long after Naḥḥās (d. 338/950) and some time after Hibatallāh (d. 410/1019) a work methodologically similar to that of Abū ʿUbayd should be written at all. The author's primary concern was with the theoretical elaboration of *naskh*, its justification as a juridical principle, and its attestation in Sunna as well as in Qur'ān. In the three chapters containing instances of Quranic abrogation the matter was introduced in the form of dispute (*ikhtilāf*) and consensus (*ijmāʿ*), and the total number of verses adduced only 59.[2] In an introductory chapter the notion of *naskh* as removal/cancellation (*rafʿ*) or cessation (*izāla*) was rejected in favour of a combination of specification (*takhṣīṣ*) and transfer (*taḥwīl*).[3] The author's conclusion may be cited:[4] ومنهم من قال كان النبى مأمورا قبل نبوته بشريعة ابراهيم ولزمه التمسك بها فى كل شئ الا فيما نسخ منها بشريعته بعد الوحى اليه وهذا هو الصحيح عندنا. That *naskh* might indeed refer to the abrogation by Muhammad's revelation of an earlier divinely revealed statute (here the 'law of Abraham') was a possibility never quite suppressed.[5]

Abrogation as supersession of earlier dispensations was of course fundamental to the character of Judaeo-Christian polemic. That the Jews allegedly rejected the specifically Islamic principle of *naskh* as in their opinion nothing more than retraction/substitution owing to the emergence of new circumstances (*badā'*) was one among a number of problems raised by Suyūṭī, himself satisfied that God was capable of reversing (*ʿaks*) any of His actions or decisions, and that such had indeed been many times attested in the history of divine revelation.[6] The allegation is puzzling, since the retraction, reversal, and change of God's word was familiar enough from Hebrew scripture, e.g. 2 Kings 9: 1–12 and Hosea 1: 4–5, as well as the crucial 'new covenant' of Jeremiah 31: 31.[7] Moreover, the integrity of the Mosaic Law, explicitly stated in Deuteronomy 13: 1 (and cf. Qohelet 3: 14), was never intended to preclude progressive modification according to altered circumstances in the community. The necessity of and capacity for modification is amply attested in the terminology of

[1] *GAL* i, 385; *GdQ* i, 54 n. 1, ii, 16 n. 5: MS Petermann I, 555.

[2] Baghdādī, MS Beyazit 445, 7^r–46^r, 46^r–71^r, 71^v–4^v.

[3] Baghdādī, 2^r–3^r.

[4] Baghdādī, 76^r.

[5] See above, pp. 192–3; and Hasan, 'Theory of naskh', esp. 182–3, where *naskh* as abrogation was denied, but acknowledged as the supersession of earlier revelation(s).

[6] *Itqān* iii, 6; see above, p. 197.

[7] Cf. Eissfeldt, *Einleitung*, 694; and above, I pp. 11–12.

Rabbinic exegesis, e.g. in the formula[1] מנהג מבטל הלכה, the antithesis[2] קיים vs ביטל or סמי, and the notion of normative, as contrasted with prescriptive, legislation contained in the terms[3] מנהג and דרך ארץ. The extent to which those formulations may be interpreted as evidence of abrogation depends of course upon the precise meaning of that term. It must by now be clear that if there was ever agreement among Muslim scholars on the semantic content of *naskh*, such would indicate general acceptance of 'change' or 'transfer', reflected in the terms *naql* and *taḥwīl*. The genuinely halakhic employment of *naskh* meant the unceasing interpretation of scripture by reference to the example of the prophet, and for the halakhists both sources were equally part of revelation. Discussions of specifically Quranic abrogation, on the other hand, represented a polemical defence of the text of scripture, and were only marginally related to the formulation of law.

And yet it was precisely that latter aspect of the Muslim doctrine of abrogation which informed Judaeo-Muslim controversy about its exegetical relevance. For example, Saadya's rejection of *naskh* consisted entirely of arguments designed to prove that there were no contradictions in the Biblical text, but only occasional passages which could be seen to require hermeneutical complement or specification, e.g. whether sacrifice or circumcision could be performed on the Sabbath.[4] Similarly, the five points adduced and rejected as evidence of *naskh* by Saʿd b. Manṣūr (Ibn Kammūna) reflect an attitude towards the text of scripture nearly unrelated to the eventual necessity of halakhic modification of its contents.[5] In his rebuttal, on the other hand, the author invoked the traditional arsenal of Rabbinic terminology to prove that such modification was possible, e.g. בת קול: بث قول.[6] Those arguments for *naskh* in Hebrew scripture adduced and so easily dismissed by Jewish apologists can hardly be said to exhibit either the subtlety or the range of Muslim discussions of abrogation. A degree of misrepresentation or, at least, of incomplete representation of opposing views is not unexpected in polemic, but that the methodological proximity, even identity, of Rabbinic and Sunnī Muslim halakhah should be ignored, or suppressed, in the polemical literature might be thought to require an explanation. Among Jewish scholars were some who did in fact acknowledge the presence of *naskh* in

[1] Bacher, *Terminologie* ii, 53–6; cf. Zunz, *Vorträge*, 54 n. (e); and Elbogen, *Gottesdienst*, 356.

[2] Bacher, *Terminologie* i, 170–2, ii, 142, 186–9, 239; Gerhardsson, *Memory*, 97 n. 7, 233 n. 2, 264, 287.

[3] Bacher, op. cit. i, 25, ii, 40–1; Gerhardsson, op. cit., 117, 182, 256, 305, 317–20.

[4] Saadya, *Kitāb al-Amānāt*, 128–45, esp. 140–5; cf. Schreiner, 'Zur Geschichte', 604–6.

[5] Ibn Kammūna, *Tanqīḥ al-abḥāth*, 45-7; cf. Steinschneider, *Polemische Literatur*, 324.

[6] *Tanqīḥ al-abḥāth*, 47.

Hebrew scripture, for example, Abraham b. David,[1] who regarded as permissible abrogation in the sense of recognizing the temporal and/or spatial limits of certain divine prescriptions, in other words *badā'* or *takhṣīṣ*. But the preoccupation of Jewish apologists was naturally, in the light of Muslim claims that predictions of the advent of Islam had been removed from Hebrew scripture, with the unassailable character of their book, and one cannot help but suspect that it was abrogation in the sense of supersession which, designated *naskh* in the polemical literature, was being unconditionally rejected.

That was not the meaning of *naskh* in Muslim halakhic exegesis, but the overtones of abrogation as reference to the supersession of earlier revelations had never been quite eliminated, e.g. in Baghdādī, and could even be derived from the principal Quranic *loci probantes* traditionally adduced in support of the doctrine: Q. 2: 106 but also 22: 52, 16: 101, 17: 76, and and 13: 39. As a contribution to the history of terminological complexity, the *lapsus calami* in the Hebrew translation of Maimonides' *Pereq Ḥeleq*, which resulted in rendering נסך not as בטול (*naskh*) but as עתק (*naql*), is not without interest: it was the abrogation of the Mosaic Law by subsequent revelation(s) which the author was concerned to deny.[2] One can hardly insist that the course of polemic on the subject of abrogation was influenced exclusively by exploitation, or ignorance, of the ambiguity inherent in the Arabic term *naskh*. It does, however, seem clear that the real dispute was not about differences of exegetical procedure, of which there were virtually none, but about the respective claims of Torah and Qur'ān to be the word of God.[3]

In the formulation of *aḥkām*, which could only retrospectively be understood as the derivation of law from revelation, the fact of a canonical text of scripture was, if not quite a hindrance, then of very little help and probably regarded as something of a challenge. No element in either the style or the structure of halakhic exegesis points unmistakably to the necessity, or even to the existence, of the canon as ultimately preserved and transmitted. It may of course be argued that the rudiments at least of a comparative method can be inferred from the chronological arrangement of scriptural passages, from the juxtaposition of *muḥkam* and *mutashābih*, and from the opposition of *nāsikh* and *mansūkh*. But the comparison was of parts to parts, not of parts to a whole.[4] As hermeneutical instruments chronology,

[1] Cf. Steinschneider, op. cit., 353 no. 5; Schreiner, op. cit., 635–8.

[2] See Hyman, 'Maimonides' "Thirteen Principles" ', 128 n. 58.

[3] And thus more approximately related to the Muslim charges of forgery (*taḥrīf*), see above, pp. 189–90; on procedural similarity it may be noted that one of Ibn Kammūna's arguments, *Tanqīḥ*, 46, against *naskh* (*sic*) was that scripture commanded obedience to the prescriptions articulated by successive prophets; see above, pp. 174–5.

[4] A halakhic *midrash* is unattested before Qurṭubī (d. 671/1272), cf. *GAL* i, 415–16, Suppl. I, 737.

analogy, and abrogation were, in respect of the existence of the canon, neutral. Similarly, the employment of traditions (*aḥādīth*) to link Sunna and Qur'ān emphasized the role of revelation but not exclusively of scripture. The dichotomy of 'Qur'ān as document' and 'Qur'ān as source' proposed by Burton, while not without a certain methodological utility, is misleading if meant to postulate the historical existence of the canonical text before it became a source of law.[1]

Logically, it seems to me quite impossible that canonization should have preceded, not succeeded, recognition of the authority of scripture within the Muslim community. Chronologically, the data of Arabic literature cannot be said to attest to the existence of the canon before the beginning of the third/ninth century. These tentative and admittedly conjectural conclusions might be thought to derive some support from the form of scripture in halakhic argumentation: the practice of adducing selected and discrete passages provides negative evidence of a kind comparable to the absence of explicit reference to the Qur'ān in other related contexts.[2] Moreover, the marginal character of lexical, grammatical, and syntactical analysis in the work of the halakhists indicates little concern for a *ne varietur* or even relatively stable text of scripture.[3] My own hypothesis, that establishment of such a text presupposed rather than prefigured acceptance of the Qur'ān as a source of law, gains some strength from the sudden efflorescence of masoretic exegesis soon after the literary formulation of the *aḥkām*.

4. MASORETIC EXEGESIS

The Quranic masorah consists basically of three elements: lexical explanation, grammatical analysis, and an agreed apparatus of variant readings. Its elaboration required two exegetical instruments: textual analogy and periphrasis, as well as the introduction of evidence from a large and conveniently flexible corpus of Arabic poetry. A single 'non-textual' component of the masorah, and curiously, the only one adduced in the 'royal' Egyptian edition of the Qur'ān, is designation of the place of revelation (*mawāṭin al-nuzūl*), the purpose and derivation of which were not masoretic but halakhic.[4] But even that material is of some comparative, methodological value for a study of the masorah proper, especially of the *variae lectiones*. Ascription and transmission, both of information on the circumstances of revelation and of reports on variant readings, were formulated exclusively as traditions from the companions of the prophet, and are thus subject to the analytical criteria appropriate to, say, legal and 'historical' traditions. It might be argued that a possible exception to this rule is

[1] 'Cranes', 251–2, 259.

[2] See above, I pp. 44–5, II pp. 82–3.

[3] See above, III pp. 100–1.

[4] See above, pp. 177–81.

represented by the existence of 'regional' codices, but those appear to be not only later than the 'companion' codices, but like them also largely fictive.[1] Of genuinely textual variants exhibiting material deviation from the canonical text of revelation, such as are available for Hebrew and Christian scripture, there are none. The Quranic masorah is in fact entirely exegetical,[2] even where its contents have been transmitted in the guise of textual variants.

An example will illustrate this not uninteresting phenomenon: in what appears to be the earliest collection of variants (*maṣāḥif*) from the consonantal text of the 'Uthmanic recension (*imām*), a chapter entitled باب الزوائد من الحروف التى خولف بها الخط [فى القرآن] in the *Faḍā'il al-Qur'ān* of Abū 'Ubayd (d. 224/838), Q. 18: 79 was rendered وكان وراءهم ملك يأخذ كل سفينة صالحة غصبا and the intrusive (non-canonical) '*ṣāliḥa*' attributed to the codex of Ubayy b. Ka'b.[3] Using the same source, Bergsträsser–Pretzl described *ṣāliḥa* (sound, in good repair) as an aetiological addition (*motivierender Zusatz*), an obvious assessment from the point of view at least of the canon's textual integrity.[4] But attribution to Ubayy was arbitrary: the reading with *ṣāliḥa* appeared not only there but also in the codices of 'Abdallāh b. Mas'ūd and Ibn 'Abbās.[5] The transparency of that device, by means of which an exegetical gloss could be construed as evidence of a textual variant, emerges from examination of Muqātil's treatment of Q. 18: 79 يأخذ كل سفينة صالحة صحيحة سوية غصبا كقوله سبحانه فلما آتاهما صالحا (7: 190) يعنى سويا يعنى غصبا من أهلها.[6] Were it not for the characteristically fluid boundaries between text and commentary,[7] the epithet *ṣāliḥa* could justifiably be regarded as scriptural and glossed by the analogous usage in Q. 7: 190. On the other hand, the further epithets *ṣaḥīḥa* and *sawiyya* (both signifying 'sound, in good repair') could be interpreted as supercommentary, with which haggadic exegesis was liberally strewn.[8] But whatever the textual state of Muqātil's scripture, the process by which 'variants' to the 'Uthmanic canon were produced and allocated to one or more of the 'companion' codices is worthy of notice. The examples collected by Goldziher can hardly be interpreted as other than exegesis to the canonical text.[9] Goldziher's understanding of those phenomena as evidence of the generosity with which the text of

[1] See above, I pp. 44–6.
[2] *Pace GdQ* iii, 108.
[3] Spitaler, 'Ein Kapitel', 7 no. 39, 9 no. 59.
[4] *GdQ* iii, 69.
[5] Jeffery, *Materials*, 143, 57, 200, respectively; Zamakhsharī mentioned both Ubayy and Ibn Mas'ūd, *Kashshāf* ii, 741 ad loc.
[6] Muqātil, *Tafsīr*, MS H. Hüsnü 17, 172r.
[7] See above, pp. 127–9.
[8] See above, loc. cit.; in Ubayy '*ṣāliḥa*' may be scriptural, Jeffery, *Materials*, 143.
[9] *Richtungen*, 4–32: consonantal, vocalic, additions, synonyms, emendations, 'scribal errors'; cf. Seeligmann, 'Midraschexegese', 159–60.

scripture was treated need not be discounted, but the chronological evolution of the *maṣāḥif* literature strongly suggests that the 'companion' codices were manufactured from exegetical material in support of an argument central to the traditional account of canonization, namely, the 'Uthmanic recension. Much of that material persisted anyway in the form of standard deviations from the canon, accommodated by the *aḥruf* doctrine,[1] evidence in my opinion of a tendency to preserve rather than to neutralize.

With the (later) delimitation of scriptural text and commentary, exegetical glosses of the sort represented by '*ṣāliḥa*' achieved a very special status tantamount to revelation, as may be inferred from Suyūṭī's observations on the 'readings' *ṣalāt al-'aṣr/wa-ṣalāt al-'aṣr ad* Q. 2: 238.[2] Citing Abū 'Ubayd's *Faḍā'il al-Qur'ān*, he ascribed the reading without the conjunctive *waw* to both Ḥafṣa and 'Ā'isha,[3] and argued that the function of the isolated variant (*qirā'a shādhdha*),[4] although basically exegetical, was of an order higher than that of mere exegesis: المقصد من القراءة الشاذة تفسير القراءة المشهورة وتبيين معانيها . . . فهو أكثر من التفسير وأقوى فأدنى ما يستنبط من هذه الحروف معرفة صحة التأويل. That the origin of the reading(s) was not textual but doctrinal, despite the apparatus of transmission, might be inferred from the juridical as well as liturgical significance of the '*aṣr* prayer.[5]

Now, elevation of the exegetical gloss to the status of 'companion' reading did not preclude the stigma which might attach to designation of such as interpolation (*mudraj*). Critical evaluation of textual variants (*maṣāḥif*) and/or readings (*qirā'āt*)[6] depended primarily, if not exclusively, upon attestation (*isnād*), as may be seen in the relevant nomenclature, e.g. *mutawātir*, *mashhūr*, *āḥād*, *shādhdh*, etc.[7] Supplementary, but secondary, criteria were grammatical feasibility (*wajh fil-'arabiyya*) and agreement with the consonantal skeleton (*muwāfaqa 'alā rasm/khaṭṭ*), the latter appropriate in practice only to modification of pointing and of vowels. In practice, too, the hierarchy of attestation and of transmission (*naql*) might include the other criteria, so that the designations *mutawātir* (generally attested) and *thiqa* (soundly attested) could be in all three respects valid for the seven major 'readings'.[8] Dānī's description of the science of *qirā'a*

1 Goldziher, op. cit., 35–51; *GdQ* iii, 106–8; and see above, I p. 45.

2 *Itqān* i, 227–8.

3 Apparently correctly, but see *GdQ* iii, 150 n. 1; cf. Spitaler, 'Ein Kapitel', 4–5 nos. 12–20, esp. no. 14, though nos. 12–13 do identify Ḥafṣa with the reading *wa-ṣalāt al-'aṣr*; for the sake of tidiness it may be added that the same reading was ascribed to yet another wife of the prophet, Umm Salama, see Jeffery, *Materials*, 235.

4 Cf. *GdQ* iii, 136–7, 155, 228–30.

5 See Goldziher, *Richtungen*, 14–15; and id. 'Nachmittagszeit', 294–302.

6 Often undifferentiated, see *GdQ* iii, 60 n. 2, but cf. Jeffery, *Materials*, 13–14.

7 See Suyūṭī, *Itqān* i, 210–29; *GdQ* iii, 149–57.

8 e.g. Suyūṭī, *Itqān* i, 225.

as one necessarily guaranteed by authority (*sunna muttabaʿa*) may be seen as theoretical acknowledgement of the primary criterion.[1] Into the conventional lists illustrating the relative ranks of 'readings',[2] examples of acknowledged interpolation might be fitted by restricting numerically the extent of attestation: Suyūṭī's *loci probantes* included '*min umm*' *ad* Q. 4: 12 and '*fī mawāsim al-ḥajj*' *ad* Q. 2: 198, and might be thought not very different from those examples allegedly derived from 'companion' codices and discussed above. That a considerable amount of exegetical gloss was not in this way relegated to the masorah, but rather left undisturbed in the text of scripture, has been proposed.[3]

The closed system of 'readings' symbolized by acknowledgement of the Seven/Ten/Fourteen authorized versions represented a generously defined consonantal text whose stabilization was chronologically fixed by recourse to the familiar device of ascription. Illustration of the product of that method is found in the collection of readings ascribed to Ḥasan Baṣrī (d. 110/728).[4] The textual standardization exhibited there, e.g. the reduction of variants to vocalic and diacritic mutation, interspersed with allegedly 'dialectal' forms, did not suppress altogether the exegetical moment, as can be seen in *yuʿbad/tuʿbad* for *naʿbud ad* Q. 1: 4,[5] and *kadib* for *kadhib ad* Q. 12: 18.[6] The role of Ḥasan as eponym in the elaboration of a Basran tradition for the science of Qur'ān reading was very significant indeed, despite his presumed insignificance (*sic*) in that very tradition:[7] it was of course as a source of *tafsīr* that he was selected to be the figurehead of a regional tradition, a tendency reflected also in ascription to him of the polemically exegetical *Risāla fil-qadar*.[8] The polarization round celebrated figures of originally anonymous dicta, whether in *ḥadīth*, *tafsīr*, or *qirā'āt*, reflects an exclusively methodological and tendentiously formulated argument of the Islamic sciences, from which objective historical data can hardly be elicited.

The same methodological tendency may be detected in the three criteria (*shurūṭ*) employed to assess the validity of a scriptural reading: acceptance for cultic purposes required authoritative and collective attestation (*tawātur/naql al-thiqāt*), which logically presupposed both agreement with the consonantal skeleton of the ʿUthmanic recension and grammatical

[1] *Apud* Suyūṭī, *Itqān* i, 211; see above, p. 169.
[2] e.g. of Ibn Jazarī, *apud* Suyūṭī, *Itqān* i, 215–16.
[3] See above, I pp. 27–9.
[4] Bergsträsser, 'Koranlesung', esp. 20–46; *GdQ* iii, 104 n. 1, 110.
[5] 'Koranlesung', 20; cf. above, III p. 108 where the 'reading' was adduced in a quite different context.
[6] 'Koranlesung', 36; anonymously adduced by Kalbī, *Tafsīr*, MS Ayasofya 118, 129r ad loc.
[7] *GdQ* iii, 165, 177.
[8] See above, pp. 160–3; the chronological conclusions of *GdQ* iii, 104 n. 1, are derived from a historical framework nowhere attested in the collection itself of Ḥasan's 'readings'.

feasibility; acceptance for exegetical purposes might waive agreement with the consonantal skeleton but such precluded cultic employment: فيُقبَل ولا يُقرأ به.[1] The distinction was later defined as that obtaining between *mashhūr* and *shādhdh*, terms related, not surprisingly, to degrees of attestation rather than to functional values. Dispute (*ikhtilāf*) engendered by contradictory readings or which employed alleged variants as proof-texts, e.g. *yaṭhurna* v. *yaṭahharna ad* Q. 2: 222, or *lāmastum* v. *lamastum ad* Q. 4: 43, could always be resolved by the customary reference to attestation, though multiple readings were seen by some to reflect the superiority of the Qur'ān over other scriptures, whose revelation (and hence, by a curious logic, their interpretation) was limited to a single 'aspect' (*wajh*): إظهار فضلها وشرفها على سائر الأمم إذ لم ينزل كتاب غيرهم الا على وجه واحد.[2] Option in that kind of dispute was more often expressed by the term *ikhtiyār* than by *tarjīḥ*, quite possibly owing to the suggestion of a *tertium comparationis* in the latter, which was essentially halakhic.[3] The extent to which the terms were interchangeable must be qualified in the same way as employment of the term *qiyās* by halakhists and masoretes respectively.[4] Acknowledgement of a multiple reading meant in theory recognition of a multiple revelation (i.e. *qirā'a* was elevated to the status of *āya*),[5] an example of which was *'ajibta* v. *'ajibtu ad* Q. 37: 12.[6] But an exegete like Zamakhsharī, preoccupied with textual tidiness, found it expedient to rationalize: the first-person pronoun must indicate indignation rather than surprise, or be interpreted as hypothetical, or be annulled by insertion of '*qul Muḥammad*'.[7]

The intrusive character of *variae lectiones* in the exegesis of Muqātil, Kalbī, and Sufyān has been noticed.[8] That the Quranic masorah had not yet been elaborated could be inferred not only from the paucity in haggadic exegesis of textual discussion but also from the elliptical form of such when found, suggestive of later redactional activity presupposing masoretic formulations. For example, Muqātil's proposal *ad* Q. 18: 44 that one may read *wilāya* (*mulk*: dominion) or *walāya* (*nuṣra*: support) is found fully documented in Farrā'.[9] Similarly, Muqātil's interpretation *ad*

[1] Suyūṭī, *Itqān* i, 213–14, 225; cf. Ibn Qutayba, *Ta'wīl*, 32; *GdQ* iii, 129.

[2] Suyūṭī, *Itqān* i, 226–7, cf. also iv, 193–4; that argument may be compared with the antithesis *munajjam*:*jumla wāḥida*, above, I pp. 36–8.

[3] See above, pp. 187–8; *GdQ* iii, 107, 129–37.

[4] See above, pp. 167–9; cf. Suyūṭī, *Itqān* i, 229 for *tarjīḥ*.

[5] Suyūṭī, *Itqān* i, 227.

[6] See Goldziher, *Richtungen*, 21–2: reference Ṭabarī, *Tafsīr* xxiii, 26 ad loc.

[7] *Kashshāf* iv, 37–8 ad loc.; the third explanation is an application of *taqdīr*, see below, pp. 219–21.

[8] See above, pp. 127, 132–3, 138.

[9] Muqātil, *Tafsīr*, 170r; Farrā', *Ma'ānī 'l-Qur'ān* ii, 145–6.

Q. 18: 80 of *khashinā* (we feared) as *ʿalimnā* (we knew) might be thought to require the documentation of Farrā', in which reference was made to the codex of Ubayy.[1] As has been noted, ascription of variants to 'companion' codices was characteristic of masoretic exegesis, in which specific authority was sought for traditions up to that point anonymously preserved and transmitted. That the equivalence *khashinā*:*ʿalimnā* for Q. 18: 80 cannot in fact be derived from the codex of Ubayy is hardly surprising;[2] some impression of the cavalier treatment of 'companion' codices can be gained from comparison of the diametrically opposed views of Ibn Ḥazm and Ibn Ḥajar on the exact contents of the codex of ʿAbdallāh b. Masʿūd (i.e. the presence/absence of the *muʿawwidhatān*).[3]

For a textual history of Muslim scripture, as opposed to doctrinal statements on the formation of the Quranic canon, the parallel passages which I have described as 'variant traditions' may be thought relevant.[4] Unlike the exclusively exegetical variant readings, glosses, interpolations, and synonym-equivalences, the variant traditions exhibit at least the components of a process by which scripture was produced from revelation. They represent the only material variants within or outside the canonical text, and were to some extent so acknowledged in the works of Horovitz (*Koranische Untersuchungen*) and Speyer (*Die biblischen Erzählungen im Qoran*). As might be expected, masoretic employment of this material was seldom explicit, but one example is Bayḍāwī's reference for the Zechariah traditions *ad* Q. 19: 10 (three nights) to the complementary locution 'three days' in Q. 3: 41: وإنما ذكر الليالى هنا والأيام فى آل عمران للدلالة على انه استمر عليه المنع من كلام الناس والتجرد للذكر والشكر ثلاثة أيام ولياليهن.[5] It could, on the other hand, be argued that the masoretes' use of both textual analogy and periphrasis involved at least implicit recognition of variant traditions, perhaps in the form of similar contexts rather than as multiple versions of a single narrative. Now, for the transmission history of Hebrew scripture the role of the Masoretes is often seen to have been mechanical rather than creative.[6] That they were working within the (perhaps not so confining) limits of a liturgical tradition cannot, and need not, be refuted. An essentially consonantal text is, however, susceptible of a variety of interpretations, semantic as well as grammatical. Establishment of a vocalized text would otherwise hardly have been necessary. Even in the selection of one of two or more purely orthographic alternatives a degree of understanding, and hence of interpretation, was essential.

1 *Tafsir*, 172r; *Maʿānī 'l-Qur'ān* ii, 157.
2 Cf. Jeffery, *Materials*, 144; *GdQ* iii, 88.
3 Suyūṭī, *Itqān* i, 221; *GdQ* ii, 41–2, iii, 179.
4 See above, I pp. 20–7.
5 Bayḍāwī, *Anwār al-tanzīl* iv, 4.
6 Cf. above, III pp. 100–1; Barr, *Comparative Philology*, 188–222.

More complex is the character of *lingua sacra* itself, for which apparently simple procedures like punctuation and segmentation could, and often did, involve a doctrinal commitment. For the textual history of Muslim scripture the activity of the masoretes was not only creative but productive: of postulates which became the foundations of both grammar and lexicography.[1] My use of the phrase 'masoretic exegesis' is intended to convey precisely those creative and productive aspects of the process by means of which revelation became scripture. The creation of a scriptural apparatus (masorah) coincided with, or was slightly posterior to, the establishment of a scriptural basis for Muslim jurisprudence, and represents acknowledgement of the authoritative status of revelation as one source of doctrine. The employment of scriptural *shawāhid* in halakhic controversy required a fixed and unambiguous text of revelation, or at least one in which ambiguity was conventionally limited. The result was the Quranic canon.

The major premiss of masoretic analogy was insistence upon the conceptual unity of the Quranic revelation.[2] Formulated as the binary opposition *muḥkam*:*mutashābih*, that premiss justified comparison of the parts to one another and eventually of the whole to its constituent parts. In its initial stages the procedure tended to be self-contained: the kind of analogy employed was thus deductive. Its basic operations were two: semantic collation (lexical) and periphrastic restoration (grammatical). The first of these found rudimentary but eminently practical expression in a work ascribed to Muqātil b. Sulaymān and entitled *Kitāb al-wujūh wal-naẓā'ir*,[3] alternatively *K. tafsīr wujūh al-Qur'ān* and *Al-Ashbāh wal-naẓīr* (*sic*) *fī tafsīr al-Qur'ān*,[4] *Al-Ashbāh wal-naẓā'ir*,[5] *Wujūh ḥarf al-Qur'ān*,[6] the last-named adduced as the title of Muqātil's work from which the extant recension was made. An undated papyrus fragment of a version of this work was published and described by Abbott as earlier than the recension preserved in Beyazit 561, itself (like Topkapı Emanet 2050) the work of one Abū Naṣr, apparently a student of Muqātil but not the transmitter of his other two exegetical treatises.[7] Neither her reasons for that conclusion, nor her reference to Muqātil's 'linguistic' *tafsīr*, inspire confidence.[8] It would be difficult indeed to characterize Muqātil's exegetical interests as 'linguistic',[9] and while there may be some connection

[1] For the Biblical Masorah Gertner emphasized, in my opinion rightly, the complementary relation between punctuation/vocalization/accentuation on the one hand, and interpretation on the other: see 'The Masorah and the Levites', esp. 244–52. His stress upon the creative work of the Levites may, however, be thought somewhat to restrict appreciation of the same quality in the activities of the post-Talmudic Masoretes.

[2] See above, pp. 166–70, but also 149–53, 155–6.

[3] *GAS* i, 37 no. 3; MS Beyazit 561, Emanet 2050.

[4] MS Beyazit 561, 1r.

[5] MS Beyazit 561, 138r.

[6] MS Emanet 2050, 1r.

[7] Abbott, *SALP* ii, 92–7; see above, pp. 144, 172: Hudhayl b. Ḥabīb.

[8] Abbott, *SALP* ii, 96, 95, 106.

[9] See above, pp. 143–4.

between his teaching and this particular work, I am inclined to regard it as an essentially independent composition and as having been composed not earlier than the beginning of the third/ninth century. Appearance (twice!) of the term *ashbāh* in Beyazit 561, but not in Topkapı Emanet 2050, poses something of a problem, and may represent an attempt to classify this treatise with the more or less contemporary *mutashābih*/*mushtabih* lexical collections.[1]

The *Kitāb al-wujūh wal-naẓā'ir* (Beyazit 561) contains 186 lemmata in no recognizable order: conceptual schemata rather than separate lexical entries. A typical example is the material assembled *sub voce waḥy*:[2]

تفسير الوحى على خمس وجوه (1) منها الوحى الذى كان ينزل به جبريل من الله على الأنبياء فذلك قوله إنّا أوحينا اليك يعنى القرآن كما أوحينا الى نوح والنبيين من بعده ثم ذكر الأنبياء فقال وأوحينا الى إبراهيم واسمعيل الى آخر الآية (4: 163) وقال وأوحى الىّ هذا القرآن لانذركم به (6: 19) ونحوه كثير (2) والوجه الثانى الوحى يعنى الإلهام فذلك قوله فى المائدة وإذ أوحيتُ الى الحواريين يعنى ألهمت الحواريين أن امنوا بى وبرسولى (5: 111) وكقوله فى النحل وأوحى ربّك الى النحل يقول وألهم ربّك النحل أن اتخذى من الجبال بيوتا (16: 68) (3) والوجه الثالث الوحى كتاب فذلك قوله فى آل عمران لزكريا فأوحى اليهم يقول كتب اليهم كتابا أن سبحوا بكرة وعشيا (19: 11!) (4) والوجه الرابع الوحى أمر فذلك قوله فى حمٓ السجدة وأوحى فى كل سماء أمرها (41: 12) وقال فى الأنعام شياطين الإنس والجن يوحى بعضهم الى بعض يقول يأمر بعضهم بعضا (6: 112) وقال فى سورة الأنعام وإن الشياطين ليوحون الى أوليائهم يعنى يأمرونهم بالوسوسة والتزيين (6: 121) (5) والوجه الخامس الوحى القول فذلك قوله فى إذا زلزلت الأرض بأن ربّك أوحى لها يعنى قال لها (99: 5). Thus, for five allegedly distinct uses of the term *waḥy*, nine scriptural passages were adduced:

1. *Waḥy*: revelation (Q. 4: 163, 6: 19)
2. *Waḥy*: inspiration (*ilhām*) (Q. 5: 111, 16: 68)
3. *Waḥy*: writing (*kitāb*) (Q. 19: 11)
4. *Waḥy*: command (*amr*) (Q. 41: 12, 6: 112, 6:121)
5. *Waḥy*: speech (*qawl*) (Q. 99: 5)

Selection of the verses was arbitrary: of seventy-two occurrences in the Qur'ān of a finite form of the verb *awḥā* and six of the substantive *waḥy*, not more than five, possibly six, separate contexts can be elicited, and those correspond roughly to the five 'aspects' (*wujūh*) of Beyazit 561. But some qualification, as well as differentiation, is necessary. The first aspect

[1] See below, pp. 212–16. [2] MS Beyazit 561, 94^r–5^v.

(revelation) is, for example, logically misleading since, as a descriptive term for divine communication, it must include the remaining four aspects. Strictly interpreted, the definition of revelation as 'that mediated by Gabriel to the prophets' cannot be reconciled with Muslim doctrine on the modes of revelation, but if that difficulty is overlooked, *waḥy*/*awḥā* as 'revelation' will account for a quarter of its Quranic occurrences (of which seven refer to Moses, and five to Noah).[1] For the second aspect (inspiration) the traditional *locus probans* was indeed Q. 16: 68; inclusion here of Q. 5: 111 presupposed a sophisticated distinction between prophets and apostles, but one well established in the tradition of Judaeo-Christian polemic, possibly the source of the semantic equivalence *waḥy*: *ilhām*.[2] Logically, the passages alluding to demonic inspiration (Q. 6: 112, 6: 121) belong here and not under the fourth aspect (command/decree), which exhibits *waḥy* as manifestation of the divine will in creation. For that function of *waḥy*, Q. 41: 12 is appropriate, as would have been inclusion of Q. 99: 5. Use of the latter to illustrate the fifth aspect (speech) is curious. In fact, a separate function of *waḥy* as speech is only significant as one component of the contrast between the fifth aspect and the third (writing), for which the choice of Q. 19: 11 might seem singularly inappropriate.[3] Incidentally, the confusion here between *Sūra*s 3 and 19 seems to reveal uncertainty about the place of variant traditions in the canon.[4] That for the third aspect *kitāb* cannot be 'decree' seems clear from the separate listing of the fourth aspect.[5] The intended reference may have been to *waḥy* as scripture, for which Q. 17: 39, 18: 27, 20: 114, 29: 45, etc. could be proposed. And Q. 19: 11 would illustrate *waḥy* as speech. Absent from the lexical analysis in Beyazit 561 is the notion of *waḥy* as dispatch (*irsāl*), for which Q. 42: 52 might have been adduced.[6] The polysemy of *waḥy* in the document of revelation is thus attested, but in a manner clearly anterior to the elaboration of sophisticated semantic analysis.

That example is characteristic of the 186 lemmata: with the exception of eleven items (the particles: *li*, *siwā*, *hal*, *fī*, *min*, *aw*, *am*, *fawqa*, *mā*, *ḥattā*, and *illā*) all may be described, within the framework of *lingua sacra*, as theological concepts, e.g. *hudan*, *kufr*, *dīn*, *ithm*, *ḍalāl*, *ṣirāṭ*, etc. But the principle by means of which the several uses of each were differentiated was of broader linguistic application: namely, the reference to context. However inappropriate the actual *loci probantes* might seem, the number of aspects (*wujūh*) for any particular item approximates very closely to the number of scriptural contexts in which the locution appears. The

[1] See above, I pp. 33–8.
[2] See above, II pp. 58–9.
[3] Thus Ibn Qutayba, *Ta'wīl*, 373–4 s.v. *waḥy*.
[4] Cf. e.g. Bayḍāwī on the same subject, above p. 207.
[5] See above, II pp. 76–7.
[6] That sense was adduced by Ibn Qutayba, *Ta'wīl*, 373–4, using Q. 6: 19.

lexical data thus isolated might more accurately be described as reference rather than as information.[1] This kind of lexicography was exclusively concerned to elucidate scriptural imagery, and hence avowedly exegetical. The type, exemplified in the primary title of Beyazit 561, *K. al-wujūh wal-naẓā'ir*, became a genre of exegetical literature and a basic component of the masorah. Ascription of its origins to Muqātil was occasionally explicit.[2] Malaṭī, too, in his *K. Tanbīh* ascribed to Muqātil a series of semantic equivalences in which much of the scriptural lexicon was reduced to a limited number of standard synonyms.[3] But the method employed there was the obverse of Muqātil's 'aspects': only one 'meaning' was adduced for each scriptural concept in whatever context (cf. the introductory formula: *kull shay' fī 'l-Qur'ān . . . ya'nī . . .*). The material includes most of what I have designated minimal units of explication, e.g. *kadhālika*: *hākadhā*, *ladaynā*: *'indanā*, *la'alla*: *likay*,[4] but also several which presupposed a rather more complex interpretation, e.g. *khātam*: *ṭab'*, *ghuluf*: *akinna*.[5] In that arrangement the informing principle was not 'aspect' (*wajh*/*wujūh*) but 'analogue' (*naẓīr*/*naẓā'ir*). Both methods are illustrated in Suyūṭī's chapter on *al-wujūh wal-naẓā'ir*, in which the *naẓā'ir* (*kull shay' fī 'l-Qur'ān*) were qualified by specifying the exceptions to their general 'meanings'.[6] Thus gradually, a more or less fixed pattern of semantic distribution was elaborated for the lexicon of scripture which included both polysemes and/or homonyms (*wujūh*) and synonyms (*naẓā'ir*).[7] Though the early stages of the process exhibit a concern primarily with substantives, the dozen or so purely grammatical elements in Beyazit 561 generated a similar but separate treatment of particles (*adāt*/*adawāt*), which in Suyūṭī's treatise ranged from the interrogative *hamza* to the vocative *yā*.[8]

The earliest uses of the term *naẓīr* vary:[9] in the works ascribed to Muqātil the 'analogy' is explicitly textual, e.g. for *bākhi'un nafsaka* (Q. 26: 3 *ad* 18: 6), for *shaṭaṭan* (Q. 38: 22 and 72: 4 *ad* 18: 14), and for *ṣaffan* (Q. 20: 64 *ad* 18: 48).[10] In Bayazit 561 the term *naẓīr* occurs *passim*, always, and not unexpectedly in view of the nature of the collection, to introduce an analogy based upon an identical word or phrase. In both H. Hüsnü 17 and Beyazit 561 the term was employed interchangeably

[1] See above, p. 142, and III, pp. 99–100. [2] e.g. Suyūṭī, *Itqān* ii, 121.

[3] See above, pp. 165–6; Malaṭī, *Kitāb al-tanbīh*, 56–63.

[4] See above, pp. 129–30. [5] Cf. above, II pp. 64–5 and 72–3, respectively.

[6] *Itqān*, *naw'* 39: ii, 121–39 (122–31 and 132–9, respectively); these specifically masoretic terms are not to be confused with the later juridical *ashbāh wa-nazā'ir*, though the principle of analogy underlying them is of course the same, cf. Schacht, *Introduction*, 114, 265.

[7] The type had an ancient pedigree from the Hellenistic schools of rhetoric and became eventually a source for both halakhic and masoretic exegesis, cf. Daube, 'Rabbinic methods', 241 n. 7; and Würthwein, *Text*, 21–2 (e.g. *Okhla we-okhla*).

[8] *Itqān*, *naw'* 40: ii, 140–259. [9] See above, pp. 127, 143, 169–70.

[10] Muqātil, *Tafsīr*, MS H. Hüsnü 17, 167^v, 168^r, 170^r, respectively.

with *mithluhā* and *ka-qawlihi*: 'textual analogies' were derived exclusively from the text of scripture. The significance of that method emerges from comparison of Muqātil with his contemporary Sufyān Thawrī. The latter's use of analogy, introduced not by *naẓīr*, but rather by *ka-qawlihi* or *mithlu* (*qawlihi*), was limited to scriptural *shawāhid* but not to *litteratim* constructions. For example, the connection between Q. 2: 28 and 40: 11 derives from the fact/assertion of resurrection but not from linguistic expression of that fact/assertion in those passages.[1] Similarly, acknowledgement of divine creation is the only link between Q. 3: 83 and 43: 87, and no attempt was made to elucidate the grammatical and lexical characteristics of one passage by reference to the other.[2] In the work of Sufyān, as it has been preserved, masoretic material is unmistakably intrusive, and the same may be said at least of Muqātil's *Tafsīr* (H. Hüsnü 17).[3] The relationship of Beyazit 561 to Muqātil is, as has been noted, problematic: its contents, like the lexical data ascribed to Muqātil by Malaṭī, signal the beginning, rather than the end or a stage along the way, of the exegetical development which I have called masoretic. With that development the term *naẓīr* came to designate syntactical/grammatical analogue generally, and not merely with reference to the language of scripture. For example, in Farrā' Q. 49: 11 عسى أن يكونوا خيرا منهم was proposed as *naẓīr* to the construction with an auxiliary verb in 18: 31 نعم الثواب.[4] The analogy was thus based upon scriptural usage but not upon an identical phrase. Similarly, Zamakhsharī introduced with *naẓīr* an analogy to Q. 4: 48 إن الله لا يغفر أن يشرك به ويغفر ما دون ذلك لمن يشاء from the *usus loquendi* (*qawluka*) إن الأمير لا يبذل الدينار ويبذل القنطار لمن يشاء by means of which the ellipsis in the scriptural passage could be resolved.[5] In Farrā' are found also the locutions *mithla*, *ka-qawlihi*, and *wa-hiya bi-manzilat qawlihi*, but more often than not to introduce analogies based upon identical wording.[6] It was that method which remained characteristically masoretic and in which exegetical use of the term *naẓīr* had originated.

From delimitation of homonyms/polysemes and synonyms it was but a short step to a distributional analysis of Quranic diction. Its formative principle was designated *mushtabih* (variant: *mutashābih*).[7] The earliest collection of data organized according to that principle is ascribed to the masorete and (seventh) 'canonical reader' Kisā'ī (d. 189/804).[8] The work

[1] Sufyān, *Tafsīr*, 3.
[2] Sufyān, *Tafsīr*, 37.
[3] See above, pp. 132–3, 138.
[4] *Ma'ānī 'l-Qur'ān* ii, 141–2.
[5] *Kashshāf* i, 519–20: an alternative to his resolution of the construction by *taqdīr*, cf. Wansbrough, 'Periphrastic exegesis', 259, and below, pp. 219–24.
[6] *Ma'ānī 'l-Qur'ān* ii, 137, 157, 5, respectively.
[7] See above, pp. 157, 165.
[8] *GAS* i, 17, 48; MS Beyazit 436, entitled *Kitāb mushtabihāt al-Qur'ān*, but given 70[r] as *Kitāb al-Mutashābih*; see also *GdQ* iii, 180, 188, and *passim*.

consists of serial enumeration by *sūra* of locutions which occur once, twice, and from three to ten,[1] fifteen, and twenty times in the text of the canon. Appropriate illustration is provided by the material assembled under the heading 'once' for *Sūrat al-Baqara*:[2] باب الواحد من سورة البقرة: يايها الناس اعبدوا ربّكم (2: 21) وسائر القرآن اتقوا ربّكم وفيها فأتوا بسورة من مثله (2: 23) وسائر القرآن مثله بغير من وفيها وادعوا شهداء كم (2: 23) وسائر القرآن من استطعتم وفيها وامنوا بما أنزلتُ مرفوعة التاء (2: 41) وسائر القرآن منصوبة وفيها النبيين بغير الحق (2: 61) وسائر القرآن بغير حق وفيها والذين هادوا والنصارى والصابئين (2: 62) وسائر القرآن والصابئون قبل النصارى وفيها لن تمسنا النار الا أياما معدودة (2: 80) وسائر القرآن معدودات وفيها لا يخفف عنهم العذاب ولا هم ينصرون (2: 86) وسائر القرآن ولا هم ينظرون وفيها بل أكثرهم لا يؤمنون (2: 100) ليس فى القرآن مثله وفيها بعد الذى جاءك من العلم (2: 120) وسائر القرآن من بعد ما جاءك وفيها يتلوا عليهم آياتك ويعلمهم الكتاب والحكمة ويزكيهم (2: 129) وسائر القرآن ويزكيهم ويعلمهم وفيها فلا تخشوهم واخشونى بياء (2: 150) وسائر القرآن بغير ياء وفيها وما اهل به لغير الله (2: 173) وسائر القرآن لغير الله به وفيها ولا عاد فلا إثم عليه (2: 173) وليس فى القرآن مثله وفيها ومن كان مريضا بغير منكم (2: 185) ليس فى القرآن مثله وفيها إن الذين آمنوا والذين هاجروا (2: 218) وسائر القرآن وهاجروا ليس فيه والذين وفيها ويكفر عنكم من سيئاتكم (2: 271) وسائر القرآن عنكم سيئاتكم بغير من وفيها ما ألفينا عليه آباءنا (2: 170) وسائر القرآن وجدنا وفيها وكلا منها رغدا (2: 35) وغيره فكلا وفيها وقلت (*sic*) يا آدم اسكن أنت وزوجك (2: 35) وفيها لا تكلف نفس (2: 233) ليس فى القرآن مثله.

In this passage twenty-one instances of 'unique' phraseology were adduced, and in all but one (the second example for Q. 2: 35) their uniqueness either reiterated (*laysa fī 'l-Qur'ān mithluhu/ghayruhu*: 2: 100, 2: 173, 2: 185, 2: 233) or contrasted with what is apparently 'normal' Quranic usage (*wa-sā'ir al-Qur'ān* . . .). The contrasts thus established are not semantic but grammatical, and turn upon the presence/absence of particles and prepositional phrases, variation in word order, in inflexion, and in orthography. As in the lexical collations of Beyazit 561 and similar works, the *shawāhid* are entirely scriptural, and no effort was made to justify a particular construction by reference to usage outside the Qur'ān. On the other hand, the selection of contrasts might be thought arbitrary: the locution *u'budū rabbakum* (Q. 2: 21) appears also in Q. 22: 77 and, in a slightly expanded form, in 5: 72 and 5: 117. If it is the apostrophe *yā ayyuhā 'l-nās* which is here operative, that appears in combination with

[1] Read so, for 'eleven', 61v.

[2] *Kitāb mushtabihāt al-Qur'ān*, 1v–3r.

ittaqū rabbakum only three times (Q. 4: 1, 22: 1, 31: 33), from which a stylistic norm can hardly be elicited. Rather more valuable would have been reference to the contrast between Q. 2: 21 and the collocation of *yā ayyuhā 'lladhīna āmanū* as the mode of address with the imperative *ittaqū 'llāh* (e.g. Q. 2: 278, 5: 35, 9: 119, 33: 70, 49: 1). But isolation and comparison of formulaic phraseology as an exercise in literary analysis was not the author's purpose, though the material assembled here may be useful to that end. Acknowledgement of variants in the form of inflexion (Q. 2: 62, but also 22: 17; only 5: 69 has *casus rectus*) and of orthography (Q. 2: 150, but the alternative spelling occurs only twice, in 5: 3 and 5: 44) exhibits concern for the conceptual unity of scripture, noticed above for the lexical category of *wujūh*. That acknowledgement emerges very clearly from the inclusion here of Q. 2: 233, whose locution لا تُكَلَّف نفس and attendant pointing with the internal passive may profitably be compared with the occurrence of لا نكَلِّف/يكَلِّف نفسا in 2: 286, 6: 152, 7: 42, 23: 62, 65: 7, but also 4: 84 لا تُكَلَّف الا نفسك. Like the variant traditions, of which these instances represent the formal aspect, the textual variations preserved in the canon might be thought to throw some light on the formation of Muslim scripture.[1] In Kisā'ī's work the principle of *mushtabihāt* was sound, its application fragmentary. Subsequent elaboration of the genre provided more complete coverage of the phenomenon.[2] It may plausibly be argued that the collation of *mushtabihāt* reflects awareness, on the part of the masoretes, not only of the Qur'ān's stylistic homogeneity but also of its structural idiosyncrasies, and finally, of the necessity to explain these in terms of intrinsic analogies.

An example is Q. 2: 35 وقلنا يا آدم اسكن أنت وزوجك الجنة وكلا منها رغدا حيث شئتما ولا تقربا هذه الشجرة فتكونا من الظالمين incompletely and incorrectly adduced by Kisā'ī. That the verse is a variant of the Adam tradition in Q. 7: 19 ويا آدم اسكن أنت وزوجك الجنة فكلا من حيث شئتما ولا تقربا هذه الشجرة فتكونا من الظالمين hardly requires demonstration. Juxtaposition of the two verses, not as *maṣāḥif* but as *mushtabihāt*, generated the following exegesis: because in the first verse the divine command was to 'dwell and feast', the co-ordinating conjunction (*wa*-) was employed to link the two actions as one divine favour, the limitless extent of which is emphasized in the terms 'copiously' (*raghadan*) and 'wherever you like' (*ḥaythu shi'tumā*); in the second verse the command was to 'take (up) residence, then nourishment', separate actions requiring

[1] See above, pp. 207–8.

[2] See Suyūṭī, *Itqān*, *naw'* 63: iii, 339–44, and the late works mentioned there, 339, to which may be added Rāghib Iṣfahānī, *Ḥall mutashābihāt al-Qur'ān*.

to be temporally distinguished by the subordinating conjunction (*fa-*), its restricted largess expressed by omission of 'copiously' and by insertion of a limiting preposition (*min*) before 'wherever you like'.[1] Whatever suspicions that interpretation might provoke, it ought to be quite clear that the presence of doublets in the text of scripture could not be an embarrassment. But all such material, absence of which could reduce the size of the canon by forty to fifty per cent, lends itself admirably to the kind of documentary analysis proposed for the Shuʿayb traditions and the 'double-garden' imagery.[2] That in the Muslim tradition recourse was had not to documentary analysis, but to exegesis, may be illustrated by considering the number of Muʿtazilites responsible for works in the genre of *mushtabihāt/mutashābihāt*.[3] An element of rhetorical criticism is also evident, at least in the later development of the genre. Repetition in scripture came to be described and evaluated in specifically aesthetic terms, and textual variation regarded as stylistic embellishment. The technical vocabulary formulated to that end, e.g. *munāsaba/irtibāṭ* (filiation) and *tafannun* (elegant variation), presupposed the structural integrity of a single document of revelation.[4] That terminological refinement, not yet expressed in the work of Kisāʾī, reflected the doctrine of *iʿjāz al-Qurʾān*, a post-masoretic phenomenon. Once acknowledged as an appropriate object of rhetorical analysis, the text of scripture was safely removed from the danger of dissolving into its original and fragmentary components.[5]

The exegetical procedures symbolized by the terms *wujūh*, *naẓāʾir*, and *mushtabihāt/mutashābihāt* were derived from a view of scripture as self-contained and self-explanatory. The logic of that view rested implicitly upon acknowledgement of *lingua sacra* as a special mode of communication. The schemata of revelation were, so to speak, *sui generis* and could gain little or nothing by reference to the elements of normal linguistic usage. To describe that mode of communication as the 'word of God' might be thought perversely dogmatic, but points none the less to the fundamental distinctiveness of the literary expression which is the subject of these studies. The manner in which originally or basically neutral elements in language (if such can ever be said to exist) achieve separate reality as the ingredients of fixed and traditional imagery (whether or not 'scriptural') is well known: all 'meaning' is related to context. Thus, the most recent attempt to analyse the lexicon of Muslim scripture derives from a semasiology not appreciably different in kind from that underlying the 'aspects' of Beyazit 561: namely, Allard's *Analyse conceptuelle du*

1 Suyūṭī, *Itqān* iii, 340.
2 See above, I pp. 20–7.
3 See *GAS* i, 618–19, 622, 626, but also 13, 44.
4 Suyūṭī, *Itqān* iii, 340, 342, and *nawʿ* 62: iii, 322–38.
5 See below, pp. 227–46, and above, II pp. 77–83.

Coran sur cartes perforées (1963).[1] Though the author was unable to resist including in his 430 cards some irrelevant information (e.g. the 'chronology' of revelation under (B) *Cadre*), the results which can be obtained from manipulation of his system are comparable to those elicited from a literary analysis (recurrent phraseology, as opposed to separate lexical items, is unfortunately accessible only through non-literary headings: *anthropologie*, *théologie*, *éthique-religion*). To establish, quickly and conveniently, statistics on conceptual distribution, the method is admirably suited; to anyone at all familiar with Muslim scripture the results are invariably predictable (e.g. quantitative emphasis upon the 'Mosaic syndrome' in Quranic prophetology).[2]

Now, in the Muslim exegetical tradition efforts to clarify the lexicon and imagery of scripture were not always confined to the material of the document itself. It is difficult, if not altogether impossible, to determine chronologically the point at which the problems of *lingua sacra* could be fruitfully referred to the data of profane literature. From what appear to be its earliest attested stages, the procedure was at first essentially lexical and methodologically atomistic. Lexical treatment in haggadic exegesis seldom consisted of more than a straightforward equivalence adduced without authorities, occasionally of a foreign etymology for *exotica* and *hapax legomena*, both practices hardly altered by the halakhists.[3] For neither may sporadic reference to ʿAbdallāh b. ʿAbbās be understood as appeal to an authority especially qualified in the sphere of lexicology. And yet, the origins of literature concerned specifically with the scriptural lexicon, not solely as the expression of theological concepts but as communication drawing upon the resources of a national language, are almost always connected with his name.[4] At least three titles of such works have been preserved: *Kitāb gharīb al-Qurʾān*, *Kitāb/Bayān lughāt al-Qurʾān*, and *Masāʾil Nāfiʿ b. Azraq*.[5] The substance of the material designated by these titles has been transmitted in several scarcely varying recensions, and is synoptically accessible in Suyūṭī's *Itqān*.[6] Whether or not the Berlin MS Petermann II, 405 is an extract from Suyūṭī, may, in view of the widespread transmission of the material and of the legendary stature of Ibn ʿAbbās, be thought quite without significance.[7]

The collection of lexical explanations known as *Masāʾil Nāfiʿ b. Azraq* exhibits an exegetical method considerably posterior to the activity of

1 Cf. also Allard, 'Une Méthode nouvelle', 5–21; a primitive, because dependent upon non-linguistic data, application of 'contextual semantics' may be seen in Izutsu, *Ethico-religious Concepts*.

2 Allard, 'Une Méthode nouvelle', 19.

3 See above, pp. 124, 143, and 181, 182, respectively.

4 See Goldziher, *Richtungen*, 69–71.

5 *GAS* i, 27–8 nos. 2, 4, 3, respectively.

6 *Itqān*, *nawʿ* 36: ii, 6–46, 47–54, 55–88.

7 MS Petermann II, 405, 93–101, and *Itqān* ii, 55–88; cf. *GAS* i, 27 no. 1 vs. *GAL*, Suppl. I, 331, and Mittwoch, 'Ahlwardt No. 683', 339–44.

Ibn ʿAbbās (d. 68/687): namely, the reference of rare or unknown words in scripture to the great corpus of early Arabic poetry.[1] That method was in fact so conscientiously and consistently applied in the *Masāʾil* as to provoke the question whether the real purpose of the work was not to furnish an ancient and honourable pedigree for what became, with the masoretes, a very important exegetical principle. Lexicology, like the other Islamic sciences, was ultimately defined in terms of traditional authority, with the customary reference to the linguistic competence of the companions of the prophet: what they did not know could not be known.[2] That one of those companions, Ibn ʿAbbās, should be able for each of 190 Quranic locutions[3] to cite a verse from Jāhilī or Mukhaḍramī poets (many anonymous) was indeed an accomplishment worthy of note. Suspicion of a *tour de force* is corroborated by appearance of the same lexica in other scriptural vocabulary lists, also ascribed to Ibn ʿAbbās but without poetic *shawāhid*.[4] That principle of which the *Masāʾil* represent an almost polemical expression was explicitly articulated in dicta attributed to Ibn ʿAbbās: الشعر ديوان العرب (Poetry is the register of the Arabs, *scil.* of their language)[5] or, in more detail, to ʿUmar b. Khaṭṭāb: عليكم بأشعار الجاهلية فان فيها تفسير كتابكم (Learn the poetry of the *Jāhiliyya*, for there you will find the interpretation of your scripture).[6] Similar exhortation, but here chronologically unexceptionable, was ascribed to Ṭabarī, Sharīf Murtaḍā, and Jubbāʾī,[7] by whose dates the practice was well established. That it was not so prior to the third/ninth century is, in my opinion, very significant.[8] A virtual *terminus a quo* may be elicited from Ibn Hishām's recension of the *Sīra*: e.g. for *bākhiʿun nafsaka* in Q. 18: 6 a line from Dhū Rumma was adduced, for *shaṭaṭan* in 18: 14 a verse from Aʿshā.[9] Application there was exclusively lexical, and thus provides a neat contrast to the haggadic method of dealing with the vocabulary of scripture. In Bukhārī's *K. Tafsīr* only one line of poetry (anonymous) was cited, for *la-awwāhun* in Q. 9: 114.[10] In Muslim a single verse was adduced, at Q. 7: 31,[11] and in Tirmidhī none in an exegetical sense.[12] Poetry was very occasionally cited, for lexical explanation, in the works of the halakhists, such as Jaṣṣāṣ and

[1] See above, pp. 142–3, and III, 97–102.
[2] e.g. Suyūṭī, *Itqān* ii, 3–4.
[3] Not 140, as in Mittwoch, op. cit. 342.
[4] e.g. Suyūṭī, *Itqān* ii, 6–54, and see below, pp. 218–19.
[5] Suyūṭī, *Itqān* ii, 55; cf. Goldziher, *Richtungen*, 70 esp. n. 3: there is on the contrary every reason for not accepting the authenticity of that report.
[6] Goldziher, op. cit. 69 n. 4.
[7] Goldziher, op. cit. 92, 116, 130, respectively.
[8] *Pace* Nöldeke, *BSS*, 11 n. 6; cf. *GdQ* ii, 192 (revised and appropriately sceptical).
[9] Ibn Hishām, *Sīra* i, 302, 304.
[10] Bukhārī, *Ṣaḥīḥ* iii, 248.
[11] Muslim, *Ṣaḥīḥ* viii, 244.
[12] A line ascribed to the prophet was incidentally included *ad* Q. 53: 32, in Tirmidhī, *Ṣaḥīḥ* xii, 173, a gratuitous insertion comparable to the line from Ḥassān b. Thābit *ad* Q. 24: 15, in Bukhārī, *Ṣaḥīḥ* iii, 297.

Ibn ʿArabī. The earliest exegetical composition in which poetic *shawāhid* were regularly employed is the *Maʿānī ʾl-Qurʾān* of Farrāʾ (d. 207/822).[1] But there application of the principle was not limited to *lexis*: grammatical phenomena were also justified by reference to profane literature. For example, the locution *wa-iqām al-ṣalāt* in Q. 24: 37 required, in the view of Farrāʾ, to be explained as an apocopate permitted by *status constructus*, i.e. for *iqāmat al-ṣalāt*. An anonymous verse containing *ʿida ʾl-amr* for *ʿidata ʾl-amr* was adduced in support of the contention.[2] The technique could be extended also to syntactical problems, accessory to the periphrastic principle known as *taqdīr/majāz*.[3]

In the related field of profane lexicography a parallel and contemporaneous practice has been noted: in Khalīl's *Kitāb al-ʿAyn* verses of ninety-nine poets together with some anonymous lines were adduced in support of the *usus loquendi*.[4] For the scriptural lexicon, however, there appears to have been some opposition to that method.[5] One title recorded for the collection otherwise known as *Masāʾil Nāfiʿ b. Azraq* is *Kitāb gharīb al-Qurʾān*,[6] but a separate work, also entitled *K. gharīb al-Qurʾān* and also ascribed to Ibn ʿAbbās, does not contain the *Masāʾil* and does *not* employ poetic *shawāhid*.[7] It is instead a plaidoyer for the exclusively Arabic vocabulary of scripture, an argument set out in the following preface:[8] عن ابن عباس فى قول الله بلسان عربى قال بلسان قريش ولو كان غير عربى ما فهموا وما أنزل الله كتابا الا بالعربية فكان جبريل يترجم لكل نبى قومه وذلك أن الله يقول وما أرسلنا من رسول الا بلسان قومه وليس لسان من ألسنة الأمم أوسع من لسان العرب والقرآن ليس فيه لغة غير لغة العرب وربما وافقت اللغة اللغات فاما الأصل والجنس فعربى لا يخالطه شئ. The conflicting interpretations of Q. 14: 4 and the ambiguity of the locution *lisān ʿarabī* have been remarked.[9] A sentiment similar to that of Ibn ʿAbbās was attributed to Sufyān Thawrī: لم ينزل وحى الا بالعربية ثم ترجم على نبى لقومه,[10] while Muqātil reported, on the authority of Saʿīd b. Jubayr that all languages were represented in the Qurʾān: ما فى الأرض لغة الا أنزلها الله فى القرآن.[11] The latter view was amplified by Suyūṭī to assert the universality of Muhammad's mission: وأيضا النبى مرسل الى كل أمة . . . (Q. 14: 4) فلا بد وان

[1] See above, p. 150.
[2] *Maʿānī ʾl-Qurʾān* ii, 254 ad loc.; cf. Vollers, *Volkssprache*, 156–7.
[3] See below, pp. 223–4.
[4] Wild, *Das Kitāb al-ʿAin*, esp. 42–51.
[5] Cf. Suyūṭī, *Itqān* ii, 55; and see below, pp. 223–4.
[6] Mittwoch, 'Ahlwardt No. 683', 341.
[7] *GAS* i, 27 no. 2; MS Atıf Efendi 2815.
[8] MS Atıf Efendi 2815, 102ʳ.
[9] See above, II pp. 53, 81, III pp. 98–9.
[10] *Apud* Suyūṭī, *Itqān* i, 130.
[11] Muqātil, *Tafsīr*, MS H. Hüsnü 17, 173ᵛ at the end of *Sūrat al-Kahf*; cf. *Itqān* ii, 106.

يكون فى الكتاب المبعوث به من لسان كل قوم وان كان أصله بلغة قومه هو.[1]
Some portion of the contradiction was neutralized by resort to the notions of coincidence between languages (*tawāfuq/tawārud al-lughāt*) and assimilation (*taʿrīb*) ascribed to Ibn ʿAbbās and Abū ʿUbayd.[2] The concept of 'pure Arabic' (*ʿarabī maḥḍ*) forcefully asserted by Abū ʿUbayda became an axiom of masoretic exegesis.[3] The link with Ibn ʿAbbās was, however, maintained. The third work of lexical character ascribed to him is entitled *Bayān lughāt al-Qurʾān/al-Lughāt fī 'l-Qurʾān*,[4] at least one manuscript version of which contains the same material as *K. gharīb al-Qurʾān*, with an identical preface.[5] They are a compilation by *sūra* of standard lexical explanations, unaccompanied by authorities or *loci probantes*, either from scripture itself or from profane literature, and similar to the list of such transmitted from Ibn ʿAbbās via Ṭabarī by Suyūṭī.[6] The central position occupied by Ibn ʿAbbās in the *lughāt/gharīb* literature emerges from examination of the data collected by Sezgin for those titles: we are confronted not by several independent traditions but by scarcely discernible variations of a single tradition.[7] The lexical data extracted from Bukhārī and alphabetically assembled by ʿAbd al-Bāqī contains the same standard material, and belongs to the same collective tradition.[8] It was not until elaboration of the genre by Ibn Qutayba (d. 276/889) and Sijistānī (d. 330/942) that the traditional stock was refurbished, substantially and methodologically.[9]

More important for the Quranic masorah than either variant reading or lexical explanation was the analysis of grammar and syntax represented by the exegetical principle *taqdīr/majāz*. The earliest formulation of that principle is found in the work of Abū ʿUbayda (d. 209/824) entitled *Majāz al-Qurʾān*.[10] In an introductory chapter the author enumerated thirty-nine kinds of *majāz* occurring in the text of scripture, illustrated by sixty *shawāhid*, ten of them adduced twice, to different ends.[11] Abū ʿUbayda's typology includes six categories of grammatical and syntactical phenomena, of which three contain solutions proposed to more or less straightforward textual problems, i.e. *lexis* (no. 28), *varia lectio* (nos. 27, 29, 38), and concord (nos. 4–13). Characteristic of the last-named category are explanations

[1] *Itqān* ii, 107.

[2] Cf. Suyūṭī, *Itqān* ii, 105, 108–19; see Kopf, 'Foreign words', 191–205, esp. 202–4; and id., 'Religious influences', esp. 34–8, 40–5.

[3] e.g. Abū ʿUbayda, *Majāz al-Qurʾān* i, 8, 17.

[4] *GAS* i, 28 no. 4; MS Esad Efendi 91; I have not seen Munajjid's edition of the Ẓāhiriyya MS (Cairo, 1946).

[5] i.e. MS Atif Efendi 2815; this preface is at 104^r of MS Esad Efendi 91.

[6] *Itqān* ii, 6–46.

[7] See *GAS* i, Indices: *Büchertitel*.

[8] ʿAbd al-Bāqī, *Muʿjam gharīb al-Qurʾān*, 1–233.

[9] *GAS* i, 48 and 43–4, respectively.

[10] *GAS* i, 48; ed. Sezgin, see Wansbrough, 'Periphrastic exegesis', 248.

[11] Abū ʿUbayda, *Majāz al-Qurʾān* i, 8–16: set out with translation in Wansbrough, op. cit. 248–54 (where the locution *awlā laka fa-awlā*, Q. 75: 34, under nos. 17 and 20, may better be rendered 'Woe unto thee, woe', see Zamakhsharī, *Kashshāf* iv, 664 ad loc.).

involving a *constructio ad sensum*, employed to neutralize contradiction between formal and conceptual reference to number, person, and gender, e.g. Q. 22: 5 (no. 4) نخرجكم طفلا (أطفالا). In another category, ellipsis (nos. 1–3), the same concept was employed to justify periphrastic restoration. One example of the latter deserves notice, Q. 12: 82 (no. 2) وسل (أهل) القرية التى كنّا فيها و (من فى) العير التى أقبلنا فيها. Insertion of 'the inhabitants of' before 'village', and of 'those in' before 'caravan' is not really essential to understanding the passage, but indicates, rather, the author's consciousness of a metaphorical construction. It is thus quite unlike the other illustrations of ellipsis included there (Q. 38: 6, 2: 26, 39: 73) and qualitatively distinguished from the examples of irregular concord. But a further category of *majāz* (nos. 14–23, 26) contains a number of rhetorical phenomena, e.g. *fictio personae*, apostrophe, chiasmus, from which together with Q. 12: 82 it would be tempting to infer that for Abū 'Ubayda the term *majāz* designated figurative usage. That it did not, however, seems clear from the bulk of his 60 *loci probantes*, and in particular for the category of idiom and/or solecism exhibited in nos. 24, 25, 30–7, most especially no. 39. Here *majāz* represents the rationalization of careless style, of syntactical ambiguity, even of grammatical error, by means of restoration according to the norms of scriptural usage.

The method is, at least implicitly, that underlying the type of analysis identified by *mushtabihāt*.[1] The functional confusion between *nomen regens* and *nomen rectum* exhibited in Q. 28: 76 (no. 24) and 2: 171 (no. 25) required justification: occurrence of the second example in the text of scripture is fairly frequent.[2] Variable function of particles (no. 30), as in Q. 2: 26, 20: 71, 83: 2, and 43: 51–2, was explained by a series of arbitrary but not quite irresponsible equations, e.g. *fawqahā*: *dūnahā*, *fī*: *'alā*, etc. On the other hand, Q. 79: 30 والأرض بعد (مع) ذلك دحاها involved a dogmatic postulate relevant to the chronology of divine creation and was recognized as one of the 'standard puzzles' of scripture:[3] substitution of 'together with' for 'after' was thus, in the precise sense of the term, exegetical. The presence of particles (nos. 31–3) was in the examples here adduced (Q. 83: 1–3, 1: 5, 16: 98) exclusively grammatical, and in the first two *majāz* represented the resolution of synthetic constructions. With regard to the third, it might well be argued that the absence/presence of *bi* after *qara'a*, contrasted in Q. 16: 98 and 96: 1, is not merely not optional but reflects, indeed, a semantic distinction. Conversely, the *majāz* proposed for Q. 20: 69 (no. 36) إنما صنعوا (إن صنيعهم) كيد ساحر indicated a genuine, and frequent, option, which may be regarded as stylistic rather than

[1] See above, pp. 212–15.
[2] See above, III pp. 113–41.
[3] As, for example, in Muqātil, *Tafsir*, MS BM Or. 6333; see above, p. 164, no. 3.

grammatical. Common, or optional, gender for collectives (no. 34) can be demonstrated by reference to Q. 26: 105 كذّبت (كذّب) قوم نوح المرسلين but not of course to 16: 66 وإنّ لكم فى الأنعام لعبرة نسقيكم مما فى بطونه (بطونها). Finally, the inconcinnity exhibited in Q. 73: 18 (no. 35) السماء منفطر به (السقف) and 55: 19 . . . 22 (no. 37) مرج البحرين يلتقيان . . . يخرج منهما (من أحدهما) اللؤلؤ والمرجان could not seriously be interpreted as figurative usage or even stylistic option. Their presence in this collection, like that of nos. 24 and 25 (Q. 28: 76 and 2: 171), can only be justified by a principle of inclusion which took account of passages requiring textual emendation.

Now, the possibility of error in the text of scripture, whether as ungrammatical usage (*laḥn*) or *lapsus calami* (*khaṭā' al-kuttāb*), was ultimately rejected.[1] In a transparently dogmatic discussion of two celebrated dicta, one attributed to 'Ā'isha: هذا عمل الكتّاب أخطئوا فى الكتاب, and the other to 'Uthmān: لا تغيروها فإنّ العرب ستغيرها, Suyūṭī argued from the authority of Ibn Anbārī and Ibn Ashtah, as well as from his own conviction, that neither report could be true since (*a*) the eloquence (*faṣāḥa*) of Muhammad's contemporaries was well known, (*b*) other equally well-known and better accredited traditions demonstrated the care taken by 'Ā'isha in the preservation and by 'Uthmān in the recension of the Quranic revelation, and (*c*) such evidence of textual instability as did exist was neither *laḥn* nor *khaṭā' al-kuttāb*, but, rather, *scriptio defectiva* or otherwise irregular orthography (خالف لفظها رسمها), or *variae lectiones* (وجوه القراءة).[2] Reference to Arab eloquence, neutralization of refractory *ḥadīth*s by other *ḥadīth*s, and accommodation of textual variants under the rubric 'seven (canonical) readings' (e.g. اختيار الأولى من الأحرف السبعة) reflect the procedural devices traditional to the solution of Quranic problems, and ought by now to be familiar.[3] It may be observed that Suyūṭī's denial of *laḥn* in the text of scripture was part of his general discussion of *i'rāb*, a term whose semantic range included not only grammatical phenomena (*aḥkām*), but also clarity (*bayān*) and euphony (*aṣwāt wa-luḥūn*).[4]

[1] Such is the substance of the first five chapters of Ibn Qutayba's *Ta'wīl mushkil al-Qur'ān* (10–75), in which the document of revelation was defended from every kind of assault upon its linguistic and literary excellence, e.g. *lapsus calami*, grammatical error, syntactic inconcinnity, semantic contradiction, and stylistic inconsistency; the author's postulates were those whose elaboration has been described here: all *qirā'āt* were equally revealed, poetry could be adduced to demonstrate analogous constructions (36–40), corruption by foreigners (*abnā' al-'ajam*) was neutralized by the reliable witness of transmission from companions of the prophet (41–2), etc.

[2] *Itqān* ii, 269–77.

[3] See above, III pp. 93–9; and 178–82, 202–8, respectively.

[4] *Itqān, naw'* 41: ii, 260–80; see above, p. 155; and III p. 104–11 for references to *Itqān* iv, 172–3, ii, 3.

It is also in that chapter that locutions permitting any one of the three *iʿrāb* vowels were listed.[1] The possibility of serious linguistic aberration in scripture was very restricted indeed.

The *locus classicus* was always Q. 20: 63 إن هذان لساحران. Suyūṭī's synthesis includes the entire spectrum of textual treatment, as well as a conventional notice of dialectal usage: (*a*) in some dialects, e.g. of B. Kināna and B. Ḥārith, the dual is expressed by *alif* in all three cases; (*b*) a pronoun anticipating the subsequent proposition (*ḍamīr al-sha'n*) has been omitted, i.e. إنّه هذان لساحران; (*c*) in addition to the ellipsis assumed in (*b*) a further omission of an inchoative of which *sāḥirān* is the predicate, i.e. إنّه هذان لهما ساحران; (*d*) *inna* in this locution signifies 'yes/surely/indeed' and thus does not require *casus obliquus*; (*e*) *hā* is here an anticipatory pronoun (*ḍamīr al-qiṣṣa*), and the remainder of the proposition an independent predication, i.e. إنّها ذان لساحران.[2] At least two other kinds of solution had been earlier articulated. In addition to citing the dialectal usage (here of B. Balḥārith b. Kaʿb), Ibn Qutayba recorded appropriate variants (*maṣāḥif*) from two 'companion' codices, namely Ubayy إنْ ذان الا ساحران and Ibn Masūd أنْ هذان ساحران or إنْ هذان ساحران or إنْ هذان لساحران.[3] The exegetical character of such ascription has been noted.[4] Of equal interest was the view, attributed by Ibn Qutayba to ʿĀṣim Jaḥdarī that one wrote إنّ هذان and read إنّ هذين, thus providing explicit support for the ʿUthmān tradition on *laḥn* in the text of scripture, i.e. وإنما فرق بين القراءة والكتاب لقول عثمان رحمه الله : أرى فيه لحنا وستقيمه العرب بألسنتها فأقامه بلسانه وترك الرسم على حاله.[5] Such was the solution proposed also by Abū ʿUbayda in slightly different terms: إن هذين لساحران فى اللفظ وكتب هذان كما يزيدون وينقصون فى الكتاب واللفظ صواب.[6] All of the 'standard' orthographic deviations, not only Q. 20: 63, but also 2: 177 (*wal-ṣābirīn*: *ṣābirūn*), 4: 162 (*wal-muqīmīn*: *muqīmūn*), and 5: 69 (*wal-ṣābi'ūn*: *ṣābi'īn*), could be and often were emended in this way.[7] Other problems, semantic rather than grammatical, might be exposed to the same treatment, e.g. Q. 56: 29 (*wa-ṭalʿin manḍūdin* for *wa-ṭalḥin*).[8]

[1] See above, III p. 108, referring to *Itqān* ii, 277–80.
[2] *Itqān* ii, 273–4.
[3] *Ta'wīl*, 36–7; see Jeffery, *Materials*, 146 and 60, respectively.
[4] See above, pp. 203–7.
[5] Ibn Qutayba, *Ta'wīl*, 37; see *GdQ* iii, 4–5.
[6] *Majāz al-Qur'ān* ii, 21–3; see Wansbrough, 'Periphrastic exegesis', 264.
[7] e.g. Ibn Qutayba, *Ta'wīl*, 37; see above, III p. 108.
[8] Goldziher, *Richtungen*, 36; Zamakhsharī adduced a scriptural analogy from Q. 50: 10, *Kashshāf* iv, 461 ad loc.

The masoretic principle of כתיב : קרי was perpetuated in the لفظ : كتبة (قراءة : كتاب) of the Muslim exegetes. Its application in the Quranic masorah may, in my opinion, be ascribed to calque rather than to inherent necessity. The methodological significance of such devices as *ketib*:*qere* and *al tiqra* is generally seen to be evidence of a fixed, immutable text.[1] For the text of Muslim scripture standard deviations were anyway accommodated by the system of 'canonical' readings, within which a distinction between *kitba* and *lafẓ* merely symbolized an option (*ikhtiyār*).[2] It will, I think, be conceded that formulation of the Biblical masorah included a period in which emendation to a still fluid text was not only possible, but in fact took place. The activities attributed specifically to the post-Talmudic masoretes exhibit only the final expression of a long and complex process, to which elements of the masorah like *tiqqunei soferim* and *miqra soferim* attest.[3] For the Quranic masorah the concept of emendation is explicit in the principle of *majāz* as employed by Abū 'Ubayda: for the solecism in Q. 20: 63 the *qere* (*lafẓ*) was expressly 'correct' (*ṣawāb*). But emendation was not by any means limited to, perhaps not even primarily concerned with, irregularities of grammar and syntax. Exegetical, often dogmatic, ends were equally served. One example, *ad* Q. 37: 12, has been noticed;[4] another was the alteration of *allāhu* to *allāha* in Q. 4: 164, producing 'Moses spoke to God' rather than 'God spoke to Moses', a change reflecting Muʿtazilī circumscription of the notion of God's speech.[5] However, very few of Abū 'Ubayda's sixty *shawāhid* required to be emended for reasons of dogma or doctrine.[6]

Masoretic *majāz*, like the grammarians' principle of *taqdīr*, had been formulated primarily with a view to obviating the angularities of scriptural syntax. The norm against which such were measured was often provided by scripture itself, but also and with increasing frequency by the data of profane literature. These might consist either of real, or contrived, examples of the *usus loquendi* (introduced by *qawluka*, *ka-qawlika*), or of *loci probantes* from Arabic poetry.[7] In support of the dialectal origins of *hādhāni* in Q. 20: 63, for instance, Ibn Qutayba adduced two lines of

[1] e.g. Barr, *Comparative Philology*, 45–6, 214–17; cf. Würthwein, *Text*, 12–22, 71–5.

[2] See above, pp. 205–7; and cf. Rabin's reference to the 'limited variability' of the text of scripture attested also in Qumran, cited Gerhardsson, *Memory*, 37 n. 2.

[3] See Barr, op. cit., 219–21; Gerhardsson, *Memory*, 33–42, 43–55; and Gertner, 'The Masorah and the Levites', 266–70.

[4] See above, p. 206.

[5] See above, I pp. 34–6, II pp. 81–4; Goldziher, *Richtungen*, 174–5: a more radical solution to the dogmatic problem which did not require textual emendation was derivation of *kallama* in this passage from *kalm* (wound); cf. Zamakhsharī, *Kashshāf* i, 590–1; but also Ibn Qutayba, *Ta'wīl*, 82.

[6] Wansbrough, 'Periphrastic exegesis', 256: three instances only, to which may be added, under no. 30, Q. 79: 30; see above, p. 220.

[7] See above, pp. 211–12, 216–18; and Wild, *Das Kitāb al-ʿAin*, 44 n. 16.

verse (anonymous) demonstrating the expression of both *casus rectus* and *obliquus* (dual) with *alif*.[1] The eventual opposition, hardly unexpected, to that technique,[2] found unequivocal expression in the observation of Ibn Munayyir to Zamakhsharī's commentary *ad* Q. 6: 137: وليس غرضنا تصحيح القراءة بقواعد العربية بل تصحيح قواعد العربية بالقراءة (Our purpose is not correction of scripture by reference to Arabic grammar, but, rather, correction/establishment of Arabic grammar by reference to scripture).[3] It need hardly be remarked, in view of the role played by 'Arabian eloquence' in Quranic theology, that this admonition remained a very dead letter indeed. Lip-service to an ideal had, however, been expressed.[4]

Another exclusively interpretative element of the Quranic masorah, and hence one which did not always require textual emendation, concerned the problem of juncture. An example was the question of pause after *kadhālika* in the messenger formula كذلك قال ربّك (قال/قالوا) (Q. 19: 9, 19: 21, 51: 30).[5] The alternatives were to read with pause making the particle disjunctive, or without pause acknowledging the formulaic locution, i.e. כה אמר יהוה. Zamakhsharī appears to have preferred the former كذلك الكاف رفع أى الأمر كذلك تصديق له ثم ابتدأ قال ربّك أو نصب بقال.[6] The term for disjunctive syntax (Zamakhsharī employed *ibtadā'*) was usually *isti'nāf*, found already in Muqātil's *Tafsīr ad* Q. 3: 7, for which verse of course the argument was doctrinal and not at all syntactical.[7] In his chapter on juncture (*al-mawṣūl lafẓan wal-mafṣūl maʿnan*) Suyūṭī provided several illustrations of that kind of theological grammar.[8] For Q. 7: 189–90 the charge of polytheism against Adam and Eve was made quite explicit by context (*siyāq*). But Adam was a prophet (*nabī'*) and therefore immune from sin (*maʿṣūm*). A solution to the dilemma was found in the change of pronoun from dual to plural, making the referent of فتعالى الله عما يشركون not the inhabitants of Eden but the pagans of Mecca. Suyūṭī called the trope thus isolated an example of 'transition and digression' (*al-takhalluṣ wal-istiṭrād*),[9] ignoring conveniently the distinct likelihood that the form *yushrikūn* reflected the pattern of verse segmentation at that point of the *sūra*. On the other hand, it may be argued that not merely

[1] Ibn Qutayba, *Ta'wīl*, 36.
[2] e.g. Suyūṭī, *Itqān* ii, 55.
[3] Ibn Munayyir, *Intiṣāf*, on the margin of *Kashshāf* ii, 69–70; cited also Goldziher, *Richtungen*, 50 n. 3; Ullmann, *Rağazpoesie*, 222–3 n. 10; see above, p. 168.
[4] See above, II pp. 78–81.
[5] See above, I pp. 12–13.
[6] *Kashshāf* iii, 6 *ad* Q. 19: 9.
[7] See above, p. 152; appearance of the technical term *isti'nāf* in Muqātil, *Tafsīr*, MS H. Hüsnü 17, 36r, may well be a consequence of later redaction, cf. above, pp. 143–4.
[8] *Itqān, nawʿ* 29: i, 252–4, an appendix to his discussion of pausal phenomena (*al-waqf wal-ibtidā'*): *nawʿ* 28: i, 230–51.
[9] See Mehren, *Rhetorik*, 130, 145.

the plural *yushrikūn* but the entire locution exhibits a formula of periodization, and need not therefore be semantically related to the preceding Adam tradition.[1]

Easily the most celebrated of such passages was Q. 106: 1 لإيلاف قريش, for which the function of *lām* as inchoative provoked some very imaginative grammatical theory.[2] To those disatisfied with exegesis, textual emendation was possible: *Sūra*s 105 and 106 were read as a syntactical unit, for which of course support could be found in a 'companion' codex (i.e. Ubayy).[3] But however the two *sūra*s were written (generally with the disjunctive *basmala*) they were understood as a narrative unit attesting to God's benevolence towards Quraysh.[4] Problems of the sort found at Q. 106: 1 have also been noted in the transmission history of the Biblical text, e.g. כספסגים vs. כסף סיגים in Proverbs 26: 23, described by Barr as a 'graphic disturbance'.[5] Ellipses and anacolutha in the Quranic text often exhibit illogical juncture rather than defective syntax: for example, Abū 'Ubayda's inclusion under ellipsis (no. 3) of Q. 39: 73, in which the second dependent clause of the *ḥattā idhā* construction is the following verse, introduced by the coordinate (!) conjunction *waw*.[6]

Abū 'Ubayda's contribution to the Quranic masorah consisted primarily in the rationalization of solecism, but also in the resolution of synthesis and the alleviation of ellipsis. The periphrastic technique, later designated *taqdīr*, was also applied to the resolution of trope (a kind of inverse metaphor, as for Q. 12: 82) and to the elimination of anthropomorphism.[7] For the history of the text of scripture one question in particular requires at least to be articulated, if not answered: was the principle of *majāz/taqdīr* understood as emendation or as exegesis? Now, copies of the Qur'ān, whether manuscript or printed, do not contain masoretic material, and may for that very reason be misleading: the impression is unmistakably that of a single *ne varietur* text. But even the most cursory examination of the masoretic literature must dispel that impression as illusory. The chronology of that literature indicates a period of approximately two

[1] See above, III pp. 113, 115, 117.

[2] Analysed in Birkeland, *The Lord guideth*, 102–30.

[3] Suyūṭī, *Itqān* i, 186; Jeffery, *Materials*, 179; sectarian appropriation of that view is significant only as an expression of opposition to the 'Uthmanic recension, cf. *GdQ* ii, 33 n. 4, 96 n. 3.

[4] e.g. Ibn Qutayba, *Ta'wīl*, 319–20; and Birkeland's interpretation, op. cit. 122–30: 'God's intervention in history as the first stage of Muhammad's prophetical experience'.

[5] *Comparative Philology*, 219; cf. also Gertner, 'The Masorah and the Levites', 247 for Exodus 23: 2.

[6] See above, III pp. 114–15; Wansbrough, 'Periphrastic exegesis', 248, 255; Brockelmann's explanation of that phenomenon, *GVG* ii, 669, as 'die Neigung des semitischen Sprachgeistes zu einfacher Satzbildung eine komplizierte Periode wieder in einfache Formen (zu zerlegen)' cannot, in my opinion, be supported by Quranic examples.

[7] Wansbrough, op. cit. 254–9.

centuries during which the text of scripture was anything but stable. The major obstacle to reconstruction of the transmission history of that period is the character of the so-called 'variant readings', which is predominantly exegetical: in other words all, or almost all, are clearly interpretations of the canon. Within the masorah their relative merits were assessed according to their respective degrees of attestation. The *apparatus criticus* resulting from such accumulation of essentially uniform materials exhibits a series of conventional modifications of one text. At the same time it conceals, and may have been meant to conceal (by means of the 'serial revelation' argument),[1] the fundamental lines of cleavage that I have called 'variant traditions'. But indirect notice of these may be thought to underlie the masoretic categories of *wujūh*, *naẓā'ir*, *mushtabihāt*, and *majāz*. Collation of parallel and divergent contexts, deductions from analogical and identical phraseology, rationalization of grammatical and syntactic irregularities: all of these presuppose a consciousness of recurring formulae and schemata. According to the theoretical postulates of the grammarians, a restored text (*muqaddar*) was at least as valid as its original articulation (*malfūẓ*).[2] Preservation and transmission of those restorations were for the masoretes tasks equal in importance to recording the canonical text.[3] The 'limited variability' of the canon was a fact, the 'Uthmanic recension an article of faith. As such, exegesis and emendation might be seen as two names for the same process, and not as mutually exclusive. Like the halakhic concept of preference (*tarjīḥ*), the masoretic principle of option (*ikhtiyār*) contained an arbitrary element which never had to conform to a single, fixed text.

And yet one feature of masoretic exegesis, as contrasted with the haggadic and halakhic types, was the practice of adducing and (usually) of commenting on the entire text of scripture. A concern for the integrity of the text and for the structural relevance to one another of its parts was characteristic even of purely lexical analysis. For the analogical restoration of grammar and syntax it was indispensable. The 'framework' of masoretic exegesis was thus neither the *narratio* (haggadic) nor the juridical/doctrinal dispute (halakhic), but the canonical text itself, perceived as a unitary document. Within that framework 'explicative elements' like *variae lectiones*, lexical and grammatical explanation, analogy, periphrasis, and *loci probantes* from poetry were typical.[4] All other elements may be regarded as intrusive, and none more than authentication of the masorah (i.e. as *apparatus criticus*) by reference to traditions and to the circumstances of revelation. That such should, none the less, figure in this genre of exegetical literature demonstrates, in my opinion, the chronological priority of the halakhah, in support of which a basis of traditional authority

[1] See above, I pp. 36–8.
[2] Wansbrough, op. cit., 257, 264–5.
[3] See above, pp. 204–5.
[4] See above, pp. 120–1.

(i.e. masorah) had to be formulated. In this context Gertner's description of the separate origins and later juxtaposition/identification of *Masorah* and *Masoreth* is of some interest for the analogous process in Muslim exegetical literature, namely, the evaluation of rationally deduced (!) 'readings' in terms of their respective degrees of attestation (the evolution *dirāya* → *riwāya*).[1] It was only after the articulation of law as divinely decreed that a scriptural canon was established, the result primarily of polemical pressure.[2] Once stabilized, the document of revelation was no longer exclusively the 'word of God' but also, and equally important, a monument of the national literature. In that capacity its service to the community, and to the cause of polemic, was unlimited.

5. RHETORIC AND ALLEGORY IN EXEGESIS

Acknowledgement of metaphor in the language of scripture could be as much an expression of piety as of aesthetic appreciation. Elimination of anthropomorphic imagery predicated of God was the primary form of that piety, practised by both Quranic and Biblical exegetes.[3] But whatever the original motive, exegetical speculation was ultimately coupled with recognition of scripture as the articulation of literary forms and related to an attested rhetorical tradition. For example, both the obvious and quite unnecessary insertion (*majāz*) of *ahl* into Q. 12: 82 and the not so obvious but equally unnecessary insertion (*taqdīr*) of *amr* into Q. 89: 22[4] were adduced by Sharīf Murtaḍā (d. 436/1044) as illustration of the particular capacity for figurative expression (*majāzāt*) of the Arabic language:[5] اعلم أن من عادة العرب الإيجاز والاختصار والحذف طلبا لتقصير الكلام واطراح فضوله والاستغناء بقليله عن كثره . . . وأنت إذا تأملت ضروب المجازات التى يتصرف فيها أهل اللسان فى منظومهم ومنثورهم وجدتَها كلها مبينة على الحذف والاختصار ولان قوله تعالى وجاء ربّك (89: 22) واسأل القرية (12: 82) مما الحذف فيه ظاهر. Stress in that passage lay on the qualities of conciseness (*ījāz*), brevity (*ikhtiṣār*), and ellipsis (*ḥadhf*) inherent in Arabic, thought for that reason *inter alia* to be superior to other languages. The shift of emphasis by means of which those and other phenomena of the scriptural style became points of departure for the elaboration of an extended corpus of literary theory is the subject of this, the concluding, section of these studies.

The standard apologia for figurative usage in scripture would seem to

[1] Gertner, op. cit., esp. 255–9. [2] See above, pp. 158–63, 194–5, 201–2.

[3] See Wansbrough, 'Periphrastic exegesis', 259 (Ibn Ḥazm), 262, 264 (Saadya), 266 (Maimonides); cf. Goldziher, *Richtungen*, 116 nn. 2, 3, 7.

[4] Wansbrough, op. cit. 254–5, 257, 259.

[5] *GAL* i, 404–5, Suppl. I, 704–6; *Amālī* ii (Takmila), 309–11.

presuppose an expressly formulated opposition to such, and occasionally indeed, that opposition was identified with scholars of the Ẓāhirī, Mālikī, or Ḥanbalī schools.[1] In fact, even the alleged opponents of Quranic *majāz* were constrained, when confronted by anthropomorphisms at least, to resort to exegetical devices like *taqdīr* for the resolution of metaphor.[2] The apologia was none the less articulated, in a form both simple and effective, by Ibn Qutayba:[3] وأما الطاعنون على القرآن بالمجاز فانّهم زعموا انه كذب لانّ الجدار لايريد (18: 77) والقرية لا تُسأل (12: 82) وهذا من أشنع جهالاتهم وأدلّها على سوء نظرهم وقلة أفهامهم ولو كان المجاز كذبا وكل فعل يُنسب الى غير الحيوان باطلا — كان أكثر كلامنا فاسدا لانّا نقول نبت البقل وطالت الشجرة وأينعت الثمرة وأقام الجبل ورخص السعر. The truism that for the mimetic function of speech metaphor was indispensable symbolized formal and collective recognition of an exegetical factor common both to halakhic dispute (*ikhtilāf*) and to masoretic emendation (*majāz*), namely that language could not be construed as having merely or exclusively an immediate (verifiable and quantifiable) relation to the data of experience it purportedly described. A good deal of halakhic exegesis turned upon that very point: e.g. derivation of a series of graded punishments for *muḥāribūn* from the syntactic sequence of Q. 5: 33,[4] or the (perhaps) extreme argument according to which a blind husband could be excluded from the provisions of Numbers 5: 13.[5] For the Quranic masorah, Abū ʿUbayda's *majāz*, when not directed to flagrant examples of grammatical irregularity, was applied to idiom and conventionally ambiguous usage, rather than to the analysis of metaphor as consciously formulated imagery.[6] Ibn Qutayba's monograph on the style of scripture exhibits the transitional employment of *majāz*: from an interpretative device to an aesthetic category.

The earlier sections of that work are concerned primarily to refute allegations of solecism (*laḥn*) and contradiction (*tanāquḍ*) in the text of scripture, and belong thus almost entirely to the masoretic tradition (i.e. chapters I–V) as exemplified by Farrā' and Abū ʿUbayda.[7] It is in the middle sections (i.e. chapters VI–XII) that the author treated the phenomena of figurative language, after a general discussion, under six headings:[8] metaphor, inversion, ellipsis, repetition and pleonasm, metonymy and

[1] e.g. Suyūṭī, *Itqān* iii, 109.

[2] e.g. Ibn Ḥazm, see Goldziher, *Ẓāhiriten*, 164–8.

[3] Ibn Qutayba, *Ta'wīl*, 99.

[4] See above, pp. 187–8.

[5] Gertner, 'Terms', 20.

[6] See above, p. 220.

[7] *Ta'wīl*, 10–75; see above, p. 221 n. 1.

[8] *Ta'wīl*, 76–229 subdivided: general (76–101), metaphor (102–41), inversion (142–61), ellipsis (162–79), repetition and pleonasm (180–98), metonymy and allusion (199–212), idiom (213–29).

allusion, idiom. At only one point (though admittedly conceivable in a number of other similar contexts) did he employ the locution *wa-majāzuhu* in the manner of Abū ʿUbayda (i.e. 'and its restoration is' or 'and it ought to read'), namely, for the not very problematic expression سنفرغ لكم Q. 55: 31, interpreted as 'And we will attend to you (*scil.* after long neglect and delay)'.[1] That for Ibn Qutayba *majāz* did not only signify metaphor (*istiʿāra*) is clear not merely from the organization of his *loci probantes* but from his express declaration: ونبدأ بباب الاستعارة لان أكثر المجاز يقع فيه.[2] His illustrations of *istiʿāra* range from examples of genuinely tropical usage, like the expression يوم يُكشَف عن ساق in Q. 68: 42, in which 'shank' is a metaphor for resolution/energy (أى عن شدة من الأمر: شمّر عن ساقه فاستعيرت الساق فى موضع الشدة),[3] across the onomatopoeic ejaculation *uff* in Q. 17: 23, explained as an instance of synaesthetic formation (وأصل هذا نفخك للشئ يسقط عليك من تراب أو رماد وغير ذلك),[4] to the standard example of ellipsis in Q. 12: 82.[5] In view of the ubiquity as *locus probans* of Q. 12: 82 in exegetical literature, it is worth recording that this and other instances of ellipsis (*ḥadhf*) were not, when unaccompanied by a change in *iʿrāb*, considered to qualify as figurative usage by the major theorist of Arabic rhetoric, ʿAbd al-Qāhir Jurjānī (d. 471/1078).[6] That argument, applied also to pleonasm (*ziyāda*),[7] drew attention to the essentially stylistic function of both phenomena by stressing the intentional dislocation of the entire utterance. Ellipsis and pleonasm were thus regarded as tropes and required to be appreciated, rather than merely clarified or emended. Ibn Qutayba's inclusion of Q. 12: 82 under metaphor (*istiʿāra*) might be thought evidence of a similar, if somewhat less sophisticated, point of view. The fact that Q. 12: 82, together with 2: 177 and 47: 13, was adduced also in his section on abbreviation/ellipsis (*ikhtiṣār/ḥadhf*) may betoken some indecision about that construction.[8] But the position of Ibn Qutayba in the evolution of rhetorical exegesis is, in my opinion, transitional, though his precise description of the nature of the ellipsis in Q. 12: 82 corresponds to that of Jurjānī, i.e. أن تحذف المضاف وتقيم المضاف اليه مقامه وتجعل الفعل له. It was that connection of ellipsis and pleonasm with syntactic function (*iʿrāb*) which was preserved in the exegetical tradition.[9]

[1] *Ta'wīl*, 77.
[2] *Ta'wīl*, 101; cf. provisional definition of *majāzāt fil-kalām*, 15–16.
[3] *Ta'wīl*, 103.
[4] *Ta'wīl*, 111.
[5] *Ta'wīl*, 129, applied also to Q. 44: 29 and 47: 4.
[6] *GAL* i, 341–2, Suppl. I, 503–4; *Asrār al-Balāgha*, paras. 26/1–3; see Wansbrough, 'Periphrastic exegesis', 255 n. 10.
[7] Jurjānī, *Asrār*, paras. 26/4–10.
[8] *Ta'wīl*, 162.
[9] e.g. Suyūṭī, *Itqān* iii, 124–5, citing Zanjānī and Qazwīnī.

Ibn Qutayba's second category of *majāz* includes two kinds of 'inversion' (*maqlūb*): one semantic, the other syntactic. The first consists primarily of locutions *per antiphrasin* (ومن المقلوب أن يوصف الشئ بضدّ صفته) employed as omen (*taṭayyur/tafā'ul*) particularly in onomastica, but also as hyperbole (*mubālagha*) and ridicule (*istihzā'*). An example of hyperbolic usage, or more correctly perhaps of litotes, was *ẓann* (conjecture) for *yaqīn* (certainty) in contexts of eschatological reference, in which of course there could be no question of 'doubt', e.g. Q. 2: 249, 18: 53, 69: 20.[1] Syntactic inversion, on the other hand, was for Ibn Qutayba hyperbaton, as in Q. 3: 40 'And old age has overtaken me' for 'I have attained old age'.[2] Although he appears to have denied presence in the Qur'ān of hysteron proteron (*maqlūb 'alā 'l-ghalaṭ*),[3] the inclusion of recognized 'problem passages' like Q. 2: 171 and 28: 76, as well as 18: 1–2, must be interpreted as tacit acknowledgement of such.[4] None of the three exhibits the rhetorical embellishment illustrated by Q. 3: 40.

Similarly, Ibn Qutayba's eight kinds of ellipsis include several examples of the rhetorically effective omission of an apodosis, e.g. in a hypothetical construction (Q. 13: 31), and in an oath (Q. 50: 1).[5] But ellipsis is also represented by zeugma, e.g. Q. 10: 71 and 17: 23, and also by sheer carelessness, e.g. Q. 38: 32 and 97: 1.[6] Mention there of the synthetic construction in Q. 83: 3 (*wazanūhum* for *wazanū lahum*) can only be understood as a survival from the masoretic tradition.[7]

In his treatment of repetition and pleonasm (*takrār wa-ziyāda*) the author distinguished on the one hand repetition of narrative passages, duly related to the doctrine of 'serial' revelation (*munajjaman/nujūman*),[8] and on the other, the verbatim repetition of specific locutions, as in *Sūra*s 55 and 109.[9] Reason for both, as for repetition of single words in verses like Q. 2: 196 and 7: 12, was emphasis and drill (*tawkīd wa-ifhām*), a view of that particular Quranic phenomenon which has informed all subsequent scholarship.[10] Unlike Jurjānī, Ibn Qutayba applied the term *ziyāda* exclusively to (in his opinion) otiose elements like the particle *bi* in Q. 96: 1,[11] but also the word *wajh* (face) in Q. 2: 115, 6: 52, 28: 88, and 76: 9,

[1] *Ta'wīl*, 142–4.
[2] *Ta'wīl*, 149.
[3] *Ta'wīl*, 154.
[4] *Ta'wīl*, 153–8; cf. Wansbrough, 'Periphrastic exegesis', 251–2 (nos. 24 and 25), and above, p. 220; Zamakhsharī, *Kashshāf* ii, 702 *ad* Q. 18: 1–2.
[5] *Ta'wīl*, 165, 173, respectively.
[6] *Ta'wīl*, 164, 167, and 174; the pronominal reference in Q. 97: 1 was in fact a matter of doctrinal significance, see above, II p. 62.
[7] Cf. Wansbrough, op. cit., 253 (no. 31) and 256.
[8] See above, I pp. 36–8.
[9] *Ta'wīl*, 180–2; see above, I pp. 25–6.
[10] See above, III pp. 111–12.
[11] Thus also Abū 'Ubayda, see Wansbrough, op. cit., 253 (no. 33) and 257.

exhibiting of course neither grammatical nor rhetorical, but rather doctrinal concern for the anthropomorphic attribute.[1]

Allusion (*taʿrīḍ*) was terminologically distinguished from metonymy (*kināya*), though Ibn Qutayba's analysis of the two was, rightly, synoptic.[2] The latter includes the *kunya* itself (onomastic), the kind of allusion commonly resolved by haggadic *taʿyīn*, e.g. *fulānan* in Q. 25: 28,[3] and finally, the generic application of the definite article, e.g. *al-ẓālim* in Q. 25: 27 or *al-kāfir* in Q. 78: 40. The last represented a rhetorical elaboration of the halakhic *khuṣūṣ*/*ʿumūm* argumentation.[4] For Ibn Qutayba, *taʿrīḍ* itself meant the kind of euphemism exhibited in Q. 18: 73 or the circumspection of Q. 34: 24. In both passages harshness was alleviated by recourse to circumlocution, but not to the extent of suppressing altogether the facts of 'forgetting/forgetfulness' and 'error/sin', respectively. The opposite of *taʿrīḍ* in that sense was *taṣrīḥ*; its synonym was *tawriya* (ورّى عن ذكرهم).[5] Of some interest for the development of rhetorical exegesis is comparison of Ibn Qutayba's treatment of Q. 34: 24 with Abū 'Ubayda's grammatical *cum* dogmatic 'restoration'.[6]

It is in the section dealing with idiomatic expressions (entitled مخالفة ظاهر اللفظ معناه) that Ibn Qutayba adhered most closely to the masoretic tradition, treating in turn problems of morphology, tempora, juncture, number, and specification.[7] Three other elements belong more properly to rhetorical analysis: (*a*) imprecation as divine utterance (e.g. *qātalahumu 'llāh* in Q. 9: 30) was interpreted as hypothetical; (*b*) rhetorical questions were analysed as signifying affirmation (*taqrīr*, as in Q. 20: 17), wonder (*taʿajjub*), or reproach (*tawbīkh*); (*c*) prohibitives/imperatives might convey threat (*tahdīd*), admonition (*ta'dīb*), even exemption (*ibāḥa*, as in Q. 62: 10).[8] Thus, *majāz* in the work of Ibn Qutayba, as for Saadya, might be understood to include not only trope, but also idiom and popular usage.[9] That the latter should be subsumed under the general rubric of rhetorical device may, in my view, be attributed to the dominant role of scriptural exegesis in the elaboration of Arabic literary theory. As in philology, so in rhetoric the tyranny of *lingua sacra* was not merely felt, but found expression as a criterion of excellence. However the dogma of *iʿjāz*

[1] Cf. Saadya *ad* Psalm 88: 15, in Wansbrough, op. cit. 264.

[2] *Ta'wīl*, 199–204; that pattern of exposition was characteristic also of the later theorists, see von Grunebaum, *Tenth-century Document*, 38–9 n. 297.

[3] See above, pp. 135–6.

[4] See above, pp. 169–70, 191.

[5] *Ta'wīl*, 210, but also the entire section, 204–12; thus considerably earlier than Zamakhsharī, *pace* Bonebakker, *Tawriya*, 27–8.

[6] Wansbrough, op. cit. 256–7.

[7] *Ta'wīl*, 213–29: morphology (228–9), tempora (227–8), juncture (226–7), number (218–26), specification (217–18).

[8] *Ta'wīl*, 213–15, 215–16, 216–17, respectively.

[9] Wansbrough, op. cit. 265–6: references in nn. 79–80.

al-Qur'ān was interpreted (theologically or rhetorically or both), comparison of the profane and sacred styles was inevitable. A perfect illustration of the double standard applied to such comparison was the observation of Bāqillānī about a line from Imru' 'l-Qays: that لما نسجتها من جنوب وشمال ought to have read . . . . . لما نسجها, and that even poetic licence could hardly justify interpretation of the pronoun *mā* as feminine.[1] Now, in the light of such examples of wayward concord as Abū 'Ubayda's nos. 34 and 35, that stricture must appear harsh if not perverse.[2] But Bāqillanī's contribution to the science of rhetoric was marginal indeed: it was his merit as a theologian to formulate the *i'jāz* argument in terms borrowed from the works of contemporary rhetorists, but not without the over-simplification inherent in synthesis.[3]

With its application to the scriptural style, rhetorical terminology exhibited evidence both of mutation and of proliferation. Much of that was the consequence of seeking, and finding, in the text of scripture at least one example of every figure known to the profane tradition. A trace of embarrassment, not quite concealed even in the assertive and confident approach of Bāqillānī, led to increasing terminological differentiation in order to prove the divine origin of all rhetorical device. A minor but none the less significant illustration of that process was the evolution of the trope known as *madhhab kalāmī*: from conceit to the syllogistic formulation called enthymeme.[4] The figure itself appears to have been originally the paronomastic epigram, of which a most artful example was composed and included in his rhetorical treatise by Ibn al-Mu'tazz (d. 296/908):[5]

أسرفتُ فى الكتمان   وذلك منّى دهانى
كتمتُ حبّك حتى   كتمتُ كتمانى
ولم يكن لى بدّ   من ذكره بلسانى

Now, to locate in the document of Muslim revelation so cunning an artifice as that would have required considerable ingenuity, and it is hardly surprising that the earliest theorists, e.g. Jāḥiẓ and Ibn al-Mu'tazz himself, denied its presence there.[6] When eventually the *madhhab kalāmī* was discovered to be of scriptural origin, the figure had altered quite beyond recognition, the work of two late scholastic theorists: Ibn Abī 'l-Iṣba' (d. 654/1256) and Khatīb Qazwīnī (d. 738/1338). The *locus classicus* was Q. 21: 22 لو كان فيهما ألهة الا الله لفسدتا (If there were in them, *scil.* heaven

[1] Bāqillānī, *I'jāz al-Qur'ān*, 161; trans. von Grunebaum, *Tenth-century Document*, 63.
[2] Wansbrough, op. cit. 253.
[3] See von Grunebaum, *Tenth-century Document*, 6 n. 43; id., *Kritik*, 87–100: the 'missing work' (97) is Ibn Wahb, *Burhān*, cf. *BSOAS* xxxiii (1970) 616.
[4] See Wansbrough, 'Note', 55–63.
[5] *GAL* i, 81; *Kitāb al-badī'*, 56; trans. Wansbrough, 'Note', 59.
[6] *Kitāb al-badī'*, 53.

and earth, gods other than God, both would have perished), that verse being interpreted as an argument for a single author of creation. The transition from epigram to dialectic (with the suppressed middle term characteristic of the philosophers' enthymeme) can only be explained by reference to the earlier inclusion under *madhhab kalāmī* of parodistic compositions ridiculing the language of philosophers and theologians.[1] In the search for Quranic *shawāhid* the element of parody had naturally been ignored, or forgotten, and each example exhibited, at least vaguely, a kind of apodictic syllogism: e.g. since the repetition of divine creation is easier than creation itself, it (*scil.* resurrection) is *ipso facto* possible (Q. 30: 27); the moon may vanish, but God does not vanish and therefore the moon cannot be God (Q. 6: 76); you are punished, but the sons (of God) are not punished, therefore you are not sons of God (Q. 5: 18).[2] For Ibn Abī 'l-Iṣbaʿ, Q. 21: 104 and all related assertions of the resurrection were employed to illustrate the *madhhab kalāmī*, the arguments an elaboration of the type employed by Qazwīnī for Q. 30: 27.[3] It seems unlikely that *madhhab kalāmī* would, without the challenge offered by scripture, have evolved much beyond its employment as caricature of technical jargon, e.g.[4]

فيك خلاف لخلاف الذى   فيه خلاف لخلاف الجميل

or

محاسنه هيولى كل حسن   ومغناطيس أفئدة الرجال

Application of the term to so serious a subject as arguments in support of monotheism (the theme common to all of the scriptural *shawāhid*) might be thought to require a very sharp divergence of the profane and sacred rhetorical traditions.[5] It could even be argued that description of the phenomenon as exegetical appropriation of a profane *terminus technicus* is facile and simplistic.[6]

Rather more complex than the mutation of *madhhab kalāmī* was the rhetorical-exegetical development of the figure originally called *tafsīr*.[7] While for *madhhab kalāmī* retention of one name for three separate phenomena might justify a hypothesis of adaptation, the evolution of *tafsīr* into *laff wa-nashr* (*inter alia*: *versus rapportati*) involved changes in form, content, and nomenclature. The specifically exegetical residue from that compound process consisted of two Quranic constructions: the first

[1] Wansbrough, 'Note', 58–62.
[2] Qazwīnī, *Īḍāḥ*, in *Shurūḥ al-talkhīṣ* iv, 369–70.
[3] Ibn Abī 'l-Iṣbaʿ, *Badīʿ al-Qurʾān*, 37–42; Suyūṭī, *Itqān* iv, 52–5.
[4] Subkī, *ʿArūs*, in *Shurūḥ al-talkhīṣ* iv, 372–3.
[5] Cf. Goldziher, *Ẓāhiriten*, 133.
[6] Cf. Wansbrough, 'Qur'anic exegesis', 469–70: it seems to me unlikely that Ibn Athīr's *maʿnā 'l-ṣanʿa* can have signified more than 'schemata' in general, cf. Heinrichs, *Arabische Dichtung*, 91 n. 3.
[7] Wansbrough, 'Qur'anic exegesis', 469–85.

represented by Q. 28: 73 ومن رحمته جعل لكم الليل والنهار لتسكنوا فيه ولتبتغوا من فضله and 30: 23 ومن آياته منامكم بالليل والنهار وابتغاؤكم من فضله; the second by 2: 111 وقالوا لن يدخل الجنة الا من كان هودا أو نصارى and 2: 185 . . . فمن شهد منكم الشهر فليصمه ومن كان مريضا أو على سفر الآية.[1] The syntactic phenomenon, of which the types were respectively designated *mufaṣṣal* (separate/diffuse) and *mujmal* (composite), was nothing more than a proposition containing a gloss in the form of a subordinate clause. Hence, its original name: *tafsīr* (*subnexio*). The difference between the *mufaṣṣal* and *mujmal* varieties lay in the ratio of elements in the gloss to those/that of the referent: in the former there were two or more in each, in the latter two or three in the gloss to one in the referent. Frequently adduced, and certainly the most graphic illustration of the *mujmal* construction was Q. 13: 12 وهو الذى يريكم البرق خوفا وطمعا.[2] Now, the exegetical moment in the *tafsīr*/*laff wa-nashr* evolution was not quite the same as that in the development of *madhhab kalamī*. In the latter the evidence suggested that Quranic *loci* had at all costs to be found for every component of rhetorical *ornatus* (*badīʿ*);[3] in the former a genuine problem of scriptural syntax, subtly identified with a trope well established in profane literature, was lent a kind of rhetorical legitimacy. One element common to both problems, however, deserves notice, namely justification of *lingua sacra* by reference to the data of profane rhetoric. In practice at least, if not in theory.[4]

For a figure conventionally represented by sequences of multiple imagery, e.g.

كيف أسلو وأنت حقف وغصن   وغزال لحظا وقدا وردفا

the role of *mujmal* constructions in exegesis remained oddly anomalous, despite the likelihood that the exegetical *laff wa-nashr* owed its name, if not its very existence, to just such constructions.[5] Scholastic elaboration of the figure produced a number of useful modifications designed to accommodate an infinitely variable ratio of gloss-elements to referent-elements, e.g. *jamʿ*, *tafrīq*, *taqsīm*, and combinations of all three.[6] The sharply defined distinctions between adverbial and relative constructions, and between explicit and implicit connection of gloss with referent, were thus gradually attenuated.[7] The final synthesis included apposition as well as attribution and predication, so long as either referent or gloss contained at least two elements. All such phenomena could be covered by the term *tafsīr*, if not always by

[1] Wansbrough, op. cit. 478–82.

[2] Wansbrough, op. cit. 475.

[3] Thus, the work of Ibn Abī ʾl-Iṣbaʿ might be described as the consummation of that begun by Ibn al-Muʿtazz.

[4] See above, p. 224.

[5] Wansbrough, op. cit. 471, 481–3.

[6] Set out in Qazwīnī, *Talkhīṣ*, in *Shurūḥ al-talkhīṣ* iv, 329–47; Mehren, *Rhetorik*, 108–11.

[7] Wansbrough, op. cit. 477–80, 483–4.

laff wa-nashr. That '*tafsīr*' was as much the product of concern for rhetoric as for 'interpretation' in general seems certain.[1] The polarity represented by *tafsīr*:*ta'wīl*, obscured in most varieties of exegetical literature, was for the most part maintained in rhetorical exegesis.

In the *Amālī* of Sharīf Murtaḍā, for example, *ta'wīl* is employed throughout for the interpretation of scripture, of tradition (*ḥadīth*), and of historical reports (*akhbār*), while *tafsīr* designates, at least in the Supplement (*takmila*), the interpretation of poetry. The essentially literary character of that work is evident even in its external structure (*āmālī*/*majālis*), within which the analysis of poetry was skilfully and felicitously blended with that of the three basic forms of Arabic prose.[2] Despite predilection for Muʿtazilī authorities and reasoning, the author's generosity in matters of dogmatic controversy is ubiquitously apparent, and quite explicit in his observations on the question of juncture in Q. 3: 7: even if the *rāsikhūn* were syntactically separated from *allāh*, and such was by no means necessary, it was essential to recall that their exegesis could in many instances be no more than conjectural.[3] Murtaḍā's method was to adduce all possible aspects (*wujūh*) equally weighted and documented, an example of which may be seen in his five proposals for reconstruction of the problematic syntax of Q. 2: 171.[4] Only one of these required acknowledgement of the equivalence *fāʿil*:*mafʿūl* (as in Abū ʿUbayda), a typically masoretic device; the others reflected solutions of common sense based upon very reasonable, and obvious, suggestions of ellipsis, e.g. 'The example of him who admonishes (*wāʿiẓ*) the disbelievers . . .'.[5] Similarly, *ad* Q. 17. 85 the haggadic tale of a 'rabbinical' test of prophethood was rejected on the grounds that a question about the Spirit (*rūḥ*), had it ever been posed, could not be a snare and therefore not the occasion which provoked the Quranic revelation.[6]

The conspicuously rationalist approach of Murtaḍā might also be applied to the logic of scriptural style, e.g. an isolated and somewhat ambiguous utterance in one of the Shuʿayb traditions:[7] (Q. 7: 89) وما يكون لنا أن نعود فيها الا أن يشاء الله ربّنا. In reply to the question: could God will sin and/or disbelief? he distinguished cultic and legal prescriptions (*ʿibādāt wa-sharʿiyyāt*) from the elements of belief or dogma (*iʿtiqādāt*), and produced seven arguments to demonstrate that for one who had professed his faith in God membership of any confessional community (*milla*) other than God's

[1] See above, pp. 121, 154–6.
[2] See Goldziher, *Richtungen*, 114–17; id., 'Fachr al-dīn al-Rāzī', 216.
[3] *Amālī* i, 439–42: *majlis* 33; cf. Jaṣṣāṣ, above, pp. 151, 154–5.
[4] Cf. Wansbrough, 'Periphrastic exegesis', 251–2 (no. 25); and above, pp. 220, 230.
[5] Sharīf Murtaḍā, *Amālī* i, 215–19: *majlis* 15.
[6] *Amālī* i, 11–12: *majlis* 2; see above, pp. 122–7.
[7] See above, I pp. 21–2: component VI in version A.

was impossible.[1] The phrase 'unless our Lord God wills it' could be understood only as acknowledgement of God's infinite mercy, not as allusion to unpredictable and capricious behaviour. Muʿtazilī theology drew its precepts from the intention, as well as from the formal expression of the theodicy. But Murtaḍā could also express interest in the parts of speech, e.g. the particle *ka* in Q. 42: 11 ليس كمثله شيء was not to be interpreted as pleonastic embellishment (*ziyāda*) to *mithl*, but as altering the quality of negation in *laysa*: from specific to generic, analogous to the relation of *mā in* to *mā*.[2] In that argument the operative factor was the function of *ka* in the entire phrase, rather than merely as (tautological) proclitic, and the reasoning may be compared with that of Jurjānī for the same construction.[3]

Save for a very few isolated vestiges of the masoretic tradition, *majāz* in exegetical writings after Ibn Qutayba signified figure or trope. That scholar's defence of metaphor in the language of revelation found expression more precise and sophisticated with Jurjānī, whose principal concern was to establish the role of context in figurative usage. His method was to stress the difference between the primitive/traditional symbolic value of separate words (e.g. *yad* as *niʿma*, or *yad* as *qudra*) and the variable function of such in extended imagery (e.g. the impossibility of saying/writing: The 'hand' (as 'benefit'/'power') manifested iteself in the land).[4] Thus was formulated the antithesis *majāz*:*ḥaqīqa* (tropical:veridical), differentiation of which required attention both to context (*ta'līf*/*naẓm*) and to the psychological participation (*ta'awwul*) of the hearer/reader.[5] The cardinal point of Jurjānī's thesis, however, lay in his insistence that the language of scripture was neither more nor less than the established lexical stock of Arabic as *habitually* employed by speakers of that tongue, and that the incidence of figurative usage, wrongly denied by some and equally wrongly exaggerated by others, corresponded to the character of the language as a whole, profane or sacred:[6] وأقلّ ما كان ينبغى أن تعرفه الطائفة الأولى وهم المنكرون للمجاز أن التنزيل كما لم يقلب اللغة فى أوضاعها المفردة عن أصولها ولم يخرج الألفاظ عن دلالتها . . . كذلك لم يقض بتبديل عادات أهلها ولم ينقلهم عن أساليبهم وطرقهم ولم يمنعهم ما يتعارفونه من التشبيه والتمثيل والحذف والاتساع. The significance of that argument can hardly be overstated. Assessment of the *lingua sacra* as partaking of the normal potential in Arabic for rhetorical embellishment and stylistic variation

[1] *Amālī* i, 402–5: *majlis* 30.

[2] *Amālī* ii (Takmila), 311.

[3] Jurjānī, *Asrār*, paras. 26/5–8; Murtaḍā did not, however, adduce the condition of change in the *iʿrāb* in order to distinguish pleonasm from trope.

[4] *Asrār*, paras. 21/1–16.

[5] *Asrār*, paras. 23/3, 23/5, 23/10; Wansbrough, op. cit., 266.

[6] *Asrār*, paras. 23/12–16, esp. 15.

was the acknowledged point of departure for the analysis of scripture as literature. Even the heavy-handed tactics of theologians concerned to demonstrate the inimitability of the Qur'ān or the divine origins of the Arabic language addressed to Muhammad never quite obscured that basic premiss. Among the several disciplines competent exegetes were expected to acquire figured the rhetorical trivium: *maʿānī, bayān, badīʿ*.[1] In his final synthesis of the Quranic sciences Suyūṭī devoted seven chapters to the components of scriptural rhetoric.[2]

In Suyūṭī's synoptic survey of the exegetical tradition categorical distinctions were inevitably effaced and terminological niceties blurred. The binary opposition *majāz*:*ḥaqīqa* was, for example, not demonstrated but merely asserted. Following what must have been the tradition from Jurjānī, *majāz* was described as either conceptual (*ʿaqlī*) or formal (*lughawī*), exhibited respectively in compound constructions (*tarkīb*) and in individual words (*mufrad*).[3] An example of the former was Q. 8: 2 'When His signs are recited to them they are increased in faith', in which the causality inherent in 'increase' was related to the fact of recitation; an example of the latter would be Q. 55: 27 'The face of your Lord endures', in which 'face' stood in place of being/essence (*dhāt*). The first example might qualify as a general illustration of tropical usage, the second only as an exegetical constant (to eliminate anthropomorphism) in the scriptural lexicon. *Majāz* had indeed become, with specific reference to the Qur'ān, a vague and general designation of all phenomena requiring to be understood other than literally, and finally included most of the textual irregularities noted in the masoretic tradition, e.g. ellipsis, repetition, concord, and morphology.[4] But in Suyūṭī's discussion, a curious and illogical blend of the material inherited from both Abū ʿUbayda and Jurjānī, there is a token effort to circumscribe the field of *majāz* by excluding or at least questioning the inclusion precisely of ellipsis, emphasis, simile, metonymy, chiasmus, and apostrophe.[5] Trope in scripture remained thus a subject of unresolved controversy. One refinement in particular deserves notice: a kind of compound *majāz* (*majāz al-majāz*) was perceived in verses like Q. 7: 26 'We have caused to descend upon you raiment', analysed as rainfall producing flax from which garments could be made.[6] That postulate of divine causality in three stages exhibits a greater concern for dogma than for rhetoric, but might be thought to reflect at least roughly Jurjānī's very subtle discussion of the fantastic aetiology (*taʿlīl takhyīlī*) amply attested in profane literature.[7] The application for theological purposes of aesthetic criteria tended to result in mechanical formulations of the sort produced

[1] According to one tradition 15 such; see Suyūṭī, *Itqān* iv, 185–8.
[2] *Itqān, anwāʿ* 52–8: iii, 109–289.
[3] *Asrār*, paras. 22/10, 25/1–2; *Itqān* iii, 109–10.
[4] *Itqān* iii, 111–23.
[5] *Itqān* iii, 124–6.
[6] *Itqān* iii, 127; cf. Isaiah 55: 10–11.
[7] *Asrār*, paras. 16/1–24.

in abundance by the later schoolmen.[1] That tendency is perfectly illustrated in Suyūṭī's discussion of *ornatus* (*badī'*), in the course of which and on the authority of Ibn Abī 'l-Iṣba' no less than forty-three separate figures were found in the text of scripture.[2] The long and complex history of most, if not all, of those figures would undoubtedly show, as for *madhhab kalāmī* and *laff wa-nashr*, some very arbitrary procedures of identification and/or of adaptation. The models, as well as the terminology, were indisputably profane in origin. The contrary might be asserted, but could not be demonstrated. Another, related instance has been noted: despite theological objections to their similarity, description of Quranic verse segmentation was derived, with very little modification, from the technical vocaculary pertinent to rhymed prose.[3]

The detection and analysis of rhetorical convention in scripture went some way towards the isolation of typical structures, but not quite so far as recognition of traditional schemata.[4] In Muslim exegetical literature the rhetoric of scripture was defined in terms of the particular historical and psychological relationship between God and His prophet. In Orientalist scholarship the cynosure was shifted just slightly from there to the relationship obtaining between the prophet and his public, a point of view already implicit and occasionally explicit in the Muslim tradition. That approach to scriptural rhetoric is adequately illustrated in the studies of Sister, *Metaphern und Vergleiche im Koran* (1931); and Sabbagh, *La métaphore dans le Coran* (1943). An element common to both is a description of imagery which could almost be called sociological: the acquisition by one man of linguistic expressions within a cultural environment whose components were familiar and verifiable because so widely and well attested. Now, the examination of available source materials, such as I have attempted in these studies, would hardly seem to support the assumption of *Urerlebnis* exhibited in the analyses either of Sister (e.g. 'Die Natur: Himmel und Gestirne, Gewitter, Farben, Landschaft, Tierwelt, Pflanzen; Der Mensch und sein Leben: Körperteile, Familie, Freudenbote, Gesellschaft, Landwirtschaft, Kunst und Handwerk', etc.) or of Sabbagh (e.g. 'La nature: l'homme: les parties du corps humain, les fonctions et l'activité du corps; la vie sociale', etc.). However, even so primitive a classification of metaphorical usage could be helpful, not of course for tracing the literary education of Muhammad nor for depicting the rustic origins of Islam, but for semasiological analysis of the scriptural lexicon.[5] Secondly, the same information might provide a statistical account of formulaic structures and

[1] See Wansbrough, 'Note', 55–7, 61.
[2] *Itqān, naw'* 58: iii, 249–89.
[3] See above, III pp. 116–17.
[4] See above, I pp. 1–33; III pp. 111–18.
[5] See above, pp. 215–16; it is precisely that element which is absent from Allard's 'analyse conceptuelle'.

systems, and hence a clue to the composition of scripture.[1] Finally, and in my view of greatest significance, would be an analysis of figure and trope in terms of archetypal patterns, that is, as the *topoi* and *schemata* of monotheistic revelation. From the premiss of *Bildungserlebnis*, in other words, the material assembled by Sister and Sabbagh, like that made available in the studies of Horovitz and Speyer, could be profitably pressed into the service of Quranic form criticism. Bound, as it has been, to the framework of a very dubious chronology, that same material is unlikely to produce more than pseudo-history.

An example of archetypal imagery in which, moreover, the source is quite explicit may be seen in Q. 62: 5 مثل الذين حملوا التوراة ثم لم يحملوها كمثل الحمار يحمل أسفارا as designation not merely of the ignorant scholar, but also (polemically) of all those unable or unwilling to perceive the 'true meaning' of God's word: חמור נושא ספרים.[2] Now the Quranic *mathal*, is primarily an extended simile, and was classified, somewhat arbitrarily, by Suyūṭī as either explicit (*ẓāhir*) or implicit (*kāmin*).[3] The term itself occurs in scripture eighty-eight times, often with *ḍarabnā* e.g. Q. 30: 58 ولقد ضربنا للناس فى هذا القرآن من كل مثل, occasionally with *ṣarrafnā*, e.g. 17: 89 ولقد صرّفنا للناس فى هذا القرآن من كل مثل.[4] Its basic function is that of *exemplum*, and as such *mathal* may be regarded as synonymous with *āya*, *ḥadīth*, and *naba'*.[5] That functional equivalence is stressed in Q. 24: 34 ولقد أنزلنا اليكم آيات مبينات ومثلا من الذين خلوا من قبلكم وموعظة للمتقين, exhibiting a parallelism of *āya* and *mathal* identical to that of *ot* and *mashal* in Ezekiel 14: 8 והשמותיהו לאות ולמשלים. On the other hand, the literary character of the Quranic *mathal* necessitates a distinction between it and the other narrative categories: it is intentionally anonymous and hence expressly symbolic.[6] Its range is thus not that of the Biblical *mashal*, which included taunt, oracle, poem, and song.[7]

It is with acknowledgement by the exegetes of the *mathal*'s symbolic quality that I am here concerned. Its functional value as *exemplum* was not thereby diminished, but rather, and perhaps predictably, enhanced. A *point*

[1] See above, I pp. 47–9.

[2] Cf. Geiger, *Was hat Mohammed*, 90; Hirschfeld, *Researches*, 94 n. 61; Sister, 'Metaphern', 126 n. 2; Speyer, *Erzählungen*, 437, 441, 461; Ahrens' proposed parallel with Matthew 23: 5, in 'Christliches im Qoran', 165, might almost be described as perverse.

[3] *Itqān*, *naw'* 66: iv, 38–45.

[4] Cf. Sister, 'Metaphern', 115–16.

[5] See above, I pp. 18–20.

[6] See Horovitz, *Untersuchungen*, 7, 25; a number of specimens were discussed, always from the point of view of the prophet's calculated appeal to his audience, by Hirschfeld, *Researches*, 83–97; and Buhl, 'Vergleichungen', 1–11.

[7] See Eissfeldt, *Einleitung*, 73–100, 106–9; Johnson, 'Mashal', 162–9; the equivalence *hijā'/rajaz*: *mashal* as taunt (*Spottlied*) was noted by Goldziher, *Abhandlungen* i, 44, 80.

d'appui was provided by Q. 25: 33 ولا يأتونك بمثل الا جئناك بالحق وأحسن تفسيرا, in which *mathal* is antithetically juxtaposed to truth (*ḥaqq*) but also to interpretation (*tafsīr*). In the polemical context of that verse, *mathal* was traditionally glossed 'falsehood' (*buṭlān*),[1] but not without allusion to the notions of challenge (*su'āl*) and enigma (*'ajab*).[2] The *mathal* contained an invitation to exegesis. From the antithesis *mathal*: *ḥaqq* was derived a number of interpretative procedures designed not only to locate figurative usage in the text of scripture but also to justify reading there several levels of symbolic meaning. Such did not ever eliminate entirely haggadic efforts to connect the *mathal* with known historical figures (*ta'yīn*), or to identify the occasion of its utterance (*tanzīl*), of which several not very persuasive examples may be read in Suyūṭī.[3] The extent to which exegetes might have perceived a distinction between historical fact and historical truth, between *Wirklichkeit* and *Wahrheit*, poses something of a problem. For the Talmudic antonyms *mashal*: *emet*, Loewe found no evidence of that distinction, though *mashal* itself was one of the thirty-two *middot*.[4] In Muslim exegesis a basic 'historical' reference was seldom neglected, though often only as prelude to excursions into allegorical analysis.[5]

As an exegetical instrument *mathal* might designate rudimentary theological symbolism derived from imagery so traditional that a consciousness of figurative usage was not even necessary to its understanding: e.g. *ḍarī'* as the unnourishing food of the damned in Q. 88: 6, or *zabad* as the foam or dross of the purifying torrent and fire in Q. 13: 17.[6] Such was described by Jurjānī as linguistic (*lughawī*), as opposed to conceptual (*'aqlī*) coinage: *ḍarī'* remained food, and *zabad* foam/dross.[7] Ibn Qutayba's description of both as *mathal* (the term actually occurs in Q. 13: 17) may be thought to have referred not to the words *ḍarī'* and *zabad*, neither of which was metaphorically employed, but to the eschatological context of both passages. The notion of 'likeness' inherent in *mathal* rested thus not upon the apprehension of metaphor, but upon assent to the author's intention. The 'parable' could be symbolic, even allegorical, but did not require analysis as metaphor. Related to the technical use of *mathal* in exegesis, and the source of some terminological confusion, was the description of certain types of metaphor as *tamthīl*. That practice can be justified by the semantic element of 'representation' common to most if not all formations from the root *m-th-l*, but is none the less misleading. Moreover,

[1] e.g. Zamakhsharī, *Kashshāf* iii, 279 ad loc.
[2] Cf. Buhl, 'Vergleichungen', 11.
[3] *Itqān* iv, 39–41; cf. also Hirschfeld, *Researches*, 87 n. 8, who could himself not resist the temptation, e.g. 95 *ad* Q. 7: 176.
[4] Loewe, 'The "plain" meaning', 172–5; see Strack, *Introduction*, 97 (no. 26); Bacher, *Terminologie* i, 121–2, ii, 121.
[5] See below, pp. 242–5.
[6] Ibn Qutayba, *Ta'wīl*, 49 and 251, respectively.
[7] See above, pp. 236–7.

the precise nature of the metaphor(s) qualified *tamthīl* was never satisfactorily defined. Zamakhsharī, for example, *ad* Q. 33: 72 'We offered (Our) covenant/trust to the heavens, the earth, and the mountains', sought to distinguish two kinds of image (*taṣwīr*): (a) *tamthīl*, derived from empirical data (*muḥaqqaqāt*), and (b) *takhyīl*, derived from hypothetical data (*mafrūḍāt*), the two being equally conceivable and equally dependent upon an exercise of imagination.[1] If Q. 33: 72 exhibited, in the opinion of Zamakhsharī, the *takhyīl* variety, other verses admitted of both interpretations, e.g. Q. 41: 11 'He addressed Himself to heaven while it was still smoke and said to it and earth "Come willingly or unwillingly" ', which contained a trope that could be either *tamthīl* or *takhyīl*: وهو من المجاز الذى يسمى التمثيل ويجوز أن يكون تخييلا;[2] or Q. 59: 21 'Had We allowed this Qur'ān to descend upon a mountain you would have seen it humbly collapse from fear of God', which was both: وهو تمثيل وتخييل.[3] It might well be argued that the operative factor in all three examples is not metaphor at all, but *prosopopoeia/fictio personae*.[4] Acceptance of the image as empirically or as hypothetically derived was not a problem of rhetoric but of dogma.[5]

The role of *tamthīl* as metaphor found better attestation in the tradition of profane rhetoric.[6] For Jurjānī metaphor was of two kinds: (*a*) those derived from physical and other sensorily perceptible data whose apprehension required no interpretative process (*ta'awwul*); (*b*) those derived from an intellectual/conceptual (*'aqlī*) relation requiring interpretation. He called the former *tashbīh*, the latter *tamthīl*.[7] An example of the *tashbīh* was 'He is a lion in battle', of the *tamthīl* 'His argument is as clear as the sun', the clarity of the sun (as opposed to its heat, brightness, etc.) requiring the additional qualification that nothing come between it and the eye of the beholder. Description of the Qur'ān as 'light' was thus *tamthīl*, and the word 'light' so employed a *mathal* for the Qur'ān.[8] The basis of *tamthīl/mathal* was not linguistic and, strictly speaking, not metaphorical, though confusion may seem inevitable. Use of *tamthīl* as analogy contributed to that confusion: appearance together of the terms *ashbāh* and *amthāl*, as well as the employment of *tashbīh* and *tamthīl* in the sense of 'assimilation'

[1] *Kashshāf* iii, 565.
[2] *Kashshāf* iv, 189.
[3] *Kashshāf* iv, 509.
[4] See Wansbrough, 'Periphrastic exegesis', 250 (no. 14).
[5] See Goldziher, *Richtungen*, 131–4; and cf. Bonebakker, *Tawriya*, 24–7 for Zamakhsharī's use of *takhyīl*.
[6] Cf. von Grunebaum, *Tenth-century Document*, 15 n. 123.
[7] *Asrār*, paras. 5/1–5, 14/1–3.
[8] Similarly, wine might be a *tamthīl* for prophecy, but hardly a 'metaphor', *pace* Wieder, *Scrolls*, 85 n. 3 citing Fāsī, *Jāmi'* ii, 52.

(juxtaposition of things similar), are amply attested.[1] That imagery draw upon 'analogous' formations could not, after all, be thought to represent a strain upon the resources of any language. But for the terminology of rhetorical exegesis it is more accurate and convenient to maintain a strict separation of *mathal* from metaphor. The latter was bound by linguistic considerations which could not be, or in practice at least were not, applied to the range of the former.

In his treatment of *mathal* Suyūṭī adduced (anonymously) the following definition:[2] فإنّ الأمثال تصوّر المعانى بصورة الأشخاص لانها أثبت فى الأذهان لاستعانة الذهن فيها بالحواس. There the role of the scriptural *mathal* is explained as an aid to comprehension, achieved by report to the personification of concepts. The reference, in my opinion, can only be to allegory, of which the prosopopoeic verses adduced by Zamakhsharī as *tamthīl/takhyīl* might be held to contain a pale reflection.[3] For those, at least, the antithesis *mathal*: *ḥaqq* is appropriate. The Talmudic application of *mashal* also included, in addition to parable, allegorical interpretation, e.g. the fables of Jotham (Judges 9: 7–20) and Joseph (2 Kings 14: 8–14).[4] Now, the designedly esoteric characterer of the Quranic *mathal* was explicit in the text of scripture (Q. 29: 43): وتلك الأمثال نضربها للناس وما يعقلها الا العالمون, an admission of *Deutungsbedürftigkeit* comparable to Matthew 13: 10–13.[5] The assumption of those exegetes not concerned with identification of dramatis personae or with relation of the *mathal* to a remembered historical event (real or fictive) was of emblematic language, by means of which levels of significance could be discerned in scripture.

These levels were not mutually exclusive, but rather, parallel and complementary. Ultimately incorporated into standard works in the exegetical tradition, that principle was concisely set out in the introduction to the *Tafsīr* of Sahl Tustarī (d. 283/896):[6] وما من آية من القرآن الا ولها أربعة معان: ظاهر وباطن وحدّ ومطلع فالظاهر التلاوة والباطن الفهم والحدّ حلالها وحرامها والمطلع إشراف القلب على المراد بها فقها من الله Every Quranic. verse had thus four 'meanings': *ẓāhir* (literal), *bāṭin* (symbolic), *ḥadd* (prescriptive), and *maṭla'* (spiritual). My translations are only approximate: in view both of their number and order of appearance correlation with the quadrivium of medieval Biblical exegesis may be justified:[7]

[1] See above, pp. 166–7; Goldziher, *Ẓāhiriten*, 104–5; Tahānawī, *Iṣṭilāḥāt*, 1193–4.
[2] *Itqān* iv, 38. [3] See above, p. 241. [4] Bacher, *Terminologie* i, 122.
[5] Also Mark 4: 10–3, Luke 8: 9–10; one of these passages, probably Matthew 13, was mentioned by Suyūṭī, *Itqān* iv, 39.
[6] *GAS* i, 647; *Tafsīr*, 3; adduced anonymously and abbreviated in Suyūṭī, *Itqān* iv, 196–7; see above, III pp. 104–5.
[7] See Lausberg, *Handbuch*, para. 900 (according to Rabanus Maurus); Richter, *Exegese*, 15, 174–90.

ẓāhir: *historia*
bāṭin: *allegoria*
ḥadd: *tropologia*
maṭlaʿ: *anagoge*

While, in the Muslim tradition, the rich possibilities of polysemy and multivalence had already begun to be exploited by elaboration of methods derived from the principles of *wujūh* and *ta'wīl*,[1] it is worth noting that the schematic arrangement of four levels of 'meaning' for every (!) scriptural verse exhibited considerable refinement of the earlier binary opposition *muḥkam*: *mutashābih*/*mushtabih*, in which theoretically (at least), only the latter were susceptible of more than one 'correct' interpretation. The fourfold system was, moreover, first formulated and invariably advocated by exegetes whose concern with the literal sense (*historia*: *secundum litteram*), even when expressly declared, was minimal. Here devoid (or nearly so) of the polemically charged connotations of halakhic usage,[2] the term *ẓāhir* was reduced to little more than a point of departure for symbolic and eschatological speculation. Coexistence of four semantic values implied both equality and independence of function: Jerusalem was thus the capital of the Jews (*historia*), the church of Christ (*allegoria*), the soul of man (*tropologia*), and the city of God (*anagoge*).[3] The Muslim designation of that phenomenon was *taṭbīq*, described by Suyūṭī as a kind of symbolic parallelism:[4] النصوص على ظواهرها ومع ذلك فيها إشارات خفية الى دقائق. An example is the interpretation imposed upon *Sūrat al-Fīl* by the Ṣūfī Ibn ʿArabī (d. 638/1240): in the historical attack of Abraha on the Meccan sanctuary was reflected the assault of the powers of darkness upon the soul of man, and in its repulsion deliverance of the soul from the snares of fantasy by the powers of intellect.[5] The exegetical principle itself might be described as *tropologia*, and its relation to *historia* defined as *taṭbīq*.[6]

Symbolic parallelism is the necessary substratum of all allegory, as well as of irony and caricature. Its success required uninterrupted consciousness of the literal 'ground', the source of whatever persuasive power the imagery of superimposed levels (whether *allegoria*, *tropologia*, or *anagoge*) might possess. The relation is one of counterpoint, present in allegory both as creative mode and as exegetical device.[7] It might not be unjustified to see in Philonic allegorism an identical set of postulates, for which *paremphasis* expressed the counterpoint between literal (*phaneros*) and symbolic

[1] See above, pp. 154–6, 208–12.
[2] See above, pp. 150–1, 152–3, 187–8.
[3] Lausberg, *Handbuch*, loc. cit.
[4] *Itqān* iv, 195; read possibly *ḥaqā'iq* for *daqā'iq*.
[5] Cited Goldziher, *Richtungen*, 242–4; see above, I pp. 42–3.
[6] *Pace* Goldziher, loc. cit., who contrasted *taṭbīq* with *ta'wīl* (the latter described as 'wirkliche Allegorie'), following Ibn ʿArabī.
[7] Cf. Frye, *Anatomy of Criticism*, 89–92: the 'contrapuntal technique'.

(*hyponoia*) levels of significance.[1] In Suyūṭī's definition of *taṭbīq*, the elements linking literal expression (*nuṣūṣ/ẓawāhir*) with arcane meaning (*daqā'iq*: ?*ḥaqā'iq*) were designated 'concealed allusions' (*ishārāt khafiyya*), or better 'signs'.[2] The linkage which followed upon apprehension of the sign was called *iʿtibār* (transition).[3] Unlike *taṭbīq* and *ishāra*, which were corollaries of the agreement to recognize manifold 'meaning', *iʿtibār* was a reference to procedure.[4] It was not, however, *iʿtibār*, but *ta'wīl* which became the generic designation of symbolic exegesis. Reason for terminological development lay, of course, in the close association of *ta'wīl* with the concepts of polysemy/homonym (*wujūh*). The antithesis *ta'wīl*:*tafsīr* acquired new significance. From an almost neutral description of rational, as contrasted with traditional, interpretation,[5] *ta'wīl* became first a collective expression for all save literal exegesis (*ẓāhir*), and finally an epithet of abuse for irresponsible, as contrasted with 'respectable' scriptural exegesis (*tafsīr*). Polemical reference to *ta'wīl* was nearly always abusive, e.g. in the writings of Ibn Ḥazm.[6] Among practitioners of *ta'wīl*, the term *tafsīr* described the necessary first step (*historia*) of any interpretation, but no more than that, e.g. in the work of Ibn ʿArabī.[7] Patronization of *tafsīr* by Ṣūfī exegetes found a complement in the criticism of their methods by opponents who perversely rejected Ṣūfī exegesis precisely because it was not '*tafsīr*'.[8]

In Tustarī's work symbolic interpretation is primitive and archetypal. The equivalence scripture:light (*qur'ān*:*nūr*) was, for example, justified by reference to the intermediate term 'guidance' (*hudā*), derived explicitly from Q. 42: 52 and implicitly from 24: 40.[9] *Ad* Q. 2: 269 wisdom (*ḥikma*) represented self-discipline in adversity, elimination of carnal appetites, and spiritual vigilance. Wisdom also comprehended all of the sciences, the basis of which was Sunna. Similarly, knowledge (*ʿilm*) was essentially arcane, and those granted access to it (*al-rāsikhūn fil-ʿilm*) the special recipients of divine favour.[10] *Ad* Q. 24: 35 the image illumination/wisdom was, not unexpectedly, elaborated in some detail: i.e. divine light, the light of Muhammad, the heart of the believer incandescent with the illumination

[1] See Loewe, 'The "plain" meaning', 143–51, esp. 148.
[2] Goldziher, *Richtungen*, 225–7: 'Hindeutungen'.
[3] Goldziher, op. cit., 245–51: 'Hinüberschreiten'.
[4] *Pace* Goldziher, loc. cit., where *iʿtibār* is defined as the halakhic application of *taṭbīq*.
[5] See above, pp. 154–5.
[6] Goldziher, *Ẓāhiriten*, 132 n. 2; id., *Vorlesungen*, 108, 159.
[7] Goldziher, *Richtungen*, 224–57, esp. 239 n. 2.
[8] See the discussion in Suyūṭī, *Itqān* iv, 194–8; that view was to some extent shared even by moderate Ṣūfī exegetes, e.g. Suhrawardī, see Goldziher, op. cit., 186 n. 1; Jullandri's unqualified description of Ṣūfī exegesis as '*tafsīr*' is simplistic and misleading, as is his distinction between 'symbolic *tafsīr*' (*ishārī/ramzī*) and 'speculative *tafsīr*' (*naẓarī*), cf. his study 'Qur'ānic exegesis', 105–19.
[9] Tustarī, *Tafsīr*, 5.
[10] Tustarī, 32–3, and 36–7 *ad* Q. 3: 7.

of divine unity, and finally, the Qur'ān as lamp: knowledge its light, commandments its wick, and purity its oil.[1]

It is precisely such straightforward substitution/transfer which characterized this earliest symbolic exegesis: e.g. *umm al-qurā* in Q. 42: 7 was both Mecca (*ẓāhiruhā*) and the human heart (*bāṭinuhā*), its environs the members of the human body; *lawḥ maḥfūẓ* in Q. 85: 22 was the breast of the believer, in which truth might abide.[2] Underlying interpretation of that kind was the acceptance of extended simile: the extent to which it may justifiably be described as allegory depends upon the nature of the scriptural passage subjected to exegesis. Tustarī's work contains almost no commentary on the 'narrative' sections of the Qur'ān, that is, those which would lend themselves most easily to the action: imagery transfer typical of allegory (e.g. *Sūra*s 12 and 18). The technique of dramatic allegorization found later and full expression in the writings of Ibn ʿArabī.[3] Earlier traces may be seen in commentaries ascribed to Jaʿfar al-Ṣādiq (d. 148/765) where, for example, the ascension of Muhammad (*miʿrāj al-nabī*) was analysed as a threefold passage: from Mecca to heaven (*malakūt*), from Medina to power (*jabarūt*), and from birth back to his creator.[4]

Recourse to symbolic interpretation was very much a characteristic of sectarian exegesis, for an important part of which the names of Jaʿfar and his father Muhammad al-Bāqir were significantly authoritative. But a more appropriate, because datable and indisputably authentic, illustration of that particular technique is found in the *Tafsīr* of Qummī (d. 309/921).[5] There, *ad* Q. 14: 24–6, the *mathal* contrasting the good and the evil word (*kalima*) with the good and the evil tree (*shajara*) was interpreted as reference to the contrasting histories of the prophetical progeny (*ahl al-bayt*) and the disbelievers (*kāfirūn*), with concomitant elaboration of the imagery derived from root, branch, and leaf.[6] *Ad* Q. 15: 87 the seven *mathānī* were understood to refer to the Shīʿī *imāms*;[7] and *ad* Q. 18: 60–82 the long dialogue between Khiḍr and Mūsā was related to a prognosis of Muhammad's appearance as herald of the true faith.[8] The device by which agency in the *narratio* was transformed into imagery appropriate to the Islamic theodicy could be construed as allegory, but because of the specifically historical mention in such exegesis, it may more accurately be described as typology.[9] The historicization or actualization of scriptural imagery is the converse and complement of allegorical interpretation, and both require assent to

[1] Tustarī, 103.
[2] Tustarī, 128–9 and 180, respectively.
[3] See Goldziher, *Richtungen*, 233.
[4] *GAS* i, 528–31, e.g. 529 no. 2; MS Nafiz Pasha 65, 70ᵛ–1ʳ *ad* Q. 17: 1; see above, II pp. 67–9.
[5] See above, pp. 146–7; and Goldziher, op. cit. 279–309.
[6] Qummī, *Tafsīr* i, 369.
[7] Qummī, i, 377; cf the emendation/exegesis *umma*: *a'imma*, above, p. 167 n. 4.
[8] Qummī, ii, 37–40; see above, pp. 127–8.
[9] Cf. Lausberg, *Handbuch*, para. 901; Seeligmann, 'Midraschexegese', 167–76.

the symbolic quality of the schemata of revelation. Definition of those schemata as the projection of cultural and spiritual ideals into history, or as the refraction of history in poetic imagery, will depend upon the use to which they are being put: whether as rhetorical device (synthetic) or as exegetical technique (analytic).

In Biblical literature the terms employed for typological exegesis originally designated the interpretation of dreams, i.e. *patar* and *peshar*.[1] The 'prognostic exegesis' of sectarian Judaism, Qumranic and Karaite, consisted exclusively of typological equivalents drawn from different but allegedly parallel historical processes.[2] While it is certainly tempting to see in the Islamic term *tafsīr* a reflex of *patar/peshar*,[3] the literary evidence provides little support for the conjecture. The *hapax legomenon* in Q. 25: 33 referred not to dream nor to scripture, but to *mathal*, and the origin of *tafsīr* as *terminus technicus* belonged to the tradition of profane rhetoric.[4] Now, the Quranic equivalent of *p-t-r* in Genesis 40: 8 and of *p-sh-r* in Daniel 5: 12 is *ta'wīl*, which occurs eight times in *Sūrat Yūsuf*, always glossed 'dream-interpretation' (*taʿbīr al-ru'yā*), and nine times elsewhere, glossed 'outcome'/'sequel' (*ʿāqiba*).[5] The eschatological and prognostic overtones of both uses render *ta'wīl* an appropriate designation of typological exegesis. That the Muslim term *tafsīr* might, on the other hand, have reflected a characteristically sectarian and polemical emphasis upon the recent fulfilment of a historical promise articulated in Hebrew scripture remains a distinct possibility. Such, indeed, was the function of all scriptural interpretation and the task imposed upon exegetes of every allegiance:

מי כהחכם ומי יודע פשר דבר

(Qohelet 8: 1)

[1] Bacher, *Terminologie* ii, 177–80, 173–4, respectively; Gertner, 'Terms', 17–18.
[2] See Wieder, *Scrolls*, 199–213; Rabin, *Qumran*, 117.
[3] Rabin, *Qumran*, 117.
[4] See above, pp. 154, 233–5.
[5] See above, pp. 156–7.

INDEX OF NAMES AND SUBJECTS

INDEX OF TECHNICAL TERMS

INDEX OF QURANIC REFERENCES (SELECTIVE)